THEATRE CENSORSHIP:
FROM WALPOLE TO WILSON

Theatre Censorship:

From Walpole to Wilson

DAVID THOMAS, DAVID CARLTON,
ANNE ETIENNE

DISCARD

OXFORD
UNIVERSITY PRESS

OXFORD
UNIVERSITY PRESS

Great Clarendon Street, Oxford OX2 6DP

Oxford University Press is a department of the University of Oxford.
It furthers the University's objective of excellence in research, scholarship,
and education by publishing worldwide in

Oxford New York

Auckland Cape Town Dar es Salaam Hong Kong Karachi
Kuala Lumpur Madrid Melbourne Mexico City Nairobi
New Delhi Shanghai Taipei Toronto

With offices in

Argentina Austria Brazil Chile Czech Republic France Greece
Guatemala Hungary Italy Japan Poland Portugal Singapore
South Korea Switzerland Thailand Turkey Ukraine Vietnam

Oxford is a registered trade mark of Oxford University Press
in the UK and in certain other countries

Published in the United States
by Oxford University Press Inc., New York

British Library Cataloguing in Publication Data
Data available

Library of Congress Cataloging in Publication Data
Data available

Typeset by Laserwords Private Limited, Chennai, India
Printed in Great Britain
on acid-free paper by
Biddles Ltd., King's Lynn, Norfolk

ISBN 978–0–19–926028–7

1 3 5 7 9 10 8 6 4 2

Acknowledgements

This volume is the outcome of an extended research project undertaken by the three authors. Generous funding for the project was provided by the Leverhulme Trust, which awarded an interdisciplinary research grant to Professor David Thomas and Dr David Carlton in 2001. This enabled Dr Anne Etienne to be appointed to a research fellowship at the University of Warwick lasting almost two years. During this period Dr Etienne undertook extensive archival and empirical research and made a substantial contribution to the writing up of the project. It also enabled the material costs of the project to be covered, including the costs of a large questionnaire survey of theatre companies and venues. For all this support the authors are extremely grateful.

The authors would like to acknowledge the help and advice given throughout the project by staff in the following libraries and archives: The British Library Department of Manuscripts (in particular Kathryn Johnson, the archivist in charge of the Lord Chamberlain's papers), the National Archives, the University of Warwick Library and Modern Records Centre, the University of Bristol Arts and Social Sciences Library and Law Library, the House of Lords Library, the University of Sussex Special Collections, and the Bodleian Library Oxford. The authors gratefully acknowledge permission to quote from manuscripts held in the British Library's Department of Manuscripts (http://www.bl.uk/collections/manuscripts.html). In each case, a full acknowledgement is made in footnote references under the following terms: © British Library Board: all rights reserved. They also gratefully acknowledge permission to quote from Crown copyright material in the National Archives (http://www.nationalarchives.gov.uk/), which is fully acknowledged in each case in footnote references. Other Crown copyright material is reproduced under the Class Licence Number printed on the title-page verso. The authors are grateful to Dr Jonathan Levy for permission to quote from his father's papers held at the University of Sussex.

The authors would like to thank the many politicians and civil servants from the 1960s and earlier who replied briefly and helpfully to their enquiries. The authors are particularly grateful to the following for their more extensive replies and comments: Rt. Hon. Michael Foot, the late Lord Jenkins of Hillhead (Roy Jenkins), Bob Morris (Home Office official), William Wilson, and Lord and Lady Kennet. William Wilson and Lord and Lady Kennet also kindly made available their personal archives. In addition, the authors very much appreciated wide-ranging interviews given to them by Sir John Mortimer (barrister and playwright) and the late Lt.-Col. Sir John Johnston (former Assistant Comptroller and then Comptroller in the Lord Chamberlain's Office).

The authors wish to acknowledge help and advice from a number of playwrights, notably John Arden, Edward Bond, and Sir Arnold Wesker, who gave extended interviews. Sir Arnold Wesker kindly made available his personal archive. The authors would also like to thank Edward Bond, Sir Arnold Wesker, and Steven Berkoff for giving permission to quote from letters sent to Dr Anne Etienne.

Many theatre managers, theatre directors, and company managers replied in detail to the authors when approached for their views on theatre censorship after the 1968 Theatres Act. The authors would like gratefully to acknowledge the significant amount of help and advice they were given. They would like particularly to thank the following for giving permission to quote from interviews they gave or written material they sent: Ashley Barnes (Dead Earnest Theatre), John Blackmore (Octagon Theatre, Bolton), Vivyan Ellacott (Kenneth More Theatre, Ilford), Sir Peter Hall, Christopher Honer (Library Theatre, Manchester), Fern Smith (Volcano Theatre), Max Stafford-Clark (Out of Joint Theatre, London), Rob Swain (Harrogate Theatre), and Graham Whybrow (Royal Court Theatre, London). The authors would also like to thank Mike Bradwell (Bush Theatre, London), Fiona Callaghan (Criterion Theatre, London), Paul Harman (Cleveland Theatre Company), Roger Hopwood (Northampton Theatres), Julia Pascal (Pascal Theatre Company), Laurence Sach (Harlow Playhouse), and James Yarker (Stan's Café) for providing valuable insights into theatre and censorship after 1968. In addition, the authors are grateful for various comments from many other theatre managers and practitioners offered on the basis of anonymity.

A number of colleagues in academic life made helpful comments and suggestions to the authors during the course of the project. In particular, the authors would like to acknowledge the help and advice given by the late Clive Barker and by Dr Nadine Holdsworth (both from the University of Warwick), and also by Dr Steve Nicholson (from the University of Sheffield). The authors are grateful for invitations to present early versions of their work at the Institute of Contemporary British History in 2001, at the University of Bristol in 2002, at Ohio State University in 2003, and at the Victoria and Albert Museum in 2004. Finally, the authors would like to thank staff at Oxford University Press (in particular Sophie Goldsworthy, Tom Perridge, and, most recently, Jacqueline Baker) for helping to bring this project to fruition in book form.

D.T.
D.C.
A.E.

Contents

Timeline of Statutory Theatre Censorship

1735   In April, Sir John Barnard's Private Member's Bill to limit the number of playhouses in London and elsewhere fails in Parliament.

1737   10 Geo. 2, c. 19. The Universities Act (19 May) restores the right of the Universities of Oxford and Cambridge to license taverns and to control the activities of players in the two locations.

In May, Sir Robert Walpole uses a dramatized version of *The Golden Rump* to persuade Parliament to support theatre censorship.

10 Geo. 2, c. 28. The Licensing Act (21 June) gives the Lord Chamberlain statutory powers of theatre censorship against which there is no appeal: previously he and the Master of the Revels exercised their censorship powers under the Royal Prerogative. The only playhouses permitted are the two patent theatres, Drury Lane and Covent Garden, and the Opera House in the Haymarket.

1755   28 Geo. 2, c. 19. The Act for Regulating Places of Public Entertainment gives Justices of the Peace powers to license places of popular entertainment in London, Westminster, and the Home Counties.

1766   Samuel Foote is given a patent for a summer theatre in London.

1767   Theatres built in provincial cities without permission are given patents from this date forward by repeal of the Licensing Act as it applies to each city.

1787   John Palmer builds the Royalty Theatre in Wellclose Square, London, but is denied permission to present spoken drama.

1788   28 Geo. 3, c. 30. The Enabling Act gives Justices of the Peace authority to issue licences to troupes of touring players in provincial playhouses.

1832   Edward Bulwer MP asks for a Select Committee to investigate the monopoly of the patent playhouses in London, protection of copyright for dramatists, and theatre censorship.

The deliberations of the Select Committee on Dramatic Literature are overshadowed by the Great Reform Bill. The Committee reports in August and does not recommend any change in censorship legislation. It does, however, recommend protection for the legal rights of playwrights and abolition of the monopoly status of London's patent playhouses.

1833   Bulwer's Dramatic Performances Bill, designed to implement the Select Committee's recommendations, fails at its Third Reading in the House of Lords.

1843   6 & 7 Vict., c. 68. The Act for Regulating Theatres is passed on 22 Aug. 1843. This Act abolishes the theatre monopoly hitherto enjoyed by the patent houses in London but confirms the Lord Chamberlain's absolute powers of censorship. The Act permits the Lord Chamberlain to forbid any play whenever he thinks it is necessary for the 'preservation of good manners, decorum or of the public peace'.

1866   The Select Committee on Theatrical Licences and Regulations recommends in its Report (28 June) that the Lord Chamberlain should be given licensing powers in respect of music halls. This recommendation is not adopted by Parliament. It recommends no change to the system of theatre censorship.

1892   The Select Committee on Theatres and Places of Entertainment recommends in its Report (2 June) that the censorship of plays has worked satisfactorily and should be extended, where practicable, to music halls. Parliament does not adopt this recommendation.

1907   In October, Harley Granville Barker's play *Waste* is banned by the censor.

A petition, signed by seventy-one dramatists protesting against censorship, is printed in *The Times*.

In November, G. B. Shaw launches a press campaign to protest against censorship.

1908   In February, a deputation of dramatists meets Herbert Gladstone, the Home Secretary, to express their concerns over censorship.

In December, Robert Harcourt introduces a Private Member's Bill on theatre censorship in the same month as H. H. Asquith issues his challenge to the House of Lords.

1909   In April, Harcourt introduces a second Private Member's Bill on theatre censorship just before David Lloyd George introduces his People's Budget.

In May, Shaw renews his press campaign on the issue of censorship.

Later in May, Harcourt asks his first Parliamentary Question about whether the Government will set up a Select Committee. Asquith responds favourably but fails to take any action.

In June, Harcourt asks his second Parliamentary Question. On this occasion Asquith agrees to set up a Joint Select Committee.

The Joint Select Committee on Stage Plays (Censorship) meets between July and September and publishes its Report in November. It recommends that the Lord Chamberlain should continue to act as a censor but that it should be lawful to perform plays without a licence from the Lord Chamberlain.

Edward VII refuses to accept the recommendations of the Joint Select Committee. Government ministers and civil servants agree that his view should prevail. The Home Office decides to avoid making any response to the Report.

1910   At a meeting between the Lord Chamberlain's Comptroller, the DPP, and the Home Office, it is agreed to leave the 1843 Theatres Act unchanged but to set up an Advisory Board for the Lord Chamberlain.

Harcourt asks a Parliamentary Question on when the Government intends to consider the Joint Select Committee Report. He is told that the Report is under consideration.

1911   Harcourt asks further Parliamentary Questions but receives inconclusive replies.

1913   Harcourt introduces a motion in Parliament asking for the abolition of stage censorship. Nothing comes of his initiative.

1914   The outbreak of the First World War brings an end to all parliamentary initiatives on theatre censorship.

1924   The first Labour Prime Minister, Ramsay MacDonald, discontinues the practice of making the appointment of the Lord Chamberlain a matter of political patronage. In future, the Lord Chamberlain is to be appointed by the Monarch.

1925   The Gate Theatre Studio opens as the first private theatre club.

1926   The Lord Chamberlain publishes guidelines to govern Dramatic Societies performing plays on Sundays.

1927   The Arts Theatre Club opens.

1930s	Various theatre managers are prosecuted for presenting unlicensed plays or plays where the actors departed from the licensed script.
1944	E. P. Smith (Conservative) asks a Parliamentary Question on theatre censorship. Clement Attlee, the Deputy Prime Minister, is incorrectly briefed to reply that theatre censorship is a matter of the Royal Prerogative and therefore cannot be raised in the House of Commons.
1946	Smith once again asks Attlee, now Prime Minister, whether he will introduce legislation to abolish theatre censorship and receives a negative reply.
1948	The first British Theatre Conference recommends the abolition of theatre censorship. After this conference, Smith and Benn Levy (Labour) plan parliamentary action.
1949	Smith is given leave to introduce a Private Member's Bill to amend the laws relating to the censorship of plays. There is little support from contemporary playwrights and strong opposition from theatre managers.
	The Government decides to oppose the Bill because of drafting flaws, because the theatre profession is divided, and because there is no space in the parliamentary timetable. The Bill falls.
1956	The Comedy Theatre reopens as a club theatre run by the New Watergate Theatre Club.
	The first performance is given of John Osborne's play *Look Back in Anger* by the English Stage Society at the Royal Court Theatre.
1958	In January, Joan Littlewood's Theatre Workshop Company is prosecuted because of departures from the licensed script of *You Won't Always be on Top*. In April, after being found guilty, nominal fines are imposed.
	On 20 April, the Theatre Censorship Reform Committee is founded but fails to agree on whether to pursue the issue of censorship in Parliament.
1962	In December, Dingle Foot makes an unsuccessful attempt to introduce a Bill under the ten-minute rule to make it optional to submit a play for censorship.
1963	Lord Cobbold is appointed Lord Chamberlain and will be the last Lord Chamberlain to exercise the role of theatre censor.

1964   In August, Osborne's play *A Patriot for Me* is refused a licence by the Lord Chamberlain and is subsequently staged as a private production by the English Stage Society at the Royal Court.

1965   In July, the Lord Chamberlain tries unsuccessfully to persuade the DPP to bring a prosecution against the English Stage Society in respect of *A Patriot for Me*.

In July, the Lord Chamberlain refuses to license Edward Bond's play *Saved*.

On 3 November, *Saved* is presented as a club production by the English Stage Society at the Royal Court Theatre.

The Lord Chamberlain presses the DPP to bring a prosecution against the English Stage Society. In December, the DPP institutes proceedings.

The Lord Chamberlain's repeated pressure on the DPP to take legal action over club performances of unlicensed plays makes it inevitable that Government ministers and Members of Parliament become involved in the issue.

In July, William Hamling (Labour) asks, in a Parliamentary Question, whether the Prime Minister will introduce legislation to abolish theatre censorship. Pressed on the matter by Jeremy Thorpe (Liberal), Harold Wilson suggests that the Lord Chancellor might investigate whether any change to the law is necessary.

On 19 November, at a formal meeting of the Home Secretary, the Lord Chancellor, and the Solicitor-General, there is agreement that the present system of censorship is no longer viable. The suggestion is made that there should be a Home Office enquiry into the matter.

On 22 November, the views of the Lord Chancellor and the Solicitor-General, as expressed in their meeting of 19 November, are communicated to the Lord Chamberlain in a meeting held at the Home Office.

On 26 November, Wilson takes the view that a Select Committee would be more suitable than a departmental enquiry.

On 3 December, the Cabinet Home Affairs Committee considers a Memorandum on Theatre Censorship written by Sir Frank Soskice, the Home Secretary. The Committee decides to set up a debate in the House of Lords to test opinion on the matter.

On 13 December, the Lord Chamberlain is informed of this decision.

On 22 December, Roy Jenkins replaces Soskice as Home Secretary.

1966   On 7 January, a meeting is called by the Lord Chancellor to discuss how best to implement the decision of the Home Affairs Committee. He reveals that he has asked Lord Annan to open the Lords debate.

On 7 January, the Lord Chamberlain calls on the Prime Minister to explain that he wishes to contribute to the Lords debate and has the Queen's authority to speak. He would like to see his censorship duties given to a Censorship Board.

On 17 January, the Prime Minister's Private Secretary asks for the Lord Chancellor's view on the Lord Chamberlain's suggestion.

On 19 January, the Lord Chancellor's Private Secretary replies that, in the Lord Chancellor's view, the suggestion of a Censorship Board would be as objectionable as the present system.

On 26 January, at a meeting of the Home Affairs Committee of the Cabinet, the decision is taken to set up a Joint Select Committee to investigate theatre censorship.

On 14 February, the case arising out of the production of *Saved* is heard at Marlborough Street Magistrates Court. The director of the play and the licensee are found guilty but given a conditional discharge.

On 17 February, the debate in the House of Lords takes place. The House approves the motion to set up a Joint Select Committee.

In July, the membership is agreed of the Joint Select Committee on Censorship of the Theatre. The Committee meets from November 1966 until June 1967.

1967   On 19 June, the Joint Select Committee publishes its Report and unanimously recommends the abolition of stage censorship.

On 19 June, at a meeting of the Cabinet's Home Affairs Committee, Jenkins proposes that the main recommendations of the Joint Select Committee should be accepted.

On 25 July, Jenkins prepares a memorandum for the Cabinet meeting to be held on 27 July. In it, he asks the Cabinet to endorse the decision of the Home Affairs Committee to accept the broad principle of the main recommendations of the Joint Select Committee.

On 27 July, at the Cabinet meeting, Jenkins is given permission to announce that the Government accepts the general principle of the recommendations of the Joint Select Committee. However, he is also invited by the Prime Minister (who had received representations from Buckingham Palace) to consider how provision could be made to deal with the problem of the presentation of living persons on the stage. Jenkins agrees to give further thought to the matter.

On 8 November, the Lord Chamberlain bans outright Bond's play *Early Morning*.

On 21 November, Jenkins prepares a memorandum for the Home Affairs Committee. He recommends that George Strauss (Labour) should be given drafting assistance for his Private Member's Bill on theatre censorship. He also reports that he has found no solution to the problem of offering protection to living persons.

On 21 November, Jenkins sends a note to the Prime Minister to explain that the problem of offering protection to living persons has been looked at from all angles, but no satisfactory method of dealing with it has so far been found.

On 24 November, the meeting of the Cabinet Home Affairs Committee accepts Jenkins's view that no solution can be found to the problem of offering protection to living persons and asks Jenkins to report back to Cabinet.

On 28 November, Jenkins prepares a memorandum for the Cabinet setting out the decision taken by the Home Affairs Committee and the reasons for it.

On 30 November, Jenkins is appointed Chancellor of the Exchequer and James Callaghan is appointed Home Secretary.

On 15 December, Callaghan prepares a memorandum for the Cabinet on theatre censorship in which he finds himself coming to the same conclusions as his predecessor, Jenkins.

On 21 December, the meeting of the Cabinet is chaired by George Brown, the Foreign Secretary, as the Prime Minister is in Australia. The Cabinet records its continuing concern over the issue of protecting living persons from attack on stage, but agrees to hand Strauss a Bill on the terms outlined in the Report of the Home Affairs Committee.

1968 On 15 January, William Gaskill, who is directing *Early Morning* for the Royal Court, asks to be given reasons why the play has been banned.

On 18 January, John Johnston (Assistant Comptroller in the Lord Chamberlain's Office) sends a detailed reply.

On 9 February, Johnston meets with Gaskill to discuss whether any changes might be made to the script.

On 16 February, Gaskill reports to Johnston that Bond is unwilling to remove all sense of historical personages from his play. When he asks whether the Lord Chamberlain would be prepared to allow club performances of the play, he is given a negative reply.

On 23 February, Strauss, who had chaired the Joint Select Committee, moves the Second Reading of the Theatres Bill. At the end of the debate, Dick Taverne, Under-Secretary of State for the Home Department, commends the Bill to the House. The Second Reading is agreed without a division and the Bill is sent for consideration by a Standing Committee.

On 25 March, Johnston discusses with the DPP's office what action might be taken if there were a club performance of *Early Morning*. The DPP's office is not supportive.

On 26 March, Cobbold informs colleagues that he has mentioned to the Queen his concerns about the present position regarding *Early Morning*.

On 27 March, only one performance of *Early Morning* is given (prior to the passing of the Theatres Act).

On 4 April, the Lord Chamberlain is informed that the police intend to interview the Royal Court authorities to warn them that the DPP is aware of and taking note of their intentions.

On 7 April, because of this pressure, the Royal Court cancels the second performance of *Early Morning*, and instead presents a dress rehearsal to critics and selected guests, followed by a teach-in on stage.

Following the dress rehearsal and teach-in on 7 April, the theatre licensee offers his resignation and demands that of Gaskill as Artistic Director: Gaskill refuses.

On 26 April, at a meeting of the Home Affairs Committee, it is agreed to oppose the amendments so far proposed on the Standing Committee to offer safeguards to living persons.

On 6 May, Lord Stonham, Minister of State at the Home Office, writes a memorandum for the Home Affairs Committee explaining why draft amendments have been rejected which would have given individuals the right to obtain an injunction prohibiting offensive references in a play.

On 10 May, Stonham's memorandum is considered at a meeting of the Home Affairs Committee. It is agreed that no amendment to the Bill to protect living persons is necessary or practicable and that the Government should support Strauss in resisting amendments for this purpose.

On 10 May, the Theatres Bill is given an unopposed Third Reading in the Commons.

On 15 May, Cobbold writes to Callaghan and explains that he would like to contribute to the Second Reading debate in the Lords, in order to express his continuing unease at the lack of safeguards in the Bill for living persons.

On 15 May, a formal reply is drafted in the Prime Minister's office for Callaghan to sign as Home Secretary. The reply makes it clear that the Government would not support an amendment to give specific additional protection to living persons and that any intervention by the Lord Chamberlain would cause considerable embarrassment to the Government.

On 22 May, a meeting is arranged between Cobbold and Stonham; because of this, the draft reply is never sent. In this meeting, Stonham makes the same points to Cobbold which were already set out in the draft letter. Cobbold argues that he is not seeking to oppose the Government and will make no reference to Her Majesty.

On 23 May, the Prime Minister agrees that Cobbold should have permission to speak in the House of Lords debate.

On 28 May, Cobbold, in the Lords debate, proposes an amendment to give protection to living persons, based on a form of words used in the 1964 Television Act. He makes it clear that this is his own personal view. His suggestion is vigorously opposed by Stonham who commends the Bill to the House. The Bill is given an unopposed Second Reading.

On 26 July, the Theatres Act 1968 (c. 54) is given the Royal Assent.

Introduction

Accounts of theatre censorship in Britain have so far explored in detail the activities of the Lord Chamberlain and his Readers. Literary critics, theatre historians, and social historians have trawled through the Lord Chamberlain's files (kept now in the British Library) and have used extensive excerpts from Readers' reports to illustrate the range of issues which, over the years, attracted the censor's blue pencil. In addition, Lt.-Col. Sir John Johnston (who served as Assistant Comptroller in the Lord Chamberlain's Office during the 1960s), published his own book of recollections.[1] Some studies have explored the effects of censorship on the work of English playwrights.[2] Others have adopted a thematic approach to the history of censorship.[3] Yet others have viewed stage censorship from a comparative or cultural studies perspective.[4] The most recent study of censorship has drawn extensively on unpublished papers and correspondence from the Lord Chamberlain's Office and the Royal Archives to examine the daily practice of censorship in the Lord Chamberlain's Office. It has also investigated the pressures exerted on the Lord Chamberlain and his Readers by public pressure groups and by government departments, the monarch, the Church, and foreign embassies.[5]

In contrast to the extensive investigation of the Lord Chamberlain's archives, the history of censorship legislation has been somewhat neglected. The only studies that have explored this topic in detail have confined themselves to

---

[1] John Johnston, *The Lord Chamberlain's Blue Pencil* (London: Hodder & Stoughton, 1990).

[2] Examples of this approach may be found in L. W. Conolly, *The Censorship of English Drama, 1737–1824* (San Marino: Anderson, Ritchie & Simon, 1976), and in John Russell Stephens, *The Censorship of English Drama, 1824–1901* (Cambridge: Cambridge University Press, 1980).

[3] See Richard Findlater, *Banned* (London: MacGibbon & Kee, 1967), and Nicholas de Jongh, *Not in front of the Audience: Homosexuality on Stage* (London: Routledge, 1992), and *Politics, Prudery and Perversions* (London: Methuen, 2000).

[4] Examples of this approach may be found in Anthony Aldgate, *Censorship and the Permissive Society: British Cinema and Theatre, 1955–1965* (Oxford: Clarendon Press, 1995), and in Arthur Marwick, *The Sixties: Cultural Revolution in Britain, France, Italy and the United States* (Oxford: Oxford University Press, 1998).

[5] See Steve Nicholson, *The Censorship of British Drama, 1900–1968*, 3 vols. (Exeter: University of Exeter Press, 2003–8[forthcoming]).

eighteenth- and nineteenth-century theatre.[6] Because of this, no significant research has been undertaken on material in the National Archives (previously the Public Record Office) relating to the various attempts to abolish theatrical censorship. The material in the National Archives relating to the abolition of censorship in 1968 was first made available for scrutiny (because of the thirty-year embargo on government records) in January 1999. The present volume is the first to make extensive use of this material.

As a result this volume offers a new perspective on British cultural history. It shows the hidden levers and tacit understandings that helped to prevent the abolition of theatre censorship until 1968 so that successive governments might be assured of a politically docile stage. Statutory censorship was first introduced in Britain by Sir Robert Walpole with his Licensing Act of 1737. By appointing the Lord Chamberlain to act as censor in 1737, he was of course building on historical tradition. The Lord Chamberlain (and earlier the Master of the Revels) had previously exercised a controlling influence on the activities of London's theatre troupes under the Royal Prerogative. By the 1730s, however, the theatre was no longer an institution controlled by royal patronage. It had become a full-blown commercial enterprise. The reassertion of the Lord Chamberlain's role as censor in statutory form was thus even then a complete anachronism. Its retention for the next two hundred years made it a uniquely repressive mechanism during a period of growing political enfranchisement and liberalization. As from the 1730s, playwrights and theatre managers remained subject to arbitrary and absolutist control. Matters relating to censorship could not even be raised by Members of Parliament because the Lord Chamberlain, although exercising his censorship powers under statute law, was an official whose authority was otherwise derived from the Royal Prerogative. Even as late as 1944, the Deputy Prime Minister (Clement Attlee) found it convenient to decline to comment in Parliament on censorship because he claimed incorrectly that it was exercised from within the Royal Prerogative. One of the major tasks facing the authors of the present volume has been to disentangle the issue of censorship exercised under the Royal Prerogative from censorship exercised under statute law. Successive governments during the twentieth century found it convenient to leave the issue as a tangled skein shrouded in impenetrable mystery.

This unique exercise in obfuscation and political manipulation had a negative and well-documented effect on the work of British playwrights for more than two hundred years. But so far, no one has explored in detail the

---

[6] These are Vincent J. Liesenfeld, *The Licensing Act of 1737* (Madison: University of Wisconsin Press, 1984), and Watson Nicholson, *The Struggle for a Free Stage in London* (London: Archibald Constable, 1906).

motives and techniques used by successive governments to keep the stage effectively muzzled and firmly under control. This present study of censorship legislation in Britain has brought together the disciplines of theatre history and political history in an attempt to illuminate an important feature of Britain's cultural history.

It became clear during the course of the investigation that attempts to reform theatre censorship legislation coincided with a wider desire for legislative reform in Britain. This was true of 1832, 1909, 1949, and 1968. However, in 1832 and 1909 the demand for constitutional reform gave rise to a profound political crisis that inevitably overshadowed the demand for the reform of theatre censorship. In 1832 it is also important to note that any desire to reform theatre censorship legislation was completely eclipsed by the wish to reform the licensing laws restricting the performance of spoken drama to London's two patent theatres, Drury Lane and Covent Garden. These antiquated licensing laws were finally repealed with the passing of the 1843 Theatres Act. In 1949, while there was no constitutional crisis, the sheer volume of political reform introduced by the Labour Government left no parliamentary time for the reform of theatre censorship.

Hitherto, most theatre historians have tended to view the issue of theatre censorship in isolation. In this volume, theatre censorship legislation and its attempted reform are placed in their wider political context. Sections outlining the political history of key periods explain why theatre censorship legislation was introduced in 1737, why attempts to reform the legislation failed in 1832, 1909, and 1949, and finally succeeded in 1968.

The project team was directed by a theatre historian, Professor David Thomas (now Emeritus Professor of Theatre Studies at the University of Warwick), who has written extensively on English and European theatre history topics from the Restoration to the twentieth century and has a strong interest in the interface of theatre, society, and politics. He took primary responsibility for researching and writing up Chapters 1 and 2 (covering the periods 1572–1737 and 1737–1892) and for writing up Chapters 7 and 8 (covering the periods 1964–8 and 1968 to the present). In addition, he has exercised editorial control over the whole volume.

A political and diplomatic historian, Dr David Carlton (sometime Senior Lecturer in Politics and International Studies at the University of Warwick), advised on political issues and took primary responsibility for researching and writing the sections on the political background of each major period. He has published monographs on major political figures from the twentieth century, notably Arthur Henderson, Anthony Eden, and Winston Churchill.

Dr Anne Etienne (Lecturer in Modern English Drama, University College Cork), whose doctoral research investigated the nature and practice of the theatre censorship exercised by the Lord Chamberlain, was appointed Research Fellow at the University of Warwick to carry out extensive archival and empirical research for the project. In addition, she had primary responsibility for researching and writing up Chapters 3 to 6 (covering the periods 1907–14; 1914–39; 1944–9; and 1952–62). She also undertook archival research for Chapter 7, the empirical research for Chapter 8 (questionnaire survey and interviews), and contributed to the writing up of Chapters 7 and 8.

In order to provide an introductory framework for this investigation into the history of statutory theatre censorship, the early history of theatre censorship exercised under the Royal Prerogative is explored in Chapter 1. Making use of an analytic and evidence-based approach, this chapter draws on already published primary source material and secondary sources to give a concise overview of the often arbitrary and inconsistent ways in which censorship (both pre-censorship and censorship after the event) was applied, prior to the Licensing Act of 1737, by the Lord Chamberlain and the Master of the Revels (for whom theatre censorship was an immediate source of earned income).

In Chapter 2 the account given of the introduction of statutory theatre censorship in 1737 makes use of previously published primary and secondary sources. In addition, a focused exposition of the historical and theatrical context explains why statutory theatre censorship was introduced in 1737 and why Walpole chose the particular form of statutory control specified in the Licensing Act. An investigative treatment of previously unpublished archival source material from the National Archives and published source material from *Hansard* is used in the latter part of the chapter to explore why no attempt was made to abolish statutory theatre censorship during the nineteenth century even though three parliamentary Select Committees made some reference to the topic in 1832, 1866, and 1892. In addition, an interpretative overview, based on previously published secondary sources, is given of the political context in which reform of theatre licensing was first discussed in 1832 and subsequently implemented in the 1843 Theatres Act.

The investigative and analytic account, in Chapters 3 to 7, of attempts to amend, repeal, or abolish statutory theatre censorship legislation during the twentieth century constitutes the major focus of the volume. This account is based on previously unpublished archival source material from the British Library, the Bodleian Library, the House of Lords Library, the National Archives, the Benn Levy Papers (University of Sussex), the Richard Crossman Papers (Modern Records Centre, University of Warwick), and the private archives of other individual politicians. In addition it draws on published material from the records of the House of Lords and the House of Commons, including Acts of Parliament, *Hansard*, and the Reports of the Joint Select Committees of 1909 and 1967. Based on careful scrutiny and selection of a very large amount of primary source material, these chapters offer a systematic investigation of why attempts to repeal statutory theatre censorship failed in 1909 and 1949 and finally succeeded in 1968. In addition, the outcomes of investigative archival research are put into their political context at key moments in the twentieth century.

Chapter 8 is in effect a coda and offers a methodologically diverse investigation of what kinds of censorship have faced the theatre since the passing of the 1968 Theatres Act. Using previously published source material, the opening section of the chapter presents a descriptive account of attempts to bring prosecutions against plays or theatre practitioners since 1968. The main focus of the chapter, however, is to explore whether, in the view of theatre companies, theatre practitioners, and playwrights, any forms of covert censorship have replaced statutory theatre censorship since 1968. This investigation uses an empirical methodology based on questionnaire returns, supplemented by telephone interviews and electronic or written correspondence. The intention of this approach is to provide a reliable snapshot of the views of theatre professionals in 2002–3. The final section of the chapter makes use of primary source material from newspapers and web pages to give a reasoned account of a new form of attempted, pressure-group censorship emerging after scenes of actual or threatened violence in Birmingham and London in 2004–5.

Much of the archival and primary source material presented in this volume has never been published before. This explains why the authors have deliberately included extensive quotations from this material so that the volume may serve as a documentary resource as well as an analytic investigation of theatre censorship legislation. Because the investigation is concerned with a deliberate policy of obfuscation, the style of presentation in the volume aims at succinct clarity of expression. The objective is to open up and reveal hitherto hidden areas of government activity in a manner that is comprehensible and transparent.

The principal aim of the present volume is then to provide a clear understanding of the way successive governments used the subtleties of Britain's largely unwritten constitution to exercise a controlling influence over the theatre as a public institution. The key issue to emerge from this study is the importance of unravelling in all its complexity the relationship between the Royal Prerogative and statute law. Only when that relationship was finally resolved in the 1968 Theatres Act could the theatre in Britain be released from the hidden web of government control that had kept it for so long in thrall.

1

Theatre Censorship under the Royal Prerogative

The history of the theatre in public playhouses begins in England during the Elizabethan period; from the outset it was inextricably bound up with the activities of the monarchy and the aristocracy. Players and writers were required by monarchs and aristocrats to provide them with courtly entertainment. In return, royal and aristocratic patrons offered generous rewards and legal protection to their favourite artists who, between their command performances, were free to pursue lucrative commercial careers in public playhouses. Favoured players became liveried servants of their patrons, which gave them protection from persecution and punishment. In contrast, common players were mistrusted by Puritan civic and county authorities and were generally viewed as troublemakers. An Act passed by Parliament in 1572 'for the punishement of Vacabondes' made it clear that players who did not belong to any Baron or person of higher estate 'shalbee taken adjudged and deemed Roges Vacaboundes and Sturdy Beggers'.[1] Even those players who enjoyed aristocratic or royal protection were not above suspicion. Because of their quick and ready wit, there was always a danger that they might give offence or cause embarrassment. This meant that they needed to be kept under some form of control. During the course of the sixteenth century, this controlling function gradually came to be exercised by the Master of the Revels, an official in the Lord Chamberlain's Office.

THE MASTER OF THE REVELS: CENSOR AND LICENSER OF PLAYS

The role of Master of the Revels was created during the reign of Henry VIII to facilitate the staging of masques, disguisings, and other courtly

---

[1] 14 Eliz., c. 5. Quoted from E. K. Chambers, *The Elizabethan* Stage (Oxford: Clarendon Press, 1923), iv. 270. This statute, revised later in Elizabeth's reign and in the reigns of King James I and Queen Anne, was to be used as the basis for the 1737 Licensing Act.

entertainment. The Master of the Revels read and viewed all plays intended for the entertainment of the Monarch. The intention was not simply to ensure that the content was suitable for royal ears but also that the standard of performance was fit for the ruler. This meant that the Master of the Revels was initially less a censor and more an arbiter of taste and a judge of quality.[2] During the reign of Elizabeth I, a royal patent issued in 1574 gave the Master of the Revels additional powers to view and approve plays intended for public performance by the Earl of Leicester's Men.[3] Because the Master of the Revels was now required to vet plays intended for public performance, the standards of taste that prevailed in the Court environment inevitably spread to the public theatres constructed in London from the mid-1570s.

The Queen's granting of a licence to Leicester's Men to perform plays (approved by the Master of the Revels) in London and elsewhere implied an extension of the Royal Prerogative into civic life, which was not welcomed by the Lord Mayor and the Common Council of London. In response, the City of London passed an Act of Common Council in 1574, which established a series of draconian punishments for any player who on stage 'vttered anie wourdes, examples, or doynges of anie vnchastitie, sedicion, nor suche lyke vnfytt and vncomelye matter'.[4] In view of this challenge to the Queen's authority, it is not surprising that the public playhouses built from 1576 onwards were all erected just outside the City boundaries. The remaining years of Elizabeth's reign were marked by a struggle for control over the theatre between the Court influenced by Renaissance ideas and the City gripped by Puritan fervour.

In 1579 Edmund Tilney was appointed to the role of Master of the Revels. He was related to the powerful Howard family, and owed his position to the patronage of Lord Howard of Effingham, Earl of Nottingham, who was to be appointed Lord Chamberlain in 1583 and Lord Admiral in 1585. Tilney did much to develop the role of the Master of the Revels into a powerful and lucrative post. In this enterprise, he was greatly assisted by a royal patent dated 24 December 1581 which gave him extended powers to license acting companies and their theatres, to censor and license plays, and to charge a fee for doing so. He and his deputy were given full power 'to order and reforme, auctorise and put downe, as shalbe thought meete or vnmeete vnto himselfe or his said deputie in that behalfe'.[5] Although the original intention behind this patent was probably to give Tilney complete control over the entertainment presented at Court, he eventually came to use his patent as the legal basis for

[2] See R. Dutton, *Mastering the Revels: The Regulation and Censorship of English Renaissance Drama* (London: Macmillan, 1991), 35.

[3] Ibid. 27.   [4] Quoted from Chambers, *Elizabethan Stage*, iv. 274.   [5] Ibid. 286.

exercising control over the commercial theatrical activity in London of the acting troupes he licensed.

Tilney was instructed to put together a new company called the Queen's Men in 1582 to provide professional theatrical entertainment at Court. Inevitably, this involved a close working relationship with some of the leading actors of the day. In addition, Tilney made it his business to work in harmony with the acting companies he licensed in London. He was paid a fee of 7s. for every play he perused or saw. There are few records of him having to suggest specific cuts in any of the plays presented to him by the acting companies. It was in both their interests to have a smoothly running system that guaranteed entertainment fit for the Queen and her powerful courtiers and that did not give rise to heated controversy in the public playhouses.

Because of this, Tilney was viewed by the players as more of a protector than a censor. The system offered an essential safeguard to the players; it meant that they were unlikely to give offence when they presented a play that Tilney had perused and approved. (Much the same kind of relationship was to exist between theatre managers and the Lord Chamberlain during the nineteenth and twentieth centuries.) The players also had an incentive to engage in their own tacit pre-censorship of plays offered to them by dramatists, knowing as they did what was likely to be approved by Tilney. For his part, Tilney saw it as in his commercial interest to peruse plays swiftly and without undue attention to detail. This meant that the system depended on a large measure of mutual trust and co-operation between the Master of the Revels and his fee-paying clients, the acting companies. All parties to this arrangement knew that matters of religion and state were not to be addressed by dramatists in any serious manner. A proclamation issued by the Queen on 16 May 1559 had expressly forbidden the performance of all plays 'wherin either matters of religion or of the gouernaunce of the estate of the common weale shalbe handled or treated, beyng no meete matters to be wrytten or treated vpon, but by menne of aucthoritie, learning and wisedome, nor to be handled before any audience, but of graue and discreete persons'.[6] By the same token, when it came to the moral or sexual values that might be explored in plays, the known standards of the Court were applied. In most cases, these were well in advance of what the Puritan civic authorities would be prepared to tolerate. Here, as elsewhere in Elizabethan society, sensitivity to current power relationships at Court, and the wish to prosper commercially by pleasing demanding, volatile, and potentially dangerous clients, required a system of protective checks and balances.

Towards the end of Queen Elizabeth's reign, relationships between the players and the twin authorities of Crown and City became noticeably fraught. The

---

[6] Ibid. 263.

Lord Mayor and Aldermen of London had always shown unremitting hostility towards the players. Viewed from their Puritan perspective, public playhouses were centres of idleness and distraction, designed to tempt the righteous and hard-working citizens of the capital on to paths that led to sin and sedition. On 28 July 1597 they petitioned the Privy Council to have all playhouses closed down because: 'They are a speaciall cause of corrupting their Youth, conteninge nothinge but vnchast matters, lascivious devices, shiftes of Coozenage, & other lewd & vngodly practizes, being so as that they impresse the very qualitie & corruption of manners which they represent . . . '[7] This approach was made at a time when all Elizabethan authorities were fearful of civil unrest and commotion. The succession to the throne had not yet been decided, which left the future stability and prosperity of the country open to question. Such considerations prompted the Privy Council to respond swiftly. On the same day they issued the following draconian order to named Justices of the Peace and to the Justices of Middlesex nearest to London:

Her Majestie being informed that there are verie greate disorders committed in the common playhouses both by lewd matters that are handled on the stages and by resorte and confluence of bad people, hathe given direction that not onlie no plaies shalbe used within London or about the citty or in any publique place during this tyme of sommer, but that also those play houses that are erected and built only for suche purposes shalbe plucked downe, namelie the Curtayne and the Theatre nere to Shorditch or any other within that county.[8]

There is no evidence that any action was taken to pull down the offending playhouses. But in the very next month a particularly provocative play, *The Isle of Dogs*, was performed at the new Swan Theatre by Pembroke's Men. A complaint was made to the Privy Council that the play was not merely lewd but also contained 'very seditious and slanderous matter'.[9] No copy is extant of this unlicensed play, performed by an unlicensed company, but its content clearly gave wide offence. Some of the players who had acted in *The Isle of Dogs* were committed to prison for a while by the Surrey magistrates. However, the Privy Council was not prepared to let matters rest there.

On 9 February 1598, Parliament was asked to pass a revised 'Acte for punyshment of Rogues Vagabondes and Sturdy Beggars' (39 Eliz., c. 4), which took away the powers of Justices to license performances of plays and authorized only those players to act who belonged to a Baron or any person of greater degree. In addition, the Privy Council, on 19 February 1598, issued a separate directive to the Master of the Revels and the Justices of Middlesex and Surrey that only two companies of players would in future be

---

[7] Ibid. 322.   [8] Ibid. 322–3.
[9] Privy Council Minute, 15 Aug. 1597. Quoted from Chambers, *Elizabethan Stage*, iv. 323.

permitted to perform in London, namely the Lord Admiral's Men and the Lord Chamberlain's Men. A further order issued on 22 June 1600 restricted these two companies to giving no more than two performances per week in two playhouses, one on the Surrey side of the Thames in Bankside (The Globe) and the other in Middlesex (The Fortune).[10] When issues of state were involved, the Privy Council was prepared to use the Royal Prerogative to intervene directly in theatrical affairs normally left to the control of the Master of the Revels. In this case, the Privy Council's intervention also had the unfortunate effect of severely restricting the income derived by the Master of the Revels from the licensing of plays. What is interesting to note here is that the performance of an unlicensed play by an unlicensed troupe had given rise to precisely the kind of offence that was normally prevented from occurring by the close working relationship that Tilney enjoyed with the players who belonged to licensed companies. (The parallel with events leading up to the Licensing Act of 1737 is striking. In 1737, however, merely the threat of an unlicensed play, blending lewdness with sedition, which was destined for performance in an unlicensed playhouse, was sufficient to provoke the Government into enacting new and powerful legislation to bring playwrights and players under the firm control of statute law.)

The death of Elizabeth I in 1603 and the accession of James I brought a number of significant changes to the way theatre companies were to be managed and licensed. The theatres had been closed, by order of the Privy Council, since just before the death of Elizabeth. Before they resumed playing in the spring of 1604, the London companies were all brought under the patronage of the royal household. The Chamberlain's Men became the King's Men; the Admiral's Men became Prince Henry's Men; Worcester's Men became Queen Anne's Men; and the Children of the Chapel became the Children of the Queen's Revels. In addition, Parliament in 1604 made further revisions to the 1572 Statute governing rogues, vagabonds, and sturdy beggars. These revisions took away the former privilege accorded to any Baron of the Realm or person of higher estate to license a company of players. In future, only the London companies, under the patronage of the royal household, would have permission to play in the capital and to tour in the provinces.[11] Glynne Wickham has argued that this intervention shows that the new monarch was determined to exercise a robust and even absolutist control over the stage.[12] In practice, however, Tilney, and Sir George Buc who succeeded him in 1610, continued to work closely and collaboratively with the cartel of licensed

---

[10] See ibid. 330–1.   [11] Ibid. 336–7.
[12] See Glynne Wickham, *Early English Stages 1300 to 1600* (London: Routledge & Kegan Paul, 1963), ii, pt.1, 90–5.

London companies. Any problems that did occur were occasioned, not by the players, but by individual playwrights. Indeed a number of plays even incurred the wrath of the Privy Council, notably *Sejanus* by Ben Jonson, *The Malcontent* by John Marston, and *Eastward Ho* by Jonson and George Chapman. The respective authors found themselves in difficulty and, in the case of Jonson and Chapman, threatened with severe punishment for what they had written because they had deliberately set out to challenge in their work the consensus-based system of theatre censorship and licensing.[13] Here too there are clear parallels with the twentieth century when theatre managers viewed the censorship exercised by the Lord Chamberlain as a safeguard against prosecution, while many playwrights resented his censorship powers because of the way it constrained their freedom of expression.

One piece of parliamentary legislation did, however, affect the day-to-day exercise of the censor's role. This was the introduction of a new statute in 1606 aimed at preventing the abuse of the 'Holy Name of God'. Puritan Members of Parliament imposed this new legal restriction on the acting companies and their playwrights in May 1606 when an 'Act to restrain the Abuses of Players' was passed by Parliament. The Act threatened any person or persons with severe financial penalties (the sum of £10 for every offence) if in any play or stage entertainment they 'jestingly or prophanely speak or use the holy Name of God or of Christ Jesus, or of the Holy Ghost or of the Trinity, which are not to be spoken but with fear and Reverence'.[14] It seems from alterations made to manuscripts and from the evidence of subsequently published editions that the theatre companies and the Master of the Revels took this injunction seriously and continued to do so for the next few decades.[15] The 1606 Act is the first example of Parliament attempting to limit the freedom of expression of licensed players by way of statute law,[16] and precise fines are specified if the provisions of the statute are wilfully ignored. Previous attempts to curtail freedom of expression on stage were contained in royal proclamations (or in proclamations issued by the Privy Council on behalf of the Monarch). However, the many exhortations, injunctions, and threats expressed in royal proclamations were made, not with the full force of statute law, but under powers derived from the Royal Prerogative. They sounded draconian but often depended for their implementation on the good will and compliance of

---

[13] See Janet Clare, *'Art made tongue-tied by authority': Elizabethan and Jacobean Dramatic Censorship* (Manchester: Manchester University Press, 1990), 111–24.

[14] 3 James 1, c. 21. Owen Ruffhead (ed.), *Statutes at Large*, (London: Henry Woodfall *et al.*, 1763), iii. 62. Quoted in Chambers, *Elizabethan Stage*, iv. 339.

[15] See Clare, *'Art made tongue-tied'*, 103.

[16] Henry VIII's 1543 'Act for the Advancement of true Religion and for the Abolishment of the contrary' had attempted to prevent *any* expression of religious views (whether printed or spoken, in books or in plays) which were contrary to those sanctioned by the King.

various civil authorities, ranging from Mayors and County Sheriffs to Justices of the Peace. Such compliance could not always be taken for granted and was frequently not forthcoming. Statute law was quite different, as persons of all ranks in society were subject to its provisions. As far as the theatre is concerned, the gradual shift from the exercise of the Royal Prerogative (through proclamation) towards a regulatory framework enshrined in statute law was to have a decisive impact on the development of the stage.

During the reigns of James I and Charles I there was discernibly less antagonism between Court and City over the control and censorship of the theatre. The most likely explanation for this is the tight control over acting troupes and theatres exercised by these Stuart Monarchs through the office of the Lord Chamberlain. In addition, the Master of the Revels came to play an increasingly proactive role in the licensing of plays, not just for performance, but also for printing. This too may have eased the anxieties of the City authorities.

During the final decade of Tilney's period of office as Master of the Revels, Buc, who obtained the reversion of the office in 1603, was impatient to benefit from it even before he formally succeeded to the post. With the help of patrons at Court, in 1606 he obtained the privilege of licensing plays for printing. (These powers were previously vested in the Church High Commission, and must have been transferred to him by warrant.)[17] Until he formally took over from Tilney as Master of the Revels in 1610, this was his main focus of activity and his primary source of income.

Buc was succeeded briefly as Master of the Revels by Sir John Astley in March 1622. Within a year, Astley had entered into an agreement with Sir Henry Herbert who was appointed his deputy in return for an annuity of £150 p.a. to be paid by Herbert to Astley.[18] Although Herbert was nominally appointed deputy, he in effect served as Master of the Revels until Astley's death in 1641. Thereafter he continued to serve formally as Master of the Revels until his own death in 1673. Herbert was energetic in his duties as a licenser but was motivated in his work more by the desire to benefit financially than by any wish to exercise draconian control over the drama. Initially he charged £1 for licensing a new play for performance; by 1632, this standard fee doubled to £2. He charged 10s. for allowing a new scene in an old play; he also charged 10s. for licensing a play for publication. In addition, the main company of actors (the King's Company) agreed to pay him a fixed benefit of £10 twice yearly with effect from 1633.[19] He normally agreed to license old plays free of charge

---

[17] See Dutton, *Mastering the Revels*, 149.

[18] See N. W. Bawcutt, *The Control and Censorship of Caroline Drama: The Records of Sir Henry Herbert, Master of the Revels 1623–73* (Oxford: Clarendon Press, 1996), 33.

[19] Ibid. 39–40.

if no alterations had been made to the text; but he was also pleased to accept the gift of a book in such cases as a gesture of good will.[20]

Because of his close working relationship with the players, there was inevitably an established framework of tacit censorship. Generally, issues of religion and state were still taboo. On those rare occasions when a politically motivated text was permitted, there were normally powerful figures at Court who had given the necessary backing. This was almost certainly the case when Herbert licensed Thomas Middleton's political satire *A Game at Chess* in 1624. The play portrayed living figures on stage, including the King of Spain and the former Spanish Ambassador to London, Diego Sarmiento. It is inconceivable that Herbert would have licensed such a play without powerful support at Court.[21] Any company that overstepped the mark, and ventured into the arena of political comment without Herbert's express permission, was subject to swift retribution.

In 1640, for instance, William Beeston's company of boy actors at the Phoenix Theatre put on an unlicensed play which referred to the King's journey to the North to prosecute the First Bishops' War of 1639. It seems likely that the mere reference to the King's struggle against Scottish dissenters was enough to give political offence. The King complained to Herbert as the official responsible for licensing. Herbert formally requested that the Lord Chamberlain should close down the theatre and imprison Beeston and other leading members of the company in the Marshalsea. While the players were swiftly pardoned and permitted to resume acting, Beeston was stripped of his position as company manager. He was not permitted to resume control of his company until late in 1641.[22]

In exercising his duties as censor, Herbert took very seriously the statute of 1606, which had prohibited the uttering of profane oaths on stage and any abuse of the Holy Name of God. Repeatedly, in his day-to-day activities as censor Herbert struck out from the play manuscripts submitted to him any oaths, references to Christ and God, and any obscene remarks. In 1633 his vigorous campaign against oaths and profane utterances led him into dispute with the playwright Sir William Davenant (later poet laureate). After perusing the manuscript of Davenant's play *The Wits*, Herbert marked a number of oaths for deletion. Davenant was sufficiently incensed that he persuaded one of his friends, Endymion Porter, who was a favoured courtier, to complain on his behalf to the King. The King took the unusual step of working through the manuscript with Herbert and allowed some of the words marked for deletion to stand, on the grounds that they were 'asservations and no oaths'.[23] Herbert had no choice but to accept the King's judgement but he did so with ill grace.

---

[20] Ibid. 45. [21] Ibid. 65. [22] Ibid. 70. [23] Ibid. 73.

THE CIVIL WAR

The outbreak of civil war in 1642 brought all theatrical activity, including the whole framework of censorship and licensing under the Royal Prerogative, to a sudden halt. After Charles I had raised his battle standards at Nottingham on 22 August 1642, there was an unbridgeable gulf between King and Parliament. Henceforward, Members of Parliament were determined to pass new legislation to control key aspects of everyday life without the previously required Royal Assent. One of the first statutes passed on 2 September 1642 was an 'Order for Stage-plays to cease':

Whereas the distressed Estate of Ireland . . . and the distracted Estate of England, threatened with a Cloud of Blood by a Civil War, call for all possible Means to appease and avert the Wrath of God, appearing in these Judgements; . . . and whereas Public Sports do not well agree with Public Calamities, nor Public Stage-plays with the Seasons of Humiliation, this being an Exercise of sad and pious Solemnity, and the other being Spectacles of Pleasure, too commonly expressing lascivious Mirth and Levity: It is therefore thought fit, and Ordained, by the Lords and Commons in this Parliament assembled, That, while these sad causes and set Times of Humiliation do continue, Public Stage Plays shall cease, and be forborne.[24]

The tone of Puritan piety is in marked contrast to the peremptory language used in previous statutes which had attempted to regulate the work of actors. But the implicit suggestion that the decision to close the playhouses was taken more in sorrow than in anger masks a deliberate and steely resolve on the part of Members of Parliament to silence what they regarded as a dangerous royalist propaganda organ.

After the major battles of the Civil War were concluded, many actors who had fought on the royalist side drifted back to London and mounted clandestine performances in different playhouses. Notably in the winter of 1648 these players attempted to form a company at the Cockpit in Drury Lane. After three or four performances they were arrested by a group of soldiers, stripped of their costumes, and then set loose again.[25] It was probably this event that prompted Parliament into issuing a draconian Ordinance on 11 February 1648 'for the utter suppression and abolishing of all Stage-Plays and Interludes'. Dispensing with the tone of Puritan piety adopted in 1642, this

---

[24] Sir Charles Harding Firth and Robert S. Rait (eds.), *Acts and Ordinances of the Interregnum 1642–1660*, (London: HMSO, 1911), i. 26–7.

[25] The details may be read in *Historia Histrionica* (1699), reproduced in Colley Cibber, *An Apology for the Life of Mr Colley Cibber* (1740), ed. Robert Lowe (London: John C. Nimmo, 1889), i. p. xxx.

statute drew on earlier legislation designed to control wandering players and extended the same provisions to *all* players:

It is ordered and ordained by the Lords and Commons in this present Parliament Assembled, and by Authority of the same, That all Stage-players and Players of Interludes and common Playes, are hereby declared to be, and are, and shall be taken to be Rogues, and punishable, with the Statutes of the thirty ninth year of the Reign of Queen Elizabeth, and the seventh year of the Reign of King James, and liable unto the pains and penalties therein contained, and proceeded against according to the said Statutes, whether they be wanderers or no, and notwithstanding any License whatsoever from the King or any person or persons to that purpose.[26]

In addition, the Ordinance went on to require the civic authorities to pull down and demolish all stages, galleries, and boxes that might be used for the viewing of stage plays and interludes. Anyone found acting after the passing of the Ordinance was to be whipped in public. Any money taken from spectators was to be given to the church wardens of the relevant parish for the relief of the poor. Finally, any spectators caught watching a play were to be fined the sum of 5*s*.; this money too would be given to the poor of the parish. This time the gloves were off and the actors were fully aware of the fact. In the immediate future, they confined themselves to giving private performances in various noble houses away from London. Later, when Oliver Cromwell dispensed with the services of Parliament, a few brave actors bribed officers of the Whitehall guard for permission to act in the one playhouse that survived relatively intact, namely the Red Bull. Even then, however, their performances were often interrupted by the soldiers.[27] Effectively, the Ordinance of February 1648 silenced the players until the restoration of the monarchy in 1660.

One enterprising theatre practitioner who found a way round the Ordinance was Davenant. Following his release from prison in 1656 (he had some years earlier been captured at sea while on a royalist mission), Davenant sought permission to mount a series of musical and visual representations initially in his own rented home, Rutland House. He used the kind offices of an old friend, Bulstrode Whitelocke (now Lord Commissioner of the Treasury), to obtain Cromwell's agreement. He began cautiously with a moral debate on theatrical entertainment set within a musical framework. The success of this *First Day's Entertainment at Rutland House* led him to plan a more ambitious event. *The Siege of Rhodes* (performed first at Rutland House in 1656 and then in 1658 at a refurbished Phoenix Theatre in Drury Lane) was the first ever opera to be presented on the London stage. This was a remarkable achievement, but it was only possible because Davenant had

---

[26] Firth and Rait, *Acts and Ordinances*, i. 1070.   [27] See *Historia Histrionica*, pp. xxx–xxxi.

noticed a loophole in the 1648 Ordinance, which prohibited the performance of 'Stage-playes' and 'Interludes'. Clearly an opera was neither a play nor an interlude and therefore fell outside the scope of the Ordinance. In addition, Davenant was fortunate in having a powerful ally who was prepared to support his case.[28]

Charles II was restored to the throne in May 1660. During the first two years of his reign, he persuaded Parliament to sweep aside and declare null and void a whole raft of statutes passed during the Interregnum, without the Royal Assent, which covered key aspects of civil and political life. Even before these Interregnum statutes were repealed by Parliament, Charles II had taken decisive action to revive theatrical activity in London. Within two months of the Restoration, in July 1660, Davenant was one of two theatrical entrepreneurs who were given permission to form theatre companies, and to find or build suitable premises in order to present theatrical entertainment in contemporary London. The other was the courtier Sir Thomas Killigrew who had followed the young king into exile in the 1650s. These two had successfully petitioned the King to be given warrants under the Great Seal that could be handed on to assigns or successors, which would effectively guarantee them and their descendants a theatrical monopoly in London. The Attorney-General wondered whether a toleration (or licence) might be more appropriate than a warrant under the Great Seal.[29] However, the King was probably mindful of the wording of the 1648 Ordinance which had dismissed in peremptory tones 'any License whatsoever from the King' and, on 21 August 1660, granted the proposed warrants for Davenant and Killigrew. Two years later these initial warrants were converted into patents.

CONFUSION OVER THE ROLE OF THE CENSOR
AT THE RESTORATION

The warrants gave permission to Killigrew and Davenant to form two companies of players, and to build or hire two houses or theatres in which to perform 'Tragydies, Comedyes, Playes, Operas & all other Entertainments of that nature'.[30] In addition, the two men were strictly enjoined 'that they doe

---

[28] See David Thomas (ed.), *Theatre in Europe: A Documentary History. Restoration and Georgian England 1660–1788* (Cambridge: Cambridge University Press, 1989), 84–5.

[29] See ibid. 9–11.

[30] Quoted from J. Q. Adams (ed.), *The Dramatic Records of Sir Henry Herbert* (New Haven: Yale University Press, 1917), 87–8.

not at any time Herafter cause to be acted or represented any Play, Enterlude, or opera, Containing any Matter of Prophanation, Scurrility, or Obscenity'. They were also authorized and commanded 'to peruse all playes that haue been formerly written, and to expunge all Prophanesse and Scurrility from the same, before they be represented or Acted'.[31] These were extensive privileges that cut right across the powers previously granted to the Master of the Revels. Herbert, having heard rumours of what was planned, petitioned King Charles II early in August. He reminded the King that his powers as Master of the Revels had previously been granted under the Great Seal and that he alone had previously enjoyed the privilege of 'ordering of plaies, players, and play makers'.[32] He went on to substantiate his case by asserting that previously: 'No person or persons haue erected any Playhouses, or raised any Company of Players, without Licence from your petitioner's said Predecessors or from your petitioner, But Sir William Davenant, Knight, who obtained Leaue of Oliver and Richard Cromwell to vent his Operas, in a time when your petitioner owned not their Authority,'[33] His attempt to discredit Davenant, pointedly referring to Davenant's theatrical activities during the Interregnum, shows that he was prepared to use any means to defend his vital interests: but his pleas fell on deaf ears. The King ignored Herbert's petition and issued the planned warrants to Killigrew and Davenant. This decision led to protracted legal battles in the courts.

Herbert was determined to safeguard his long-established source of income for perusing and licensing old and new plays, and brought numerous lawsuits against individual actors and the two company managers. Eventually, Killigrew and Davenant were forced to settle with him. Killigrew settled first and agreed to pay Herbert his customary fees for perusing plays. He also agreed to pay him damages. Herbert, for his part, relinquished any claim to license playhouses and players and agreed not to molest Killigrew any further.[34] The effect of this settlement was to safeguard Herbert's main source of income but to diminish the stature of the office of the Master of the Revels. Until his death in 1672, Herbert continued to read and censor play manuscripts submitted to him, but without the assiduous attention to detail he had shown in the 1630s. As in previous generations, matters of state and religion were generally avoided by playwrights. However, the libertine temper of the age meant that dramatists could be audacious in their exploration of contemporary patterns of behaviour. Leading playwrights such as John Dryden, William Wycherley, Sir George Etherege, and Aphra Behn (Britain's first female professional playwright) pushed forward in their comedies the boundaries of what might be said and seen on London's stages without offending

---

[31] Ibid. 88.　　[32] Ibid. 85.　　[33] Ibid.　　[34] See Thomas, *Theatre in Europe*, 14.

contemporary audiences. The advent of the first actresses on the Restoration stage also led to the appearance in contemporary plays of lively and outspoken female protagonists whose language and behaviour were as uninhibited as that of any of their male sparring partners. For the first time in the history of the theatre, playwrights and actors were permitted to operate within a relatively permissive system of control and censorship. On rare occasions when an actor or playwright managed to give offence (as when the actor John Lacy, in 1667, embellished a part in which he was meant to satirize the King and comment on the corruption of the Court), the Lord Chamberlain would intervene, closing the offending playhouse and imprisoning the guilty player for a short period.[35]

INTERVENTIONS BY THE LORD CHAMBERLAIN

As from 1673, Killigrew became Master of the Revels, which meant that the powers of censorship previously exercised by Herbert were now handed over to one of the two patent holders. This further weakened the role and stature of the office of Master of the Revels, particularly when the two acting companies (the King's Company and the Duke's Company) were amalgamated in 1682. In effect, the United Company was alone responsible for ensuring that nothing performed in its playhouses offended the King and his Court. This system of tacit censorship generally functioned well during the final decade of the seventeenth century. However, there were some difficulties for playwrights and players during the politically troubled years of the early 1680s, when the Lord Chamberlain took a more proactive role than had previously been the case. Because of the political unrest associated with the exclusion crisis, a number of duly licensed plays were banned after a few performances. These included Nathaniel Lee's *Lucius Junius Brutus,* Nahum Tate's *Richard the Second,* and John Crowne's *Henry the Sixth.*[36] In these cases, it was the Lord Chamberlain, not the Master of the Revels, who stepped in to issue the banning order.[37] This new role taken on by the Lord Chamberlain would eventually lead to increasing tension between the acting companies and successive Lords Chamberlain. In addition, towards the very end of the 1690s and the early decades of the eighteenth century, other

---

[35] Ibid. 128, 132.

[36] See Susan J. Owen, *Restoration Theatre and Crisis* (Oxford: Clarendon Press, 1996), 12.

[37] See Liesenfeld, *Licensing Act,* 11.

subtle changes began to take effect, which would transform the whole basis of the laissez-faire approach to censorship that characterized the Restoration period.

By the turn of the century, the theatre was attracting a new kind of audience with very different tastes from before. The boisterous, but intelligent audience of the Restoration had been replaced by an increasingly middle-class audience which was less well educated and far less sophisticated in its tastes. Writing in 1702, the critic John Dennis described how the Restoration delight in satirizing 'all the sheer originals in town' had turned into a contemporary obsession with politics, 'For from Westminster to Wapping, go where you will, the conversation turns upon politics.'[38] In addition, the tired businessmen who now frequented the theatres wanted light entertainment, not food for thought: hence the increasing amount of farce, dance, and music included in the contemporary repertoire.[39] Moreover, the middle-class women who had begun to attend theatre performances had tastes that were distinctly more prudish than those of their Restoration counterparts. Hence, there was a growing desire to see the stage reformed to reflect the changing values of this new audience. Contemporary playwrights such as Colley Cibber and Sir Richard Steele reflected this shift in temper in their work as they abandoned the satiric approach of Restoration playwrights in favour of a moralizing sentimental approach to comedy.

A dissenting High Church clergyman called Jeremy Collier captured and focused this distinctive change of attitude in his vitriolic critique of the stage published in 1698, *A short View of the Immorality and Profaneness of the English Stage*. His attack (which provoked even the most distinguished playwrights of the age such as William Congreve and Sir John Vanbrugh to defend themselves in print) summed up the feelings of many in the middle classes. The popularity of Collier's views led to a spate of attempted prosecutions against individual actors for uttering profane language on stage. These various prosecutions were based on the statute originally enacted by Parliament in 1606 aimed at preventing the abuse of the Holy Name of God. When one minor player, George Bright, was convicted and fined £10 with costs, he complained bitterly to the Lord Chamberlain in 1701. As a result, Queen Anne entered a *nolle prosequi* in respect of the other cases, in order to prevent a spate of vexatious prosecutions.[40] In taking this action, she effectively reasserted the Crown's absolute control over the patent theatres by virtue of the authority vested in the Royal Prerogative. In addition, the Lord

---

[38] Quoted from Thomas, *Theatre in Europe*, 187.   [39] See ibid. 187.
[40] See ibid. 189–90.

Chamberlain sent reminders to the players about the need to have their plays properly licensed.[41]

The first two decades of the eighteenth century saw the theatre in London fractured by violent disputes between actors and managers. The figure of Christopher Rich looms large in most of these disputes. He was a devious and avaricious lawyer who had managed to acquire both royal patents by the 1690s and had used his monopolistic powers to exploit his actors. An actors' rebellion in 1695 had already led to the aged Thomas Betterton and other leading players successfully petitioning the Lord Chamberlain for a licence to form a new actors' company at the old Lincoln's Inn Fields playhouse to rival that controlled by Rich at Drury Lane. When these actors rejoined Rich at Drury Lane in 1708, after the opening of the Opera House in 1705 (the Queen's Theatre in the Haymarket), further ructions followed. Once again, the players petitioned the Lord Chamberlain. This time, the Lord Chamberlain intervened more vigorously and 'silenced' Rich altogether. He gave permission to the actors to resume their living, but Rich had to wait until a change of monarch in 1714 before he was allowed to take renewed control of a theatre. The upshot of this turbulent period was to occasion the Lord Chamberlain's increasing involvement in the day-to-day management of the patent company. In its turn, this inevitably led to unresolved tensions. When Rich was silenced, for instance, his fellow shareholders considered taking legal action to question the validity of the Lord Chamberlain's silencing order.[42] This had been made, not backed by the full authority of statute law, but under powers derived from the Royal Prerogative.

Further complications arose when Steele was given a new patent for the Theatre Royal, Drury Lane, in 1715. He claimed that the wording of his patent (identical to that used in the Killigrew and Davenant patents) gave him full authority to peruse and hence to approve all plays for performance at this theatre. In view of this, he declined to submit plays for licensing by the Master of the Revels or the Lord Chamberlain. By 1717 this refusal led to a full-scale conflict with the Lord Chamberlain who, with the King's permission, eventually revoked Steele's licence in 1720 and silenced the theatre. Once again, the Lord Chamberlain had acted using powers derived from the Royal Prerogative. The three actor-managers at the time agreed to accept the Lord Chamberlain's authority and they were given a licence to reopen the theatre without the involvement of Steele as patentee. Steele, who saw this as an affront to his status as a Member of Parliament, was furious at his exclusion but was not reinstated as patentee until 1721,

---

[41] Quoted from ibid. 22.   [42] Ibid. 25.

when his friend and ally, Sir Robert Walpole, was made Chancellor of the Exchequer.[43]

CHALLENGES TO THE AUTHORITY OF THE LORD CHAMBERLAIN

The tribulations experienced by patent holders, such as Rich and Steele, underscored the need, in the minds of shareholders and would-be theatrical entrepreneurs, to find a way of breaching the Crown's monopolistic control over theatrical activity. The growing importance of commercial activity in London fuelled this pressure. The first breach in royal control over all theatrical activity in London came in 1720 when John Potter, a carpenter, constructed a new theatre building known as the Little Theatre in the Haymarket. His intention was to make the building available to visiting foreign companies rather than to form a new permanent company. Throughout the 1720s this was how the playhouse was used, and it attracted little attention from the authorities.

In 1729 Thomas Odell built the next fringe theatre in the capital, the Theatre in Goodman's Fields in the East End of London. In contrast to the opening of the Little Theatre in the Haymarket, the construction of this new playhouse led to shrill protests from nearby residents and from the City of London. Odell was summoned to a meeting with the Lord Chamberlain and received written instructions from the latter 'not to presume to Act or Represent any Comedies Tragedies or other Theatrical performances for the future, as you will answer the contrary at your Peril'.[44] After a fortnight's period of closure, Odell took legal advice and reopened his playhouse in May 1730. The Lord Chamberlain's threat, although it sounded impressive, proved to be completely empty. His failure to act was clear proof that his authority did not extend to unlicensed players and playhouses.

1730 also brought a significant change to the status of the Little Theatre in the Haymarket. In that year, Henry Fielding leased the theatre in order to mount a season of topical satirical plays. His plays, *The Author's Farce* and *Tom Thumb*, proved to be highly successful and ensured that all of London society and government authorities were now aware of the Little Theatre in the Haymarket. In 1731 Fielding's *Welsh Opera* and *The Fall of Mortimer* set alarm bells ringing in government circles. In *The Welsh Opera*, the royal family was mocked in the figures of Squire Apshinken (George II)

---

[43] Ibid. 26.   [44] See ibid. 206.

who has to cope with a shrewish wife (Queen Caroline), an awkward son, Owen (Frederick, Prince of Wales), and the machinations of Robin the Butler (Walpole). In *The Fall of Mortimer*, set in the time of Edward III, Mortimer (Walpole) was shown conspiring with his brother Horatio (Charles Townshend: Walpole's brother-in-law) and the Queen to deceive King and country.[45] This posed a real dilemma for the Government. The Little Theatre in the Haymarket was not a patent house and therefore did not fall under the direct control of the Lord Chamberlain: the building was unlicensed, as were the players. In addition, the former authority of the Master of the Revels to license all companies of players and all theatre buildings had been successfully challenged at the Restoration. The only recourse that might be had was to bring a charge against named players under the most recent statute relating to rogues, vagabonds, and sturdy beggars, passed in 1714 in the reign of Queen Anne (12 Anne, stat. 2 c. 23). In this latest revision of the original statute dating from Tudor times, 'all Fencers Bearwards Common Players of Interludes... shall be deemed Rogues and Vagabonds...' and subject to arrest, whipping, and hard labour.[46] In July 1730 the Justices of Westminster met to consider whether the players at the Little Theatre in the Haymarket might be prosecuted under the terms of this statute. Some argued that members of a company resident in London could hardly be considered vagrants, but others wanted to bring charges. Attempts were made to detain members of the company, but the players somehow managed to evade arrest.[47]

In the event, a court case was finally brought in 1733 against a named member of the company, but not by the Government. The case was brought by the new patentee of Drury Lane, John Highmore, with the aim of protecting his monopoly from commercial competition. In November 1733, a writ was issued for the arrest of John Harper, a player at the Little Theatre in the Haymarket, which accused him of being a vagrant under the terms of the statute passed in the reign of Queen Anne. At his trial, the jury found him not guilty. Harper's acquittal meant that in future neither the Government nor the patent holders could use the vagrancy laws as a means of keeping unlicensed theatres and players under control.

These events, an unsuccessful test case and the Lord Chamberlain's failure to impose his will on the unlicensed Theatre in Goodman's Fields, form the immediate prelude to the Licensing Act of 1737. In addition, contemporary playwrights, such as John Gay and Fielding, had subjected Walpole and members of the royal family to withering satirical attack during the late

---

[45] See Liesenfeld, *Licensing Act*, 17.   [46] Quoted from ibid. 163.
[47] See ibid. 19.

1720s and early 1730s. It was the vitriolic force of these attacks, combined with the unstable political climate of the decade, which finally persuaded Walpole's administration to introduce draconian legislation to curb the new-found freedom of the stage. With the passing of the 1737 Licensing Act, day-to-day control over the theatre was removed from the Royal Prerogative and enshrined instead within the clearly defined and completely constricting framework of statute law. However, by giving the Lord Chamberlain statutory censorship powers, Walpole set up a system of censorship that could neither be challenged in the law courts nor in the House of Commons, as the Lord Chamberlain derived his authority from the Royal Prerogative. The legal uncertainties and confusion caused by this were exploited by successive governments as a powerful disincentive to reform right up to the Theatres Act of 1968. By comparison with the haphazard control of the theatre previously exercised under the Royal Prerogative, the new censorship powers introduced by Walpole were used for the next two hundred years as an effective and blunt instrument to suppress, on the English stage, any expression of serious thought on religious, moral, or political issues that might offend contemporary sensibilities or cause concern to the royal family or those in government.

2

Statutory Theatre Censorship, 1737–1892

THE POLITICAL BACKGROUND TO THE 1737
LICENSING ACT

The Licensing Act of 1737 was seen by few contemporaries as being of seminal importance. Ironically, however, this particular Act outlived Walpole and his critics in a way that little else from the era did. As the historian Dorothy Marshall noted in 1962, just one year before Harold Wilson became Leader of the Labour Party:

Walpole is remembered for his economic legislation and for his supposed influence on constitutional forms, though the one has been swept away and the other overlaid; it is his determination to smother, by the Playhouse Bill, unfriendly criticism from the stage, which, more than any of these, remains an active part of English life today.[1]

The mundane truth was that Walpole, who had risen to power as First Minister in 1721 during the reign of George I, had become little more than George II's political manager by the 1730s.[2] Whatever high-minded goals he had had during the 1720s had all been long ago achieved and embedded. First, the Hanoverian dynasty, imported in 1714 on the death of Queen Anne, had come to be, if not loved, at least universally accepted in England. Only a few romantics claimed to believe that the Jacobite (and Roman Catholic) 'King over the Water', James Edward Stuart, had any serious chance of seizing the Crown. With acceptance of the Hanoverians came also the comforting knowledge that the age of the divine right of kings was long gone; that Roman Catholicism had been marginalized; and that religious issues in general usually mattered little in day-to-day life. The so-called 'mixed' constitutional arrangements, enshrined in the settlement of 1689 and involving a partnership of King, Lords, and

---

[1] Dorothy Marshall, *Eighteenth Century England* (London: Longman, 1962), 162.
[2] On Walpole see J. H. Plumb, *Sir Robert Walpole*, 2 vols. (London: Cresset Press, 1956 and 1960). A third awaited volume, to cover the period after 1734, did not appear before the author's death. See also H. T. Dickinson, *Walpole and the Whig Supremacy* (London: Hodder, 1973).

Commons, were not only broadly acceptable to the nation but had proved an effective tool of government. In addition, Walpole had presided over the restoration of economic stability in the aftermath of the so-called South Sea Bubble, which had inflated and burst during 1720 with ruinous consequences for many investors. He was at least initially untroubled by the fact that in cultural matters there was in Great Britain a good measure of freedom of expression, certainly more so than in any other leading country at that time. True, occasionally a newspaper would be sued for seditious libel, but none was permanently closed down by government order.

As for the stage, Walpole only reacted when he was subject to sustained personal attack. According to Marshall, 'he had invoked the powers of the Lord Chamberlain to stop performances of [John] Gay's *Polly*'.[3] *Polly* (1729) had been written by Gay as a sequel to his popular piece *The Beggar's Opera* (1728). The latter had caused deep embarrassment to Walpole who was associated in it, through nicknames, with the activities of London's underworld. Although Walpole had bravely attended a performance of *The Beggar's Opera*, only to find the audience gazing at him every time there was an allusion to him,[4] he was clearly determined that he would not find himself mocked a second time in one of London's patent houses. Marshall quotes Lord Hervey as recording at the time: 'Sir Robert Walpole resolved, rather than suffer himself to be produced for thirty nights together on the stage in the person of a highwayman, to make use of the authority of his friend the Duke of Grafton as Lord Chamberlain to put a stop to the representation of it.'[5] But this was an exceptional move and, prior to 1737, managers were not deterred from putting on many other plays that lampooned politicians and which were frequently 'crude and licentious'.[6]

The problem for opposition factions during the early 1730s was that Walpole seemed invincible. With great cynicism, he frequently retreated in the face of strong opposition to specific proposals and he raised the art of bribery to levels never previously experienced. Some rather ambitious and talented Members of Parliament, such as William Pulteney and John Carteret, remained in the political wilderness for many years. Gradually they and their associates became ever more desperate and wild in their public denunciations of the First Minister. Moreover, Frederick, the Prince of Wales, also threw his lot in with the Opposition.[7] Unsurprisingly the resulting polarization in London society eventually spread to the worlds of literature and theatre. For example,

---

[3] Marshall, *Eighteenth Century England*, 161.
[4] See Charles Macklin's account of Walpole's visit to the theatre in Thomas *Theatre in Europe*, 195.
[5] Marshall, *Eighteenth Century England*, 161.   [6] Ibid.
[7] On Frederick see Michael De-la-Noy, *The King Who Never Was: The Story of Frederick, Prince of Wales* (London: Peter Owen, 1996).

journals like *The Craftsman*, the *London Journal*, the *London Evening Post*, together with various provincial newspapers, were able to build up a strong following of readers because of their increasingly ferocious denunciations of the 'Robinocracy'.[8] Numerous talented writers at various times rallied to their assistance; these included Gay, Fielding, Dean, Jonathan Swift, Alexander Pope, and John Arbuthnot. From time to time particular issues became the subject of fierce dispute. In 1733, for example, Walpole brought forward an Excise Bill, which would have increased the price of wine and tobacco. Basil Williams recounted the result:

It was put about that the new scheme was only the beginning of a plot to impose an excise tax on every article of consumption by means of an army of excise-men scouring the country-side and prying into every shop, nay, every home . . . In the face of . . . widespread opposition Walpole for the first time found his majorities dwindling in the House of Commons and, bowing to the storm, withdrew the bill after the Second Reading.[9]

However, a far more serious crisis built up in 1736–7, which brought together a number of disparate issues. There was firstly the Gin Act, which was intended to put an end to the availability of cheap gin to the poorer classes, whose levels of drunken excess were visible in all major cities. The prospect of this legislation caused much rioting in the streets, especially in London. Other London riots took place in Shoreditch and Spitalfields because the local population were persuaded that Irish immigrants were taking their jobs. Walpole was convinced that Jacobite agitators were behind these disturbances.[10] Further riots had taken place in Edinburgh, which culminated in a mob lynching an army captain who had ordered his soldiers to fire on a rioting crowd protesting over the execution of a smuggler. After the lynching of Captain Porteus in September 1736, a regiment of foot soldiers was sent to Edinburgh to restore order.

In addition, the behaviour of the royal family was causing some dismay to the general public. After the dissolution of Parliament in May 1736, the King absented himself from England for an extended period, in order to be with his German mistress in Hanover. Initially, public sympathy lay with the Queen, but as the months went by, even the Queen found herself subject to public criticism because of the King's unpopularity. This unfortunate state of affairs was ruthlessly exploited by Frederick, Prince of Wales, who was at loggerheads

---

[8] See Paul Langford, *The English Satirical Print, 1600–1832: Walpole and the Robinocracy* (Cambridge: Cambridge University Press, 1986), and Dickinson, *Walpole*, 140–1.

[9] Basil Williams, *The Whig Supremacy, 1714–1760* (Oxford: Clarendon Press, 1939), 182.

[10] See Liesenfeld, *Licensing Act*, 62.

with his father. Making no secret of this in public, Frederick went out of his way to win popular acclaim. For instance, he helped to extinguish a fire in the Inner Temple and gave money to those who were helping to fight the blaze. He also donated £500 to the Lord Mayor of London to be used for releasing poor freemen of the City who were in prison. While his mother was hissed at the opera, the Prince of Wales avidly attended performances of plays to bask in popular support.[11]

After the King's much delayed return to England in January 1737, Frederick caused deep embarrassment to his father and to Walpole by permitting the Opposition to raise in Parliament the issue of the allowance paid by the King to the Prince of Wales. Frederick received only half the allowance of £100,000 per annum which had been paid to his father when he had been Prince of Wales. Frederick was now mired in debt and was desperate to have more funding. Walpole attempted to find a compromise, but without success. The issue of raising the allowance paid to the Prince of Wales was put to both Houses of Parliament in February 1737. Walpole opposed any increase and regarded the outcome as in effect a vote of confidence in his government. Right up until the last minute, the outcome was seen as too close to call. In the event, Walpole won the vote in the Commons with a majority of thirty; the majority in the Lords was even larger. The result of the vote, however, was to ensure an even closer alliance in future between the Prince of Wales and the Opposition.

The cumulative effect of these various difficulties was to convince Walpole that the stability of his Government and even the country was under some threat. This was the frame of mind in which he found himself at a time when London's theatres were increasingly presenting scurrilous satires on his policies and the behaviour of the royal family. Although Walpole frequently trimmed in the face of prevailing winds of opinion, he also hit back when it was safe to do so against those he saw as factious and unprincipled critics both within and outside Parliament. This explains his decision to introduce a bill in 1737 to stifle attacks on him, the Government, and the King in London's playhouses. It was, as will be seen, a measure intended to restore a perceived loss of control over the stage rather than a central challenge to ancient English liberties. It was, in short, a rather desperate gesture of defiance by a man who had been in office rather too long and who sensed that enforced retirement was looming. It certainly was not to be part of any general assault on liberty such as Charles I had mounted during the early part of his reign. Before long even Walpole had had enough. His supporters had lost ground in the general election of 1741: in February 1742, despite the pleas of George II, he resigned his offices and quietly retreated to the House of Lords.

[11] Ibid. 65–9.

THE THEATRICAL BACKGROUND TO THE 1737
LICENSING ACT

It was against this tense political background that the small commercial theatres in London, as has already been noted in Chapter 1, had secured for themselves in the 1730s total freedom from any kind of control or censorship exercised under statute law or the Royal Prerogative. The realization that London's small commercial theatres were not subject to any kind of legal censorship or control prompted Fielding, who had already had a successful season of satirical productions in 1730–1, to take out a lease for the Little Theatre in the Haymarket in April 1734. His Great Mogul Company opened their season with his ballad opera *Don Quixote in England*. He had originally written the piece, with its topical allusions, as a comedy for Drury Lane. For the next two seasons, he offered his audiences a feast of satire. Some of his barbs were aimed at fellow writers and theatre managers: in *Tumble-down Dick, or Phaeton in the Suds*, Fielding satirized the mindless entertainment offered contemporary audiences in pantomimes performed at the patent houses. However, his most vitriolic barbs were aimed at contemporary politicians, notably Walpole, in *Pasquin* and in *The Historical Register for 1736*. The latter piece gave particular offence as it linked accusations of bribery against Walpole with claims of crass stupidity aimed at well-known figures in the theatrical world such as Colley Cibber.

Although Walpole had been the primary target of the satirists since 1728, he was prepared to bide his time and wait for a suitable opportunity to take action. Given the general animosity felt towards the theatre by civic authorities and Justices of the Peace in the City of London, he may well have calculated that the lack of any legal framework for controlling the activities of London's burgeoning unlicensed playhouses was eventually bound to attract parliamentary attention. This is precisely what happened in 1735. In February 1735, an announcement was made in the *Daily Post* that a new playhouse was to be built in the parish of St Martins le Grand (just north of St Paul's Cathedral) and members of the public were invited to subscribe to this new venture. The journalist and former theatrical entrepreneur, Aaron Hill, insinuated in *The Prompter* (13 May 1735) that the announcement was a government ploy designed to outrage local magistrates.[12] He may well have been correct. Walpole was a master of bribery and corruption, and he may have been prepared to pay handsomely to help spread any rumour that would

---

[12] Ibid. 25.

focus renewed attention on the activities of London's unlicensed theatres. Wealthy merchants, Justices of the Peace, and even members of the nobility had already been vociferous in their opposition to the Theatre in Goodman's Fields when it opened in 1728. The prospect of yet another playhouse being opened, with undesirable social consequences (alehouses and brothels had been opened near the Theatre in Goodman's Fields), would give grave cause for concern to local citizens. If Walpole was indeed responsible for planting the announcement about a new playhouse, then his ploy worked. Sir John Barnard, a Justice of the Peace and one of London's independent Members of Parliament, asked leave in March 1735 to introduce a Private Member's Bill to limit the number of playhouses in London and elsewhere. Barnard was a staunch puritan from a Quaker family and was to become Lord Mayor of London in 1737. His opposition to unlicensed playhouses was therefore motivated by puritan sentiment rather than any sympathy for Walpole and his administration.

Barnard's motion to bring in a bill to limit the number of playhouses was supported unanimously and without a division. The Committee selected to prepare the bill included members from both sides of the House.[13] However, the fact that the First Minister, the Master of the Rolls, the Attorney-General, and the Solicitor-General chose to serve on the Committee indicates very clearly that this bill would enjoy full Government support at every stage of its drafting and progress through Parliament.[14] Following well-established precedent, Barnard's bill envisaged the vagrancy laws as the most effective method of bringing London's unlicensed playhouses under strict legal control. Barnard's main aim was to limit theatrical activity in London to the two patent playhouses (Drury Lane and Covent Garden) and the opera house (the King's Theatre in the Haymarket) by closing down all other unlicensed playhouses. His bill was designed to achieve this aim by redefining the scope of the statute against vagrancy passed in the reign of Queen Anne. In future, anyone acting in a playhouse without a royal patent would be deemed a vagrant and would be liable to the punishments specified in the vagrancy laws. The bill was therefore intended to reverse the adverse judgement in the test case that, as we have seen, Highmore had brought in 1733. Legal enforcement of the bill's provisions would be in the hands of Mayors, Bailiffs, and Justices of the Peace.

After an unopposed Second Reading, the bill was considered in detail by a Committee of the Whole House. Petitions were received from various parties, including the actors in Goodman's Fields (who feared unemployment), Henry

---

[13] For a detailed account of the bill's progress through Parliament, see ibid. 25–54.

[14] There is a fascinating parallel here with the 1960s when George Strauss's Private Member's Bill to abolish theatre censorship was given full Government support.

Giffard (who now owned Goodman's Fields), and John Potter (who owned the Little Theatre in the Haymarket). In addition, a wandering player, Anthony Aston, was allowed to make a personal plea, rather than through counsel, on behalf of players in the provinces. His witty and amusing presentation (almost a theatrical performance in its own right), in which he explained that the bill would lead to the ruin of all wandering players, seems to have been taken seriously by the House. An amendment was presented that would allow for performances outside London.[15] The other pleas fell on deaf ears.

At this point, Walpole, who had carefully overseen and engineered the bill's smooth progress through Parliament, overplayed his hand. In breach of normal parliamentary practice, he introduced a substantive new amendment at the Committee stage (in effect a completely new clause), which would give the Lord Chamberlain the power to censor and license plays. He also let it be known that the King (presumably on his advice) would be unlikely to give the Royal Assent to the bill, if this amendment was not approved.[16] Barnard objected strongly to giving any new statutory powers to the Lord Chamberlain. His bill had envisaged a regulatory framework for London's playhouses controlled by local officials and Justices of the Peace. It was certainly not his intention to grant statutory legal powers to a crown officer whose authority was derived from the Royal Prerogative.[17] He therefore made it clear to Walpole that he would prefer to see his bill fall, rather than include the clause insisted on by the First Minister. As neither was prepared to compromise, the bill lapsed through a tactical procedure in April 1735.[18] The bill's failure had the immediate effect of strengthening the legal freedoms enjoyed by London's unlicensed playhouses. In addition, the defeat of Walpole's attempt to introduce a censorship clause into Barnard's bill was interpreted by contemporary playwrights as giving them the green light to intensify their satiric attacks on the First Minister and his administration.

Walpole did not accept defeat gracefully, but he was prepared to wait. As time passed, he saw a clear link between the subversive attacks directed against him on stage and the civil disorders that were experienced in London and Edinburgh during 1736 and 1737. Reports from his spies on the ground confirmed his worst suspicions that Jacobite agitators in London were exploiting the grievances associated with the Gin Act and with worries over unemployment. By the autumn of 1736 civil unrest grew to the point where troops had to be called out to bring order to the streets of the capital. At precisely the same point in time Walpole was subject to a barrage of satire emanating from London's

---

[15] See Liesenfeld, *Licensing Act*, 45.   [16] Ibid. 49–50.

[17] See Watson Nicholson, *The Struggle for a Free Stage in London* (London: Archibald Constable, 1906), 59.

[18] See Liesenfeld, *Licensing Act*, 53, and Nicholson, *Struggle for a Free Stage*, 59.

unlicensed fringe theatres. The increasing ferocity of these satirical attacks (directed against him and against George II) only served to strengthen his resolve to conclude the unfinished business of introducing statutory theatre censorship.

Events played into his hands. The growing problem of vagrancy and aggressive begging in London and other cities led to the setting up of a Parliamentary Select Committee in the early part of 1737 to consider how best to reform and tighten up the statute on vagrancy passed in the reign of Queen Anne (12 Anne, stat. 2 c. 23). Prior to Highmore's test case in 1733, this statute had also been used, as we have seen, as the primary means of controlling players in unlicensed playhouses. Walpole took the view that a new and carefully worded statute on vagrancy would provide the ideal means of overturning the adverse judgment in the Highmore test case and would in addition provide a convenient peg on which to hang the mantle of all-encompassing theatre censorship. By March 1737, reports in the press, notably the *Daily Post*, suggest that similar thoughts had occurred to London's players. They were beginning to voice their concerns that the proposed new statute on vagrancy might include amendments that would remove their freedom to work in unlicensed playhouses.[19] The fact that this was reported in the press suggests that the matter was under active discussion in government circles.

The next relevant parliamentary event was a petition from the University of Cambridge in March 1737 relating to the opening of a new permanent playhouse in the town.[20] Since the days of Queen Elizabeth, the Vice-Chancellors of Oxford and Cambridge had been given authority to license or forbid plays within a clearly defined geographical limit extending, in each case, from the city or town centre. In Cambridge, the only regular theatrical entertainments had been linked to the Stourbridge fair in September of each year. (The charter to hold the fair on Stourbridge Common outside the city boundaries dated back to 1211.) Attempts to control these performances were not generally pursued with great vigour as they were of an ephemeral nature. In 1736, however, one Joseph Kettle had erected a permanent playhouse structure for use during the fair and possibly at other times. This caused great alarm to the university authorities who now sought parliamentary permission to suppress this new playhouse. In addition, an unforeseen consequence of the Gin Act (which had permitted those distillers deprived of their livelihood through the Act to pursue any other legitimate trade, including the setting up of ale houses) had led to the proliferation of new taverns in Cambridge. Previously, the licensing of taverns had been a privilege exercised by the

---

[19] See Liesenfeld, *Licensing Act*, 105.
[20] Cambridge did not acquire its charter as a city until 1951.

university authorities. Here too the university authorities sought redress from Parliament. On 10 March 1737, the House of Commons ordered a bill to be prepared to prevent the 'unlawful Playing of Interludes within the Precincts of the University of Cambridge' and also asked for a clause to be inserted to restore to the university its traditional control over taverns.[21] Walpole and Thomas Townshend (Member of Parliament for Cambridge and the son of Walpole's brother-in-law) were appointed by Parliament to prepare the bill.

The speed at which a bill was drafted suggests that a template for imposing strict control on theatrical performances was already in existence. The new bill was given its First Reading on 24 March and its Second Reading on 1 April. After the Second Reading, petitions from interested parties (including Kettle) were heard but not heeded. In mid-April, the University of Oxford submitted a petition to be granted the same authority in respect of players and taverns as the University of Cambridge. This request was duly granted. When the bill was considered by a Committee of the Whole House at the beginning of May, it was significantly Walpole who chaired the Committee and not Townshend.[22] The Third Reading took place on 4 May, after which the bill was sent for approval to the Lords. The Lords made some minor amendments, which were accepted by the Commons, and the bill became law on 19 May 1737 (10 Geo. 2, c. 19). The progress of this bill from First Reading to Royal Assent within a mere two months was quite exceptionally swift. Not only did this statute restore to the Universities of Oxford and Cambridge their right to license taverns in their respective areas, it also gave them unparalleled control over the activities of any players in the two locations. Exploiting the time-honoured device of equating unlicensed actors with rogues and vagabonds, the bill specified draconian punishments for any player who attempted to give any kind of theatrical performance within five miles of the centre of either Oxford or Cambridge. Anyone attempting to earn a living by acting in either of these two locations could in future be imprisoned on the sole authority of the relevant university Chancellor or Vice-Chancellor: there was no provision for bail, remand, or appeal. The automatic punishment specified was a month's hard labour in a house of correction.[23] Walpole clearly viewed this bill as a dress rehearsal for the Licensing Act that he was already planning and which was shortly to follow. He must also have been greatly encouraged by the lack of any serious opposition to the bill in either the Commons or the Lords.

The draconian measures specified in the Universities Bill need to be seen in the context of the activities of contemporary playwrights, players, and journalists in the spring of 1737. Walpole seemed convinced that the satiric

---

[21] Liesenfeld, *Licensing Act*, 86–90.   [22] Ibid. 113.
[23] The full text of the Bill is quoted in ibid. 187–8.

plays of, above all, Fielding (which were performed to great acclaim in London's fringe theatres) posed a real threat to the stability of the state. Fielding's dramatic method in the various pieces he wrote at the time was to base the action around the rehearsal of a fictitious play. This permitted him to make satirical links between the theatrical world and the world of politics by using characters who were critics or authors to comment on aspects of the action that needed particular emphasis. The names of characters in the fictitious pieces contained hidden (but fairly obvious) references to leading figures in the theatre and in politics. Inevitably, Walpole (known as the great man) figured repeatedly in the action of these rumbustious satirical farces.

On 14 March 1737, Fielding's company performed the newest of his farces at the Little Theatre in the Haymarket. It was entitled *A Rehearsal of Kings; or, The Projecting Gingerbread-Baker. With the unheard-of Catastrophe of MacPlunderean, King of Rogusmania: And the ignoble Fall of Baron Tromperland, King of Clouts.* No printed version of the text has survived, but the resonant names of the main characters (and other characters in the piece) suggest an irreverent attack on the First Minister, as a king amongst rogues, and on George II, as a king with a short fuse and a willingness to deliver kicks and clouts. On 21 March 1737, Fielding's company performed his *Historical Register for the Year 1736* at the Little Theatre in the Haymarket. The barbs in this piece were directed equally at politicians and leading figures in London's theatre world. Walpole surfaced in the guise of various characters and was accused of bribing Members of Parliament to buy their support for his policies. Much of the satire, however, was anarchic in tone and the play lashed too many disparate targets to be seen as a sustained political piece.

Fielding's next play was more overtly political in its overall thrust. Called *Eurydice hiss'd: or, a Word to the Wise*, it was performed at the Little Theatre in the Haymarket on 13 April 1737. Supposedly, the piece referred to Fielding's earlier play *Eurydice; or, The Devil Henpeck'd,* which had been hissed at Drury Lane in February by rioting footmen. However, frequent parallels between theatrical and political events made it clear that the real target of the piece was Walpole's Excise Bill of March 1733, which had been effectively 'hissed' out of Parliament by opposition in the House and in the town. That is how Fielding's contemporaries interpreted the play, which was even attended by the Prince of Wales (who was of course at loggerheads with the King and with Walpole). One immediate consequence was an attack on Fielding in the *Daily Gazetteer* (a paper supporting the Government) on 7 May 1737. He was accused of bringing politics on to the stage in order to expose the Government to public ridicule and resentment; this was seen as an abuse of liberty which 'might make a RESTRAINT necessary'.[24] Fielding published a vigorous defence of his approach a few days later in a 'Dedication to the Public', prefaced to the first editions of *The Historical Register* and *Eurydice Hiss'd*. But the defiant tone of his dedication could not entirely disguise his awareness that his use of satire to ridicule 'vice and imposture' was only feasible 'while the liberty of the press and stage subsists'.[25]

The attack on Fielding implied that he might be guilty of seditious libel. The seditious libel laws made it an offence to bring the Government into hatred or contempt, or to foment public resentment against the Government in print, or to publish writings which subverted the authority of the King. For the press, which enjoyed considerable liberty, and for authors and publishers, this was a serious charge, which (if proved) could lead to heavy fines, punishment at the pillory, and a banning order.[26] Given the rumbustious and farcical nature of Fielding's pieces, this charge, if pressed, would have seemed heavy-handed. However, at precisely the same moment in time when Fielding's satires were performed at the Little Theatre in the Haymarket, an anonymous attack on Walpole and the King was published, entitled *The Vision of the Golden Rump*, which clearly did fit the definition of seditious libel. The publication of *The Vision of the Golden Rump* may well have made Walpole suspect a link between Fielding and its anonymous author. The scabrous satire was published in two parts (on 19 and 26 March 1737) in a new journal called *Common Sense*, which was allegedly funded by James III, the Old Pretender.[27] The Jacobite link would have fuelled Walpole's worst suspicions and may have led him to associate Fielding with those who genuinely wished to undermine the stability of the Hanoverian dynasty. In *The Vision of the Golden Rump*, Part One, George II is depicted as a foul-tempered idol or Pagod whose golden rump is kept in proper working order by a High Priestess or Tapanta (the Queen) administering *Aurum Potabile* mixed with pearl powders through a clyster-pipe (an anal syringe). The Pagod's awful temper leads him, on occasion, to kick those near him, particularly if the High Priestess fails to apply her soothing mixture to his golden rump in good time. Assisting the High Priestess is the Chief Magician (Walpole) who carries his wand (or staff of office) which he waves back and forth and which changes into a dragon if laid upon the floor (Walpole's Excise Bill was often referred to as a dragon). Part One concludes with the Pagod demanding tributes of gold and silver and with the Chief Magician promising, on behalf of the congregation (Parliament), to

---

[24] Quoted from ibid. 118.   [25] Ibid. 120.

[26] A number of journalists were successfully prosecuted for seditious libel during the eighteenth century. Full details may be found at: 'Treasury Solicitor: miscellaneous Papers on Sedition Cases (1732–1901)', National Archives.

[27] See Liesenfeld, *Licensing Act*, 92.

obey the Pagod's commands. A procession of Knights of the Golden Rump then follows. In Part Two, the Chief Magician strokes the Pagod's golden rump with his magic wand; this causes it to grow to an enormous size, which pleases the idol greatly. The various Knights approach the Chief Magician who gives them tickets entitling them to various privileges. Not all are satisfied with their tickets, but the process is smoothed over with more processions that conclude the piece.[28]

Both parts were intended as a scurrilous allegory of George II's reign and his behaviour towards his courtiers and politicians. It was public knowledge that the King had suffered from a combination of piles and an anal fistula when he returned from Germany at the beginning of 1737. This had doubtless caused his unusually foul temper at the time, which had led him to aim kicks at some of his closest courtiers. His profligacy was also much resented by both the Government and the public. However, Walpole had no option but to find the money to cover his excessive expenditure. In addition, his long-suffering Queen, who was left abandoned in England while he spent long periods of time in Hanover, was nevertheless expected to minister to his every physical and sexual need as soon as he reappeared in London. Despite his appalling behaviour, courtiers and Members of Parliament were bought off with bribes and perquisites handed out by Walpole, the First Minister. The whole system functioned on the basis of greed and graft and any problems were papered over with empty but impressive rituals.

This was the figurative meaning of *The Golden Rump*, which would have been widely understood in contemporary London. It was plainly intended as a seditious libel, inasmuch as its aim was to destroy any credibility which the King and his First Minister might otherwise have enjoyed. However, rather than bring a prosecution against the offending journal in which the piece was published, Walpole must have realized that this gross satire gave him the opportunity he needed to justify theatre censorship legislation. All that was required was to persuade some anonymous hack to turn the prose version of *The Golden Rump* into a play script for performance; this is exactly what happened. It seems that Henry Giffard, the financially embarrassed owner of the theatres in Goodman's Fields and Lincoln's Inn Fields, was bribed to furnish Walpole with a dramatized version of *The Golden Rump*. Whether he simply handed over the text of a play that had been presented to him for performance, or whether he played a more active role in procuring or even commissioning a dramatized version of *The Golden Rump* is far from clear. What does seem clear is that he was promised a handsome reward by Walpole,

[28] For a detailed account, see ibid. 92–101.

which was honoured only in part.[29] Armed with this incriminating evidence, Walpole calculated that his fellow Members of Parliament would support the introduction of a formal system of theatre censorship. Walpole's preferred vehicle for such an undertaking, as already noted, was an amendment to the vagrancy laws that Parliament had been considering since the early part of 1737. The amendment, which had been mooted in the press since March, would thereafter become known as the Licensing Act of 1737.

THE LICENSING ACT OF 1737

The passage of Walpole's Licensing Act showed the First Minister's true virtuosity as a parliamentary operator. Nothing was left to chance. The detailed wording of the bill was prepared well in advance, but Walpole's intentions were not made clear. Quite deliberately, the bill was introduced at a very late stage in the parliamentary year, when members of both Houses were preparing for the summer recess. Finally, key figures in the theatre were bribed to provide Walpole with the ammunition he needed to win over Opposition Members of Parliament who might otherwise have opposed him. These not only included Giffard (as noted above), but there is also a hint that Fielding's silence was procured with the promise of financial recompense. In 1741, in the preface to his poem 'Of true Greatness', Fielding wrote: 'I have been obliged with Money to silence my Productions, professedly and by Way of Bargain given me for that Purpose.'[30]

Having carefully prepared the ground for the smooth passage of his bill through Parliament, Walpole acted with deft precision on the floor of the House. On 20 May 1737, Parliament agreed to the First Reading of a bill designed to revise the laws relating to rogues, vagabonds, and sturdy beggars passed in the reign of Queen Anne (12 Anne, stat. 2 c. 23). After reading that section of the bill, which classified itinerant actors as vagrants, the House gave leave 'to bring in a Bill to explain and amend so much of [12 Anne, stat. 2 c. 23] . . . as relates to common Players of Interludes'.[31] This deliberate hijacking of Parliament's consideration of a vagrancy statute, in order to bring in a new bill to control theatres and actors, was clearly planned in advance. At this stage of the proceedings, however, Walpole's name was not formally linked with the suggested bill. A mere four days later (24 May), his close associate, Henry

---

[29] See Nicholson, *Struggle for a Free Stage*, 74.

[30] Henry Fielding, *Miscellanies*, ed. by Henry Miller Knight (Oxford: Clarendon Press, 1972), i. 248. See Liesenfeld, *Licensing Act*, 133.

[31] See Liesenfeld, *Licensing Act*, 123.

Pelham, a brother of the Duke of Newcastle, presented to the House the text of a bill whose intention, like the Universities' Act, was to use the provisions of the vagrancy laws as a means to control players who might attempt to perform in unlicensed playhouses. There was, however, no reference at this stage to theatre censorship. The main effect of the proposed bill would be to silence London's unlicensed playhouses, as had been envisaged in Barnard's bill of 1735. Given the widespread support there had been in Parliament for the 1735 bill, it is not surprising that Parliament approved the First Reading of the proposed new bill without a division.

The Second Reading of the bill was ordered for the following day, 25 May 1737. It was at this reading that Walpole announced his intention of adding a clause to the bill that would introduce theatre censorship. To demonstrate the necessity for censorship, he circulated copies, before the debate, of extracts from a dramatized version of *The Golden Rump*. During the debate, he also read out further extracts from the piece, which had the desired effect of causing a general sense of disgust amongst Members of Parliament at the scurrility of the attack on the King. Even Walpole's opponents were now persuaded of the need to bring order and decency back to the London stage. Much the same view was taken by the King, when Walpole read extracts of the farce to him. In Walpole's capable hands, *The Golden Rump* was utilized as a public relations coup which effectively undermined all opposition to his proposed legislation.[32]

A letter to *The Craftsman* published on 28 May insinuated that the farce may have been written to order so as to justify stage censorship.[33] In response, rumours were spread from the Government that Fielding was responsible for the farce. Fielding vigorously denied that this was the case.[34] Meanwhile, consideration of the bill proceeded swiftly in the House of Commons. Pulteney objected to the notion of theatre censorship on the grounds that it would serve as 'a certain preamble to the taking away the Liberty of the Press in general'.[35] However, there is no evidence that the House even moved to a division at the end of the Second Reading on 25 May. The following day, the House was convened as a Committee of the Whole House to give detailed consideration to the proposed bill. The new clause on censorship required theatre managers to submit copies of new plays to the Lord Chamberlain fourteen days before they were acted, and not to perform them without a licence from the Lord Chamberlain or risk a fine of £50, and the loss of their licence for the playhouse.[36] The Lord Chamberlain was in addition to be given absolute authority to prohibit the acting, performing, or representing of any

---

[32] See ibid. 129.   [33] See ibid. 131.   [34] Ibid. 132.
[35] Quoted from ibid. 132.   [36] See ibid. 139.

kind of play, opera, farce, or any stage entertainment.[37] When the clause was voted on, 185 Members of Parliament voted in favour and 63 against. A second clause added to the bill in committee restricted the location of playhouses to the City of Westminster and to such places where the King or his heirs might in future reside and then only during the period of such residence. The effect of this clause would be to force the closure of the various unlicensed playhouses in London and to prohibit the erection of any playhouses in the provinces.

The bill was given an unopposed Third Reading in the House of Commons on 1 June 1737; on the same day it was sent to the House of Lords, where it was given its First Reading. The Second Reading in the House of Lords took place the following day. During the debate after this Second Reading Lord Chesterfield made a brilliantly crafted speech opposing the bill. He began his speech by attacking the unseemly haste with which the playhouse bill had been rushed through Parliament. He also complained of the late stage in the parliamentary session when the bill was introduced. He then went on to argue that current laws were sufficient to deal with any plays containing seditious libel. The problem was not with current laws, but with the failure of those in authority to bring forward prosecutions. He went on to predict that a bill designed to introduce strict theatre censorship would be a prelude to a further bill in which Parliament would be asked to ban the printing of plays, and then novels containing seditious libel. Finally, Parliament would be asked to approve a bill placing 'the Press under a general Licence, and then we may bid adieu to the Liberties of *Great Britain*'.[38] Looking back to the time of Charles II, when the stage operated under licence, he commented that the only plays permitted were those that reflected the views, the follies, and the vices of the Court. The same would be true in future. With the Lord Chamberlain exercising theatre censorship on behalf of the Government, the only views permitted would be those of the court party. In a far-sighted passage, he argued that wit is a kind of property (probably the first ever mention of intellectual property), 'the property of those who have it and too often the only property they have to depend on'. It was the duty of Parliament to protect wit, 'whosoever's property it may be'. The only effect of the proposed legislation will be 'to prevent every man of a generous and free spirit' from writing for the stage. Chesterfield's prophecy in this respect was to prove to a large degree accurate.

The more ominous prophecy with which he concluded his speech was less convincing and proved to be overstated. Chesterfield warned the House that

---

[37] Ibid.   [38] Ibid.

arbitrary power was normally introduced into a country by slow degrees, so that people might not be made aware of its approach:

The stage, my Lords, and the press are two of our out-sentries; if we remove them, if we hood-wink them, if we throw them in fetters, the enemy may surprise us. Therefore I must look upon the bill now before us as a step, and a most necessary step too, for introducing arbitrary power in this kingdom. It is a step so necessary that if ever any future ambitious king, or guilty minister, should form to himself so wicked a design, he will have reason to thank us, for having done so much of the work to his hand, but such thanks, or thanks from such a man, I am convinced, every one of your lordships would blush to receive and scorn to deserve.[39]

In setting out this apocalyptic vision, Chesterfield gave clear evidence of his rhetorical skills. But he also diluted the arguments he had made against theatre censorship by submerging them in a vision of a hypothetical future state in which all ancient laws and liberties were swept aside. Clearly their Lordships were unimpressed by such a vision, which seemed utterly far-fetched. The proposed bill was intended, as they saw it, not as an attack on liberty but as a return to proper and effective control over the theatre. It was viewed as a necessary restraint on playwrights who were intent on using seditious libel to foment public unrest. The following day, 3 June, the House of Lords, sitting as a Committee of the Whole House, considered the bill clause by clause and approved it without amendment. Chesterfield's rhetoric had fallen on deaf ears. This was confirmed a few days later when the House of Lords gave the bill its Third Reading. After the Reading, a division was called; those in favour of the bill numbered 37 and those against (including Chesterfield) numbered 5.[40]

The parliamentary session ended on 21 June 1737. The King, in the presence of both Houses, gave the Royal Assent to the Licensing Act (10 Geo. 2, c. 28). In his speech to the assembled Lords and Commons, George II made it clear that he saw the passage of the Act as a necessary defence of good order. In words that echoed the sentiments of his First Minister, he pointed to a clear link between civil disorder and disorder on the stage:

You cannot be insensible what just Scandal and Offence the Licentiousness of the present Times, under the Colour and Disguise of Liberty, gives to all honest and sober Men; and how absolutely necessary it is to restrain this excessive Abuse, by a due and vigorous Execution of the Laws. Defiance of all Authority, Contempt of Magistracy, and even Resistance of the Law, are become too general, although equally prejudicial to the Prerogative of the Crown, and the Liberties of the People; the Support of the one being inseparable from the Protection of the other. I have made the Laws of the Land the constant Rule of My Actions; and I do with Reason expect, in Return, all that

---

[39] Ibid. 214.   [40] See Liesenfeld, *Licensing Act*, 150.

Submission to my Authority and Government which the same Laws have made the Duty, and shall always be the Interest, of My Subjects.[41]

By implication, the King's statement confirmed that control over the stage, exercised by the Lord Chamberlain under the ill-defined authority of the Royal Prerogative, had proved insufficient to safeguard the stage from abuse. The flagrant defiance of the King's authority and prerogative power, exercised by the Lord Chamberlain, had been prejudicial to good order and government. It was now time to bring the stage under the stricter control of statute law to which all citizens were subject.

The final version of the Licensing Act (10 Geo. 2, c. 28), in its opening clause, effectively undid the judgement given in the Highmore test case of 1733. The Act established that every person should be deemed a rogue and a vagabond (and liable to a fine of £50 for each offence) for presenting any play or entertainment for 'Hire, Gain or Reward' in a place where such person had no legal settlement, 'or performed without Authority by virtue of Letters Patent from His Majesty, his Heirs, Successors or Predecessors, or without Licence from the Lord Chamberlain of His Majesty's household'.[42] This clause meant that in future any player attempting to act for hire, gain, or reward in any of London's unlicensed playhouses would face an immediate fine of £50. The clause also meant that the managers of London's two patent houses (Drury Lane and Covent Garden) were in effect given monopoly rights over all future stage performances in the capital, while the actors and managers from London's unlicensed playhouses at a stroke lost their livelihoods. A later clause in the Act confirmed the full extent of the monopoly powers given to the two patent theatres. Performances might only be given in future in patent houses or in playhouses licensed by the Lord Chamberlain within the City of Westminster, or in such places where the King or his successor was residing during the period of their residence. The aim was clearly to curtail any new theatre building in London for the foreseeable future.

The wording of the opening clause, however, also affected the provinces. As a result, the extensive proliferation of theatre buildings which took place in the provinces during the latter part of the eighteenth century was initially undertaken in breach of the law. The process began with the building of the Orchard Street Theatre in Bath (erected in 1750), and continued with the construction of new playhouses in major cities from the 1760s onwards in places as disparate as Edinburgh, Norwich, York, Liverpool, Manchester, and Bristol. Few prosecutions were attempted as these provincial ventures were

---

[41] *Journals of the House of Lords*, xxv, June 1737, 151.

[42] 10 Geo. 2, c. 28. *Statutes at Large* (1764), vi. 275. The Act is also reproduced in Thomas, *Theatre in Europe*, 207–10.

widely supported by their local communities and viewed favourably by local magistrates. But there was a successful prosecution in Bath in 1754, which led to the temporary closure of the Orchard Street Theatre. When it reopened shortly afterwards, theatrical performances in Bath were advertised as Concerts of Music.[43] As from 1767, however, the Licensing Act was amended to bring it back into line with actual practice. For each of the provincial playhouses already constructed, and for new ones about to be constructed, the Licensing Act was repealed in as far as it applied to the relevant city. The new playhouse was then given a formal patent and the title of Theatre Royal.[44] However, in every case the manager of each Theatre Royal was strictly required to perform only plays, operas, or other kinds of performance licensed by the Lord Chamberlain.[45] The flouting of the licensing provisions of the Act with impunity in the provinces confirms that the real target of the legislation was London's politicized fringe theatres which had proliferated during the late 1720s and early 1730s.

The censorship provisions of the Act were included in Clauses III and IV. Clause III required that any new work intended for performance should be submitted, with an accompanying note from the relevant theatre manager, to the Lord Chamberlain for approval at least two weeks before the intended performance. Failure to comply with this requirement would entail an immediate fine of £50 in every case and the loss of the licence and grant under which the relevant playhouse operated. This was a draconian punishment that no manager would in future be prepared to risk.

Clause IV of the Act went on to spell out the far-reaching powers of censorship that were now given to the Lord Chamberlain:

It shall and may be lawful to and for the said Lord Chamberlain for the time being, from time to time, and when, and as often as he shall think fit, to prohibit the acting, performing or representing any Interlude, Tragedy, Comedy, Opera, Play, Farce or other Entertainment of the Stage, or any Act, Scene or Part therefore, or any Prologue or Epilogue.[46]

This clause meant that the Lord Chamberlain could in future prohibit whatever he wished, and whenever or how often he thought fit. No limits were set to his authority and nor was he required to justify any of his decisions. His powers of censorship were absolute and arbitrary and there was no provision for any appeal against them. Without once mentioning playwrights, the wording of the Act ensured that they were placed in a uniquely disadvantaged position

[43] See ibid. 222.   [44] See ibid. 222–3.
[45] As an example of this, see the patent for establishing a playhouse in the City of Edinburgh (1767), reprinted in ibid. 223.
[46] 10 Geo. 2, c. 28. *Statutes at Large* (1764), vi. 276.

in English society. Books (including plays) and newspapers were published without pre-censorship. Authors were then only liable to prosecution if their work was deemed to contain seditious libel. But the charge of seditious libel would need to be proven at law. In the case of playwrights intending their plays for performance rather than for publication, they were required to submit their work for pre-censorship and might expect to see their works banned or censored by the Lord Chamberlain whose decisions could not be challenged. No redress was open to them in law, nor did Parliament have any powers to question the decisions taken by the Lord Chamberlain. Although these powers given to the Lord Chamberlain were not a prelude to a more general attack on freedom of speech (as Chesterfield and others feared), they did amount to an arbitrary imposition of authoritarian control over the stage.

In previous centuries, the Master of the Revels and later the Lord Chamberlain had exercised the roles of censor and licensor in respect of theatrical activity in London under the ill-defined authority of the Royal Prerogative. Any interventions by the Master of the Revels or later by the Lord Chamberlain to ban plays or players were undertaken on behalf of the monarch both before, but more frequently after production. In drafting the Licensing Act, Walpole may have intended no more than a formal reinstatement of the traditional powers (exercised by members of the royal household) to license plays and players as part of the Royal Prerogative. However, by giving the Lord Chamberlain sweeping powers which were defined in statute law, Walpole established a cast-iron legal framework of control that could only be relaxed or broken if Parliament, at some future date, was minded to repeal the Licensing Act. As we have seen, some of the provisions of the Act relating to the licensing of provincial playhouses were relaxed in practice and eventually formally repealed during the late eighteenth century. In addition, the provisions of the Act relating to the licensing of new theatre buildings in London were eventually repealed by the Theatres Act of 1843. However, the censorship powers vested in the Lord Chamberlain by the Licensing Act of 1737 were not repealed until the Theatres Act of 1968. This was the astonishing outcome of Walpole's attempt to bring back some semblance of control to London's theatres at a time of general unrest in the 1730s.

THE AFTERMATH OF THE 1737 LICENSING ACT

The Licensing Act did not specify how the Lord Chamberlain was to undertake his censorship duties, although clearly the Lord Chamberlain himself could not be expected to read and judge the merits of the many play manuscripts that would be submitted to him. As head of the King's Household, he had far too many other tasks that would demand his daily attention. It was therefore decided to appoint a licensor and also an Examiner of Stage Plays to the Lord Chamberlain's staff to undertake his censorship role on his behalf and to license approved plays. There is no record of what advice the Lord Chamberlain took in arriving at this solution. However, it seems reasonable to assume that he would have consulted Walpole who was after all responsible for the drafting of the censorship clauses in the Licensing Act and for steering the Act through Parliament.

It was probably Walpole who saw to it that the man appointed to peruse and censor plays on behalf of the Lord Chamberlain was Odell, the former manager of the playhouse in Goodman's Fields. Back in 1728, Odell had brazenly defied the authority of the Lord Chamberlain (the Duke of Grafton) when the latter attempted to silence his newly erected, unlicensed playhouse. Now, as Examiner of Plays, Odell was to become one of the closest allies and most trusted servants of the very same Lord Chamberlain whose authority he had previously challenged.[47] Astute as ever, Walpole was well aware that in political life it is often wise to encourage a former poacher to turn gamekeeper. Odell proved to be a reliable and zealous censor; there were also financial advantages to be gained from his new role. Although the Act made no mention of a licensing fee, such a fee had traditionally been paid to the Master of the Revels. Custom and practice therefore dictated that a fee would now be paid to the Examiner for every play (or new scene in an old play) given a licence for performance.[48]

In financial terms, the main beneficiaries of the Licensing Act were the patentees of London's two licensed playhouses (Drury Lane and Covent Garden). Instead of having to form an illegal cartel to control the theatrical life of the capital, they were given the free gift by the Government of a total theatrical monopoly. Under these circumstances, they naturally supported the new Act and firmly rejected the arguments that Chesterfield (and the Opposition) had made against it. The economic argument in favour of the Act is made explicit by Colley Cibber (a former patentee) in his autobiography:

What Advantage could either the Spectators of Plays or the Masters of Play-houses have gain'd by its having never been made? How could the same Stock of Plays supply four Theatres, which (without such additional Entertainments as a Nation of common Sense ought to be ashamed of) could not well support two? Satiety must have been the

---

[47] See Thomas, *Theatre in Europe*, 216.
[48] Some theatre historians have suggested that the levying of a fee was illegal, but this ignores the importance of custom and practice in such matters. See L. W. Conolly, *The Censorship of English Drama 1737–1824* (San Marino: Anderson, Ritchie and Simon, 1976), 16.

natural Consequence of the same Plays being twice as often repeated as now they need be; and Satiety puts an End to all Tastes that the Mind of Man can delight in. Had therefore this Law been made seven Years ago, I should not have parted with my Share in the Patent under a thousand Pounds more than I received for it—So that, as far as I am able to judge, both the Publick as Spectators and the Patentees as Undertakers, are, or might be, in a way of being better entertain'd and more considerable Gainers by it.[49]

Cibber was understandably dismissive of Fielding's plays in which he had been repeatedly satirized: hence his comments about the kind of entertainment offered in the unlicensed houses as an affront to common sense. However, the main thrust of his argument was that there were not enough quality plays available to justify the existence of more than two licensed playhouses in London. In Cibber's view, it was to everyone's advantage to have London's theatrical life controlled by a small cartel of two patent playhouses. This was not a view shared by those actors who had just lost their livelihoods or by the audiences who had given their enthusiastic support to the work of the unlicensed playhouses. In addition, the monopoly powers exercised by the patent holders were to prove damaging to the work of new playwrights. The patentees' stranglehold over the London stage for the next hundred years was to give rise to a powerful form of covert censorship exercised alongside the overt censorship undertaken by the Examiner and Deputy Examiner of Plays.[50]

Some few years after the passing of the Act, the unfortunate managers of London's (now silenced) unlicensed playhouses sought to find ways round the statute. Giffard was the prime mover. Having failed to secure the financial reward he had expected for providing Walpole with a dramatized version of *The Golden Rump*, he may have assumed (or even been told) that the authorities would overlook any breach of the Act on his part. He reopened the Theatre in Goodman's Fields on 15 October 1740, claiming to charge only for the music and offering the play for free. For the remainder of the season, his ruse seemed to work. However, when he engaged the young David Garrick as a member of his company in the autumn of 1741, large crowds flocked to see this talented young player in *Richard III*. Soon audiences were competing for tickets at Goodman's Fields, and ignoring the programmes offered at the patent houses. At this point, the patentees were stirred into action and, with the support of Sir John Barnard in his role as a magistrate,

---

[49] Cibber, *An Apology*, i. 297–8. Cibber had previously been co-manager at Drury Lane with John Wilks and Barton Booth; he had sold his share in the Drury Lane patent to John Highmore for 3,000 guineas in 1735. By the late 1730s he was in semi-retirement and was primarily concerned with writing his autobiography.

[50] See Conolly, *Censorship*, 2.

threatened to lay a formal complaint against Giffard and Garrick, invoking the 1737 Act. Both Giffard and Garrick bowed to the inevitable and accepted engagements offered at Drury Lane. The Theatre in Goodman's Fields closed once again.[51]

Similar tactics were attempted by the actors Charles Macklin and Theophilus Cibber in the 1743–4 season, when some of the leading Drury Lane players (including Garrick) rebelled against their manager Charles Fleetwood. After Garrick and other actors had backed down (which led to a fierce pamphlet war with those who refused to compromise), Macklin formed a company of young actors at the Little Theatre in the Haymarket. Initially, the declared intention was to establish an academy of acting. The opening performance of the young actors on 4 February 1744 was advertised as a concert, to be followed by *Othello*. By the autumn of 1744, Macklin had returned to Drury Lane and was obliged to apologize in public for his rebellion. Cibber was now left in sole charge of the company of young players at the Little Theatre in the Haymarket. He tried the ploy of advertising a concert, to be followed by a free public rehearsal given by his pupils. Like Giffard, who had been threatened with a prosecution under the Licensing Act, Cibber was formally warned by a Justice of the Peace that he would be liable to prosecution as a vagabond if he continued with his scheme. Faced by this prospect, he gave up his attempted defiance of the Act and joined Rich's company at Covent Garden.[52]

Initially, the absolute powers of censorship vested by the Licensing Act in the Lord Chamberlain were used cautiously by the Examiner and his Deputy. Although Fielding had ceased writing political satires (presumably for the financial reasons mentioned above), other playwrights were keen to follow his example and subject the Government to ridicule on stage. For the first two years after the passing of the Act, several plays were allowed by the Examiner which had included satiric attacks on Walpole.[53] However, after 1739 (one imagines following discreet but firm representations from the First Minister), Odell began to act more resolutely and even recommended that several plays be banned outright which included anti-government sentiments in the dialogue. The first was Henry Brooke's *Gustavus Vasa*, which was banned by the Lord Chamberlain in March 1739. This was soon followed by James Thomson's tragedy *Edward and Eleonora*: both plays contained obvious coded references to Walpole and his corruption.[54] Further bans were issued during 1739 and the early 1740s; other plays, which attacked Walpole, were published but were not even submitted for licensing. With Walpole's resignation from office in

---

[51] See Nicholson, *Struggle for a Free Stage*, 73–6.   [52] Ibid. 78–80.
[53] For a detailed account of such attacks, see Conolly, *Censorship*, 47–54.
[54] See ibid. 54–9.

1742 and with the Jacobite invasion in 1745 stirring strong feelings of patriotic support for King and Government, playwrights lost interest in politics. For the remainder of the eighteenth century, the few men who still bothered to write for the stage simply avoided politics altogether.[55]

It is a remarkable fact that a period of great turbulence in English political history in the 1770s and 1780s attracted no attention from the stage whatsoever. The American War of Independence and the loss of the American colonies led to frequent changes of government and even the threatened abdication of George III.[56] On the London stage, there was not as much as a passing reference to these momentous events. One of the few plays of literary merit written during this period, R. B. Sheridan's *School for Scandal* (1777), shows the image of a society that is completely obsessed with its own trivial, day-to-day concerns, namely gossip, money, inheritance, and adultery. Sheridan's portrait of an inward-looking, self-engrossed society was probably completely accurate. Members of London's fashionable society (known as the *ton*) were more than content to concentrate their attention on guessing which figures from the contemporary social whirl surrounding the Duchess of Devonshire were depicted in Sheridan's play. Mrs Crewe, as one of the Devonshire House Circle, wrote to Lady Clermont: 'I can assure you that the Farce is charming; the Duchess of Devonshire, Lady Worseley and I cut very good figures in it.'[57]

After the outbreak of the French Revolution in 1789, there were stirrings of republican feelings in Parliament and the press. The mood turned, however, after the execution of Louis XVI and his family and after war broke out between France and Britain in January 1793. The general tide of opinion in the country was for King and Church. Nevertheless, to ensure domestic peace and to prevent the spread of seditious views, the Prime Minister William Pitt armed himself with additional powers. In 1794 habeas corpus was suspended; and in 1795 an Act was passed that made writing or even speaking treason a criminal offence.[58] Against a background of this kind of repressive legislation, there was little incentive for playwrights even to attempt any reference in their work to contemporary events. Furthermore, the Lord Chamberlain and his Examiner would have immediately banned any material that was considered politically sensitive. Despite this gradual erosion of freedom of expression, there was no groundswell of opposition to the principle of theatre censorship at any point during the eighteenth century: nor was there to be any during the nineteenth century. Individual playwrights might complain of the way

[55] For a detailed account, see ibid. 65.
[56] See Asa Briggs, *The Age of Improvement, 1783–1867* (London: Longman, 2000), 65–8.
[57] Quoted from Amanda Foreman, *Georgiana, Duchess of Devonshire* (London: HarperCollins, 1999), 50.
[58] See Briggs, *Age of Improvement*, 118.

they were treated by the Examiner, but none of them went on to demand the abolition of theatre censorship.[59] Viewed in retrospect, it is clear that the system of theatre censorship introduced by the Licensing Act was remarkably effective in stifling any expression of political criticism on the London stage from the eighteenth century until the beginning of the twentieth century.

The main issue of contention that was to arise out of the Act was the monopoly given to the London patent theatres. Initially, pressure for change came from the provinces. In principle, any performance of drama-related material for hire, gain, or reward needed the permission of the Lord Chamberlain and was to be confined to patent playhouses (or playhouses licensed by the Lord Chamberlain) in the City of Westminster. However, in the provinces custom and practice dictated that permission for ad hoc performances would continue to be given (as previously) by local Justices of the Peace. As the historian Asa Briggs has pointed out, throughout England justices wielded a powerful control over local affairs: 'It was the local Justices of the Peace rather than the Cabinet who symbolized "authority" to most Englishmen, and in this view of the matter most Englishmen were right... the Justices of the Peace combined judicial and administrative functions which gave them far greater local power to control or compel than that wielded by ministers at the centre.'[60]

The role of the justices was to preserve property, rank, and good order in society. Unless their powers in specific areas were clearly defined in statute law, they exercised their authority on the basis of historical precedent and common sense. Inevitably, they also took into account local circumstances, which might vary considerably in different parts of the country. In some areas, there were reports of disorders, unruly behaviour, and even plays being performed that had not been formally licensed by the Lord Chamberlain.[61] Eventually, these reports attracted the attention of Members of Parliament and led to two further Acts of Parliament, which were both intended to clarify an increasingly confused situation rather than to apply new restrictions to current licensing practice. The first, known as the Act for Regulating Places of Public Entertainment (25 Geo. 2, c. 36), was passed in 1752. Initially, it was approved for a trial period of three years, and then in 1755 it was renewed and made permanent (28 Geo. 2, c. 19).

The Act was intended to provide clear guidelines for magistrates when granting licences to places of popular entertainment both in the Cities of London and Westminster and within a twenty-mile radius of the two cities.

---

[59] Some examples of complaints made by playwrights are given in Conolly, *Censorship*, 169.

[60] See Briggs, *Age of Improvement*, 86–7.

[61] See John Russell Stephens, *The Censorship of English Drama, 1824–1901* (Cambridge: Cambridge University Press, 1980), 7.

Such locations included permanent structures such as Sadler's Wells (closed briefly in 1744 after prosecution as a disorderly and disreputable house), and in addition rooms, gardens, and parts of taverns used for performances of popular acts (including singing and dancing). Section 2 of the Act makes it clear that it was prompted in part by complaints of disorderly conduct, including thefts and robberies, in these mushrooming places of entertainment 'for the lower sort of people'.[62] In future, all such places would be required to obtain a licence from four Justices of the Peace, sitting in their Michaelmas Quarter Sessions. These justices 'are hereby authorised and empowered to grant such licences as they in their discretion shall think proper'.[63] The licence must be displayed at the entrance to the relevant place of entertainment, and it must include the statement that no entertainment may be offered 'before the hour of five in the afternoon'. In effect, this Act gave the force of statute law to powers already exercised in an ad hoc manner by Justices of the Peace in London and Westminster and the Home Counties. It also standardized their practice so that any breach of the law would make it easy to bring a prosecution on the charge of keeping a disorderly house. However, the unlimited discretionary powers now given to justices by statute ensured that they could give proper consideration to local circumstances in arriving at their decisions.

The second piece of legislation, known as the Enabling Act of 1788 (28 Geo. 3, c. 30), was likewise intended to give the force of statute law to powers previously exercised by magistrates on an ad hoc basis in towns and cities throughout England. By the 1780s, various provincial cities had successfully obtained letters patent for a permanent theatre building (most of which had been erected in quiet defiance of the law). In each case, as we have seen, the granting of a patent involved the repeal of the 1737 Act in as far as it applied to the city in question. This left unresolved the issue of licences granted by justices to troupes of touring players for occasional performances of plays, operas, and light entertainment. The 1788 Act gave justices statutory powers to license such occasional performances 'for any number of days not exceeding sixty days'.[64] As in the case of the patents granted for theatres in specified cities, this Act makes it clear that all dramatic entertainment presented by troupes of players in the provinces must also have been approved and licensed by the Lord Chamberlain. In giving statutory authority to the powers already exercised by the justices, the Act in addition clarified and tightened up the censorship requirements in respect of all licensed performances.

Following the passing of the Enabling Act, the extensive powers of local justices to license all kinds of performance throughout the length and breadth

[62] The Act is reproduced in Thomas, *Theatre in Europe*, 225–6.
[63] Quoted from ibid. 226.   [64] Ibid. 231.

of the land were formally acknowledged. What had previously been a de facto power exercised through custom and practice (almost a judicial equivalent of the Royal Prerogative) now received the blessing of statute law. However, if the intention behind the legislation was to clarify an increasingly confused situation, the opposite effect was actually achieved. Enshrined in statute law, there was now a shared jurisdiction, operating in parallel, which gave both Justices of the Peace and the Lord Chamberlain powers to license different kinds of performance. The Lord Chamberlain was given responsibility for licensing theatres (including the patent theatres) in the City of Westminster; and the patent theatres were the sole theatres entitled to present spoken (or 'legitimate') drama in the City of Westminster. However, Justices of the Peace now had formal powers to license other types of popular theatrical establishments and popular entertainment (non-legitimate drama) within a twenty-mile radius of London and Westminster. They could also license performances of 'legitimate' drama (providing the scripts had been approved by the Lord Chamberlain) outside the twenty-mile radius of London and Westminster for limited periods of time in any provincial town or city. Not surprisingly, enterprising theatre entrepreneurs (who resented the monopoly of the patent houses) did their best to exploit this tangled skein of legislation to their own advantage: some did so even before the Enabling Act reached the statute books.

The first of these was the actor John Palmer who built the Royalty Theatre in Wellclose Square in 1787 with the firm intention of presenting a repertoire that included 'legitimate' drama. Palmer's theatre was situated just east of the Tower of London. The site fell within the jurisdiction of the Governor of the Tower who gave his approval for the construction of the playhouse. In addition, Palmer had obtained a licence for performance from the magistrates of Tower Hamlets under the terms of the 1752/1755 legislation. This would have permitted him to perform popular entertainment, such as burlettas (plays with musical elements), dances, and pantomimes. As soon as he announced that his repertoire would include legitimate drama, the patentees publicly threatened him with legal action in articles published in the press. Because of this threat, the players whom Palmer had engaged declined to fulfil any contract (for hire, gain, or reward) that would make them liable to prosecution as vagrants and vagabonds. In order to avoid the immediate threat of litigation, Palmer was obliged to announce that the proceeds of his opening night would be devoted to the London Hospital. On 20 June 1787 the theatre duly opened with a performance of Shakespeare's *As You Like It*, followed by an afterpiece. At the end of the evening Palmer came on stage and made an eloquent speech to a supportive audience in which he outlined his case for presenting 'legitimate' drama. He explained the nature of his licence (from the Governor of the Tower of London and the magistrates of Tower Hamlets); he then went on to accuse the patentees of acting in bad faith by waiting until the last moment to raise objections to his scheme. With some bitterness he commented to the first-night audience: 'Tumblers and Dancing Dogs might appear unmolested before you: but the other performers and myself, standing forward to exhibit a moral play, is deemed a crime.'[65] Palmer concluded his address by announcing that the theatre would remain closed until he could establish what kind of entertainment might be offered without the threat of prosecution. When the theatre reopened on 3 July 1787, its repertoire consisted of burlettas, dances, and pantomimes, which could quite properly be licensed by a magistrate under the terms of the 1755 legislation.[66] Nevertheless, the patentees continued to harass Palmer and his company if they considered there was any infringement of the strict terms of the Licensing Act.

In the following year, 1788, Sadler's Wells attempted to proceed down the parliamentary route and to make a bid to be given letters patent. This was a path that had already been followed with considerable success by a number of theatres in provincial cities. A bill was given its First Reading on 10 March in the House of Commons which would have permitted letters patent to be granted to Sadler's Wells for the kind of entertainments at present licensed by justices. However, viewed from the perspective of the patentees, Sadler's Wells was situated close enough to Westminster to be seen as a potential competitor. The playwright Sheridan, who was now a patentee of Drury Lane and a Member of Parliament, spoke vigorously against the proposed bill. He argued with some shrewdness that Sadler's Wells was merely requesting monopoly rights over certain kinds of light entertainment. He went on to move a postponement of the Second Reading until April, knowing full well that this would delay consideration of the Bill until after the new season had started at Sadler's Wells. After these delaying tactics instigated by Sheridan, William Mainwaring, who had moved the original bill, introduced a new bill known as the Interlude Bill on 8 April 1788. The aim behind this bill was to clarify and amend current legislation in respect of theatre licences outside Westminster. A clause was added to bring Sadler's Wells within the scope of the bill and soon other theatres petitioned the House to be included in the new bill. These included the Royalty Theatre, Astley's, and the Royal Circus. The House of Lords in June 1788 agreed amendments that would have extended patent rights for light entertainment not only to Sadler's Wells but also to these other performance venues. When the bill returned to the House of Commons, however, it was rejected on 25 June 1788.[67]

---

[65] Quoted from Nicholson, *Struggle for a Free Stage*, 106.
[66] For a detailed account of the opening of the Royalty Theatre, see ibid. 98–112.
[67] See Thomas, *Theatre in Europe*, 226–7, and Nicholson, *Struggle for a Free Stage*, 127–37.

Throughout the eighteenth century the patentees defended their monopoly rights in London with hawk-eyed vigilance. The only breach in the monopoly rights granted to the patent houses by the 1737 Act occurred in 1766. It was, however, sufficiently limited in scope as to cause no real concern to the patentees. Between 1747 and 1756, the comic actor Samuel Foote had offered one-man shows during the summer season at the Little Theatre in the Haymarket. Presented on an irregular and erratic basis, his shows were tolerated by the patentees because of their eccentric nature. They were also mounted during the summer season when the patent theatres were closed. This situation changed in July 1766, when Foote was given, by grace and favour, a patent to present every year a summer season of plays at the Little Theatre in the Haymarket, situated in the City of Westminster. The patent was granted by the Lord Chamberlain (the Duke of Portland), apparently at the request of the Duke of York. It seems that the latter felt a keen sense of personal responsibility for a riding accident in which Foote was seriously injured and subsequently had one of his legs amputated. The grant of a patent was therefore viewed as a means of compensating the actor for the loss of a limb.[68] The real significance of this grant lay in the fact that the Lord Chamberlain, in approving Foote's patent, for the first time used the discretionary licensing powers given him in the 1737 Act. However, in granting a patent (rather than a licence) to Foote, the Lord Chamberlain in effect reasserted the authority of the Royal Prerogative over theatrical activity in the City of Westminster. This added yet further confusion to the whole issue of licensing legislation.

More confusion was to follow in the early nineteenth century. In the first few decades of the nineteenth century, there was increasing pressure from theatre managers and actors in London to abolish the monopoly powers of the patent holders. The theatres at Covent Garden and Drury Lane burnt down in respectively 1808 and 1809 and were replaced by significantly larger structures. The increased capital investment required for these new buildings ensured that the patentees and their shareholders would in future fight even more resolutely to preserve their monopoly rights. However, these large new theatres also involved significantly increased running costs. To cover these, Charles Kemble at Covent Garden attempted to put up the prices of admission when his new building opened in 1809. This provoked 'old price' riots which lasted several months. This was clearly not a viable course of action. The only other recourse open to the patentees was to broaden the appeal of their repertoire by admitting popular forms of entertainment. But in turning to pantomimes, acrobats, and performing animals, they were hardly proving to be stout defenders of legitimate drama, which they alone were legally entitled

---

[68] See Nicholson, *Struggle for a Free Stage*, 88–9.

to present to London audiences. This led in 1810–11 to a concerted attempt in Parliament to introduce legislation that would have permitted the building of a new, third patent theatre in London. The arguments advanced in favour of the Third Theatre Bill included the lack of choice available to London's theatregoers and the poor quality of the repertoire offered by the patent houses. However, the rights of the patentees were stoutly defended by some Members of Parliament, including Sheridan, who had a vested interest in seeing the status quo preserved. Both the bill itself and subsequent motions to investigate the present state of 'Dramatic and Scenic representations'[69] in London were defeated. In 1813 the attempt to break the monopoly of the patent houses by legislating for a third theatre in London was finally quashed.

While this activity was taking place in Parliament, pressure was building on the patent theatres from another quarter. With the inexorable growth of London's population, market forces dictated that theatrical entrepreneurs would find alternative ways to meet the demands of a growing audience base. The provinces had seen a veritable explosion of theatre building since the 1760s so that, by the turn of the century, all major cities and most towns of any significance now had their own theatres. Similar developments began to take place in the outskirts of London, although the licensing arrangements here were different from those that obtained in the provinces. Within twenty miles of London and Westminster, magistrates could license theatres and other buildings offering *only* light entertainment. Within the cities of London and Westminster, such licences were given, not by magistrates, but by the Lord Chamberlain.

By the early years of the nineteenth century, there was a steady growth in what became known as the minor theatres, offering different kinds of light entertainment to local audiences in and around London. Inevitably, those serving as Lord Chamberlain during the first few decades of the nineteenth century found themselves on the receiving end of countless petitions and requests from theatrical entrepreneurs for new and additional licences for theatres in the City of Westminster. Some were accommodating to the demands of the minor theatres. Most notable was the Earl of Dartmouth, who served as Lord Chamberlain from 1804 to 1810 when the position of the minor theatres was greatly strengthened.

Successive Lords Chamberlain granted restricted licences (for supposedly musical burlettas, melodramas, and other kinds of light entertainment) to new theatres opened within the City of Westminster, namely the Adelphi, the Olympic, the St James's, and the Strand.[70] At the same time, magistrates south

---

[69] Quoted from ibid. 242–3   [70] See Stephens, *Censorship of English Drama*, 7.

of the Thames gave permission for similar performances at Sadler's Wells, Astley's Circus (later the Royal Circus and, later still, the Surrey), the Coburg, and the Sans Pareil. Gradually, the quality of work presented at these minor theatres improved markedly. At the same time, the work offered by the patent houses declined in quality. In addition, the minor theatres stretched the definition of a burletta to the point where it was almost indistinguishable from that of a play. A few chords played inaudibly in the background might suffice for the claim to be made that a piece was a burletta and not a tragedy or comedy. Inevitably, this led to a barrage of complaints to the Lord Chamberlain by the patent holders. One example from the Lord Chamberlain's files may suffice here to illustrate the point. On 2 November 1815, the proprietors of Drury Lane and Covent Garden complained to the Lord Chamberlain about the repertoire of the Olympic Theatre: 'Instead of confining the performance to the regulations of Burletta, as directed by your Lordships Licence, Dialogue is substituted for Recitation in Rhyme, and carried on without accompaniment by the orchestra.'[71]

THE 1832 SELECT COMMITTEE

By the early 1830s, it was increasingly clear that the theatre licensing system in London needed to be reformed. The final push for reform, however, came not from representatives of the minor theatres but from playwrights who felt increasingly that their livelihoods were being adversely affected by the monopoly restrictions imposed by the 1737 Act. Meetings convened by playwrights were held in late 1831 and early 1832 at which resolutions were formulated and passed to be forwarded to Parliament. The second meeting, held on 24 February 1832, was chaired by Edward Bulwer MP[72] (who was himself a playwright) and he carefully noted the various comments and objections made by his fellow authors. On 22 May 1832 Bulwer presented a petition to the House of Commons asking for a repeal of legislation restricting the performance of legitimate drama in the capital. He announced his intention of moving for a Select Committee to examine the state of the laws affecting dramatic literature, with a view to bringing in a bill based on the Select Committee report.[73] The proprietors of Drury Lane and Covent Garden responded on 30 May with a petition asking for the protection

---

[71] NA (National Archives), LC7/4, Part 1, 1767–1823 (Lord Chamberlain's papers).
[72] When he succeeded to the Knebworth Estate in 1843 Bulwer added Lytton to his surname. He become Baron Lytton in 1866.
[73] See Nicholson, *Struggle for a Free Stage*, 323–5.

of their rights. On 31 May Bulwer duly moved the appointing of a Select Committee. In his speech, he alluded to the way that the minor theatres were constantly threatened with prosecution, even when trying to present work that was modest and uncontroversial. In contrast, the patent houses had shown themselves poor guardians of the legitimate drama. Their vast size meant that tragedies and comedies could no longer be seen or heard by an audience: hence the introduction of spectacular shows with mountebanks and animals. In a key passage in his speech, he went on to question the need for a dramatic censor:

He was at a loss to know what advantages they had gained by the grant of this almost unconstitutional power. Certainly, with regard to a Censor, a Censor upon plays seemed to him as idle and unnecessary as a Censor upon books . . . The only true censor of the age, was the spirit of the age. When indecencies were allowed by the customs of real life, they would be allowed in the representation, and no Censor would forbid them. When the age did not allow them, they would not be performed, and no Censor need expunge them. For instance, while the Licenser at this moment might strike out what lines he pleased in a new play, he had no power by strict law to alter a line in an old play . . . The public taste, backed by the vigilant admonition of the public Press, might, perhaps, be more safely trusted for the preservation of theatrical decorum, than any ignorant and bungling Censor, who (however well the office might be now fulfilled) might be appointed hereafter.[74]

Sir Charles Wetherell (an ardent opponent of all reform), in speaking against the motion, asserted that it interfered 'very unnecessarily with the prerogative of the Crown, which had hitherto been exercised with great judgment'.[75] He then went on to comment that 'the house had Reform enough upon its hands without also reforming the prerogatives of the Crown and all the theatres'.[76] This astute observation (made almost as an aside) helps to explain why the push for reform of the theatre was likely to be viewed as a matter of low priority at a time when Parliament faced the crisis of the Reform Bill of 1832. Nevertheless, the motion was agreed to and the Committee was appointed.

Throughout 1831 and the early part of 1832, not only Parliament but the whole country was transfixed by the attempt made by Earl Grey's Whig administration to introduce a bill that would reform the whole basis of enfranchisement. What was proposed was not wholesale democracy (one person, one vote) but a reform that would sweep away the rotten boroughs and extend the right to vote to men with even modest property. The convulsions in Parliament that this proposal engendered meant that the Reform Bill had to be

---

[74] *Hansard* (Commons), 31 May 1832, vol. 13, cols. 244–5.
[75] Ibid., col. 248.   [76] Ibid.

rewritten three times, an election was fought in March 1831 to strengthen the position of the reformers, and Grey tendered the resignation of his Government when the House of Lords voted against the third version of the bill early in May 1832. King William IV asked various Tory politicians, including the Duke of Wellington, to form an alternative administration, but without success. By mid-May, Grey was able to extract a reluctant promise from the King to create sufficient additional peers to guarantee the passing of the bill, if required. In the event, this proved unnecessary. Faced with this threat, the Lords gave the bill its Third Reading on 4 June 1832 and it received the Royal Assent on 7 June.[77]

It was in the very midst of this crisis that Bulwer and his supporters in Parliament moved the appointing of a Select Committee on 31 May 1832 to investigate the laws governing dramatic literature. The demand for the reform of theatre legislation was clearly part of a far wider desire in the country for legislative reform. The same pattern can be detected in 1909, 1949, and 1966–8. However, in 1832 and in 1909 the demand for constitutional reform engendered a political crisis of such far-reaching proportions that any tangential demands for reform or liberalization (such as the desire to reform theatre legislation) were bound to suffer in consequence.

Bulwer's Select Committee duly met and heard evidence from a wide range of witnesses, including authors, actors, and theatre managers. It also gathered a significant amount of evidence about the licensing of theatres in and around London and the prices paid for admission. By August, the Committee had completed its investigation and prepared its report for the House of Commons.[78] The report was cautious and addressed a number of contentious issues in a measured tone. Its main findings were summarized in eight paragraphs. The key recommendation was the abolition of the monopoly status of Drury Lane and Covent Garden. Equally important was the suggested rationalization of all theatre licensing in and around London and Westminster. Instead of the previous overlapping jurisdiction of the Lord Chamberlain and local magistrates, the Committee recommended that the Lord Chamberlain should have exclusive licensing authority in the metropolis and within a twenty-mile radius. No less important was the recommendation that all theatres licensed by the Lord Chamberlain should be free to present the legitimate drama. Perhaps influenced by the extension of voting rights proposed in the Great Reform Bill that had just become law, the Committee recommended that resident householders in any large parish or district should be entitled to press for a new theatre to be given a licence by the Lord

---

[77] See Briggs, *Age of Improvement*, 205–23.
[78] Report from the Select Committee on Dramatic Literature, 2 Aug. 1832.

Chamberlain in their locality. Other important recommendations included a clarification of the status of the censor (subject to the discretion of the Lord Chamberlain); a suggested sliding scale of fees for different kinds of submission to the censor; and protection for the legal rights of dramatic authors. The one issue the Committee did not comment on, despite Bulwer's early statement to the House of Commons, was the matter of whether or not there was a need for censorship at all. Presumably any recommendation for the complete abolition of theatrical censorship would not have commanded majority support in the Committee. It is even more unlikely that such a proposal would have been supported by the House of Commons. Reform was in the air in 1832, but opposition to reform was also strong and vociferous.

In the following parliamentary session, permission was given to Bulwer on 12 March 1833 to introduce a bill 'for licensing theatres, and for the better regulation of dramatic performances in the cities of London and Westminster, and within twenty miles thereof'. This became known as the Dramatic Performances Bill.[79] In substance, the bill attempted to address the recommendations made by the Select Committee in paragraphs 2 and 3, which would have given the Lord Chamberlain the sole right to license theatres in and around the metropolis and would also give local communities the right to be involved in the licensing of new theatres. However, there were significant drafting errors which gave rise to extended debate (notably a partial and flawed list of theatres to be included in the legislation) and, at the Second Reading, a London Member of Parliament succeeded in introducing an amendment that exempted the City of London from the legislation. At its Third Reading (24 July 1833), a small number of dedicated supporters were present in the Chamber and voted for the bill to be sent to the House of Lords (the vote was 38 for and 7 against).[80] The First Reading of the bill in the House of Lords was uncontested. However, at the Second Reading, on 2 August, an extended debate occurred in which the usual arguments in favour of the minor theatres on the one side and the monopoly proprietors, on the other, were duly repeated. The Bishop of London took everyone by surprise when he launched into an extended attack on the immorality of the stage and protested vigorously against any legislation that would sanction an increase in the number of playhouses. Clearly, his intervention struck a chord in the Upper House so that their Lordships refused to sanction this new piece of legislation, which would have brought much-needed reform to London's theatres. At its Second Reading in the Lords, Bulwer's bill was rejected by five votes.[81] It would take another decade of internecine warfare between the

---

[79] See Nicholson, *Struggle for a Free Stage*, 339.   [80] Ibid. 346.   [81] Ibid. 354.

major and minor theatres, and of petitions and pleas directed to the Lord Chamberlain, before reforming legislation was again presented to Parliament.

THE POLITICAL BACKGROUND TO THE ACT
FOR REGULATING THEATRES OF 1843

There were broader political reasons for the delay. One was that the House of Lords had, in the view of many of its members, been humiliated by William IV's reluctant threat to create sufficient new peers in 1832 to enable the Grey administration to force through the Parliamentary Reform Act. In consequence, it was in a mood to be obstructive on a relatively minor question which even Grey and his colleagues were unlikely to deem worthy of a principled showdown.[82] A second reason was that during 1833 and 1834 the Government was far from united about its agenda for further reform. The coalition of Whigs and Radicals that had carried through the Parliamentary Reform Act had always been an uneasy one: hence further reforming measures were slow in coming. True, one unambiguously radical Act passed in 1833 was a first step to curtailing the slave trade; there was a Factory Act in the same year; and the New Poor Law was introduced in 1834. Most Whig Members of Parliament elected to support a measure of parliamentary reform were by no means root-and-branch extremists or even supporters of the kind of democracy that arrived in Great Britain during the twentieth century. They were not, for example, in favour of universal suffrage or the abolition of the House of Lords. On the other hand, they did tend to give a cautious welcome to measures that dealt with anomalies, with blatant corruption, and with anachronistic practices. There was, however, a hysterical minority of Tories which had feared that, for example, Catholic Emancipation in Ireland (granted in 1829) or the Parliamentary Reform Act itself would have catastrophic consequences for the social fabric of Britain. In view of this, it is perhaps unsurprising that during the 1830s 'reform' proceeded slowly rather than rapidly after these traumas.

Another distinguishing feature of the era after the passing of the Parliamentary Reform Act was a prolonged lack of stability and assured continuity at the highest levels of government. This too helps to explain the lack of any progress to implement the recommendations of the Select Committee on theatrical

---

[82] On the passing of the Parliamentary Reform Act see Michael Brock, *The Great Reform Act* (London: Hutchinson University Library, 1973), and Edward Pearce, *Reform! The Fight for the 1832 Reform Act* (London: Jonathan Cape, 2003).

matters. During 1833 bitter quarrels arose in the Cabinet about the best means of dealing with continuing discontent and disaffection in Ireland. In May/June 1834 several ministers resigned from Grey's Government on the issue. Shortly thereafter, in July, the Prime Minister himself resigned.[83] His successor was Viscount Melbourne, who turned out to be little more than a caretaker. The King soon lost confidence in him and effectively dismissed him. He decided in December 1834 to appoint in his place Sir Robert Peel, a Tory. The latter did not, however, have a working majority in the House of Commons. A general election was accordingly called early in 1835. This failed to give Peel sufficient gains for him to be able to continue. Hence in April Melbourne returned to the premiership, but with only a precarious majority; perhaps for this reason, he showed little appetite for introducing contentious legislation. This was also a period of economic stagnation and even depression. It is thus unsurprising that the only important radical measure to reach the statute book in the mid-1830s was the Municipal Corporations Act. The accession of a new monarch, Queen Victoria, on 20 June 1837 only increased the sense of political immobility. Melbourne was willing in 1839 to step aside in favour of Peel, whose followers had gained some further seats in the general election occasioned by Victoria's accession. He was, however, prevailed upon by the monarch not to do so for what in hindsight seems the absurd reason that she did not want to countenance replacing Whig Ladies of the Bedchamber with Tory ones.

Only in the summer of 1841 was the deadlock broken when a further general election resulted in a decisive Commons majority of ninety-one for Peel. Many of his supporters looked back to the Younger Pitt's Peace Ministry as a model to be followed, and few were any longer obsessed by the now-distant French Revolution. Hence, as Charles Greville wrote in his journal: 'There was a general feeling of satisfaction and security by the substitution of a real working government for the last batch.'[84] A period of intense legislative activity was at last possible. Few if any of the measures were particularly radical as seen through the eyes of, say, a Chartist. But rationalization of anomalies and the ending of anachronisms undoubtedly appealed to Peel.[85] Hence, for example, an efficient income tax system was introduced in 1842; a Bank Charter Act was passed in 1844; the Ten Hours' Factory Act also came into force in 1844; and the chaotic state of the Church in Scotland was tackled. Eventually Peel, with Whig support and to the despair of many of his own followers, famously

---

[83] For details see Norman Gash, *Aristocracy and People: Britain 1815–1865* (London: Edward Arnold, 1979), 170–1.

[84] Quoted in Briggs, *Age of Improvement*, 330.

[85] See Norman Gash, *Sir Robert Peel: The Life of Sir Robert Peel after 1830* (London: Longman, 1972).

steered through the Repeal of the Corn Laws in 1845–6. This was the brisk and businesslike context in which the 1832 report of the Select Committee concerning theatres was revisited and new legislation was prepared and passed in 1843.

THE ACT FOR REGULATING THEATRES OF 1843

In the early 1840s, as in 1832, it was the playwrights who took the initiative in pressing for reform of theatre legislation. Their grievances, which had not been addressed in the interim period, remained the same: namely, the lack of copyright protection in respect of performances of their work and, above all, the fact that only the two patent theatres in London could legitimately perform new plays. A number of playwrights submitted a petition to the Member of Parliament and historian Lord Mahon (later 5th Earl Stanhope) in 1842 asking for their grievances to be considered by Parliament. Mahon introduced their petition to the House of Commons on 30 June 1842. In his prefatory comments, Mahon gave a brief historical overview of the way the patents granted by Charles II to Killigrew and Davenant had served 'as a foundation for the statute laws by which the stage was regulated'.[86] He went on to show how, over the years, the monopoly granted to the patent houses had led to a whole range of damaging consequences. Small, unlicensed premises had proliferated in defiance of the law; playwrights and actors found themselves driven to work in breach of the law; and the outstanding playwrights of the eighteenth and early nineteenth centuries had their work rejected by the patent houses and were only performed in unregulated theatres. For their part, the managers of the patent houses found it increasingly difficult to derive any profit from their large undertakings. He went on to cite the significant losses recently incurred at both Drury Lane and Covent Garden. He concluded by asking for copies of any communications sent to the Secretary of State for the Home Department on the state of law in reference to the drama to be made available to Parliament.

His motion was seconded by H. Gally Knight who had served on the 1832 Select Committee. Gally Knight asserted that the Select Committee had investigated the topic very thoroughly: the problems highlighted by the Select Committee, and the conclusions it reached, were similar to the issues just raised. He felt that there were three matters that could and should be addressed and which would all help to overcome the unnecessary obstacles placed in the

---

[86] *Hansard* (Commons), 30 June 1842, vol. 64, col. 791.

path of dramatic literature: 'first, the size of the theatres at which the legitimate drama is alone allowed to be performed; second, the state of the law with respect to the licensing of theatres; third, the laws which affect the copyright of dramatic works.' His analytic account of the first problem summarized, briefly and effectively, the negative, long-term effects of the theatrical monopoly in London:

the two theatres to which the legitimate drama is restricted, are become too large for anything but scenery and show. The minor theatres are restricted to what is technically called 'the burletta'—a species of composition not very easy to define; but the general understanding is, that burletta must always be accompanied by music, which, of course, places the legitimate drama out of the province of the minor theatres . . . it was impossible not to see that the size of the theatres, in which the legitimate drama may be represented, had operated unfavourably on dramatic literature.[87]

Having outlined the nature of the problem caused by granting the two patent houses monopoly rights to perform legitimate drama, he reminded the House of the Select Committee's preferred solution:

the committee came to the opinion that, with regard to this point, some improvement might be made if the licensing powers of the Lord Chamberlain, which are now limited to the city of Westminster, were extended, and if the right of representing the legitimate drama were no longer confined to the two patent theatres.[88]

Finally, he turned his attention to the issue of copyright protection for plays in performance, and outlined the kinds of disadvantage under which playwrights laboured. Although he argued passionately the need to safeguard dramatists from commercial exploitation and piracy, he studiously refrained from expressing any criticism of the need for censorship. In describing the Select Committee's deliberations on the matter, his choice of words suggests an awkward division of opinion amongst committee members:

With regard to the copyright, the dramatic author, is certainly obstructed by peculiar and unnecessary vexations. In the first place, he must submit works to a censor; but, after having fully considered that subject, the committee could not come to the opinion that the censorship could be dispensed with. But dramatic authors enjoy less protection than is granted to authors in any other branch of letters, and are exposed to hardships which others have not to encounter. They have to make the best bargain they can with the manager, and have often great difficulty in obtaining the payment of the moderate compensation which may have been allowed. The management changes before the payment is complete; the piece is considered a stock-piece of the theatre, and no redress can be had from the new manager. Successful plays are often pirated by the provincial theatres.[89]

---

[87] Ibid., col. 797.　　　　[88] Ibid., col. 798.　　　　[89] Ibid.

The Home Secretary, Sir James Graham, entered the House during Gally Knight's speech and made it clear that, without committing himself to any specific course of action, he was perfectly willing to consider any plan which Mahon might wish to bring forward. This public expression of interest, if not support, set in train a process of behind-the-scenes discussions that led a year later to the First Reading of the bill for regulating theatres (29 July 1843). The bill was given an unopposed Second Reading on 31 July 1843: it was then considered by a Committee of the Whole House on 4 August 1843.

During the course of the debate, Graham made it clear that the bill was brought forward with Government support with 'the intention to improve the dramatic art'.[90] In his speech he implied that the patent houses had failed in their duty to present the 'chief plays of the country'.[91] At present, the plays of Shakespeare, for instance, could only be seen at the Haymarket Theatre (which was in effect London's opera house) and not at one of the two patent houses supposedly dedicated to legitimate drama. He took the view that the best way of protecting the future of the drama was by 'placing the power of making regulations for the drama in the hands of one responsible person',[92] namely the Lord Chamberlain. After an unopposed Third Reading, the bill was sent, without amendments, to the House of Lords on 7 August 1843. A few minor issues were discussed during the committee stage of the Lord's deliberations on 11 August but no alterations were made. It was only at the Third Reading of the bill in the House of Lords on 15 August that an issue of substance was raised and a brief but significant alteration was made to a crucial clause in the bill defining the Lord Chamberlain's powers of censorship.

Clause 15 of the bill (which became Clause 14 of the Act) reaffirmed the sweeping censorship powers given to the Lord Chamberlain in the 1737 Licensing Act:

And be it Enacted, That it shall be lawful for the Lord Chamberlain for the Time being, whenever he shall think fit, to forbid the acting or presenting any Stage-play, or any act, scene or part thereof, or any prologue or epilogue, or any part thereof, any where in Great Britain, or in such Theatres, as he shall specify, and either absolutely or for such time as he shall think fit.[93]

Hitherto, no one in either House had raised any objections to this wording. However, at the Third Reading in the Lords, Lord Campbell of St Andrews proposed a substantive amendment to this clause. Campbell, who saw himself as a moderate Whig, had taken silk in 1827, and had served as Attorney-General from 1834 to 1841. He was elevated to the peerage in 1841 in order to serve

[90] *Hansard* (Commons), 4 Aug. 1843, vol. 71, col. 232.   [91] Ibid.   [92] Ibid.
[93] NA, HO 45/496 (Home Office Papers).

as Chancellor of Ireland, a post he held, because of changes in government, for a mere ten days. During the 1840s, when he held no government post, he intervened frequently in debates in the House of Lords on matters of law. Had it been accepted, his amendment would have significantly curtailed the powers of censorship given to the Lord Chamberlain. In moving his amendment, Campbell stated:

He was quite ready to invest the Lord Chamberlain with full powers to prevent any performances which were calculated to offend public decency, or to peril the public peace; but beyond this he did not think that officer ought to interfere with a manager's arrangements. He did not propose to omit any of the words of the clause, but merely to guide the Lord Chamberlain in his exercise of this power, by proposing these words before the existing clause: — 'Be it enacted, that for the preservation of good manners, decorum, and of the public peace, it shall be lawful for the Lord Chamberlain, for the time being,' the rest of the clause remaining as at present.[94]

Lord Wharncliffe, the Lord President of the Council, immediately objected that this amendment would restrict the powers of the Lord Chamberlain, whereas the object of the bill was to extend them. The Lord Chancellor intervened to suggest a judicious compromise that would remove all objections to the amendment:

He recommended that the words, 'whenever in the opinion of the Lord Chamberlain it was necessary for the promotion of good manners and decorum, or of the public peace, to forbid the performance of any stage play, farce, &c.'[95]

Campbell accepted this alteration to his amendment, which was then adopted and inserted into the bill. The effect of the Lord Chancellor's wording was to restore to the Lord Chamberlain his absolute powers of discretion in deciding when to censor a play or performance piece. Nevertheless, Campbell's amendment did, for the first time since 1737, provide the Lord Chamberlain with working guidelines for the exercise of his powers of censorship. His role as censor was henceforth to forbid the performance of a play or other work 'whenever he shall be of opinion that it is fitting for the Preservation of good Manners, Decorum, or of the public Peace so to do'.[96] For the first time, the two interlocking areas of private and public decorum were formally defined as his primary concern. These guidelines were to remain unchanged (though not unchallenged) until the passing of the Theatres Act in 1968.

Apart from this change to the previously undefined and absolute powers of censorship vested in the Lord Chamberlain, the main concern of the bill was to abolish the theatrical monopoly hitherto enjoyed in London by

---

[94] *Hansard* (Lords), 15 Aug. 1843, vol. 71, col. 689.   [95] Ibid., col. 690.
[96] Act for Regulating Theatres 1843 (6 & 7 Vict., c. 68), section 14.

the patent houses and to extend the Lord Chamberlain's powers to license theatres in and around London and Westminster. The Act for Regulating Theatres (6 & 7 Vict., c. 68) was given the Royal Assent on 22 August 1843. In Clause 3, the Lord Chamberlain was given powers to license not only the patent theatres but all theatres in the Cities of London and Westminster and in the Boroughs of Finsbury, Marylebone, Tower Hamlets, Lambeth, and Southwark. In Clause 5, it was established that in every other county, riding, city, or borough beyond the limits of the authority of the Lord Chamberlain, Justices of the Peace were given powers to license houses for the performance of stage works. Clause 12 stipulated that any work 'intended to be produced and acted for Hire at any theatre in *Great Britain*' shall be sent to the Lord Chamberlain at least seven days before the intended first performance. Clause 13 stipulated that the Lord Chamberlain might in future charge a fee for all works submitted for examination and that he could fix a scale of fees that seemed appropriate although not exceeding the sum of two guineas in any one case. These provisions swept away the previously overlapping jurisdiction of the Lord Chamberlain and local magistrates. They abolished any distinction between the patent houses and the minor theatres in respect of their repertoire. They also placed provincial theatres on the same footing, in respect of play licences, as the theatres in and around London. At a stroke, this Act liberated the theatres in and around London from the shackles that had previously stunted the development of their repertoire. It brought to an end the fierce and prolonged battle between the major and minor theatres in London that had raged unabated since the beginning of the century. This did not prevent the patentees from sending anguished petitions and claims for compensation to the Government,[97] but their pleas went unheeded.

The Act had brought a long overdue reform to the whole business of theatre licensing. In contrast, it reaffirmed the censorship powers vested in the Lord Chamberlain in the 1737 Act, but with the addition of some basic working guidelines. Its full implications were spelled out to the Lord Chamberlain in a letter from the Home Secretary drafted on 25 August 1843. Graham wrote:

By this Act the power vested in your Lordship as Lord Chamberlain to license theatres within the City of Westminster has been extended, and all theatres within the limits of the City of London and of the Metropolitan Boroughs have been placed under the control of your Lordship.

Your Lordship is aware that before the passing of this Act, there existed no authority competent by law to license the representation of any dramatic performances either within the Metropolis or within the distance of twenty miles from the Metropolis,

---

[97] See NA, HO 45/496.

except in the City of Westminster, to the limits of which City, and to such places as may be the residences of Her Majesty . . .

From this anomaly in the law a custom has grown up under which, altho' not sanctioned by law, a licence granted by Justices of the Peace for music and dancing has been considered sufficient to enable parties to open Houses for the representation of theatrical events. And a large amount of capital has thus been invested on the security that where the Law had not for a long period interfered to restrict these performances, the Law would not be put in force against them.

It has been considered advisable to bring these theatres within the power and the protection of the Law; and while a needless and inoperative restriction on the amusements of the people has thus been abolished, a large discretionary power has been vested in your Lordship for the purpose of enabling your Lordship as Lord Chamberlain to secure decency and good order within all the theatres of the Metropolis generally to prevent the representation of such dramatic performances as may be considered by your Lordship calculated to outrage morality or to give an incentive to crime.

These extensive powers have been granted by the Legislature in the full conviction that the High Officer of State to whom they have been confided by his impartiality, and by the careful restriction of the exercise of his authority to cases in which the interests of morality and of good order demand his interference, justify the course which has thus been pursued.

Permit me to add that I am convinced that this Confidence has not been misplaced, but that by the wise and cautious exercise of the large powers entrusted to the Lord Chamberlain, decency and order will be maintained within the Theatres under his superintendence and the public will be secured against the performance of representations of an immoral and vicious character, at the same time that no unnecessary restriction on the amusements of the people will be enforced.[98]

In the final paragraph of his letter Graham makes it clear that the Government hoped to see the Lord Chamberlain exercise his authority as censor wisely and judiciously. His extensive powers were to be viewed as a safeguard in those exceptional cases where plays or performance pieces were manifestly intended to outrage morality by offering entertainment of a deliberately immoral and vicious nature. In effect, his letter attempted to narrow the scope of the Lord Chamberlain's powers in much the same manner as had been intended by Campbell when he had earlier proposed his amendment to the censorship provisions in the bill. However, a pious hope expressed in a confidential letter from a Home Secretary to the current Lord Chamberlain did not have the same weight as a clause enshrined in statute law. In later years, successive Lords Chamberlain were to use their extensive powers neither judiciously nor sparingly.

[98] Ibid.

THE SELECT COMMITTEES OF 1866 AND 1892

Two further Select Committees were appointed in the late nineteenth century to consider theatres and places of entertainment and their licensing and regulation. (The 1854 Select Committee on Public Houses, &c.[99] was primarily concerned with licences for the sale of intoxicating liquor and made only fleeting references to the issue of theatrical licences.)[100] The first reported on 28 June 1866 and the second on 2 June 1892. Both Committees took evidence from a significant number of witnesses and produced detailed reports and recommendations. In neither case, however, were the recommendations adopted by Parliament. The policy of inertia in respect of theatre legislation now seemed set in stone. The primary concern of both Select Committees was the vexed question of how best to control the rapidly proliferating music halls which catered for working-class audiences. In 1866 the Committee recommended that the best way forward was to give the Lord Chamberlain licensing powers over metropolitan music halls similar to those he enjoyed over the theatres. The proceedings of the 1892 Committee make it clear, however, that the Lord Chamberlain had declined to take on this additional burden of responsibility with its attendant workload. Instead, the licensing powers previously exercised by magistrates in the metropolitan area had now passed, since the Local Government Act of 1888, to the local authorities. The Committee found itself in broad agreement with this development, but did not share the view recently expressed by the London County Council (LCC) that licensing control over those theatres situated in London should pass from the Lord Chamberlain to the LCC. The Committee furthermore expressed its satisfaction with the involvement of the Metropolitan Board of Works in the licensing process. Since 1878, the Board of Works had responsibility for framing regulations governing the positioning and the structures of theatre buildings so that members of the public might be protected from the danger of fire. The Committee saw no reason to change any of these overlapping responsibilities. The predictable upshot was to confirm an administrative framework that had emerged organically from previous, interlocking pieces of legislation.

When the two Committees turned their attention to censorship, their endorsement of the status quo was quite unambiguous. The 1866 Committee heard evidence from several witnesses on the operation of theatre censorship under the Lord Chamberlain. Some of these expressed grave reservations.

---

[99] Report from the Select Committee on Public Houses, &c, 13 July 1854.
[100] See ibid., pp. xxiv–xxvi.

In particular, the manager and playwright Dion Boucicault gave examples of capricious decisions taken by the Lord Chamberlain and contrasted the situation in England with that of the United States, where public opinion was the sole check upon playwrights.[101] Similar points were made by the writer Shirley Brooks. However, the Lord Chamberlain and his staff countered that very few plays were refused licences, citing a total of only nineteen plays in thirteen years. Theatre managers, such as John Baldwin Buckstone (proprietor of the Haymarket Theatre), expressed the view that censorship was necessary to prevent immorality and objectionable political material in dramatic literature.[102] The Select Committee concurred and resolved: 'That the censorship of plays has worked satisfactorily, and that it is not desirable that it should be discontinued. On the contrary, that it should be extended, as far as practicable, to the performances in music halls.'[103]

The 1892 Select Committee heard a similar range of views for and against the Lord Chamberlain's role as censor. On this occasion, the critic William Archer argued robustly against the intrusion of a censor and concluded that the public is the only reliable judge of the worth of a play. Any indecency on stage should be a matter for the police. Once again, however, the Select Committee endorsed the status quo. In the General Recommendations, the report dealt with censorship in the very last paragraph. The Committee contented itself with repeating, in quotation marks, the recommendations made by the 1866 Select Committee.[104] The fact that the 1892 Committee had nothing to add or any comment to make on these earlier recommendations is in itself a striking demonstration of the policy of inertia that informed parliamentary thinking on the topic of theatre censorship throughout the nineteenth century.

Underpinning the consistent support for censorship shown by Members of Parliament during the nineteenth century was the fear that an uncontrolled stage might be given over to indecency or objectionable political material. Occasionally this fear was articulated in the evidence of those appearing before the Select Committees held from time to time. It was also clearly expressed in the detailed guidelines given to the Lord Chamberlain for the exercise of his role as censor in the 1843 Act. It was as if the distant memory of Fielding's rumbustious political satires and the obscene and scurrilous attack on King and First Minister in *The Golden*

[101] Report from the Select Committee on Theatrical Licences and Regulations, 28 June 1866, 4147–57.

[102] Ibid. 3564–74.   [103] Ibid., Resolution 8.

[104] Report from the Select Committee on Theatres and Places of Entertainment, 2 June 1892, 4.

Rump in 1737 had become grafted on to the genetic memory-bank of Britain's governing classes. It would take almost another century of attacks on theatre censorship, mainly spearheaded by dramatists, before the resistance to change, on the part of anxious Members of Parliament, began to crumble.

Another factor that may have deterred Members of Parliament from pressing for reform was the mistaken assumption that the Lord Chamberlain exercised his censorship duties as part of the Royal Prerogative. This point was made by Wetherell when Bulwer questioned the need for a censor in his 1832 speech to Parliament. As we have seen, Wetherell expressed a view that many other Members of Parliament would have shared, namely that to query the role of the Lord Chamberlain as censor was to interfere with the 'prerogative of the Crown'. Under the terms of the 1737 Act, the Lord Chamberlain was given statutory powers of censorship; he did not therefore exercise his role as censor as part of the Royal Prerogative. In 1832, this distinction was lost on Members of Parliament and dramatists alike. The same confusion was to persist in the minds of Members of Parliament and government ministers until the latter half of the twentieth century.

Finally, the key feature of any campaign to oppose censorship was largely absent during the nineteenth century, namely concerted opposition from contemporary dramatists. True, it was pressure from dramatists in 1832 and 1843 that led Parliament, in the first instance, to set up the first of the nineteenth-century Select Committees on theatrical matters and then to pass the 1843 Act for Regulating Theatres. Equally, dramatists who gave evidence to the 1866 and 1892 Select Committees on theatrical matters were unanimously opposed to censorship, but there was no breadth or depth to their opposition. They were essentially lone voices, which was hardly surprising. The monopoly powers retained by the patent houses until 1843 made the chances of having a new play accepted for performance slim in the extreme. Any play that was accepted was then subject to detailed scrutiny by the Lord Chamberlain's Examiner of Plays who would ensure that any material of serious social or political significance would be censored. This had the long-term effect of discouraging serious writers from even considering writing plays at all. The unholy alliance of monopoly powers granted to the patent houses and strict theatre censorship was broken in 1843. Thereafter, playwrights could submit plays to a far wider choice of theatres, but their work was still subject to the strict control of the theatre censor. It was not until a new generation of dramatists emerged towards the beginning of the twentieth century, inspired by the work of above all Henrik Ibsen, that serious pressure for change in the system of theatre censorship was applied. The group of playwrights who insisted on change found themselves confronted by a combination of ignorance and arrogance on the part of government ministers and their civil servants, but in the first decade of the twentieth century there was nevertheless a real struggle to liberate the stage from the suffocating grip of censorship.

3

The 1909 Challenge to Statutory Theatre Censorship

THE EDWARDIAN ERA: DEMANDS FOR REFORM IN THE THEATRE AND PARLIAMENT

The 1892 Select Committee on Theatres and Places of Entertainment had chosen to recommend no change to the law on theatre censorship. In the closing years of Queen Victoria's reign, it is not really surprising that a parliamentary Select Committee should choose to support the status quo in matters concerning public taste, decency, and morality. The Lord Chamberlain was clearly viewed as a safe pair of hands, whose control over the output of dramatic authors had ensured that audiences were not offended by the content of plays performed in public and politicians were spared the prospect of facing critical comment from the stage. The cosy assumptions of Victorian society, however, about family life, marital relationships, politics, and patriarchy were soon to be challenged by a new generation of English and Irish playwrights, following the lead already given by Scandinavian, French, and German playwrights, but above all by the Norwegian playwright Ibsen.

Beginning with A Doll's House in 1879, but even more blatantly in Ghosts in 1881, Ibsen had unpicked the myths surrounding contemporary marriage and family life. He showed marriage as a commercial transaction, in which women were the victims of patriarchal attitudes and behaviour. In London, the supporters of Ibsen (branded as 'Ibsenites' by the Daily Telegraph critic Clement Scott)[1] were to spearhead the rebellion against theatre censorship that culminated in the early 1900s. The actress Janet Achurch led the way with her production of A Doll's House in 1889, which caused a furore in London. The process continued with J. T. Grein, a Dutch journalist, who founded his Independent Theatre in 1891 to give a private production of Ghosts, which had not been, and clearly would not be, licensed by the Lord Chamberlain. This

---

[1] See William Archer, 'The Mausoleum of Ibsen', Fortnightly Review, 54 (1893). Quoted from James McFarlane (ed.), Henrik Ibsen: A Critical Anthology (London: Penguin Books, 1970), 151.

private production at the Royalty Theatre caused real outrage. An editorial in the *Daily Telegraph* (14 March 1891) labelled the play: 'an open drain . . . a loathsome sore unbandaged . . . a dirty act done publicly . . . a lazar-house with all its doors and windows open.' Such polemical attacks were countered by a thoughtful and measured assessment of Ibsen's work in George Bernard Shaw's *The Quintessence of Ibsenism* (1891). Shaw saw Ibsen as a passionate moral reformer. Other contemporary critics shared his enthusiasm for Ibsen's plays, notably Edmund Gosse, who had written warmly of Ibsen's work in a series of essays published from the 1870s onwards, and William Archer, who began publishing essays on Ibsen and translations of his plays from the 1880s onwards. Ibsen's work also had a decisive impact on Shaw's career as a playwright. It inspired him to write his early plays revolving around social problems and moral issues, notably *Widower's Houses* (1892) and *Mrs Warren's Profession* (1893). Ibsen gave Shaw the confidence to deal with the kind of controversial topics that Victorian society preferred to avoid.[2]

Shaw, along with his fellow playwright, Harley Granville Barker, was to play a key role in the struggle against censorship during the first decade of the 1900s. Many other dramatists joined the protest as it gathered momentum. However, as in 1832, the attempt by a group of committed dramatists to change the law governing freedom of expression in the theatre and the issue of theatre licensing coincided with a turbulent period in English politics when other serious constitutional issues were at stake.

In 1832 the issue which had divided the Lords, Commons, and the monarch was the Reform Bill. This led to threats to increase the number of peers to force through the Reform Bill which the Commons had already approved. In 1909, the immediate trigger for conflict was the People's Budget prepared by the Liberal Chancellor of the Exchequer, David Lloyd George. But this time, the real issue was the right of the House of Lords to veto legislation approved by the Commons. What was at stake was a serious challenge to the 1689 settlement which had provided for a 'mixed' if largely unwritten constitution, in which power was to be shared among King, Lords, and Commons.

THE LIBERALS VERSUS THE LORDS AND THE MONARCHY, 1906–1912

Edward VII became king at the age of 59 in 1901. Such constitutional guidance and precedents as he derived from the lengthy reign of his mother, Queen

---

[2] See David Thomas, *Henrik Ibsen* (London: Macmillan, 1983), 157–8.

Victoria, were reactionary in the extreme. For example, as late as 1894 she was outraged by a speech made by her last Liberal Prime Minister, Lord Rosebery. Following the House of Lords' rejection of an Irish Home Rule Bill, earlier approved by the House of Commons, he had spoken of an 'intolerable situation' and had suggested that the next general election might be fought on the issue. But the Queen made clear to Henry Campbell-Bannerman, one of Rosebery's colleagues, that she was alarmed by the danger 'of increasing the power of the H of C [Commons] and having no force to resist the subversive measures of the so-called Liberals but better called destructives'. She added that she 'could never agree to taking from the Lo. [Lords] their power to alter or reject measures—this might be obtained from a president but not from her'.[3] As Edward Pearce has put it: 'The assumption of the Lords that they not only might, but should reject bills proposed by elected governments, bills which had figured in election programmes, would give one eminent personage no problems at all.'[4] It should not surprise or shock us, then, to find that Edward VII was of basically the same opinion and saw it as his duty to seek compromises between the two Houses rather than support the elected one over the hereditary one. This outlook was widely shared in the Conservative Party and in the Establishment generally, but it was anathema to members of the Liberal Party.

The Liberal Party, so hated by Queen Victoria, came to office in December 1905 following the resignation as Prime Minister of Arthur Balfour, whose Conservative and Liberal Unionist administration had foundered on the issue of tariff reform. The new Prime Minister, Campbell-Bannerman, then sought and was granted a dissolution and proceeded to obtain a landslide victory in the general election of January 1906. Campbell-Bannerman's administration came to power with a series of manifesto pledges that was expected to keep Parliament busy for years: most related to domestic matters. The main legislative burden was initially carried by the Home Secretary, Herbert Gladstone, who has been described by John Grigg, David Lloyd George's biographer, as having 'a radical record second to none in the Campbell-Bannerman Government'.[5]

The fact was, however, that some manifesto commitments were unpopular with the electorate. The Liberals had won the general election not on their broad programme but because they had stood for free trade and because their opponents had been seen as too evidently divided to be fit to govern.

---

[3] Edward Pearce, *Lines of Most Resistance: The Lords, the Tories and Ireland, 1886–1914* (London: Little, Brown, 1999), 176.

[4] Ibid. 175.

[5] John Grigg, *Lloyd George: The People's Champion, 1902–1911* (London: HarperCollins, 1997), 149.

The Leader of the Opposition, Balfour, and his 'poodle', the Conservative-dominated House of Lords, were aware of this and hence felt emboldened to block or drastically amend measures they judged to be unpopular even if they had been in the Liberals' manifesto. On the other hand, the Lords were more circumspect with measures they thought had a wider following. Thus over time a cat-and-mouse game developed. The Conservatives hoped that the Liberals would fall into the trap of confronting the Lords over matters that would be unpopular with the electorate. The Government, on the other hand, sought a way of fighting a general election occasioned by an unpopular use of their veto by the peers. For some years there was an effective stalemate, which seemed to be serving Balfour's interests. Gradually the Government became unpopular and, particularly after H. H. Asquith had succeeded the dying Campbell-Bannerman as Prime Minister in April 1908, began to lose by-elections on a regular basis.

Meanwhile some members of the Government expressed their frustration by making public attacks on the Lords and even on the hereditary principle. This raised the temperature generally and alarmed Edward VII in particular. Winston Churchill, still only a junior minister, spoke in June 1907 of the House of Lords as 'a one-sided, hereditary, unprized, unrepresentative, irresponsible absentee'.[6] Lloyd George had asked an audience at Oxford in December 1906 whether the country 'was to be governed by the King and the peers or by the King and the people'.[7] The King objected to being brought into the argument in this fashion and secured a grudging apology from Lloyd George but thereafter was increasingly at odds with both his Liberal Prime Ministers for their failure to prevent such outbursts. His irritation was demonstrated when Asquith took over. The new Prime Minister was compelled to visit the vacationing King in France in order to kiss hands.

Once Asquith had settled into Number Ten, it was only to be a matter of time before a showdown between the Commons and the Lords occurred. The first test of nerves came almost immediately. Asquith as Chancellor of the Exchequer had prepared a Budget and he decided to deliver this even though he was now Prime Minister. It provided for the introduction of state-funded pensions for those over 70 who were without adequate means: the first modest building block in what has become today's welfare state. Because it was part of a Budget package, the Liberals claimed that it was covered by the convention that the Lords did not reject money bills and certainly not a Budget. But many Conservatives saw it as sharp practice to introduce so novel a departure in this way. In the event, however, the Budget was allowed to pass. Yet it was only a dress rehearsal for what was to happen a year later when Lloyd

---

[6] Roy Jenkins, *Mr. Balfour's Poodle* (London: Collins, 1954), 55.   [7] Ibid.

George, the new Chancellor, introduced his so-called 'People's Budget'. The battle lines were drawn up at a dinner held at the National Liberal Club on 11 December 1908. The Prime Minister invited a large group of supporters 'to treat the veto of the House of Lords as the dominating issue in politics—the dominating issue, because in the long run it overshadows and absorbs every other'.[8]

It was just six days later (as we shall see) that a first attempt was made by the MP Robert Harcourt to promote in the Commons a Private Member's Bill on theatre censorship. He was to make another attempt at introducing a Private Member's Bill on theatre censorship in the following April, just before Lloyd George's historic Budget was presented as a dramatic challenge to the Lords. As was demonstrated in 1832, a period of fierce disagreement on constitutional issues was not the most opportune of moments to raise the topic of the control and censorship of the theatre.

Lloyd George's People's Budget was presented to the Commons on 29 April 1909. Its most controversial provisions involved new ways of raising national finance: super-tax on income intended to 'soak' the rich; new taxes on alcohol and tobacco; and, above all, taxes on the ownership and inheritance of land. In his four-and-one-half-hour speech Lloyd George also provocatively set out a vision of what Liberal budgets over a series of years would create: a modern welfare state such as Germany already possessed. The sick, the widowed, the unemployed, and the orphaned would be sustained, and by implication, in considerable measure at the expense of the wealthy, who had just been shown the thin end of the wedge with the new forms of taxation.

Never did a Budget take so long to pass all its stages in the Commons. Seventy parliamentary days were consumed in a debate with 554 divisions; the usual summer recess did not take place. In fact, not until 4 November 1909 did it pass its Third (and final) Reading in the Commons.[9] The temperature was also raised by the rhetoric used by ministers, and particularly by Lloyd George himself, in public meetings throughout the long months of controversy. In particular, he spoke most disrespectfully about Dukes: they were 'the first out of the litter' and 'a fully-equipped Duke costs as much to keep up as two dreadnoughts but less easy to scrap'.[10] This was a view that enraged Edward VII, who was after all just as much the first out of a litter as any Duke. In the Lords, a majority came to share the view of the courtier, Lord Cawdor, as expressed to the King: 'The Lords had a constitutional duty to afford the electorate an opportunity to pronounce its views upon what was, in reality,

[8] Quoted from Colin Cross, *The Liberals in Power, 1905–1914* (London: Barrie & Rockcliff, 1963), 82.

[9] Ibid. 84.

[10] Philip Magnus, *King Edward the Seventh* (London: John Murray, 1964), 430.

an important piece of social legislation masquerading as a Finance Bill.'[11]
The upshot was that to nobody's surprise on 30 November 1909 the Lords,
contrary to all modern precedent and convention, rejected the Budget by 350
votes to 75.

On 2 December 1909 the Government asked the King for a dissolution and
proceeded to fight a general election in support of the Budget and seeking
a mandate to curb the power of the Lords. At the same time, the Palace
realized that if the Government were re-elected the King was likely to be asked
permanently to transfer the power to create peers to the Prime Minister; or,
alternatively, to promise himself to create enough new peers to force through
the necessary legislation. Lord Knollys, the King's Private Secretary, thought
this 'outrageous' and held that the former course would 'tend to weaken the
Monarchy so considerably that it would be better that the King should abdicate
than agree to it'.[12] The King himself soon began to think along similar lines
about abdication, though, according to his biographer, Sir Philip Magnus, he
was not wholly serious.[13]

Asquith for one was not unduly disturbed by the King's attitude and
approached the general election campaign in a determined frame of mind. In
particular, he stated in the Albert Hall: 'We shall not assume office, and we
shall not hold office, unless we can secure the safeguards which experience
shows to be necessary for the legislative utility and honour of the party of
progress.'[14] It was widely but incorrectly assumed that he was confident that,
following an election victory, he would be able to count on the King being
willing to create enough peers to force through legislation curbing the powers
of the Lords.

In the event Asquith did not secure a convincing victory in the general
election of January 1910. The Liberals lost no fewer than 104 seats and their
majority over the Conservatives and Unionists fell from 220 to a mere 2.
The Liberals continued in office but were now dependent for survival on the
rather unpredictable support of the Labour Party (with 40 seats) and the Irish
Nationalists (with 82 seats). The Irish, in particular, wanted early action on
Lords reform and on Home Rule. The outcome of the general election was thus
rather demoralizing for the Liberals and encouraged the King and the Lords
to continue their resistance to constitutional change. All the same, Asquith
felt that he had no alternative but to continue the contest. He accordingly
insisted that the King's Speech to the new Parliament contain only two items:
the delayed Budget from the previous April and a Parliament Bill to secure
the reform of the House of Lords.[15] The Budget was by far the lesser problem,

---

[11] Ibid. 436.   [12] Ibid. 438.   [13] Ibid. 439.
[14] Quoted from Pearce, *Lines of Most Resistance*, 283.   [15] Cross, *The Liberals in Power*, 111

as there was now no appetite in the Lords to carry on the fight. Both Houses finally approved the Budget at the end of April 1910, just one year late.

The reform of the Lords, on the other hand, was to cause much more trouble. Edward VII made no secret among his intimates of his pleasure at the Liberals' failure to retain an overall majority in the Commons. He refused even to contemplate giving any guarantee to create hundreds of peers unless and until a precise bill had been drafted. This, as he would have known, was in itself a divisive issue in Liberal circles: would they concentrate on the composition or on the powers of the Lords or attempt to tackle both? Eventually, the Cabinet settled on a not particularly radical measure. No challenge for the present was to be offered to the hereditary principle but the Lords' veto on any bill repeatedly approved by the Commons would be overridden after a two-year delay. In addition, money bills, certified as such by the Speaker of the Commons, would automatically become law. Of course Asquith next had to face up to the likelihood that the Lords would reject these changes. Accordingly, he informed the Commons on 14 April 1910: 'If the Lords fail to accept our policy . . . we shall feel it our duty immediately to tender such advice to the Crown as to the steps which will have to be taken if that policy is to receive statutory effect *in this Parliament.*'[16] The Prime Minister knew, as the general public did not, that this would greatly anger the King. For he had already been privately informed that the latter was minded to insist that a further general election must be held before there would be any question of the Lords being coerced by the creation of new peers. So we can safely say that Asquith was, in the last resort, willing to enter upon a duel with Edward VII on a major constitutional issue. On the other hand, on less crucial issues (including, as we shall see, the issue of theatre censorship), he was certainly not prepared to open a second front in his war with the monarch.

It must indeed remain a matter for speculation how matters would have resolved themselves in the growing confrontation between Asquith and Edward VII. Rather suddenly, however, the King was taken seriously ill and was pronounced dead on 6 May 1910. The new King, George V, was less obstinate than his father and more ready to take advice. All the same, he too was extremely reluctant to start his reign by controversially threatening to create hundreds of new peers, and no doubt Asquith could see the force of this argument. The upshot was that the Liberal and Conservative leaderships each nominated four representatives who were given the task of privately trying to reach agreement on how to handle what was now a full-blown constitutional crisis without embarrassing the new monarch. Discussions dragged on from 17 June to 10 November 1910, effectively putting most other business on hold.

---

[16] Magnus, *Edward The Seventh*, 452. Italics supplied.

Eventually, however, the differences between the two main political parties could not be reconciled in private discussions. This meant that Asquith was driven back to Buckingham Palace in the quest for a solution: the outcome was a compromise. The Prime Minister abandoned the line he had taken on 14 April 1910 and agreed that if the Lords remained obdurate in their opposition to the Parliament Bill another general election would indeed have to be held. For his part, George V, who incidentally later regretted that he had allowed Knollys to influence him away from the harder line of dismissing Asquith and sending for Balfour, agreed in principle to grant the Liberals a dissolution. Thereafter he would permit Asquith at a moment of his choosing to announce that he had a royal promise that peers would be created if that became necessary to prevent the will of the Commons being frustrated.

As the Lords showed no sign of yielding, this led rapidly to Parliament being dissolved on 28 November, with the subsequent general election being completed before Christmas 1910. Naturally the constitutional question dominated the electioneering as it was correctly expected that the Parliament Bill would dominate parliamentary business during 1911, provided Asquith retained Number Ten. Asquith did in fact retain Number Ten. The outcome of the general election, however, was no better from his point of view than on the previous occasion; the Conservatives and Unionists actually drew level with the Liberals in terms of number of seats as against a previous deficit of two. As a result, the Opposition, not yet aware of the King's attitude, decided to offer total and outright resistance to the Parliament Bill. Thus another parliamentary year was consumed with bitter controversy. The Commons, for example, took until 15 May 1911 to deal with the bill and had 'to pick its way between more than 900 amendments tabled for the committee stage'.[17] The Lords then proceeded with relish to wreck the bill with numerous amendments of their own. Asquith now had no alternative but to drag into the controversy George V, whose coronation had fortunately already taken place on 21 June 1911. On 20 July Asquith privately informed the Opposition leaders of the existence of the royal pledge to create peers without any further general election and attempted, amid scenes of great disorder, to make the matter public in the Commons four days later. The Lords now had to decide whether to yield or to face being overridden by hundreds of new Liberal colleagues. Nobody could foretell the outcome. But in conditions of near-hysteria the 'hedgers' in the Lords defeated the 'ditchers' by 131 votes to 114 on 10 August 1911. The Lords reluctantly agreed to relinquish their veto over Bills approved by the Commons. In the midst of all this commotion and uncertainty, Robert Harcourt

---

[17] Roy Jenkins, *Asquith* (London, 1964), 225.

(as we shall see) on 19 July asked in the Commons whether legislation on theatre censorship was contemplated and unsurprisingly received a severely discouraging answer.

With the ending of the Lords' veto, the way was open for the Liberal Government during the remaining three years before the outbreak of the First World War to push ahead with a plethora of bills that might otherwise have been on the statute book much earlier. Many were controversial and were delayed for as long as possible by Opposition tactics in both the Commons and the Lords. They included various measures to build a welfare state as foreshadowed by the People's Budget of 1909. There was, above all, starting in 1912, an attempt to pass an Irish Home Rule Bill that provoked threats of armed resistance from many in Ulster who were not without encouragement from powerful elements in the Conservative and Unionist Party in London and in the armed forces. Even civil war might have been a possibility, had war with Germany not supervened in August 1914. In the same period there was growing labour unrest that brought a series of strikes to the United Kingdom as a whole. There was also an increasingly violent campaign mounted by militant suffragettes. Finally, the international scene was becoming steadily more ominous with the outbreak of the Balkan Wars in 1912 and the ongoing naval arms race with Germany.

THE DRAMATISTS' BATTLE AGAINST THEATRE CENSORSHIP

It was against this turbulent political background that the dramatists of Edwardian England began their campaign to have theatre censorship removed. The immediate trigger for the dramatists' protest over censorship seems to have been the banning of Granville Barker's play *Waste*. The Examiner of Plays, Alexander Redford, wanted the deletion of all outspoken references to the sexual relations between the main characters, a man and a married woman; in addition, he wanted the deletion of all references to an abortion. Granville Barker felt unable to comply.[18] As a result, *The Times* announced, on 18 October 1907, that 'the Examiner of Plays has refused the licence for the new play, entitled *Waste*, by Mr Granville Barker, which was to have been produced at the Savoy Theatre on 19 November'.[19] A letter written by Shaw

---

[18] See C. B. Purdom, *Granville Barker* (London: Rockliff Publishing, 1955), 73–4.

[19] *The Times*, 18 Oct. 1907. This is the only evidence indicating when *Waste* was refused a licence as the correspondence file is not to be found in the Lord Chamberlain's archives.

to Gilbert Murray on 10 October 1907 refers to an imminent campaign: 'We shall get in one blow, and one only; and it must be a smasher . . . It is the length and completeness of the list that will make the impression.'[20] Shaw's letter was written while Redford and Granville Barker were engaged in their fruitless exchange of views over *Waste*, which suggests that the writers close to Granville Barker had anticipated a negative outcome.

On 28 October 1907, seventy-one dramatists addressed a petition to the editor of *The Times* in which they outlined their reasons for wishing to protest against theatre censorship. This first published statement expressed very clearly the deep sense of grievance felt by contemporary dramatists. It also set out what they wished to achieve with their campaign. They condemned the extensive powers of the censor as arbitrary. They also deplored the fact that censorship placed them in a uniquely weak legal position, with no right of appeal to any other body. They asked for their art to be placed on the same footing as every other art and that 'they themselves be placed in the position enjoyed under the law by every other citizen'.[21]

Home Office files in the National Archives and files in the Royal Archives suggest that, from the outset, Home Office officials were hostile to any change in the law on theatre censorship. As soon as the dramatists' petition had been published in October 1907, Home Office officials assessed the importance of the dramatists' movement and the implications of the abolition of the censor, even though the initial assumption was that 'the Prime Minister will probably give no encouragement to this'.[22] The reasons suggested were numerous: previous Home Secretaries considered that the late nineteenth-century Select Committees were right in advocating no change; the dramatists' movement was small, 'only a few faddists among the theatrical reporters and other unpractical persons'; and the press as well as theatre managers and proprietors were mostly in favour of censorship. What was even more significant was the argument advanced for maintaining the censor: 'It is a question . . . of keeping down undesirable personal and political skits and criticisms . . . [a question of] how far caricature or ridicule of British or Foreign public personages, or nations, or national customs should be allowed.'[23] Censorship was clearly viewed by Home Office officials as an essential political tool to ensure that the theatre should be denied any opportunity for subjecting public figures to ridicule.

[20] George Bernard Shaw, *Collected Letters 1898–1910*, ed. Dan H. Laurence (London: Max Reinhardt, 1972), 715.
[21] 'Censorship of Plays', *The Times*, 29 Oct. 1907.
[22] NA, HO45/10545/159288. Note drafted by legal Assistant Under-Secretary Henry Cunynghame, Oct. 1907.
[23] Ibid.

Shaw kept up the pressure for reform by launching a press campaign. He made the first contribution by publishing a letter in *The Nation* in November 1907, in which he mounted a ferocious attack on the principle of censorship and on the Lord Chamberlain's Examiner of Plays, Redford:

You want a man who will undertake to know, better than Tolstoy or Ibsen or George Meredith or Dickens or Carlyle or Ruskin or Shakespeare or Shelley, what moral truths the world needs to be reminded of—how far pity and horror and tragedy dare be carried—on what institutions the antiseptic derision of comedy may be allowed to play without destroying anything really vital in them. Now it is clear without argument that no man who was not a born fool would pretend for a moment to be capable of such a task; and the reason that some censors have been born fools.[24]

Although Shaw took great pleasure in subjecting the Examiner to withering scorn, he also put the case for the defence of freedom of speech and iden- tified a key problem in the exercise of censorship: 'the Lord Chamberlain's department, corrupted by endless reading of plays, has become as sensitive in the wrong place as an 18th century duenna.'[25] In a letter to *The Times* published later that same month, the playwright John Galsworthy reiterated the main points of the dramatists' protest: 'It asks for no free stage . . . It bases itself on hatred of an unfair, un-English institution . . . It is the office that offends.'[26] He summed up what made the protest unique in the history of the theatre: 'This protest is a collective outcome of the bitter and just resentment felt at the affront so long laid upon the whole profession of writers for the stage.'[27]

Between November 1907 and February 1908, the letter pages of *The Times* were full of polemical discussion on the issue of censorship. Not all theatre professionals agreed with the dramatists. In particular, the theatre managers strongly supported the safeguards offered by the system of formal censorship. In response to the dramatists' campaign, the Theatrical Managers' Association made their support for the Lord Chamberlain publicly known in a resolution that was forwarded to the Prime Minister, the Lord Chamberlain, and the London County Council. Their support for the role of the Lord Chamberlain as censor was to remain unchanged in subsequent debates on the issue of censorship during the twentieth century. For theatre managers, the Lord Chamberlain's role as censor was seen as a necessary safeguard against the threat of vexatious prosecutions. In addition to supporting the present system of censorship, they also took the opportunity to press for stricter regulation of performance venues that were not licensed by the Lord Chamberlain so that 'the conditions attached to the licences of theatres for stage plays should apply

---

[24] *The Nation*, 16 Nov. 1907.   [25] Ibid.   [26] *The Times*, 1 Nov. 1907.
[27] Ibid.

to all buildings where stage plays are permitted'.[28] As in the eighteenth century, theatre managers were keen to use the licensing system to protect themselves from unwanted competition. Their target on this occasion was music-halls managers who were illegally presenting stage plays. The theatre managers were also concerned at the growth of 'private' (and hence unlicensed) productions mounted by dramatic societies, as a means of circumventing the law.

The Times gave some support to the dramatists' case, publishing an account of the 1737 and 1843 Acts in December 1907 and, in January 1908, an account of the Select Committees that discussed censorship in the nineteenth century. Its conclusion was that censorship was now a matter of concern to 'serious' drama. Support for the dramatists' campaign also came from a pressure group of sympathetic playgoers. In a letter to *The Times* in February 1908, 'The Committee for the Abolition of the Office of Dramatic Censor' expressed their 'sympathy with the dramatic authors in their demand for the abolition of the present system of the censorship of plays'.[29] Members of the group included Max Beerbohm, Clemence Housman, Walter Raleigh, T. Fisher Unwin, Beatrice and Sidney Webb, as well as Churchill.[30] They not only sent their petition to *The Times*, they also forwarded a booklet to the Home Office stating the case for the abolition of theatre censorship. This sustained press campaign eventually helped to persuade the Government to hear the dramatists' case, and a meeting was finally agreed between the dramatists and the Home Secretary, Gladstone, on 25 February 1908.

Prior to Gladstone's meeting with the deputation, a private memorandum to prepare the Home Secretary was written by Redford, the Examiner of Plays. In it, Redford listed the dramatists' complaints, and then went on to counter every one of their claims:

Point 1: 'power lodged in the hands of a single individual'

> The Official is selected with proper qualifications and experience. He is responsible to the Lord Chamberlain and acts on his behalf . . . He has no powers of his own, and he is not even mentioned in the Act. It follows therefore, that the Examiner of Plays must be entirely in accord with the Lord Chamberlain . . .

Point 2: 'judges without a public hearing'

> Every case about which there can be any possible doubt or question is laid before the Lord Chamberlain . . . before any final decision is given. The Manager of the Theatre is invariably given the opportunity to alter or modify the play . . . He is never left in doubt as to the cause of withholding a Licence . . . In the majority of cases the Author's name is not even known to the Examiner . . .

Point 3: 'against whose dictum there is no appeal'

---

[28] *The Times*, 20 Nov. 1907.   [29] Ibid., 24 Feb. 1908.
[30] Churchill's inclusion in this list is curious as he was at the time a government minister.

No public inquiry is possible, and under the Act no appeal is provided for, but there is no secrecy.

Point 4: 'cast a slur on the good name'

The Author suffers no injustice nor is there any 'slur cast on his good name'. The Manager of the Theatre alone is responsible and the Lord Chamberlain is not in any way officially concerned with Authors. It would be impracticable for the Lord Chamberlain to deal directly with Dramatic Authors.

Point 5: 'not exercised in the interests of morality, relieves the public of moral judgement'

The censorship is always exercised in the interests of morality, and is much more likely to err in the direction of broadness and liberality rather than narrowness and drastic severity. As for a 'free Theatre' and 'the Public being the best Censors',—the mischief is done when a play is once produced, and the only means the public would have of expressing their reprobation of a play would probably result in an unseemly disturbance in the Theatre, which would certainly be deprecated in the interest of the Managers.[31]

Gladstone did not use any of Redford's arguments when he met the deputation, which suggests that his own views on the issue may have been neutral.

The Lord Chamberlain's response to the dramatists' protest was to suggest a way of appeasing the dramatists rather than to agree their demand for the abolition of all pre-censorship. It was relayed to the Home Secretary by Henry Cunynghame, the Legal Assistant Secretary in the Home Office:

The Lord Chamberlain asked me unofficially to say that he proposed on the next occasion on which complaint is made of rejection of a play by the Reader, to appoint a small committee of reference consisting of the Comptroller of the Household, and the Assistant Comptroller, Mr Pinero (principal spokesman at the deputation to you), Mr Bram Stoker and Sir Douglas Straight. Both of the latter have legal as well as literary qualifications . . . He did not propose to make the Committee perpetual but to choose the members as the occasion arose.[32]

This suggestion was likewise passed over in silence when Gladstone met the deputation.

Gladstone and Herbert Samuel (Parliamentary Under-Secretary) received the dramatists' deputation on 25 February 1908. J. M. Barrie introduced the group, and A. W. Pinero presented the case for their protest against 'the arbitrary action of a single official who was neither responsible to Parliament nor amenable to law [and] from which there was no appeal'.[33] He mentioned that the deputation represented roughly 80 per cent of all dramatic

---

[31] NA, HO45/10545/159288, 13 Feb. 1908.　　[32] Ibid.
[33] *The Times*, 26 Feb. 1908.

authors. He disputed the notion that dramatists were being sentimental about their plays: 'The fact that several acknowledged masterpieces were under the censor's ban was sufficiently ridiculous and would be incredible in any other civilised country.'[34] Sir William Gilbert proposed, as a compromise, an amendment to the current system rather than its abolition, namely that 'the office of the Examiner of Plays should take the *status* of a Court of first instance, from whose decision there should be an appeal to a Court of arbitrators constituted under the Arbitration Act of 1894, and consisting of three members'.[35] Gladstone commented diplomatically that his personal view was benevolent, but that his role was to make notes and report to the Prime Minister, adding that theatre censorship 'was one of those curious questions, not infrequently found in the British constitution, which seemed not to belong to any distinct Department of State'.[36] To conclude the discussion, Murray reminded the Home Secretary that the system proposed was a compromise and that 'a great many dramatic authors seriously disliked the censorship altogether'.[37]

Following this meeting, opinions drafted by civil servants in the Home Office make it clear that they wanted legislation to be avoided. On the other hand, they recognized that the Government would have to make an effort to meet the dramatists on some common ground because 'the objection to the existing system arises wholly from the anomalous nature of the Lord Chamberlain's jurisdiction'.[38] This was the first, albeit tentative, acknowledgement that there was indeed something anomalous in the Lord Chamberlain undertaking the statutory role of censor under the terms of the 1843 Theatres Act when the authority of his Office derived from the exercise of the Royal Prerogative. The principal clerk at the Home Office, W. P. Byrne, considered that 'the more moderate section admit that some sort of censorship is necessary'; because of this, he suggested the following compromise: 'An arrangement by which in all cases where refusal to license is contemplated the S of S [Secretary of State] would be consulted would go far to meet the outcry, because the S of S can be questioned in Parliament.'[39] This was not a view that was likely to commend itself to any Home Secretary. The prospect of becoming embroiled in disagreements on the day-to-day exercise of theatre censorship was something that a Home Secretary would wish to avoid at all costs. The main advantage to government in having the Lord Chamberlain as theatre censor was precisely the fact that his decisions could not be questioned in the Commons.

---

[34] Ibid.   [35] Ibid.   [36] Ibid.   [37] Ibid.
[38] NA, HO 45/10545/159288. Note drafted by W. P. Byrne, on 18 Apr. 1908.
[39] Ibid.

The Prime Minister, Campbell-Bannerman, died in the very same month that these Home Office opinions were drafted. Inevitably, this meant that Gladstone had to brief the new Prime Minister, Asquith, on the deliberations that had so far taken place on the issue of theatre censorship. In a note to the Prime Minister written on 30 June 1908, Gladstone stated categorically that 'it is not proposed to legislate'. The view of Home Office officials had clearly prevailed and he was minded to follow the advice he had been given by his civil servants. He then went on to address the Lord Chamberlain's suggestion of an Advisory Body to hear appeals. In his view, this would 'further weaken a very weak position'. He continued:

I do not think the Government should be brought in and made responsible for an arrangement in which subsequently they have no voice. Short of altering the law, if a new arrangement is come to, it should be on the responsibility of the Lord Chamberlain—who would not act without His Majesty's approval—and should be of a nature which would commend itself to the public as combining competence to deal with higher morality problems, and commonsense in regard to the ordinary questions of decency. The Government cannot relieve the Lord Chamberlain of his responsibility, but may be expected to help him with advice. The nomination of an Advisory body by the Lord Chamberlain would still expose him to a charge of packing. I am inclined to suggest therefore, that if such a body is set up it should be composed of three or five persons nominated by such bodies as the Playwrights, Managers, and the London County Council with one or two added by the Lord Chamberlain himself. . . If something of this sort is done it would probably settle the controversy.[40]

In response, the Prime Minister wanted clarification as to the workings of the future Advisory Board:

I presume that the Examiner of Plays would continue to perform his present duties, and that the advisory body would only be called in upon a reference from him in a case of doubt, or by way of appeal, when the person interested in the play was dissatisfied with an adverse decision by him. Subject to this, I am disposed to agree with you.[41]

This exchange of notes indicates that the dramatists had succeeded in provoking the Government into considering how to improve the workings of censorship but not into changing the law. In the short term, no action was taken and no formal reply was sent to the playwrights. The well-established policy of inertia was followed in the hope that the dramatists' campaign would eventually run out of steam. Two years later, however, in 1910, the Lord Chamberlain did set up an informal Advisory Board along the lines he had first suggested in his note to the Home Office.

---

[40] Ibid. Gladstone's comments on 30 June 1908.
[41] Ibid. Asquith's comments on 22 July 1908.

The dramatists' campaign did not run out of steam. In the absence of any formal response from the Government, Robert Harcourt MP, who was also a writer of comedies, began a series of parliamentary interventions. Harcourt came from a distinguished family of Liberal politicians. His father, William Harcourt, had served as Home Secretary in Gladstone's administration, and his half-brother Lewis Harcourt was First Commissioner of Works in Asquith's government. Although Members of Parliament had raised the issue of theatre censorship from time to time during the early 1900s (some wanted more rigorous censorship, others questioned the validity of individual decisions taken by the Lord Chamberlain),[42] Harcourt was the first to address the matter in a serious and focused manner. On 17 December 1908, he introduced a Private Member's Bill, which set out 'to abolish the powers of the Lord Chamberlain in respect of stage plays and to transfer to the local authority the powers of the Lord Chamberlain in respect of the licensing of theatres in London'.[43] It was given its First Reading that same day. On 23 December, *The Times* stated that the bill had now been printed and quoted the memorandum attached to the bill:

The object of this Bill is to abolish the censorship of plays exercised in Great Britain under the authority of the Lord Chamberlain, and to transfer to the London County Council as the local authority the power of licensing and controlling theatres exercised by the Lord Chamberlain in the central parts of the Metropolis. As to the censorship of plays, it is proposed to make theatrical performances subject to the same control as performances in music-halls. In the case of music-halls no censorship exists, but any impropriety can be dealt with by the police or by a refusal of the licence by the licensing authority, which in London is the London County Council. The censorship of plays does not exist in Ireland. As to the licensing of theatres, this power is now exercised by or under the control of the local authority in practically the whole of Great Britain where theatres are to be found, except the central district of London, the University cities of Oxford and Cambridge, and places where his Majesty resides. Further, even in the central district of London, the London County Council as the local authority has already extensive powers over the structure of theatres under the Metropolis Management Act, 1878.

The bill was supported by Members of Parliament from different parties, including Alfred Mason and Arthur Ponsonby (Liberals), T. P. O'Connor (Irish Nationalist), and Ramsay MacDonald (Labour). However, the Second Reading and printing of the bill, scheduled for the day after, never took place. One possible explanation for the disappearance of the bill was lack

---

[42] See *Hansard* (Commons), 9 Apr. 1900, vol. 81, col. 1522; 15 May 1900, vol. 83, cols. 276, 282–3, 297–8; 11 July 1901, vol. 97, cols. 92–3; and 24 June 1902, vol. 109, col. 1517
[43] Ibid., 17 Dec. 1908, vol. 198, col. 2161.

of parliamentary time, as the Christmas recess began on 22 December 1908. In addition, this first attempt to promote a Private Member's Bill to abolish theatre censorship coincided with Asquith's speech at the National Liberal Club in which he had made his determination clear 'to treat the veto of the House of Lords as the dominating issue in politics'. No less important was the fact that the Home Secretary had decided to block any progress on the bill.

Harcourt's introduction of his Private Member's Bill on 17 December 1908 came as something of a shock to the Government. The first reaction to it, interestingly, came from the King and was conveyed to the Lord Chamberlain, not to the Government. On 24 December, 1908, the King's Assistant Private Secretary, Sir Frederick Ponsonby, wrote to the Lord Chamberlain, Lord Althorp:

> The King says he will not agree to the theatres being removed from the jurisdiction of the Lord Chamberlain and he thinks you might speak to L. Harcourt respecting his Brother's officiousness. The latter does not represent a Metropolitan Borough so what business is it of his? I don't know how far the House of Commons has power in a matter of this sort.[44]

This initial response suggests that the King still saw the exercise of censorship by the Lord Chamberlain as part of the Royal Prerogative. The reference to the House of Commons and its powers, however, also indicates that the King's Assistant Private Secretary was by no means certain on this point. While the monarch appears to have assumed incorrectly that the Lord Chamberlain's role as censor was part of the Royal Prerogative, since the Licensing Act of 1737 (as we have seen) this was no longer the case. In addition, the King had powerful personal reasons for wishing to see strict theatre censorship retained. His marital infidelities had led to widespread adverse comment in contemporary society. He would doubtless have been fearful that a stage, freed from any royal control, might subject his behaviour to satirical critique of the kind that had plagued royalty in the early eighteenth century. This was an outcome that he would have been eager to avoid at all costs. This perhaps explains the vehemence of his response and his refusal to countenance any change in the law on censorship, whatever the constitutional propriety of such an action.

While there is no record of whether the King discussed the matter with the Prime Minister, his wishes were swiftly brought to the attention of the Home Office. Althorp wrote to Byrne, officially liaising between the two departments:

> It [the bill] was obviously brought in as a 'feeler' with the purpose of getting up some kind of agitation against the Lord Chamberlain retaining jurisdiction over

---

[44] RA (Royal Archives), Box 251 (1909 Censorship Committee). Handwritten letter to Althorp from Sandringham dated 24 Dec. 1908.

Metropolitan Theatres. I did not make out if the bill proposed to abolish the Lord Chamberlain's censorship over plays, or if it only referred to structural supervision and such like. But my impression is that the object was to abolish all control except that of police over theatres under the jurisdiction of the Lord Chamberlain. As I believe that this jurisdiction is one of the prerogatives of the Crown, I should like to know if it is possible for the H. of Commons to vote upon it. I am totally ignorant of what powers the Commons have in such a matter. Probably all power, only it seems to me that a debate on the prerogative of the Crown founded on a bill to abolish the Lord Chamberlain's control over theatres in the Metropolitan area would be very regrettable even were it possible. I of course do not know what view the Home Secretary takes of this bill . . . but I know that the proposed abolition of the Lord Chamberlain's jurisdiction would be very distasteful, to use no stronger expression.[45]

Althorp's note indicates that he, as Lord Chamberlain, was unaware that he exercised his powers of censorship under statute law. He therefore emphasized the fact that any attempt to abolish the control of the Lord Chamberlain over the theatres would raise the whole issue of the Royal Prerogative. In his view, this was clearly undesirable, presumably because, as Asquith had made clear, at the time the country already faced a constitutional struggle of serious magnitude. Any further constitutional challenge was therefore something to be avoided at all costs.

The main points in Byrne's draft response were the following:

If the Bill is reintroduced in its present shape it will be opposed by the S of S. It removes all censorship over plays and puts nothing adequate in its place . . . The transfer of the licensing of theatres to the LCC is not generally approved, it is a question which is now sleeping and it would be a pity to arouse it.[46]

The Permanent Under-Secretary Edward Troup agreed that the system should not be abolished 'unless something better can be substituted'. The last note in the file was signed by the Secretary of State. It reads:

Reply as proposed. Personally I don't think the present arrangement is at all satisfactory in principle though it has worked tolerably well in practice. All depends upon the judgement of the authorities concerned. But it is one of these questions which should be allowed to sleep as long as possible.[47]

Gladstone and his officials were clearly intent on following the same policy of inertia, in respect of theatre censorship, that had characterized any scrutiny of the issue by Parliament during the nineteenth century. The object was to avoid any change, if possible, and to delay any serious consideration of the issue for the foreseeable future. The last thing anyone wanted in the Home Office,

---

[45] NA, HO 45/10416/173738, 29 Dec. 1908.
[46] Ibid., 16 Jan. 1909.   [47] Ibid., 20 Jan. 1909.

whatever the merits of the dramatists' case, was to open the Pandora's box of theatre censorship legislation at a time when the country faced the prospect of a serious constitutional struggle between the monarch, the Lords, and the Commons.

In the continued absence of any formal response from the Government, Harcourt decided to renew his attempt to introduce a Private Member's Bill: on 22 April 1909, his second Private Member's Bill on theatre censorship was given its First Reading. It was entitled: 'Theatres and Music Halls—Bill to abolish the powers of the Lord Chamberlain in respect of stage plays, and to vest in local authorities the licensing of theatres, music halls, and places of public entertainment.'[48] The Second Reading was scheduled for 27 April 1909, but once again, it never took place. The planned date was a mere two days before Lloyd George's People's Budget was presented as a dramatic challenge to the Lords. It would be difficult to imagine a less auspicious moment to attempt any change in legislation on the issue of theatre censorship. Passions were running high in the Lords and the Commons because of Lloyd George's Budget and because of the implied threat that the Government would no longer tolerate the veto of the Lords if it were exercised on a matter of such central importance. It is therefore hardly surprising that in such a frenzied atmosphere, Harcourt's bill should disappear without trace. On this occasion too, as we shall see, the Home Secretary had decided to block any progress on the bill. Officials in the Home Office and the Home Secretary responded to this new bill in much the same manner as they did to Harcourt's first bill. Troup, the Permanent Under-Secretary, and Samuel, the Parliamentary Secretary (who was later to chair the Select Committee), drafted the Home Office view that, 'though not on the same lines, the same objections, if no others, apply to this Bill as to the other one, and it should be blocked'.[49] A further note states that the draft was 'seen by S of S, who agrees that the Bill must be blocked'.[50]

The memorandum attached to the bill made it clear that its intention was to abolish the censorship of plays and transfer the licensing of the theatres, including those London theatres under the Lord Chamberlain's jurisdiction, to local authorities. It would also abolish the distinction between theatres and music halls, as there would only be one licence for all buildings to cover every kind of entertainment. Byrne was asked to draft a memo summing up the Lord Chamberlain's views, so that both departments 'should express views in harmony'. In respect of the proposal to bring together music halls and theatres

---

[48] *Hansard* (Commons), 22 Apr. 1909, vol. 3, col. 1675.
[49] NA, HO 45/10416/173738. Draft prepared by Principal Clerk J. Pedder, 26 Apr. 1909.
[50] Ibid., 29 Apr. 1909.

under one licensing authority, he wrote about the current situation in respect of music hall sketches:

a) That these Dramatic sketches are mostly undoubted stage plays and their production in music halls which are not licensed as theatres is clearly illegal.

b) But that the Lord Chamberlain does not in existing circumstances want, and does not intend, to be drawn into a policy of prosecuting them.

c) That these Dramatic sketches are in themselves objectionable as being presentations either of unlicensed stage plays or of condensed and mutilated versions of licensed plays, which versions the Lord Chamberlain has never seen and cannot hold himself responsible for.

d) That they are further objectionable as being injurious to the National Drama, a fact which has been repeatedly and urgently pressed upon you by West End managers.

e) That they injure the theatre proper both financially and artistically. They withdraw from the theatres many who are tempted by the freedom, the smoking, the promenade and the drinks in the auditorium of the music hall, privileges which the theatre cannot have. Some of these people will not go to a theatre if they can see actors and actresses in the halls in 'sketches'. And they tend to produce a degraded taste for hurried and frivolous and brainless drama. The theatre is thus impoverished and hampered in its own proper work which it is to the interest of all should be kept at a high level.

f) That for these reasons the Lord Chamberlain, though unwilling to restrict the presentation of any harmless and refined form of recreation in the music halls, is opposed to any extension of the Dramatic sketch beyond the limits fixed by the modus vivendi established 2 years ago, and would object to 'mixed licences' allowing every form of entertainment.

As Byrne had been told that the matter was to be submitted to the King, he added:

If I am right in thinking these are the views held by your Dpt (and possibly also in the highest quarters) I shall be very glad to lay them before the HO [Home Office] and H. Samuel, in the hope that they will support them in Parliament when occasion offers.[51]

The occasion arose rather sooner than Byrne might have anticipated. Harcourt and his fellow dramatists decided on a two-pronged approach. Shaw renewed his press campaign against censorship on 24 May 1909, and two days later Harcourt put a formal Parliamentary Question to the Prime Minister. In his press campaign, Shaw complained about the censoring of his plays *The Shewing-up of Blanco Posnet* and *Press Cuttings*.[52] He also chose to highlight

    [51] NA, HO 45/10416/173 738. Memorandum drafted by Byrne, 14 May 1909.
    [52] 'Mr Shaw and the Censor', *The Times*, 24 May 1909; and 'The Censor's Revenge', *The Times*, 26 June 1909.

Waste as an example of a play wrongly censored. Shaw opened this second press campaign on the topic of censorship by pointing out the errors of censorship and by mischievously accusing the King of being responsible for the Lord Chamberlain's mistakes:

I have just had occasion to make a public statement concerning the prohibition of one of my own plays . . . It was necessary for me to be scrupulously correct in defining the authority with which I was in conflict. As that authority happened to be the King, several journalists proceeded to lecture me severely, evidently believing that I had committed a gross solecism by mentioning the King instead of mentioning the Minister representing the Government and responsible to the House of Commons. They also expressed a sense of wounded chivalry at the spectacle of a defenceless monarch attacked by an all-powerful and merciless playwright . . . I therefore wish to point out that when we speak of Mr Redford as the Censor, and the Lord Chamberlain's function as a censorship, we are taking a liberty with these gentlemen . . . To hold them responsible for the control of the theatres is really as great a solecism as it would be to hold the King responsible for the Budget . . . I have no remedy except to state my grievance; and because this grievance happens to lie technically against the King I am told that it would be in better taste for me to suffer in silence.[53]

A spate of letters on censorship and on Shaw's assertions now appeared in *The Times*.[54] Shaw was particularly pleased to receive support from an eminent lawyer: 'Sir Harry Poland's opinion that the Lord Chamberlain is a private and irresponsible monopolist to whom Parliament, in a fit of insanity, gave despotic powers over the theatre, including the levy of taxes, is, I hope, as sound as might be expected from so eminent a lawyer.'[55] A letter from Redford attempted to counteract Shaw's earlier satiric piece with literal-minded earnestness: 'I have never described myself as "The King's Reader of Plays". Mr Shaw has possibly gone to the "Dead Letter Office" for his facts.'[56] The dramatist Galsworthy joined in with a spirited attack on censorship,[57] and, in some exasperation, Granville Baker wrote about the manifest absurdity of conflicting decisions on censorship emanating from the office of the Lord Chamberlain:

How is one, unenlightened, to distinguish between *Salome* with the head of John the Baptist (censored) and the same *Salome* with a blood-dripping sword (licensed); or between *Eagerheart* with the Holy Family in it (licensed) and *Bethlehem* with the Holy Family in it (censored); between *Monna Vanna*, wholly clothed in a single garment (censored) and *The Devil* in which the same situation is suggested (licensed)? . . . How was I to tell, in writing *Waste* that, while almost every variety of adultery, seduction

---

[53] *The Times*, 29 May 1909.
[54] Letters were printed on 29 May, 1–5 June, 10 June, 17 June, 26 June, and 30 June 1909.
[55] *The Times*, 4 June 1909.   [56] Ibid., 5 June 1909.   [57] Ibid.

and debauchery may be vividly presented in the theatre, yet an illegal operation might not even be mentioned? . . . It is for the public good to have vice painted in glowing colours, but for the public harm that its consequences should ever be referred to.[58]

Shaw's intention in co-ordinating this new press campaign was to maintain political pressure on the Government.

Similar pressure was applied by Harcourt in Parliament. On 26 May 1909, he asked the Prime Minister:

whether his attention has been called to recent incidents in connection with the existing dramatic censorship, and also to prosecutions of music-hall managers for the performance of stage plays; whether the Government contemplates any legislation on these subjects; and, if not, should the House consent to give a Second Reading to the Bill introduced by the hon. Member for the Montrose Burghs and supported by members belonging to all political parties; whether he would be prepared to appoint a Select Committee to examine the Bill, and hear evidence, on the understanding that the Bill would not be further pressed during the present Session.[59]

The draft answers prepared by the Home Office for the Prime Minister's reply to Harcourt's formal question of 26 May 1909 took into account the views of the Lord Chamberlain, the Home Secretary, and the King:

To ask the Prime Minister whether his attention has been called to recent incidents in connection with the existing dramatic censorship and also to prosecutions of music-hall managers for the performance of stage plays;

Presumably yes.

Whether the Government contemplate any legislation on these subjects;

No: there is no time and the present is, in the Lord Chamberlain's opinion, by no means a favourable moment for legislation. The theatrical world is hopelessly divided and muddled on the question.

If not, should the House consent to give a Second Reading to the Bill introduced by the hon. Member for Montrose Burghs and supported by Members belonging to all political parties,

The Bill is to be opposed.

Whether he would be prepared to appoint a Select Committee to examine the Bill, and hear evidence, on the understanding that the Bill would not be further pressed during the present Session.

No need for a Committee: there was a very good committee in 1892 which dealt with the question after hearing all sides.[60]

---

[58] *The Times* 10 June 1909.   [59] *Hansard* (Commons), 26 May 1909, vol. 5, col. 1183.
[60] NA, HO 45/10416/173738. Draft prepared by C. E. Troup, 25 May 1909.

This draft was signed by the Prime Minister's private secretary. As far as the Home Office was concerned, it was in everyone's interests for the Prime Minister to give a series of negative responses to Harcourt's set of questions.

Much to everyone's surprise, however (and the same thing was to happen in the 1960s in the case of Harold Wilson), the Prime Minister responded positively in the Commons to the suggestion that a Select Committee be appointed: 'I do not know what may be the fortunes of [the bill] but I am disposed to agree that the time has come for some such inquiry.'[61] This answer of course forestalled any further discussion of the bill, but the Government then remained silent. Parliament was fully preoccupied at the time by the furore caused by Lloyd George's People's Budget. Presumably Asquith hoped that a positive response to Harcourt, followed by complete inertia, would permit the matter gently to fade into oblivion. He had reckoned without Harcourt's stubbornness. In a second Parliamentary Question he put to Asquith on 22 June 1909, Harcourt insisted on a more precise response from the Prime Minister. Presumably, he hoped that a favourable Joint Select Committee verdict could be considered at leisure by a new Parliament in which the Liberals had unambiguously won the constitutional battle between the 'peers and the people'. He therefore pressed the Prime Minister on the issue of a select committee:

Is the Prime Minister prepared to appoint a committee of enquiry into the working of the censorship over stage plays previous to production, and also the forms of licence granted respectively to theatres and music halls, with a view to considering whether legislation is desirable?[62]

The answer this time was unambiguous: 'I think the time has come when a further inquiry into these matters might well be held. The best instrument for such an inquiry will be a Joint Committee of the two Houses.'[63]

Asquith's reply was given at the end of the dramatists' second press campaign, a campaign that had begun when Harcourt first asked the Prime Minister about his views on legislation. Asquith's decision in June 1909 to support the establishment of a Select Committee of both Houses was unexpected and yet, in retrospect, unsurprising. At a time when a fundamental constitutional confrontation was in prospect over the People's Budget, the Prime Minister did not want theatre censorship to be a subject of complicating controversy for King, Lords, and Commons. Establishing a Joint Select Committee to look into the issue effectively kicked the topic of theatre censorship out of sight for a significant period of time.

[61] *Hansard* (Commons), 26 May 1909, vol. 5, col. 1183.
[62] Ibid., 22 June 1909, vol. 6, col. 1545. [63] Ibid.

When Harcourt asked his second Parliamentary Question, Asquith's draft reply, setting out the terms of reference for the Joint Select Committee, was copied to the Lord Chamberlain:

To inquire as to the expediency of the Censorship of stage plays as established by the Theatres Act, 1843, and as to the operation of the Acts of Parliament relating to the Licensing and Regulation of Theatres and places of public entertainment, and to report any alterations of the law or practice which may seem desirable.[64]

Between giving his two parliamentary answers, the Prime Minister had reported to the King that 'questions as to suggested changes to the censorship of dramatic performances' had been discussed in the Cabinet meeting but that 'the Cabinet did not come to any decision'.[65] He further asked to submit 'informally certain considerations' to the King, presumably at one of their weekly audiences. These were never set down in writing, but were doubtless intended to reassure the King that Asquith had no intention of engaging in a second constitutional skirmish with the monarch when he was fully preoccupied with the issue of the Lords' powers to veto legislation. He may well have concluded, and persuaded the King to acknowledge, that setting up a Joint Select Committee was an astute move. The fact was that every previous Joint Select Committee had recommended that the Lord Chamberlain continue to exercise his role as censor. Setting up a Joint Select Committee therefore permitted the Prime Minister to appear open-minded, while killing off a Private Member's Bill that parliamentary session and placating an irate monarch.

THE 1909 JOINT SELECT COMMITTEE

The Joint Select Committee was composed of five commoners and five peers. Hugh Law (Irish Nationalist), Colonel Mark Lockwood (Conservative), Alfred Mason (Liberal), Robert Harcourt (Liberal), and Herbert Samuel (Liberal) were the commoners. Samuel, who served as Chairman had been recently appointed Chancellor of the Duchy of Lancaster and, as a result, had a place in the Cabinet. He had previously been Parliamentary Secretary to the Home Office and had accompanied Gladstone to meet the dramatists' deputation in February 1908. Lord Newton, Lord Willoughby de Broke, Lord

---

[64] RA, Box 251 (1909 Censorship Committee). Letter from Vaughan Nash to Althorp, 21 June 1909.

[65] NA, CAB 41/32/19 (Cabinet Papers), 27 May 1909.

Ribblesdale, Lord Gorell, and the Earl of Plymouth represented the Lords. The Committee sat from 21 July to 2 November 1909, and forty-nine witnesses were examined between 29 July and 24 September 1909. The report was printed in November 1909 but was never formally considered by either the Lords or Commons.

The witnesses were divided into two opposing factions. Generally, actors and theatre managers (and a minority of playwrights) expressed the view that a centralized censorship of plays prior to production was essential. Prior censorship avoided the threat of prosecutions by the police when a play was touring in the provinces and effectively prevented local authorities, and especially their watch committees, from meddling with the theatre. It was reassuring for theatre managers to have the support of the Lord Chamberlain, so that they were spared the effort and responsibility of being censors. All these points were made by Sir Herbert Beerbohm Tree when he argued that:

To constitute the local authorities as *censores morum* and committees of taste, would be to create a state of things absolutely intolerable to managers and to authors, and would substitute mob law for a beneficent, or at least benevolent, autocracy . . . And it must be plain that if plays were to be subject to the arbitrament of a mixed audience, a new terror would be added to the production of a play. At the moment the Lord Chamberlain has the responsibility, and his action naturally carries with it the moral weight of that high office; were the censorship abolished, the responsibility would fall on the managers.[66]

As a distinguished actor-manager, his evidence was representative of the opinion of both professions (actors and managers) and was well articulated compared to that of his colleagues. He admitted that he 'did not hold that the acts of the censorship have invariably been above criticism'.[67] But he then went on to undermine this viewpoint by asserting: 'I do not think the drama in England has suffered very severely through the prohibition of plays like certain dramas of [Eugène] Brieux or plays like *Monna Vanna* and *Blanco Posnet*.' In effect, Tree suggested that the censor had been correct to ban plays that were challenging. Theatre managers wanted their businesses to operate smoothly and effectively, and without the threat of controversy and any ensuing legal action.

In contrast, the dramatists claimed that the censor tended to allow indecent plays and to refuse plays that were morally educating. Yet, there was no clear set of rules to guide them in their creative process, and they never knew whether they were going to be censored or not; as a result, they

---

[66] Report of the 1909 Joint Select Committee, Q. 2601, 151.   [67] Ibid.

sometimes worked a long time in vain. The critic Archer explained the dramatists' plight:

The effect [of censorship] is to depress and to mutilate and actually to keep out of existence serious plays; because many authors will not write serious plays under the threat of having them destroyed by a single veto of the Censor. On the other hand, it is in the nature of the censorship to be indulgent, shall we say, to all the lighter forms of frivolity which sometimes trench very closely upon indecency and impropriety.[68]

The same inconsistency was also mentioned by Granville Barker in his evidence,[69] where he quoted the testimony of such writers as Thomas Hardy, Henry James, H. G. Wells, and Joseph Conrad. Galsworthy confirmed that a national drama could not exist as long as the censor posed a threat to creativity.[70] Also significant was the evidence given by J. M. Barrie. He was a respected dramatist who had led the deputation to the Home Secretary and he had never been censored. He therefore could not be accused of 'sentimentality' when he declared:

I think we are at the root of the matter if we accept the following as true, that the important objections to abolition are not founded on what is best for the drama, but on practical difficulties, real or imaginary, of running theatres without such an official to simplify matters for the manager.[71]

This was in many ways the nub of the matter. While the dramatists were making a case for what was best for the drama, those who supported censorship (and in particular theatre managers) were primarily concerned for the financial stability and well being of their business.

Generally, the dramatists who were called to give evidence proved to be more articulate than both actors and managers. In addition, there were two star witnesses: G. K. Chesterton and Shaw. Chesterton was a critic, novelist, and poet. His view was simple: 'I am for the censorship, but I am against the present Censor.'[72] When asked to reflect on the situation of the theatre managers if the censor was abolished, his answer was: 'I represent the gallery, but certainly not the manager. It is a horrible thought.'[73] His solution was to suggest an elected jury:

I will take my chance with a democratic censorship, knowing at least the absurdities of Jones will be balanced by the absurdities of Smith, and the eccentricities of Robinson will be balanced by the insanities of Tomkinson. But I cannot take my chance with a person who could suppress those two last plays of Bernard Shaw.[74]

---

[68] Ibid., Q. 658, 34.   [69] See ibid., Q. 1224, 71.   [70] See ibid., Q. 2262, 127.
[71] Ibid., Q. 1764, 101.   [72] Ibid., Q. 6141, 342.   [73] Ibid., Q. 6159, 343.
[74] Ibid., Q. 6168, 345.

The plays in question were *The Shewing-up of Blanco Posnet* and the political sketch *Press Cuttings*; both were refused a licence in 1909.

When Shaw was asked, early in his testimony, which form the law of the land should take to control the theatre, he made a formal request for his prepared statement to be read by the Committee before he was examined; he quoted the precedent of Henry Irving in 1892. The room was cleared and the Committee decided, after deliberation, not to allow Shaw's statement as part of the evidence. Shaw famously called this episode an 'anti-Shavian panic': 'As far as I can guess, the next thing that happened was that some timid or unawakened member of the Committee read my statement and was frightened or scandalized out of his wits by it.' His testimony nevertheless allowed for his conclusions to be heard. (He then decided to print the forty-seven-page 'rejected' statement as part of the preface to published editions of *Blanco Posnet*.) Three of his plays had been censored for the three different taboos: sex, religion, and politics. Yet, he was known to be prudish in sexual matters, an attitude he shared with Samuel.[75] He was an articulate witness for the cause of the dramatists, but he put forward views and solutions that were unmistakably his own. Based on his experience with the censor he declared that 'it is exceedingly difficult to find out sometimes what the mind of the Censor is and what his politics are'.[76] This is the reason why he advocated that the law of the land be applied to the theatre as a control *after* production:

The Censor is a species of anarch, if I may say so. He is not a person administering the law in any sense. When you go to the magistrate you have not only shifted the control, but, for the first time, you have created what is real legal control. You have created law where there was nothing before but the chaos of the Censor's mind.[77]

His testimony was well documented and his conclusions were to the point. He also took delight in mocking Redford and in explaining the correct meaning of the words 'moral' and 'immoral':

at the present time a great many immoral plays (and I am using the word now in the correct English sense; I had almost said in the sense in which it is *not* used from one end of the Bible to the other) are now passed and performed because the Censor (I do not know how to put this quite politely) is not sufficiently an expert in moral questions to know always when a play is moral and when it is immoral.[78]

---

[75] In *Liberalism*, Samuel wrote: 'the publication of books and pictures, and the performances of plays which incite to sexual immorality are properly forbidden.' Quoted from Bernard Wasserstein, *Herbert Samuel: A Political Life* (Oxford: Clarendon Press, 1992), 49. Correspondence in the House of Lords Library between Shaw and Samuel suggests that they saw each other socially.

[76] Report of the 1909 Joint Select Committee, Q. 931. Shaw's testimony is reprinted in 'Shaw on Censorship: A Readable Bluebook', *Shavian Tract no.3* (London: Shaw Society, 1955).

[77] Ibid., Q. 930.   [78] Ibid., Q. 897.

After deliberating until November, the Committee, contrary to all expectation, recommended that a change to the law was needed:

We conclude that the public interest requires that theatrical performances should be regulated by special laws. We conclude that the producers of plays should have access, prior to their production, to a public authority which should be empowered to license plays as suitable for performance. We conclude that the licensing authority, which we desire to see maintained, should not have power to impose a veto on the production of plays. We conclude that the public authority should be empowered by a summary process to suspend the performance of unlicensed plays which appear to be of an improper character, and that, where it is confirmed that they are of such a character, the producers should be liable to penalties. We conclude that the authority to decide on the propriety of the future performance of an unlicensed play should be the Courts of Law in cases where indecency is alleged, and, in other cases, a mixed Committee of the Privy Council.

Based on these conclusions, the Committee recommended the following:

The Lord Chamberlain should remain the Licenser of Plays. It should be his duty to license any play submitted to him unless he considers that it may reasonably be held—

a) To be indecent;

b) To contain offensive personalities;

c) To represent on the stage in an invidious manner a living person, or any person recently dead;

d) To do violence to the sentiment of religious reverence;

e) To be calculated to conduce to crime or vice;

f) To be calculated to impair friendly relations with any Foreign Power; or

g) To be calculated to cause a breach of the peace.

It should be optional to submit a play for licence, and legal to perform an unlicensed play, whether it has been submitted or not.

If the Director of Public Prosecutions is of opinion that any unlicensed play which has been performed is open to objection on the ground of indecency, he should prefer an indictment against the manager of the theatre . . . and the author of the play. It should be illegal for any further performances of the play to take place until the case has been heard and decided.[79]

Finally, the Committee also looked into the position of the music halls: 'We recommend a single licence for both classes of houses, giving them freedom to produce whatever entertainment may best conform to the tastes of the public which they serve.'[80]

---

[79] Ibid., Q. 897, p. xii.   [80] Ibid., p. xvi.

Though the report was unanimous, the draft copy indicates that some members of the Committee had to compromise on certain points. Ribblesdale moved that the report should omit the reasons why a play might be refused and insert as the sole reason: 'not to be fitting for the preservation of good manners, decorum, or of the public peace.'[81] However, this phrase was borrowed from the 1843 Theatres Act, and playwrights had already complained that it was too vague. His motion was therefore not supported. Newton suggested a motion to delete the sentence: 'It should be optional to submit a play for licence, and legal to perform an unlicensed play, whether it has been submitted or not.'[82] His motion was not supported. Samuel, who chaired the Committee, made a number of detailed suggestions, which were all accepted by the Committee. The most surprising motion was proposed by Gorell, namely:

We consider that the choice, therefore, lies between control prior to, or subsequent to, performance, and that, having regard to all the difficulties of the matter, the system of licence before production should be abolished and that reliance should be placed on subsequent effective control.[83]

Only Harcourt supported this motion, which would have swept away all prior censorship.

The arguments put forward by the dramatists seem to have carried more weight than the pleas made by actors and managers. What was completely unexpected was the fact that the Committee recommended that it should be optional for dramatists to submit plays for licence. This was a conclusion that no one in the Government had anticipated before the Committee began its work. Though the Committee had been called upon to enquire into the system of theatre censorship and to recommend legislation if need be, the assumption in Government had been that the Committee would not recommend any significant change. The Government had then done everything in its power to steer the process towards this outcome.

This attempt to influence the conclusions of the Committee can be discerned during the period when the Committee was conducting its deliberations. Firstly, the Lord Chamberlain's Office was in close contact with the Home Office, and particularly with Byrne, as well as with Samuel. Secondly, Sir Douglas Dawson (the Lord Chamberlain's Comptroller, was in constant correspondence with all interested parties: he wrote to the witnesses supporting the Lord Chamberlain in order to check their opinions; he also kept in close contact with Byrne. As he had to testify himself,

[81] Draft Report of the 1909 Joint Select Committee, §21.   [82] Ibid.
[83] Ibid., §19.

Dawson asked the help of Byrne, who sent him a précis of his evidence and added:

I do not think you could say anything better with respect to the disputes between the theatres and the music halls than what is set out in the letter which I wrote to you some time ago, conveying what I understood to be the Lord Chamberlain's views and your own. I am inclined to think that the Committee will adopt those views . . . They were all very polite and, I think, practically unanimously sympathised with our views.[84]

In contrast to the care taken to brief Dawson for his evidence, the help provided to Redford suggests that there was no love lost between the Lord Chamberlain and his Examiner: 'There is one very strong point which you will never lose sight of and it is that the Lord Chamberlain is the (so called) "Censor" and the Examiner of Plays is not. . . . I think you have slid into the practice by degrees somewhat unconsciously.'[85] In addition, 'Lord Althorp . . . advised Mr Redford to make his replies as brief as possible. Lord Althorp warned Mr Redford that he would be likely to be heckled. Mr Redford should take care not to be carried away, and to volunteer no information.'[86] In the event, the evidence given by Dawson and Redford proved damaging as it demonstrated a lack of co-ordination within the Lord Chamberlain's Office.

Althorp's assistants seem to have taken pains to find witnesses who would not only recommend continued censorship but who would also be willing to attempt to influence the outcome of the hearings:

It could be a good thing to approach either Alexander or Tree confidentially and suggest to them that it might help their views if the theatre managers were to petition Mr Samuel against any idea of separating them from the Lord Chamberlain either as regards the theatres themselves or as to stage play licences.[87]

The evidence shows that the Lord Chamberlain was against any alteration in the workings of censorship. His intention was to retain the system of pre-censorship without appeal: 'There must be no appeal against the final decision of the Lord Chamberlain. This decision to be arrived at only after consultation with an Advisory Board with [sic] closed doors.'[88]

Throughout, Althorp was intent on serving the interests of the King. When privately told by Samuel that the Committee might want to hear him give evidence, Althorp requested the King's view: 'HM told me not to offer myself to give evidence, but if I was invited to do so by the Committee that I was to

---

[84] RA, Box 251 (1909 Censorship Committee). Confidential letter from Byrne to Dawson, 29 July 1909.
[85] Ibid. Letter from Tupper to Redford, 20 July 1909.
[86] Ibid. Report on Redford's meeting with Althorp, 28 July 1909.
[87] Ibid. Private letter from Tupper to Dawson, 27 Aug. 1909.   [88] Ibid.

go before it.'[89] In a private and confidential note to Samuel, Althorp added: 'I rather demur to being made a stalking horse for advertising authors! I could not agree to alterations . . . limiting the powers conferred by Act of Parliament on the Lord Chamberlain representing the Sovereign in this respect.'[90] Despite the tight liaison between Samuel, the Lord Chamberlain, the Home Office, and the King, the Lord Chamberlain's Office in late September 1909 still misinterpreted the likely conclusions the Committee would reach:

I believe that important members of the Committee have long ago realised the nonsense of the whole thing, and are fretting over the ridiculous waste of time and the prominence which has been, quite needlessly, given to the subject.[91]

The King was less confident than his Lord Chamberlain that the deliberations of the Committee were running as hoped. In August 1909 Althorp forwarded to Asquith a communication which he had received from the King's Private Secretary, Knollys:

The King hopes you [Althorp] are keeping an eye on his interests in the matter, and that it is clearly understood that the ultimate decision rests entirely in his hands. While H.M. will be only too glad to consider any recommendation of the Commission, and to discuss with the Prime Minister the best solution of the question, he hopes that no attempt will be made to force his hand. I have answered saying that of course the King must be told by the Prime Minister when the report of the Committee is presented what plan is suggested.[92]

The receipt of the letter was acknowledged by an official: 'The Prime Minister has made a mental note of what you said in reply and I will bring your letter to his recollection when the report is presented.'[93] This seems to suggest that the King was beginning to fear by this juncture that the enquiry might arrive at an unwelcome conclusion. Once again, he attempted to put pressure on the Prime Minister to ensure that the Committee would not encroach on what he mistakenly regarded as his Prerogative. His biographer, Magnus, confirms that he took very seriously matters relating to his Prerogative:

It is true that King Edward was extremely sensitive about anything which touched his prerogative even remotely, and that he had declined, for example, in June [1909] to surrender the Lord Chamberlain's right to censor plays. 'The question', Knollys explained (4 July) to Asquith, 'involves a point of his Prerogative, as both the Lord Chamberlain and the Reader of Plays are in his Household'.[94]

[89] Ibid. Note from Althorp to Dawson, 5 Sept. 1909.   [90] Ibid., 8 Sept. 1909.
[91] Ibid. Dawson to a potential witness, G. W. E. Russell, 25 Sept. 1909.
[92] Ibid. Letter from Althorp to Asquith, 18 Aug. 1909.
[93] Ibid. Letter from Nash (Downing Street) to Althorp, 19 Aug. 1909.
[94] Magnus, *Edward the Seventh*, 439.

The assertion that the ultimate decision rested in the King's hands was in clear breach of all constitutional propriety. It was intended, and was doubtless understood, as a warning to Asquith that any attempt to encroach on what the King regarded, however mistakenly, as his Prerogative would unleash a second constitutional crisis at a time when Asquith was already fully preoccupied with the long-running constitutional battle over the Lords' veto. If the Government had had the slightest interest in resolving the matter, the issue of theatre censorship and the Royal Prerogative could have been referred, for a formal ruling, to the Lord Chancellor, as happened in 1949. In reality, Asquith had no desire to pursue the question any further.

Althorp was anxious that the King, as promised by Asquith, should be informed of the Committee's conclusions before they were published:

There are numerous paragraphs in yesterday's newspapers purporting to give the main points of the report of the Committee. I am particularly anxious that there should be no mistake about the King seeing the report before it is seen by anyone. I have received very strong comments on this point, and I am sure that you will understand the importance of this.[95]

The Prime Minister did indeed understand the importance of this and ensured compliance. This careful system of liaison nevertheless failed to achieve the result desired by the Lord Chamberlain and the King. On 18 October 1909, Byrne sent the following note to Dawson: 'I hear from H. Samuel that the Censorship Committee have agreed unanimously to the substance of their report. I am rather surprised and not altogether pleased to hear it.'[96] Dawson answered, underlining the difficulty: 'I agree with you a <u>unanimous</u> report from the Committee looks ominous, although I can hardly believe seriously that the views of the extremists are shared by the rest of the Committee.'[97] The Lord Chamberlain's Office was alarmed about a unanimous report which, 'if carried into effect, will completely destroy the position of the Censor and turn it into ridicule'.[98] Still, the Home Office advised against making a hasty reply:

Troup . . . is strongly of the opinion that it would be inexpedient for the Lord Chamberlain to express any <u>immediate</u> opinion or to tender any <u>immediate</u> advice to H.M. in the matter but that it would on the contrary be advisable to allow opinion gradually to form and express itself, the opinion both of the public and of persons specially concerned.[99]

---

[95] RA, Box 251 (1909 Censorship Committee). Althorp to Nash, 3 Oct. 1909.
[96] Ibid., 18 Oct. 1909.   [97] Ibid., 19 Oct. 1909.
[98] Ibid. Undated comment from the Lord Chamberlain's Office.
[99] Ibid. Byrne to Dawson, 12 Nov. 1909.

The Home Office was fully aware of the King's obdurate views on the matter but wanted to let the dust settle before any action was taken. Significantly, no mention was made in the Home Office note of the views of Parliament. This suggests that a deliberate decision had already been taken to avoid, if possible, any discussion of the report in the Commons. Instead, the Home Office wanted to judge the public's response to the report. In addition, the far more serious constitutional crisis over the People's Budget was drawing to its climax. At the end of November, the Lords caused uproar by voting against Lloyd George's Budget. Within days, Asquith had asked the King for Parliament to be dissolved so that a general election could be fought on the issue of curbing the power of the Lords. The Home Office was well aware that this course of events would leave no time before Parliament's dissolution for Harcourt and his supporters to ask when the recommendations of the Committee might be implemented.

THE GOVERNMENT'S RESPONSE

Because of the dissolution of Parliament in December and the ensuing general election, there was no formal consideration of the Joint Select Committee report by any government officers until January 1910. Even then, it was Dawson (the Lord Chamberlain's Comptroller) who took the initiative to set up a first meeting to discuss the Joint Select Committee report. On 3 January 1910, he wrote to Sir Almeric Fitzroy (Clerk of the Privy Council) to propose a meeting for this purpose, and the meeting was duly held on 7 January 1910. It was attended by Dawson, Fitzroy, Sir Charles Mathews (Director of Public Prosecutions) (DPP), and Byrne from the Home Office. The meeting concluded that no immediate action should be taken on the issue of censorship. The Theatres Act should be left alone, although an Advisory Board for the Lord Chamberlain should be established. The views of the King were seen as paramount:

Both Sir Charles Mathews and Mr Byrne were of opinion that were the King to express it as his wish that things remained in status quo the Government would be bound to fall in with that view as there was no real backing to the agitation which started the enquiry.[100]

Dawson subsequently confirmed to Mathews that the King did not wish for any change: 'The King wished me to tell you specially that H.M. quite agreed

---

[100] Ibid. Minutes of the meeting held on 7 Jan. 1910.

with you that things should remain in status quo.'[101] Mathews's reply to the effect that 'every effort will be made to fulfil His Majesty's wishes' was submitted to the King five days later.[102] This exchange suggests a degree of collusion between the Home Office and the DPP that was quite improper as its stated aim was to fulfil the wishes of the King to avoid any change in legislation on the question of theatre censorship. The lame excuse given was that there was no real support for the 'agitation' that started the enquiry. By comparison with the unyielding views of the King on this matter, the published views of a Parliamentary Joint Select Committee clearly counted for nothing and were deliberately brushed aside. Significantly, after this confidential meeting, there was no mention in Parliament or in the press of the Joint Select Committee report or the decision to ignore its findings.

The new session of Parliament in 1910 was preoccupied with only two issues: the delayed implementation of the People's Budget and reform of the House of Lords. The frenzied atmosphere in both Houses left little or no time for serious consideration of other issues. Matters were further complicated by the sudden death of Edward VII in May 1910. Despite King George V's accession to the throne, there was no immediate resolution to the constitutional crisis that had paralysed Parliament. As we have seen, the crisis was to drag on throughout the autumn and would lead to yet another general election in December 1910. Even after this election, the crisis would still preoccupy Parliament until August 1911. Inevitably, in such a turbulent period, other issues were pushed aside.

Undeterred by the crisis, Harcourt asked the new Home Secretary, Churchill, on 14 June 1910 whether legislation on theatre censorship would be introduced. Churchill answered that the report of the Joint Select Committee was under his consideration,[103] but failed to reveal that there was no plan for any immediate action. This point emerged from a chance encounter between Churchill and the Lord Chamberlain the following day: 'The Lord Chamberlain met Churchill in the street, who told him that he was not opposed to the abolition of the Censorship, but that there was to be no legislation this year. Churchill promised to do nothing without letting the Lord Chamberlain know. Byrne's abroad.'[104] Not only did Churchill confirm that no legislation was planned, he also promised that nothing would happen without the Lord Chamberlain's prior knowledge. Although Churchill was not opposed to the abolition of censorship, he nevertheless swiftly adopted the Home Office policy of inertia in all things concerned with theatre legislation.

[101] Ibid. Dawson to Mathews, 21 Jan. 1910.
[102] Ibid. This reply was submitted to the King on 26 Jan. 1910.
[103] *Hansard* (Commons), 14 June 1910, vol. 17, col. 1185.
[104] RA, Box 251 (1909 Censorship Committee). Memorandum, 15 June 1910.

Having failed to elicit any meaningful response from the Government, a new press campaign was launched by various playwrights and by Harcourt in September 1910. The immediate trigger for this was the banning of Housman's historical play *Pains and Penalties*, set in the reign of George IV. Housman wrote an angry letter to *The Times*: 'If reference to past Monarchs is henceforth forbidden on the English stage, it is evident that in this country historical drama is dead; and the power which kills it is the Court-flunkeyism of the Lord Chamberlain's Office.'[105] Although there was no chance of Housman's play being licensed, his supporters blamed the censor through the press. Harcourt, in his letter to *The Times*, asked on which of the recommendations given by the Joint Select Committee the play was banned; whether the Lord Chamberlain had followed the correct procedure as given in evidence by his Comptroller Dawson; and whether the play had been referred to the Advisory Committee which was presented as the answer to everybody's doubts. The key section of Harcourt's letter was the introduction:

The inevitable Act of Parliament which will carry out the considered judgment of a Joint Committee of both Houses. . . will relieve the Lord Chamberlain of his veto. The Home Secretary is at home: he gets his *Times* regularly; . . . and he is even now preparing to legislate. Or if not, there will be trouble.[106]

More support was shown for Housman's play in further letters,[107] but to no effect. The real reason for this lack of response was spelled out by another correspondent:

It is contrary to public interest in these critical times that an episode damaging to the present dynasty should be presented on the stage. . . The exigencies of the dramatic art make it improbable that the presentation of the episode should be really fair and true to history.[108]

Housman finally ended the campaign by announcing that he would give 'as public and as dramatic a reading of my play as I like, with no excisions whatsoever'.[109]

In November 1910, Churchill was asked a Parliamentary Question on an alleged breach of the Theatres Act by music halls. He gave a written answer

[105] 'Mr L. Housman and the Censor', *The Times*, 26 Sept. 1910. (Letter from Housman to the Editor.)

[106] Ibid., 28 Sept. 1910. (Letter from Harcourt to the Editor.)

[107] Other letters than those quoted were published on 28 and 29 Sept., on 1 and 3 Oct. (a petition in favour of the play was also signed that day), and on 10 and 12 Oct. 1910.

[108] 'Mr L. Housman and the Censor', *The Times*, 6 Oct. 1910. (Letter from W. S. Robinson to the Editor.)

[109] Ibid., 10 Oct. 1910. (Letter from Housman to the Editor.)

in response which clarified the Government's current intentions in the matter of legislation for theatre licensing and, by implication, for theatre censorship: 'Legislation is at the moment impracticable, and I do not think any useful purpose would be served by my receiving a deputation.'[110] Clearly, the severe constitutional crisis in 1910 left no parliamentary time to debate an item that was politically less important but potentially equally divisive. A further attempt by Harcourt on 19 July 1911 to press the 'proposal for a single licence for all places of public entertainment which was made unanimously by Mr Samuel's Committee' met with another negative answer. This time the ground had shifted from the excuse of a crowded parliamentary timetable to the suggestion that there was no unanimity of opinion amongst the interested parties. Churchill replied:

I am aware of the support which the proposal receives, but . . . the proposal was opposed before the Joint Committee of 1909, and is still opposed, by influential theatre and music hall managers, by representative associations of such managers, and by those concerned in the administration of the present law.[111]

Harcourt put a supplementary question: 'Is the right hon. Gentleman referring to representations which officially reached him at the Home Office, and which are directly contrary to my information?'[112] He received no reply to this further intervention. Once again, Harcourt's formal intervention came at a time of extraordinary crisis in Parliament: Asquith was to announce a few days later that the King had promised to create sufficient new peers, if necessary, to ensure that proposed reform of the House of Lords would be carried in both Houses.

Harcourt continued to raise the matter of theatre censorship after the main constitutional crisis was resolved in August 1911, when the Lords finally accepted a limit to their powers of veto. In November he pressed Reginald McKenna, who had succeeded Churchill as Home Secretary, on the issue of theatre censorship legislation. McKenna conveyed an answer from the Prime Minister confirming that: 'As at present advised, I do not propose to take any steps with regards to the dramatic censorship.'[113] Harcourt raised the issue again in Parliament in December 1911, this time following the appointment of Charles Brookfield, the author of a much-condemned farce adaptation, to the post of Assistant Examiner of Plays. Pressed by Harcourt and other Members of Parliament supporting abolition, McKenna, on 1 December 1911, finally suggested a compromise as the way forward:

---

[110] *Hansard* (Commons), 24 Nov. 1910, vol. 20, col. 450.
[111] Ibid., 19 July 1911, vol. 28, col. 1027.
[112] Ibid.   [113] Ibid., 27 Nov. 1911, vol. 32, col. 25.

Would it be right to hold out the smallest hope that in the next Session of Parliament—which is already fully mortgaged—I could make myself responsible for a Bill . . . I can only say that if in discussing this question personal matters are left out and hon. Members and the Government combined can produce a measure which will not arouse controversy, but which will be generally acceptable, then it might be a desirable thing to push such a measure through.[114]

Despite this suggestion that a way forward might be found, there is no evidence that civil servants or the Home Secretary devoted any time or energy to discuss possible new legislation.

Members of Parliament continued to press that the recommendations of the Joint Select Committee be implemented. In February 1912 McKenna gave Asquith's official answer: 'I see no prospect of introducing legislation on this subject this session.'[115] This did not prevent Members of Parliament from mentioning more anomalies of the censorship system on 26 February, and on 4 and 25 March 1912. This renewed campaign led to a petition signed by dramatists, critics, theatre practitioners, and Members of Parliament who protested against the censor's refusal of a licence for Eden Philpott's *Secret Woman*. The Home Secretary reiterated that the session was too crowded to allow for any prospect of legislation. Finally, in April 1913, Harcourt introduced a motion stating:

That the attempt to maintain by means of antiquated legislation a legal distinction between a theatre and a music hall, and to differentiate between productions called stage plays and other dramatic performances, is unworkable; that the system of licensing stage plays before production in Great Britain, though not in Ireland, by means principally of the perusal of a manuscript should be abolished; and that, as regards stage exhibitions of whatever kind or wherever given, reliance should be placed on subsequent effective control.[116]

The recommendations of the Committee were quoted at length during the ensuing debate. Ellis Griffith, Parliamentary Secretary to the Home Office, represented the Government position. It became clear during the debate that the Government had no intention whatsoever of amending the law. The official reason given was that 'there is such diversity of opinion among experts that it is very difficult as yet in the present situation to know on what lines you could legislate'.[117] All Members present but one voted in favour of the motion. By way of compromise, the second clause was changed to quote the

[114] Ibid., 1 Dec. 1911, vol. 32, col. 959. For the first parliamentary protest on the appointment of Brookfield, see cols. 580–2.
[115] Ibid., 21 Feb. 1912, vol. 34, col. 615. Members of Parliament had intervened prior to this answer on 7 and 13 Dec. 1911 and 19 Feb. 1912.
[116] Ibid., 16 Apr. 1913, vol. 51, col. 2036.   [117] Ibid., col. 2059.

1909 report: 'that the system of compulsory licensing of stage plays before production in Great Britain should be abolished.'[118] Though the motion was approved, it led to no further debate and no further action on the part of the Government. This was to be the last intervention of Harcourt in his repeated but ultimately unsuccessful attempts to effect some change in theatre censorship legislation.

The attempt described in this chapter to abolish or at least to amend the role of the Lord Chamberlain as theatre censor coincided, as we have seen, with an unusually turbulent period of domestic political history. The larger constitutional issues undoubtedly overshadowed the less crucial issue of theatre censorship. Nevertheless, it is difficult to avoid concluding that what primarily prevented any change to the system of censorship was above all the insistence of Edward VII on his Prerogative and the resulting unwillingness of Asquith to confront the King on this issue when he was intent on pursuing his wider constitutional challenge to the authority of the Lords. The King's repeated interventions in this matter were in breach of Walter Bagehot's definition of the three rights of a constitutional monarch: 'the right to be consulted, the right to encourage, the right to warn.'[119] Even after the death of Edward VII, Asquith clearly did not wish to open the Pandora's box that was the Royal Prerogative. He had compromised with George V over the issue of the role of the Lords, and was presumably unwilling to raise any further constitutional matters. It is remarkable, however, that the unanimous recommendations of a Joint Select Committee were ignored by the Government, as were the views of playwrights and Members of Parliament, and that the Home Office preference for a policy of inertia won the day. This was a superb demonstration of the hidden levers in English politics moving quietly and unobtrusively to thwart the clearly expressed recommendations of a Select Committee of both Houses of Parliament. Those in authority initially used the excuse of a lack of parliamentary time. Later they argued, with some justification, that there was no unanimity amongst experts in the matter. Eventually, their firm embrace of political inertia in this matter coincided fortuitously with the outbreak of hostilities in the First World War. The dramatists and their supporters in Parliament were all seen off by a combination of unfortunate political 'events' (all associated with the constitutional crisis of 1909–11); the obdurate attitude of a reactionary monarch; the refusal of the Prime Minister to challenge the monarch on a

---

[118] *Hansard* (Commons), 24 Nov. 1910, vol. 20, col. 2077. Proposal made by the Unionist MP Walter Guinness.

[119] Walter Bagehot, *The English Constitution*, 4th edn. (London: Kegan Paul & Trench, 1885), 75.

second constitutional matter when he was already locked in a constitutional battle for reform of the Lords; the implacable opposition of theatre managers to any suggestion that theatre censorship should be abolished; and finally the well-rehearsed arguments in favour of inertia that characterized Home Office policy. There would be no further challenges to Britain's well-tried system of censorship for many years to come.

4

The Inter-War Years

The declaration of war in 1914 put an end to Harcourt's attempts to change theatre censorship legislation. In the post-war period, a new generation of playwrights seemed to be less concerned as a group with the issue than was the case with playwrights in the 1900s.[1] Other factors contributed to a period of relative calm and stability during the inter-war period. In the immediate aftermath of the 1909 Joint Select Committee, there were significant changes in personnel in the Lord Chamberlain's Office; there were also changes in censorship practice; most important of all, there were changes in taste and changes in theatre practice.[2]

THE LORD CHAMBERLAIN'S OFFICE

In 1911, the Examiner of Plays Redford resigned one month after an assistant Examiner had been appointed: this may have been a diplomatic way to ease him out of the post, as he was much disliked. He went on to become the first president of the British Board of Film Censors and applied to cinema the same unimaginative criteria he had applied to the theatre. In 1912, Lord Althorp resigned as Lord Chamberlain: this was unusual, as normally the Lord Chamberlain remained in post until death or a change of government. Lord Sandhurst, who succeeded Althorp and served until 1921, made it his duty to follow the recommendations of the 1909 Joint Select Committee on the licensing of plays. A new licence form was issued, and he also retained the services of the Advisory Board set up by Althorp in 1910 to help with difficult cases. Some of the causes of complaint of the dramatists in 1907 were therefore at least in some measure addressed by the Lord Chamberlain.

---

[1] Individual playwrights continued to question any decision to ban one of their plays through the relevant theatre manager.

[2] See Nicholson, *Censorship*, i. 159, 298–9, 304.

Lord Cromer succeeded Lord Atholl in 1922 and served as Lord Chamberlain until 1938. Much in the censorship system changed while Cromer was Lord Chamberlain. Whenever a play raised any issue that might give offence, he consulted the Advisory Board; his aim was to avoid any adverse criticism in the press. In addition, during his period of office plays previously censored were at last given a licence for performance. When he was appointed Lord Chamberlain in 1922 by the Conservative Prime Minister, Andrew Bonar Law, Cromer was the last to be given office as Lord Chamberlain upon a change of government. The appointment of the Lord Chamberlain by the Prime Minister, when a new ministry came into being, had been the normal practice since the passing of the 1737 Licensing Act. The tradition was discontinued for practical reasons when the Labour Prime Minister Ramsay MacDonald came to power in 1924, as George V's official biographer explained:

Hitherto the senior offices of the Court had been regarded as political appointments, made on the advice of the Prime Minister in power. Mr Ramsay MacDonald, not having at his disposal a sufficient number of candidates anxious to assume such functions, proposed that this practice be abandoned and that in future the King should appoint or retain such Court officials as he thought fit . . . Lord Balfour . . . was opposed to the abolition of these political appointments since it was of assistance to a Prime Minister, when forming a Government, to possess some sops wherewith to reward those supporters who were not qualified for ministerial office. Mr Asquith . . . was entirely in favour of these offices becoming permanent and independent of political or party fluctuations.[3]

This change allowed for greater continuity in the licensing process as both the Lord Chamberlain and the Examiner remained in office for an extended period of time.

CENSORSHIP AND GOVERNMENT

Even though the office of the Lord Chamberlain was no longer a political appointment as from 1924, the censor remained keen to work in harmony with successive governments. When Cromer asked whether his jurisdiction was affected by the decision to make his office a non-political one, the Home Office attempted to reassure him. In respect of the Royal Prerogative, however, the comments were completely erroneous; in view of Edward VII's previously voiced objections, they may have been deliberately disingenuous:

[3] Harold Nicolson, *King George V: His Life and Reign* (London: Constable, 1953), 390.

[it] does not make any fundamental change in the exercise of his duties of censorship, because the censorship has always been regarded as attached to the Royal Prerogative . . . The change indeed has some advantage in making the position clearer. It will no doubt be convenient that the Secretary of State shall continue to answer questions in the House of Commons when they arise. For that reason the Lord Chamberlain should keep in close touch with the Home Office, and consult the Secretary of State beforehand as to any matters which are likely to arouse public comment but the Secretary of State will take no responsibility for the decisions of the Lord Chamberlain.[4]

When in doubt about plays which were likely to give rise to controversy, Cromer not only took advice from the Home Office; he also consulted the King (on royal matters), the Archbishop of Canterbury (on religious drama), and other relevant government departments (when politics or policies were discussed in a particular play).[5]

This process of liaison between the Government and the Lord Chamberlain's Office seems to have led to an accepted (although hidden) code of practice. Unlike the guidelines suggested by the report of the 1909 Joint Select Committee and subsequently applied by the censor, this process was not revealed to the public. The hidden relationship that linked the Crown, the Lord Chamberlain's Office, and the Government was clearly set out by Cromer in a letter to the Home Secretary William Joynson-Hicks in 1925:

It will, I feel, be a matter of gratification to the King to know that the Government would certainly be reluctant to see any alteration in the existing system, which, in spite of the criticisms that must necessarily be levelled from time to time against any system, seems to work quite well in practice. I need hardly assure you that in matters governing questions of policy or legal points I should always work in consultation with the Home Office, and I am very grateful to you personally for your kind assurance of advice and assistance in case of need.[6]

The changes in custom and practice in the exercise of censorship in the inter-war years meant that there was greater consistency and continuity than before. There was also a process of consultation, with advice being sought before decisions were reached. As a result, some of the basic complaints of earlier dramatists were addressed. What also helped to smooth things over was the fact that Cromer believed in a policy of subtle and hidden censorship. Steve Nicholson summed this up as follows:

----

[4] NA, HO 45/12254. Reply of 5 Jan. 1925 to Cromer's letter of 16 Dec. 1924.

[5] See Nicholson, *Censorship*, i. 240–2, 256–8, 269–71, 276–9, and Anne Etienne, *Les Coulisses du Lord Chamberlain: la Censure Théâtrale de 1900 à 1968* (unpublished Ph.D. dissertation, Université d'Orléans, 1999), 171–8, 216, 224, 227–8, 237.

[6] NA, HO 45/12254. Letter from Cromer to Joynson-Hicks, 30 Jan. 1925.

For Cromer, the real art of censorship was that as much of it as possible should remain unseen and therefore unacknowledged. Sometimes a relatively innocuous play would be refused a licence in order to discourage others on the same theme; sometimes he would politely but deliberately request such widespread and detailed changes that a play was almost certain to be withdrawn without his having to ban it. Often discussions between Cromer or his representative and a theatre manager negotiated changes which would be incorporated within a new and clean script, which could then be licensed without any endorsements or evidence of censorship. On occasions, he even encouraged managers to send in scripts informally, in order to test whether it was worth their while submitting them officially . . . Such practices disguised the true extent of theatre censorship.[7]

In addition, the inter-war years also saw a distinct shift in public taste. The popularity of light entertainment during the war years carried over into the 1920s. Musical comedies, bedroom farces, and revues characterized the commercial theatre of the inter-war period. The West End theatres catered for middle-class audiences, who were perfectly content with a largely unchallenging repertoire. Noël Coward's morally ambiguous comedies from the 1920s, notably *The Vortex* (1924), caused the censor some problems. But even the best plays of the inter-war period by Coward, Somerset Maugham, and Terence Rattigan had a gentler feel to them than the socially committed plays of the 1900s written by Shaw and Granville Barker. These earlier dramatists who had fought so vigorously against the censor were by now respected authors who were regarded as modern classics. The plays of the old guard were therefore not only warmly appreciated by the critics, though still not necessarily by the majority of playgoers, they were now licensed by the Lord Chamberlain. The only groups who expressed repeated opposition to the predominantly innocuous plays written during the inter-war years were isolated reactionaries and members of the London Public Morality Council.[8] Indeed, during his term of office, Cromer had to deal with increasing pressure from this body, which had been formed in 1899 'to combat vice and indecency in London and to assist in their repression by legal means'.[9] Its members included representatives of the Church of England, Roman Catholic and nonconformist churches, and of the Jewish faith, leaders in education, medicine and charitable associations, and others supporting reform. By 1913, the London Public Morality Council had created a Stage Plays Committee to enable an efficient check to be made on improper stage productions. The Council regularly appealed to the Lord

---

[7] Quoted from Nicholson, *Censorship*, i. 153–4.

[8] For details of the complaints made by members of the London Public Morality Council, see ibid. 158–60, 182–4, 206–7, 229–30, 232–4, 238–9.

[9] See London Metropolitan Archives: Public Morality Council, Constitution: A/PMC/1/1–2. The online catalogue may be found at: http://www.a2a.org.uk/html/074-apmc.htm.

Chamberlain on the issues of private performances and nudity, and made
occasional complaints to the Home Secretary: such complaints were generally
regarded as vexatious by the Home Office.[10]

DRAMATIC SOCIETIES AND THEATRE CLUBS

For the minority audiences who wanted to see more demanding plays,
private performances provided a useful safety valve. By the 1920s private
performances of unlicensed plays had become a well-established method of
evading censorship. The 1843 Theatres Act had specified in section 15 that it
was illegal to act or present an unlicensed play 'for Hire'. Private performances,
where no money was exchanged, were not for hire: they were therefore outside
the scope of the Act. The performances were deemed to be private as long as
only members of the dramatic society were allowed inside the theatre and the
stage was hired at a minimal rate. This loophole in the 1843 legislation was
discovered as early as the 1880s, when enterprising individuals or groups of
enthusiasts had mounted, from time to time, 'private' productions of plays
that were unlicensed. Dramatic societies usually gave only one performance
of a play because theatre managers could only afford to let their theatre
on a Sunday. There was also always the threat of intervention by the Lord
Chamberlain, which could mean the loss of a theatre licence.

By the mid-1920s, the activities of the dramatic societies were complemented
by the creation of private theatre clubs. These offered a more long-term means
of circumventing the censorship provisions of the 1843 Theatres Act. The
New Lindsey Theatre Club, the Watergate Club, the Torch, the New Lyric
Club, and the Bolton's opened during the 1920s in small theatres, situated
outside the West End to benefit from lower rents; they were financed by their
members in the same way as dramatic societies.[11] The two most prominent
clubs, however, competed with commercial theatres on their own territory.
The Gate Theatre Studio (which was the first theatre club to open in 1925)
and the Arts Theatre Club were located in the heart of the West End. Clubs
developed in the 1920s because the theatrical context of the inter-war period
demanded it. The First World War had changed the face of the West End
theatre, which had previously been dominated by famous actor-managers, as
Normal Marshall explained:

---

[10] See NA, HO 45/22797.
[11] For more details on productions by theatre clubs, see Norman Marshall, *The Other Theatre*
(London: John Lehmann, 1947).

Before 1919 the playgoer was served by managers running their own theatres according to their own taste and policy . . . During the war of 1914–18 theatres became just another asset on the list of properties held by business magnates . . . One of the most serious results of the crazy economics of the post-war theatre was that it prevented the return of the independent manager prepared to rely on his own taste and judgment.[12]

Because of the marked commercialization of London's theatre, innovative plays of artistic merit, whether British, European, or American, could only rarely be found outside the repertoire of dramatic societies and theatre clubs. The growth of the theatre club movement was therefore provoked, not just by the censorship decisions of the Lord Chamberlain, but also by the timidity of commercial managements. The advantage of clubs over dramatic societies (and it explains their soaring number in the 1920s) was that they worked on the basis of at least three-week runs while societies had to limit themselves to a Sunday performance and, sometimes, a Monday matinee.

The Gate Theatre Studio (the 'Gate to Better Things') was a novelty when it was opened by Peter Godfrey and Molly Veness in Floral Street on 30 October 1925.[13] It was the first truly private theatre club, which meant that plays, whether licensed or not, were performed every night for two to three weeks. At the time, the decision to open a private theatre club, when it was safer and easier to hire the stage of a licensed theatre for one private performance, was something of a pioneering act. However, it had nothing to do with Godfrey's boldness or any wish to evade the censor's jurisdiction. Marshall, who later took up the lease of the Gate, explains why the premises opened as a private theatre:

It was not originally Godfrey's intention to run the Gate as a private theatre . . . The Gate was opened as a private theatre not to escape from the jurisdiction of the Lord Chamberlain, but because the London County Council not unnaturally refused to license as a public theatre a loft in Floral Street to which the only entrance and exit was a rickety wooden staircase. The decision to run the theatre as a private club was a bold one and entirely new . . . This was the first time that anyone had conceived the idea of using the privileges of a theatrical club not merely for one or two performances but for a nightly run of two or three weeks.[14]

The Lord Chamberlain had so far tolerated one-off private productions by dramatic societies as long as the plays were of artistic merit and were aimed at a minority audience. Godfrey may have calculated that his venture would be

---

[12] Ibid. 15–16. [13] It was relocated two years later to Villiers Street.
[14] See Marshall, *The Other Theatre*, 43.

tolerated on the same grounds, as his primary aim was to present innovative plays of clear artistic merit to a private club audience.

In the same way as Godfrey, Marshall produced plays that appealed to his own taste, and the success of the policy was simply due to the fortunate fact that, as he himself expressed it, 'there were a few thousand people in London who happened to like the same sort of plays that I liked myself'.[15] His tastes were undeniably more suited to English audiences and embraced a wider range of theatrical narratives than Godfrey's. In addition, whereas Godfrey was mostly interested in plays which were refused by commercial managements, Marshall produced quite a few censored plays. Consequently, the audiences knew that the Gate was the only place where they would ever see such plays.

The Arts Theatre Club, which opened its doors in Great Newport Street on 20 April 1927, continued to function until the 1960s. The unusual feature of the Arts Theatre interior lay in the fact it could seat 324 people but had 'the smallest stage in Central London with a proscenium opening of under 21 feet and a height of $14\frac{1}{2}$ feet'. There was never any competition between the two clubs although the membership of the Arts was adversely affected when the Gate enjoyed renewed popularity under Marshall's management. The real weakness of the Arts was the fact that its founders Walter Payne, Bronson Albery (both with managerial positions in the commercial theatre world), and W. E. Gillespie had no clear artistic vision.

Theatre clubs produced many plays after they had been refused a licence and sometimes before they were submitted for licensing. As long as they were not presented 'for Hire', this did not contravene section 15 of the 1843 Theatres Act. The real advantage for the clubs was that no time was wasted in waiting for the Lord Chamberlain's Office to issue a licence or discuss changes to the text of a play. Furthermore, most private performances had the legitimate aim of presenting plays of artistic merit, some of which happened to be banned, to discerning audiences. In contrast, some dramatic society productions exploited the sense of scandal associated with particular plays to attract an audience whose tastes were less than wholesome. On such occasions, seats were sometimes sold to people who were not members of the dramatic society.

This raises the question why the Lord Chamberlain failed to apply section 14 of the 1843 Theatres Act, which gave him authority to forbid any play anywhere in Great Britain 'either absolutely or for such Time as he shall think fit'. This seemingly absolute authority to ban any play at any time and at any place in Great Britain was, however, given to the Lord Chamberlain in respect

---

[15] Ibid. 108.

of the *public* performance of plays 'for Hire', as set out in section 12 of the Act. It was therefore a conditional and not an absolute power. In addition, the Lord Chamberlain probably concluded that members of theatre clubs represented an insignificant portion of the already tiny minority of the population who went to the theatre in England. According to the 1843 Theatres Act, one of the primary purposes of censorship was to preserve the public peace. The Lord Chamberlain presumably took the view that since the number of spectators and performances was so limited, so was any threat of public disorder that could hypothetically arise from private performances. The audiences of the theatre clubs were mainly composed of people who had a genuine interest in innovative theatre styles and in the drama of ideas written by English and foreign playwrights.

The second reason for the Lord Chamberlain's tolerant attitude was a lack of clear guidance in the 1843 Theatres Act in respect of private performances. Section 2 specified that all theatres for the 'public Performance of Stage Plays' must be licensed by the Lord Chamberlain or by Justices of the Peace or have received letters patent from the monarch. Performances of plays for members only at the private premises of theatre clubs were clearly not public performances and were therefore not in breach of the Act. The one grey area was the definition of the word 'for Hire'. Section 12 of the 1843 Theatres Act made it clear that no play was to be performed 'for Hire' before it had been licensed or after it had been prohibited by the Lord Chamberlain. Yet, numerous unlicensed plays were presented privately by dramatic societies, and later by theatre clubs, without any legal proceedings being brought against them, because in theory they were not presented for hire. The definition of 'for Hire' in section 16 of the Act was sufficiently opaque as to open up loopholes for enterprising theatre practitioners:

in every Case in which any Money or other Reward shall be taken or charged directly or indirectly, or in which the Purchase of any Article is made a Condition for the Admission of any Person into any Theatre to see any Stage Play, and also in every Case in which any stage play shall be acted or presented in any House, Room or Place in which distilled or fermented Liquor shall be sold, every Actor therein shall be deemed to be acting for Hire.

As long as dramatic societies and theatre clubs were able to claim that no money was charged directly or indirectly for their private performances, they argued that they were not in breach of the letter of the law. Nevertheless, from time to time, there were sporadic attempts to bring prosecutions against both dramatic societies and theatre clubs whenever any production might be construed as being for hire.

PRIVATE PRODUCTIONS IN BREACH OF THE 1843 THEATRES ACT

In 1928, the directors of the Gate Theatre Studio, Godfrey and Velona Pilcher, were prosecuted on two counts at Bow Street police court. The first summons was for permitting unlicensed stage plays to be produced at the theatre; the second summons was for keeping the theatre for the public performance of stage plays without letters patent or a licence. The plays in question, Eugene O'Neill's *The Hairy Ape* and Kaiser's *From Morn to Midnight*, deemed to be of a 'high brow' character, were not a matter for concern. The case had come to the attention of the police because:

In December last some unauthorized person advertised, offering for sale admission tickets to the Gate Theatre Studio. The defendants at once went to Bow-street with a view of preventing 'outsiders' gaining admission in this way. It was apparently this voluntary communication which drew the attention of the authorities to the matter, for very shortly afterwards the police began to obtain evidence. The defendants did not know that they were contravening the law, or they would never have gone to Bow-street in this way.[16]

The defence was based on the membership process of clubs, and it was argued that there was no proof of a production 'for Hire'. However, police officers who had attended the performances testified that they had been admitted directly on payment at the box-office. As a result, the magistrate ruled that the plays had been presented for hire. This was the first prosecution of a club and therefore of crucial importance for similar organizations. The magistrate fined each defendant on the first summons and agreed to outline a case for the High Court regarding the second summons. There is no report of a High Court decision in this case. One can only assume that the matter did not go beyond the police court. As a result of this case, theatre clubs took greater care to prevent non-members from entering.

RULES ARE DRAWN UP TO DEFINE PRIVATE PRODUCTIONS

The legal distinction between a private and a public performance under a statute which failed to mention private performances continued to give concern to the Lord Chamberlain's Office. As the popularity of private

[16] 'Gate Theatre Studio. Case stated in High Court', *The Times*, 22 May 1928.

performances and clubs gathered momentum, the lack of any clear definition gave equal concern to the government departments to which he turned for legal advice. As early as 1903, the Law Officers expressed the opinion that 'the Lord Chamberlain's jurisdiction did not extend to a genuinely private performance'.[17] They omitted, however, to identify what they deemed to be a genuinely private performance.[18] In 1918, the Home Office suggested to the Lord Chamberlain that 'action should be taken under the existing law to deal with performances to which admission is in fact public'.[19] Once again, no explanation was provided, nor any action taken.

The spread of private performances inevitably gave rise to questions in Parliament. In 1918, the Unionist MP John Butcher raised the issue of the private production of *Salomé* in connection with the libel court case that followed:[20]

people who cannot get the leave of the Censor to produce plays in the ordinary way are able, apparently, as the law stands, to produce them in this sort of fashion privately by subscriptions or by some way in which, apparently, they cannot be stopped, and that . . . it ought to be made impossible for plays of this kind to be produced before any audience.[21]

Sir George Cave, the Home Secretary in the coalition government led by Lloyd George, replied in a non-committal manner though he differentiated between *genuine* private performances and *so-called* private performances. In 1921, the Labour MP Robert Richardson stated that the system of censorship was 'being held to ridicule'. Edward Shortt, now the Home Secretary in the same government, denied that there was anything wrong with the Lord Chamberlain's censorship.[22]

However, in 1926, when the issue was mentioned again in Parliament,[23] the Home Secretary, Joynson-Hicks, was able to say that the matter was under consideration. In order to reply to the oral question put by the Liberal MP, J. M. Kenworthy, Joynson-Hicks had asked the Law Officers for an interpretation of the 1843 Theatres Act; he wanted to establish whether the Lord Chamberlain had the authority to prevent the private performance of an unlicensed play. The advice given was contradictory and was at odds with the practice of the Lord Chamberlain thus far. According to the Law Officers, a performance to which the public was admitted free was a 'public performance'

---

[17] NA, HO 45/22797.
[18] In Oct. 1946, the Home Office provided the following interpretation: 'a performance paid for and witnessed only by the members of a bona fide Society and their invited guests', NA, HO 45/24954.
[19] NA, HO 45/22797.   [20] See *The Times*, 5 June 1918.
[21] *Hansard* (Commons), 16 July 1918, vol. 108, col. 879.
[22] See ibid., 13 Apr. 1921, vol. 140, col. 1136.   [23] See ibid., 25 Feb. 1926, vol. 192, col. 684.

within the meaning of section 2 of the Act. The number of performances given need not be superior to one for proceedings to be initiated. In contrast, their reading of sections 12, 14, and 15 led them to conclude that 'the mere fact that a play has not been licensed by the Lord Chamberlain does not make the performance of such a play in a duly licensed theatre an offence against the Act if such performance is not for hire'.[24] One striking omission is the fact that the Law Officers failed to address the legality of productions by theatre clubs.

Having failed to obtain a clear and unambiguous opinion from the Law Officers, the Home Office and the Lord Chamberlain decided that same year to draw up their own guidelines 'to govern the performance of stage plays on Sunday':[25]

The use for a dramatic performance given on a Sunday of a theatre which holds the Lord Chamberlain's licence shall . . . be allowed only in the case of a bona fide society established for the private performance of stage plays.

The admission to a drama performance given on a Sunday shall be by ticket procurable only by members of the society presenting the proposed play at its office or address. In no circumstances shall money be taken or tickets supplied at the theatre for admission to the performance.

No ticket shall be issued except to members of such a society who have been duly elected . . . annual members thereof at least 7 days before the proposed performance.

Tickets issued to such members either for their own use or the use of guests of members up to a reasonable number shall be issued only in accordance with these conditions.

No payment, directly or indirectly, beyond an honorarium for expenses shall be paid to the actors or performers for their services . . . [26]

These published conditions were only aimed at occasional productions in licensed theatres, and there is no mention here of theatre clubs. The purpose of this measure may have been to control the spread of sensational performances by dramatic societies when a play was refused a licence because of indecency. Genuine dramatic societies and theatre clubs, with annual programmes planned in advance and with a list of fee-paying members, were therefore informally given the Lord Chamberlain's approval to cater for the minority audiences who were interested in drama of artistic merit. In the 1920s, the theatre clubs were attracting a select membership and were not attempting to offend public opinion by producing banned plays. In reality, they represented a useful safety net, from which everyone benefited.

---

[24] NA, LO 3/817 (Law Officers). Opinion signed by Douglas McGarel Hogg and T. W. H. Inskip. Received on 27 Feb. 1926 and returned to the Home Office on 1 Apr. 1926.

[25] *Hansard* (Commons), 25 Mar. 1926, vol. 193, col. 1350. Statement by the Home Secretary, Joynson-Hicks.

[26] *The Times*, 25 June 1926.

Educated theatregoers were permitted to view private productions of challenging plays, which made them less likely to complain about the practice of censorship.

But the issue was far from being settled. Joynson-Hicks admitted only a year later that 'whether a particular performance is public or not and for hire or not can only be decided on the facts of the case'.[27] The decision taken in 1926 to issue guidelines to cover genuine private performances was not so much a legal move (as it had no basis in statute law), but a political one. The Home Office and the Lord Chamberlain had jointly taken this initiative in response to interventions by Members of Parliament and from pressure groups, notably the London Public Morality Council, who were in favour of extending theatre censorship. The Lord Chamberlain took a pragmatic view in assessing the positive role of private performances:

When a play which is regarded with some importance by a certain section of the theatrical community is refused a licence, there is always a good deal of comment and agitation in the press concerning it. The next move is that the play is presented privately at a Sunday performance, or at the Arts Theatre . . . In very many cases the play is badly reviewed by the press, and the producers realise there is no commercial value in the play so nothing is heard of it. The Lord Chamberlain is strongly of opinion that this is all for the good, as they act as a sort of safety valve so far as this department is concerned.[28]

The Lord Chamberlain's pragmatism helped to maintain a deeply flawed system, but one which had sufficient checks and balances built into it to ensure its continued survival.

INADEQUACIES OF THE SYSTEM LEADING TO COMPLAINTS AND PROSECUTIONS

As we have seen, the 1926 guidelines did not cover the activities of theatre clubs. These remained a cause of contention in the continuing political debates on censorship. Unsurprisingly, most Parliamentary Questions that were raised on the subject of stage performance concerned theatre clubs.[29] Questions were also raised in the House of Lords in 1926 which indicated some degree of dissatisfaction with Cromer's role as censor. Cromer was asked:

[27] *Hansard* (Commons), 28 Nov. 1927, vol. 211, col. 32.
[28] BL, LR Corr 1926/2 *The Shanghai Gesture.* Note from Comptroller C. L. Gordon to S. W. Harris (Home Office), 11 June 1929.
[29] See, for instance, *Hansard* (Commons), 25 Feb. 1926, vol. 192, col. 684.

If his attention has been called to the production of certain plays in London, which have been described in the Press by dramatic critics and others as 'immoral', 'degrading', 'demoralising'. Will he make inquiries into this matter and take appropriate action to suppress what is deemed indecent and objectionable? Will he state what are the principles upon which the Censor of Plays acts, and upon which plays are granted a licence for performance?[30]

During the ensuing discussion, Lord Newton (who had been a member of the 1909 Select Committee) suggested that a 'really sensible woman' be appointed to the Advisory Board. As a result, Asquith's daughter Lady Violet Bonham Carter became a member of the Board.

In 1926, the London Public Morality Council suggested that all theatre licences should be granted by local authorities and that stricter regulation should prohibit the performance of indecent or immoral plays. Joynson-Hicks replied that 'police action and censorship can only deal with the more gross offences against public taste'.[31] This was in effect an admission that the censor's powers were not absolute, but that a pragmatic implementation of current laws was preferable to new legislation.

A few theatre managers were prosecuted in the 1930s. In most cases, the play script in question departed from the version licensed by the censor. In 1932 and 1933, for instance, the theatre producer William Henshall was reported to the police by a member of the audience for altering a sketch dealing with the paternity of a baby. The revue *Restez la Nuit* was presented at the Empire Theatre, Liverpool: 'In some cases, the words were complained of, in others the actions of the performers, and in others the lay-out of scenery and effects.'[32] Henshall argued that the actors were responsible for alterations to the script, but he was fined £25 in 1932 and £100 in 1933. In 1933, a member of the audience objected to lines allegedly added by the actors to a licensed play called *The Signalman's Daughter*. A representative of the Lord Chamberlain visited the Victoria Palace and stated that the lines would never have been licensed. The manager of the theatre and the company pleaded guilty and were fined £25 each with costs. The fact that the Lord Chamberlain had no staff to check whether scripts were being performed as licensed was regarded by an official in the Home Office as 'one of the weak spots in the present system' and one where there might be 'scope for the London Public Morality Council to do useful work'.[33] As it was, the Lord Chamberlain had to rely

[30] See *Hansard* (Lords), 10 June 1926, vol. 64, col. 366.
[31] 'Home Secretary and Clean Plays: Letter to Public Morality Council', *The Times*, 4 Mar. 1926.
[32] 'Theatrical Producer Fined', *The Times*, 14 Jan. 1933. Henshall had previously been fined £10 in Glasgow for similar reasons.
[33] See NA, HO 45/12254.

entirely on informants, whether they were members of the audience or the police.

In 1934, summonses were brought under section 5 of the 1843 Theatres Act following the performance of a revue *In Town To-Night* at the Empire Theatre, Finsbury Park. The magistrate fined the theatre managers for allowing dialogue that was not in the original script to be spoken on stage, but imposed no other penalty. The magistrate 'did not think it was necessary to impose the maximum penalties, or in any way to suspend the licence of the theatre'. In other cases, local authorities objected to the production of licensed plays in their town. In 1920, two complaints were brought to the attention of the Home Secretary. In Eastbourne, the production of *One Law for Both* and *Just a Wife or Two* had 'offended some of the inhabitants including the Chief Constable'.[34] No proceedings were brought partly because there was no evidence that anything other than the licensed script had been performed. In addition, the Home Office noted that in Eastbourne 'the Population was largely well-to-do, middle class and elderly'.[35] By implication, it was assumed that such an audience would be easily offended.

The oversight of theatrical activity by, amongst others, police watch committees in provincial cities was discussed at a meeting between officials of the Home Office and representative Chief Constables in 1920:

Sir Malcolm Delevingne saw the Chief Constables of Manchester, Newcastle and Merthyr Tydfil. They all said that plays are produced from time to time which are objectionable or in which objectionable actions are introduced by the players.

At Manchester there are special inspectors appointed by the Watch Committee to supervise theatres and music halls. At Newcastle the licensing of theatres rests not with the Watch Committee, but with the General Purposes Committee, which appoints inspecting officers who act independently of the Police.[36]

The difficulty which presented itself to these committees was deciding what to do with plays when 'the objectionable features are not sufficiently bad to warrant a prosecution for indecency, and the only method of punishment is to forfeit the theatre licence'.[37] This was seen as so drastic a penalty that it was difficult to impose it. Instead, local authorities from time to time resorted to banning a specific production. In 1936, for instance, the Bournemouth authorities decided that Coward's *Fumed Oak*[38] was unsuitable for local audiences and prohibited a planned production of the play by Sybil

[34] Ibid.   [35] Ibid.   [36] Ibid.   [37] Ibid.
[38] Subtitled 'an unpleasant comedy in two acts', the play shows a father quitting his dysfunctional family.

Thorndike's company. This ban was imposed despite the fact that the play had been duly licensed by the Lord Chamberlain.[39]

These examples suggest that the exercise of theatre censorship was full of contradictions. As we have seen, the rules governing theatre societies were no more than a compromise, an attempt by the Lord Chamberlain to satisfy high-brow theatregoers and to avoid complaints about censorship. They had no legal basis in statute law. In those cases mentioned above, where managers were prosecuted for departing from licensed scripts, magistrates failed to apply the penalties specified in the 1843 Theatres Act. The withdrawal of a theatre licence was a measure that no court was willing to apply for a trifling offence. However, the fact that a play was licensed by the Lord Chamberlain did not prevent local authorities from attempting their own censorship when they thought fit. Despite some liaison between the Home Office, the police, and the Lord Chamberlain's Office, the overlapping jurisdiction of the Lord Chamberlain and the local authorities was an issue that remained unresolved. Whenever the Home Office was consulted on this matter, its responses simply confirmed the ambiguity of the legal position:

It is not by any means clear that a licensing authority could not refuse to renew a licence if they took objection to a play which had been passed by the Lord Chamberlain. In exercising their jurisdiction they are acting judicially and not in a ministerial capacity, and if they could show that their action had been conducted not by caprice or favouritism but by reasonable exercise of discretion their action might be defended. An appeal would lie to the High Court, who might of course decide that the passing of a play by the Lord Chamberlain was sufficient guarantee of its fitness for production, but so far as I know the point has not yet been raised before the courts.[40]

The only way to put an end to these legal uncertainties, whether they related to public or private performances, was to amend or repeal the 1843 Theatres Act. The post-war Labour Government was to be offered just such an opportunity to legislate in 1949 with the Censorship of Plays (Repeal) Bill.

---

[39] For other examples of prosecutions, see Nicholson, *Censorship*, ii. 24–5, 105–7, 173–5.

[40] NA, HO 45/12254. Home Office memorandum, signed by A.L., to the Lord Chamberlain, 14 Apr. 1925.

5

The 1949 Bid to end Statutory Theatre Censorship

THE POST-WAR PERIOD AND THE LABOUR GOVERNMENT OF 1945

The first attempt to repeal censorship legislation in Parliament in the twentieth century had coincided with the serious constitutional crisis of 1909. This had effectively undermined any possibility of reform. The inter-war years had seen a period of relative stability in the theatre, which had brought no sustained challenges to the system of censorship exercised by the Lord Chamberlain. The 1940s were to see renewed challenges to this system, culminating in a Private Member's Bill in 1949 that would seek to repeal the 1843 Theatres Act. This time the attempt to repeal censorship legislation coincided with a post-war period when the United Kingdom faced enormous financial, social, and political challenges. The country was also governed by a Labour administration which, under Clement Attlee's leadership, had won a surprising electoral victory in 1945.

By 1949, when a new attempt was made in Parliament to repeal censorship legislation, the Labour Government's leading personalities can be seen at least in retrospect to have resembled a row of near-extinct volcanoes. Almost all were elderly; several were in failing health; and most, because of service in the wartime coalition administration, had been in high office for almost a decade. They had come to power in the general election of July 1945 after most of them had expected Churchill and the Conservatives to win. They had found themselves committed to ambitious pledges made in the Labour Party's famous manifesto entitled *Let Us Face the Future*, which had been forced on them by activists at the Labour Party Conference of December 1944. Apart from promising full employment and stressing the need for government intervention in the economy, it also committed the party to a National Health Service, a major housebuilding programme, and price controls. In addition, and rather against the inclinations of a timid leadership, the manifesto undertook to 'nationalize the iron and steel industry, along with coal, gas, electricity, transport, and the Bank of England'.[1] Once elected, whatever private reservations some of the Labour leaders may have had, they faithfully and determinedly set about implementing this programme with its heavy legislative load and by 1949 were by no means near the end of their labours.

By mid-1949 the Labour Government was entering the final year of its parliamentary term and thus had to contemplate a possibly difficult general election during 1950. The collective approach of the senior leadership to this prospect was to emphasize their not inconsiderable achievements and to talk principally of 'consolidation' as their watchword for a new term of office. The corollary was that they were certainly not interested in responding in whole or in part to pleas to adopt a radical social or libertarian agenda from backbench Members of Parliament and Labour Party activists.

In 1949 Attlee was already 66 years old. He had become the Labour Party's Leader as long ago as 1935. He had served as Deputy Prime Minister in Churchill's wartime coalition administration from May 1940 until May 1945 and had then become Prime Minister in July 1945. By 1949, therefore, he was inevitably no longer at his best. His health was to become something of a problem, leading to his hospitalization in 1948 and again in 1951.[2] Unlike most Labour Members of Parliament of a pre-1945 vintage, he had a middle-class education at public school and Oxford. He was, however, no less an adherent of 'respectable' and 'petty bourgeois' values than most of his less privileged colleagues. Indeed, Kenneth O. Morgan has written of a government 'which made much of duty, moral earnestness, and respectability, embodied in the prim, puritanical form of Attlee himself'.[3] Thus he was quite unlikely to have been personally attracted to a radical social agenda of the sort that came to be associated in the fullness of time with his young backbench colleague Roy Jenkins (first elected to the Commons in 1948). Indeed, he appears not to have been greatly interested in the arts in general or to have been a regular playgoer. It is thus unsurprising that he appointed no minister with responsibility for the Arts or Culture as has became customary since 1964.

Key figures in Attlee's Cabinet, such as Ernest Bevin and Herbert Morrison, came from working-class backgrounds. Both were social conservatives loyal to the nonconformist, working-class values of the era. Neither would have wished to see the Labour Party adopt a libertarian programme congenial to 'Hampstead intellectuals'. Of a very different background was the Chancellor

---

[1] Kenneth Morgan, *Labour in Power, 1945–1951* (Oxford: Oxford University Press, 1984), 33.
[2] Kenneth Harris, *Attlee* (London: Weidenfeld and Nicolson, 1982), 425–6, 447, 472.
[3] Morgan, *Labour in Power*, 298.

of the Exchequer in 1949, namely Sir Stafford Cripps. He had been educated at Winchester and University College, London, and subsequently became a barrister before being elected to the House of Commons in 1931. The 1940s were for him, as for others in Labour's leadership, a decade of exceptionally strenuous activity. He was first sent as a Labour Member of Parliament of Marxist reputation to serve as British Ambassador in Moscow between 1940 and 1942, 'a lunatic in a country of lunatics' as Churchill unflatteringly put it,[4] with subsequent spells as Lord Privy Seal and Leader of the House (1942) and Minister of Aircraft Production (1942–45). He then served in Attlee's Cabinet as President of the Board of Trade before becoming Chancellor of the Exchequer in 1947. A vegetarian and a teetotaller, he appears to have undermined his health by working absurdly long hours. At all events, at the age of 60, while still holding the Chancellorship, he had to attend a Swiss sanatorium during the summer of 1949. His resignation from office in 1950 and his death in 1952 ensued. Rather more attracted to social libertarian ideas than many of his Cabinet colleagues, he nevertheless could not be expected to play an active role over theatre censorship or any other similar issue given his general exhaustion, his ill health, and of course his heavy responsibilities at the Treasury at a time of acute crisis for the British economy. Although he did express himself in favour of ending theatre censorship, he was a devout Christian and it is not obvious that he would have been particularly comfortable with the permissive consequences of abolishing all forms of censorship.[5]

Another leading Labour figure to whom social reformers would have looked for some support was Hugh Dalton. Son of a Dean of Windsor (who had served as tutor to the sons of Edward VII) and educated at Eton and King's College, Cambridge, Dalton had moved in circles that were libertarian in every sense. He had, for example, been a friend of Rupert Brooke and knew many members of the Bloomsbury Group. During the late 1940s (and later) Dalton befriended many younger Labour Members of Parliament and parliamentary candidates who were later to serve in Harold Wilson's Cabinets. But by 1949 Dalton, though in the Cabinet as Chancellor of the Duchy of Lancaster, was no longer particularly influential. He had been disgraced in 1947, when Chancellor of the Exchequer, by carelessly leaking part of the contents of a budget to a journalist before it was actually delivered to the Commons. Resignation and a spell on the backbenches had been inevitable, and he was

---

[4] Quoted from David Carlton, *Churchill and the Soviet Union* (Manchester: Manchester University Press, 2000), 76.

[5] For biographies of Cripps see Colin Cooke, *The Life of Richard Stafford Cripps* (London: Hodder and Stoughton, 1957); and Peter Clarke, *The Cripps Version: The Life of Sir Stafford Cripps, 1889–1952* (London: Allen Lane, 2002).

never fully to recover. By 1949 he was 62 and also in uncertain health.[6] It seems fair, then, to place Dalton among the virtually extinct volcanoes, who by then had little to offer to the cause of social reform.

In Attlee's post-war government, the role of Home Secretary was occupied by James Chuter Ede. This post is traditionally considered to be one of the great offices of state and its occupant a figure of real political importance. Unfortunately, Ede was a mediocrity with no charisma and with no great authority in Cabinet. He was a former schoolmaster who had first entered the Commons in 1923 and who in 1949 was 67 years of age. He was responsible for only one major piece of legislation during his time at the Home Office. This was the Criminal Justice Bill of 1948 whose most significant radical feature was probably the outlawing of corporal punishment.[7] It was unlikely that this particular Home Secretary would be enthusiastic about calls for radical measures of a libertarian character. Nevertheless, and somewhat surprisingly, Ede was in favour of reform of theatre censorship when the issue was raised. Rather less surprising, as we shall see, was the fact that his handling of the issue in Parliament was completely inept.

Two younger Cabinet ministers might have been expected to identify themselves with backbenchers interested in issues of libertarian social reform but in the event neither became seriously involved. One was Wilson, aged only 33 in 1949. He had been an Oxford don before working in Whitehall with Lord Beveridge and entering the Commons in 1945. He was, however, not markedly less of a philistine and a puritan than older working-class Labour Members of Parliament, probably as a result of his early upbringing in a lower middle-class nonconformist home in West Yorkshire and his marriage to the daughter of a Congregationalist Minister.[8] Another was Aneurin Bevan, who, despite his origins as a working-class miner in South Wales, had moved far since being elected to the House of Commons in 1929. Still only 52 in 1949, he had become a seriously civilized and well-read man with friends in a variety of social circles. From the mid-1930s, he had been on friendly terms with both Michael Foot and Benn Levy, both elected to the Commons in 1945, both married to actresses (Jill Craigie and Constance Cummings respectively), and both supportive of the ending of theatre censorship and other libertarian causes. Foot, in his biography of Bevan, recalls their being guests of Bevan and his wife Jennie Lee:

No one who was a frequent visitor . . . ever forgot the magic of those evenings . . . Out of the topics of the day he could spin a wonderful delicate web of theory, a grand

---

6 Ben Pimlott, *Hugh Dalton* (London: Jonathan Cape, 1985), 564.
7 Morgan, *Labour in Power*, 55–6.
8 For biographies of Wilson see Ben Pimlott, *Harold Wilson* (London: HarperCollins, 1992); and Philip Ziegler, *Wilson: The Authorised Life of Lord Wilson of Rievaulx* (London: Weidenfeld and Nicolson, 1993).

perspective on the forces shaping society... Not that politics always or even usually played a predominant part on those occasions; he would talk about everything and anything with varying degrees of knowledge and unvarying assurance. He was an encyclopaedist, fervently holding that all branches of knowledge were parts of the same tree... Benn Levy and Constance Cummings were among the most frequent visitors in those days. 'Everything was laughter and fun and larger than life', says Constance.[9]

Foot's own biographer, Mervyn Jones, has recorded that what his subject and Bevan had in common went beyond normal politics: 'They responded eagerly to the arts, to music, to poetry, to the theatre.'[10] Thus in 1949 Levy and Foot may have been disappointed at Bevan's apparent lack of fervour in the cause of ending theatre censorship, even though he supported the change. The fact was, however, that their hero was obsessed at that time with his departmental brief, which was of course to establish and sustain a free National Health Service and to secure the funding necessary to its success in a period of economic austerity and crisis.

One other Cabinet minister deserves mention in connection with the bid to end theatre censorship in 1949, namely the Lord Chancellor, Earl Jowitt. His role would have been crucial in securing Lords' approval for any Private Member's Bill that might pass the Commons. He was not opposed to ending theatre censorship in principle but would not have offered any enthusiastic support to those keen to see its abolition.

The remaining six members of the all-male Cabinet in 1949 can only be described as elderly lightweights. They were long-serving in the Labour Movement and, apart from Philip Noel-Baker, were of 'respectable' working-class origins with no experience of public school or university education. They tended to be conscious of their limitations in the presence of well-informed civil servants and hence easily influenced. Deference towards authority was inbred among such men. They were thus mostly men whose radicalism was of a strictly limited and rather dated character.

Such social conservatism was also strongly represented on Labour's back-benches, especially so among the more senior of those who had been elected before 1945. But there was a different atmosphere among younger Members of Parliament, some of whom had by 1949 become junior ministers outside the Cabinet. Many were not of working-class origin and had been educated at university; some had a good knowledge of abroad and of the European Labour Movement (traumatized by events in the 1930s not least in Central Europe and in Spain) giving them, for good or ill, a less insular outlook; and

---

[9] Michael Foot, *Aneurin Bevan: A Biography* (London: MacGibbon and Kee, 1962), i 164.
[10] Mervyn Jones, *Michael Foot* (London: Victor Gollancz, 1994), 40.

many who had won seats in the 1945 landslide not normally considered in Labour's sights were not nominees of trades unions. It was in these circles that progressive social policies came to be favoured. But most of the radicals were distracted from agitating on this front during the Attlee era as a consequence of public discussion being dominated by the parlous condition of the British economy and the onset of the Cold War.

The preoccupation of Attlee and his senior colleagues with the great issues relating to the management of the British economic crisis and to matters of war and peace inevitably gave them little time to consider less urgent domestic questions. But it should not be thought that backbench Members of Parliament had little to do. For, as has been seen, the Labour Government had a full legislative programme. According to Bullock, 'In all, the Parliament elected in 1945 put 347 Acts on the Statute Book.'[11] By 1949 much time-consuming legislation was still in progress. In particular, there was the bill to nationalize the steel industry, which faced determined resistance in the House of Lords:[12] also important in 1949 was a Housing Act. Thus the Government's business managers were certainly correct in seeing difficulties in facilitating the passing through all its stages of any Private Member's Bill, and particularly any such bill that would be contentious. Hence the attempt to end theatre censorship in 1949 through a Private Member's Bill can clearly be seen to have been inopportune. This is, however, by no means the full explanation for the fact that almost a further two decades had to elapse before the Lord Chamberlain's blue pencil was to be laid aside.

PARLIAMENTARY QUESTIONS IN 1944 AND 1946

The slow progression towards the attempt to repeal censorship in 1949 began with questions in Parliament in 1944 and 1946. In much the same fashion that the attempt to repeal censorship provisions was spearheaded in 1909 by one energetic Member of Parliament, Harcourt, the same happened again in the 1940s. On this occasion, the Member of Parliament was the Conservative representing Ashford, E. P. Smith, who was also a novelist and playwright. In contrast to 1909, however, there was in the 1940s no underlying groundswell of support from contemporary playwrights of the kind that might have forced the Government to contemplate legislation. In 1944 and 1946, when he asked

---

[11] Alan Bullock, *Ernest Bevin: Trade Union Leader, 1881–1940* (London: Heinemann, 1960), 52.

[12] George W. Ross, *The Nationalisation of Steel* (London: MacGibbon and Kee, 1965).

Parliamentary Questions, Smith was very much a lone figure protesting when individual playwrights found their work censored.

In December 1944, Smith asked the Prime Minister 'whether he will consider making provision whereby the censorship of plays may be transferred to a Minister of the Crown responsible to Parliament'.[13] His intervention was motivated by the Lord Chamberlain's refusal to license the historical fantasy by Monckton Hoffe, *Mr Lincoln meets a Lady*. The play was developed from Hoffe's *The Immortality Club*, a series of sketches which had also been performed in Canada and on New York radio. The story of President Lincoln and Queen Victoria was therefore well known and well received before the developed script was submitted to the Lord Chamberlain. It was refused a licence on 2 January 1944 despite the fact that the Examiner of Plays, George Dearmer, had a favourable opinion of it. The American businessman, Hayes Hunter, who had commissioned the play, then turned to the Lord Chamberlain for an explanation as other plays portraying Queen Victoria had been allowed since 1937. Both he and Hoffe were willing to alter the script to suit Lord Clarendon's wishes. They were given to understand that previous plays, such as *Victoria Regina*, had been licensed by Cromer, but that Clarendon's policy as to representation of historical figures was quite different.[14]

Hoffe contacted Smith in September 1944, who subsequently wrote a confidential letter to the Home Secretary, Morrison, in October:

It is sheer nonsense that 'Victoria Regina' should have been licensed and a tremendous popular success 'Mr Lincoln Meets a Lady' (a fantasy in which President Lincoln and Queen Victoria are introduced and which was written solely to further good Anglo-American relations and has been a big broadcasting success in the U.S.A) should be refused a licence apparently on the personal prejudice of my Lord Clarendon. The present position is one which enrages the serious worker for the theatre; and, if you will grant me a short personal interview, I will undertake, not merely to prove the case as regards this particular play, but to explain to you the peculiar technique whereby unscrupulous writers get their 'bawdry' through the Lord Chamberlain's Office.[15]

Though a meeting was organized two days later, no correspondence or minutes remain giving details of the encounter. However, Smith's question to the Prime Minister on 6 December 1944 was the direct result of the meeting. Attlee, the then Deputy Prime Minister, was asked to reply on behalf of the Prime Minister. His answer was prepared by the Home Office.

Before drafting a statement for Attlee, Morrison's Private Secretary, J. A. R. Pimlott, contacted the Lord Chamberlain's office to enquire why the play had

[13] *Hansard* (Commons), 6 Dec. 1944, vol. 406, col. 525.
[14] NA, HO 144/23024. Letter from Hoffe to Smith, 30 Sept. 1944.
[15] Ibid. Letter from Smith to Morrison, 4 Oct. 1944. Underlining by Morrison.

been banned. The explanation, though it had to be kept secret, was perfectly rational and in line with past policy:

The script of the play, 'Mr. Lincoln meets a Lady', was submitted to the King and Queen who did not like it. His Majesty's Private Secretary, returning the script, wrote, 'There is a great difference between a strictly biographical record and a purely fantastical one. In the present instance the portrayal of the Queen passes in the majority of the scenes from the realm of fantasy to that of absurdity. Moreover, the general public would probably assume that the instance of scenes in the play had a biographical basis and that it was actually a record of certain authentic episodes in the Queen's life.'[16]

Because of royal disapproval, a fantasy, which had been broadcast on the radio in the United States and in the United Kingdom, without any complaint or any question about its historical accuracy or inaccuracy being raised, was banned from the stage. In his briefing to Attlee, Pimlott went on to suggest the following:

It cannot be claimed that the arrangements for censorship either of films or of plays are particularly logical, but both work reasonably well and probably better than any alternative likely to be acceptable . . . The author's agent was fully informed of the reasons for the refusal of the licence—but not of course that the script had been submitted to Their Majesties and disapproved by them. Mr Morrison would suggest that the PM's answer to Smith should be to the effect that the censorship of stage plays has always been a matter of the Royal Prerogative and not of ordinary ministerial responsibility and that, as at present advised, he is not disposed to make any change.[17]

The comments on the Royal Prerogative follow the line taken by the Home Office throughout the 1920s. They were factually incorrect and completely misleading. In his reply in the House of Commons, Attlee followed to the letter the advice given in Pimlott's briefing. He stated:

The Censorship of stage plays has always been a matter of the Royal Prerogative and not of Ministerial responsibility; as at present advised, the Prime Minister is not disposed to recommend any change.[18]

Because of the misleading advice he had been given, Attlee in his turn inevitably misled Members of Parliament on the legal status of the Lord Chamberlain's censorship powers. No one in the Commons challenged his statement, and it therefore had the effect of colouring the way Members of Parliament viewed the role of the Lord Chamberlain. When pressed by Smith on the subject of freedom of speech, Attlee admitted that 'there is a lot to be said on both sides',

---

[16] NA, HO 45/24954. Home Office Memorandum, 4 Dec. 1944.
[17] Ibid. Letter from J. A. R. Pimlott to Miss E. M. Watson (one of Churchill's private secretaries), 5 Dec. 1944.
[18] *Hansard* (Commons), 6 Dec. 1944, vol. 406, col. 525.

but nevertheless concluded that 'the present arrangements work out fairly well on the whole, taking into consideration the enormous difficulty which always arises where there is any censorship'.[19] But Smith, a well-known novelist and dramatist, was not to be so easily brushed aside.

Supported by Bevan (then a backbencher), he expressed his dissatisfaction and declared that he would raise the matter on the Adjournment later that month (the Christmas Adjournment debate). The Home Secretary, Morrison, delegated Robert Grimston, the Assistant Postmaster-General, to deal with the Adjournment. Accepting Attlee's misleading assertion at face value, namely that the Lord Chamberlain's censorship powers were part of the Royal Prerogative, Smith suggested a way to divest the Lord Chamberlain of his censorship powers without having recourse to legislation: 'At the present time this is a Royal Prerogative. Let us suppose that His Majesty chooses to divest himself of this particular Royal Prerogative and hand it to the Home Secretary for the time being. Would that necessarily require legislation?' This suggestion caused pandemonium. He was ruled out of order by the Deputy-Speaker John Milner because the House could not discuss 'the functions of a Court official, which is the matter of the Prerogative' and 'If the hon. Gentleman is proposing that an alteration should be made and that some minister should be responsible, that would be a matter for legislation, and again cannot be raised on the Adjournment.'[20] Through this 'abortive but amusing little debate',[21] Smith had successfully pressed home the point that censorship should not be left in the hands of an official who was not answerable to the Commons. Well satisfied with the attention his intervention had received, Smith commented in a letter to Morrison: 'This is one of those rare occasions when the reply doesn't matter (because one knows what it will have to be beforehand) but the statement of care does.'[22]

Morrison replied in a letter dated 4 January 1945: 'Strictly biographical representations of Queen Victoria have been permitted since 1937, but *Mr Lincoln* is a fantasy, and members of the public might well have thought that some of the imaginary scenes were authentic episodes in the Queen's life.'[23] Morrison nevertheless omitted to mention that *Mr Lincoln meets a Lady* was banned at the specific request of the King George VI and his consort.

A briefing memorandum prepared for Grimston by Home Office officials on the occasion of Smith's Parliamentary Question reveals that the censorship exercised by the Lord Chamberlain was regarded as a tool which could be

---

[19] Ibid.   [20] Ibid., 20 Dec. 1944, vol. 406, col. 1912.
[21] NA, HO 45/24954. Letter from Smith to Morrison, 8 Jan. 1945.
[22] Ibid. Letter from Smith to Morrison, 17 Dec. 1944.   [23] Ibid.

replaced should its usefulness cease to be greater than the inconveniences it created:

No doubt in the last resort, if the Lord Chamberlain proved to be totally out of touch with popular opinion in the matter of the licensing of plays, it would be necessary for the Government to make representations with a view to his removal and replacement by someone better qualified, and so long as this power exists in the background there are advantages in leaving the responsibility for particular decisions to someone who is not answerable to the House of Commons...

   All that can be asked for is that broadly speaking the censorship shall be exercised in accordance with principles which are acceptable to public opinion in general: so far as the experience of the Home Office for the last 20 years goes, there have been no serious complaints against the general method by which the censorship has been exercised. Complaints have been rare, and as already stated, complaints in particular cases are inevitable.[24]

The last paragraph accounts for the Government's reluctance to abandon the system; the first paragraph explains just as bluntly that the Government did not consider the Lord Chamberlain to be irreplaceable if public opinion turned against him. The key advantage from the Government's perspective was the fact that the Lord Chamberlain was not answerable to the House of Commons.

   It was in this spirit that officials in the Home Office outlined in note form a case for supporting the role of the Lord Chamberlain as censor:

The [1909] recommendations were not acceptable then and would be equally unacceptable now.

   The following considerations, raised in 1924, still hold good today:—

(1) Link with Crown much valued by theatrical profession

(2) Maximum continuity of policy as Lord Chamberlain would no longer change with the Government

(3) No Minister should be expected to take direct responsibility for decisions with regard to the censorship of individual plays

(4) Local Authority censorship would be cumbersome and vexatious to theatrical interests on account of expense, delay, and variations in policy

(5) Censorship by a special Board would have little advantage over censorship by Lord Chamberlain

(6) The Lord Chamberlain works in close consultation with the Home Secretary on matters involving questions of law or policy or likely to be the subject of general controversy.[25]

---

[24] NA, HO 45/24954. Memorandum prepared by the Permanent Under-Secretary of State, Alexander Maxwell, and approved by Morrison, 18 Dec. 1944.

[25] Ibid. Undated and unsigned memorandum entitled, 'Censorship of stage plays'.

A pencilled note scribbled opposite the last point asked the question: 'Is this dangerous?' The Government was keen to deny any involvement in the process of censoring plays, since the Lord Chamberlain was supposed to hold a non-political office. The question implies that to make this kind of admission arguably gave away too much about what in practice happened behind closed doors.

This episode shows two essential factors that served to maintain the censorship system. Firstly, as a Member of Parliament without government support, Smith proved unable to press for reform of theatre censorship legislation within the format of the interventions allowed in the Commons. The role of the Lord Chamberlain and, therefore, his censorship duties could not be discussed in the House of Commons. The Royal Prerogative enjoyed the same privilege. Secondly, the legal basis of censorship seemed to have been unclear to Government ministers. The Home Office briefed Attlee to declare that censorship was exercised under the Royal Prerogative, whereas in fact it had been exercised under statute law since 1737. Had it been simply a question of devolving the Royal Prerogative with respect to censorship to the Home Office, this could have been achieved without legislation. But the Home Office would have been loath to take on the responsibility. Indeed, the last thing it wanted was direct responsibility and accountability for the exercise of stage censorship. This was made crystal clear in the memorandum prepared by Alexander Maxwell, the Permanent Under-Secretary of State at the Home Office, for Morrison on 18 December 1944:

It would be quite intolerable if questions or debates could be raised in the House of Commons on particular decisions which must frequently be merely matters of opinion and can be hotly argued both ways by partisans. If, for example, the censors allowed a play with a Fascist tendency or quite properly interfered with a play with a Communist tendency on the grounds that it contained offensive personalities or did violence to the sentiment of religious reverence, or was calculated to cause a breach of the peace, suggestions would certainly be made that the interference was based on political prejudice, and it would be most undesirable that a Minister belonging to a particular political party should be the final arbiter on the question whether the play should be licensed or not.[26]

This explains very convincingly why no Home Secretary would ever wish to have direct or devolved responsibility for theatre censorship.

In December 1946, Smith once again asked Attlee (this time as Prime Minister) whether legislation would be introduced to abolish the system of theatre censorship. His question, as on the previous occasion, was prompted by a decision taken by the Lord Chamberlain. He had disallowed the satirizing

[26] Ibid.

of Cabinet ministers in the revue *Between Ourselves* performed at the London
Playhouse, objecting in particular to a song entitled 'Left Honourables'. At
the end of much negotiation, the lines considered to be most offensive by the
censor were deleted. In an article by Beverley Baxter, the Conservative MP
for Wood Green, the suggestion was made that it was a policy of the Lord
Chamberlain's to prohibit political satire. Most newspapers reacted strongly
to this. The *Daily Mail, Daily Mirror, Daily Telegraph, Evening Standard, News
Chronicle,* and *Daily Worker* expressed the opinion that the Lord Chamberlain's
'pettifogging interference' should be abolished. The generally shared view was
that his intervention was an infringement of 'an essential part of our liberties
that we should be free from political restrictions in deciding what we should
say about our politicians—on the stage or anywhere else'.[27]

The Home Office considered the censorship exercised by the Lord Chamberlain in this particular matter 'possibly mistaken'.[28] Maxwell commented: 'I
doubt myself whether the censorship does any good . . . the illogicalities of the
present system are patent.' Yet, Smith's plea for the abolition of censorship
was answered negatively in Parliament because 'it [the censorship] saves a lot
of trouble'.[29] A Home Office note of 6 December 1946 suggested that Smith's
interest in the theatre was excessive: 'Now all Smith asks is that the existing system of censorship should be abolished!'[30] Officially, the Parliamentary Under-
Secretary of State for the Home Office, George Oliver, stated in a Commons
written answer that the Home Secretary was in no position 'to suggest that there
is a prospect of legislation on this subject'.[31] The role of the Lord Chamberlain
as censor was once more supported by the Government on the grounds that
he represented the lesser of two evils. As in 1944, the Home Office was most
reluctant to accept any suggestion that a minister should assume responsibility
for theatre censorship. Fortunately for the Government, the press was unaware
that different Government departments were consulted by the Lord Chamberlain whenever he was in doubt about a play. Nor did they know that the
Lord Chamberlain would always follow the advice given by the Government.
The responses of Home Office officials to Smith's parliamentary interventions
make it clear that there were distinct advantages in following a deliberate policy
of obfuscation in respect of theatre censorship. The system, as it operated
in practice, gave the Government a crucial but secret advisory role in the
day-to-day exercise of censorship by the Lord Chamberlain. Any transparency
in the system of theatre censorship would have laid the Government open to
repeated challenges against individual decisions in the House of Commons.

---

[27] *News Chronicle*, 3 Dec. 1946.   [28] NA, HO 45/24954. Minutes, 6 Dec. 1946.
[29] Ibid. Memorandum prepared by Maxwell and countersigned by Ede, 9 Dec. 1946.
[30] Ibid.   [31] *Hansard* (Commons), 10 Dec. 1946, vol. 431, col. 216, written answers.

THE 1949 ATTEMPT TO REPEAL STATUTORY THEATRE CENSORSHIP

The next event to put the issue of censorship back on the agenda was a resolution passed in 1948 by the first British Theatre Conference, which recommended the abolition of theatre censorship. This Conference was called as a result of yet another initiative taken by Smith. In March 1947 Smith asked in Parliament whether the President of the Board of Trade 'will appoint a working party to investigate and report upon conditions prevailing in the theatre industry'.[32] Although the reply was negative, the idea of an enquiry resurfaced in June during the debate on the Finance Bill. A. P. Herbert (Independent MP for Oxford University) proposed a reduction of entertainment duty to alleviate some of the financial problems facing the theatre industry. Levy (Labour MP for Eton and Slough) was against the notion of a cut in entertainment duty but, like Smith, was keen to see an enquiry. Levy was a well-known playwright and was to become the second parliamentary champion in this period of the move to abolish censorship. Dalton, who was still Chancellor of the Exchequer at the time, responded positively to this suggestion:

What I should like to do would be to have a discussion between now and next year between . . . my hon. Friend the member for Eton and Slough, who has great knowledge of the matter, and others, including the hon. Gentleman the Member for Ashford [Smith] if he cared to join in. I should like us to constitute ourselves an unofficial working party, to consider what steps should be taken within the fiscal field . . . to sustain and assist the British living theatre in the years to come. Of course, if an official working party could be appointed, perhaps they would do the work for us. I should be very happy to take part in an inquiry of the kind I have described . . .[33]

Dalton's subsequent resignation as Chancellor meant that the working party failed to materialize.

Smith and Levy responded with alacrity to Dalton's suggestion of a working party by encouraging the theatrical profession to call a preparatory conference. The suggestion was enthusiastically supported by the theatrical profession, represented by the Federation of Theatre Unions.[34] The Conference was planned to meet under the chairmanship of the playwright, J. B. Priestley, and with the collaboration of Basil Dean (Producer), Geoffrey Whitworth (Chairman of the British Drama League), Gordon Sandison (Secretary of

[32] Ibid., 11 Mar. 1947, vol. 434, col. 1139, oral answers.
[33] Ibid., 16 June 1947, vol. 438, col. 1640.
[34] See 'Theatre working party', *The Times*, 3 July 1947.

British Actors Equity Association), and Levy. Though his name appeared among the members of the preparatory committee in an article published in *The Times* on 4 December 1947, Levy did not wish to be seen as too closely involved in the organization of the Conference:

My feeling has been that the holding or announcement of the Conference at this juncture will either be seized upon as a pretext for Government inaction (especially if its conclusions are divided or indeterminate) or, less likely but worse, be regarded as a pressure group's attempt to bounce them into a decision on matters which are already sympathetically under discussion.[35]

The Conference took place between 5 and 8 February 1948,[36] and over 300 representatives from every branch of the industry attended, although the theatre managers declined repeated invitations to attend the Conference. The few managers who did attend did so in an unofficial capacity. Walter Payne, the chairman of the Theatres' National Committee, explained the managers' decision to the new Chancellor of the Exchequer, Cripps. According to Payne, the character and procedure of the Conference 'make it impossible, in the absence of a preliminary factual survey of many of the subjects, for our delegates to consider and vote on behalf of our seven organisations upon questions which the promoters of the conference have said should be brought to a climax in order to approach Government departments'.[37] The stated aim of the Conference was not only to make recommendations but also 'to authorize an appeal to Government departments on problems requiring action or investigation'.[38] Payne concluded his explanation with a personal attack on Priestley:

Apart, however, from all this I am to add that the Chairman of the conference has already published such abusive and ill-informed criticism of those who are sometimes described as commercial managers that very many of our manager members strongly opposed acceptance by my committee of any invitation to take part in any conference over which he might preside.[39]

Clearly there was no love lost between commercial theatre managers and some of the playwrights who felt that their plays were not given the consideration they merited.

[35] BLP (Benn Levy Papers), University of Sussex Special Collections, Sx MS 37, file 3/2. Letter to Ossia Trilling (British Theatre Conference), 20 Oct. 1947.
[36] Some 77 resolutions were discussed in committee after being forwarded by members of representative organizations.
[37] 'Theatre Managers' Boycott', *The Times*, 6 Feb. 1948.
[38] 'Fostering interest in the theatre', *The Times*, 20 Jan. 1948.
[39] 'Theatre Managers' Boycott', *The Times*, 6 Feb. 1948.

One of the questions raised by different interest groups and studied by the preparatory committee was that of theatre censorship. The resolution to abolish censorship was proposed by Sir Lewis Casson for Equity and by Smith for the League of Dramatists. It was carried at the Theatre Conference by all present except three. This meant that some 300 delegates, representing all branches of theatre practitioners except theatre managers, backed an appeal to the Home Office to abolish theatre censorship.

Cripps had been invited to open the plenary session. He chose to remain non-committal on the likely response of Government to resolutions passed at the Conference, but made the kind of placatory and encouraging noises that might be expected from a Cabinet minister facing a potentially hostile gathering. In his speech, he stated: 'What I can and will say is that any unanimous decisions coming from such a representative and well qualified conference as this will be taken into serious consideration by the Government.'[40] However, he sounded a note of caution about the Government's ability to respond, drawing attention to the lack of parliamentary time in a period of economic reconstruction and stressing the Government's reluctance to interfere in cultural matters. Nevertheless, he expressed his personal concern at the economic and artistic difficulties facing the British theatre. Significantly, he also declared that one 'must avoid all tendency either directly or indirectly to teach or censor the artist'.[41] His presence at the Conference was important, as it ensured that views expressed at the Conference would at least be familiar to a senior member of the Cabinet. It also meant that the dialogue between Government and the Arts, set in motion by the newly created Arts Council, was given a further boost. The Conference strongly supported the creation of this new body and called for it to be strengthened.

Smith and Levy were delighted with the outcome of the Conference, as emerges from a letter Levy wrote to Smith shortly after the Conference on 11 February 1948:

I entirely agree that the Conference far exceeded my best expectations. Not only did it pass all the most important resolutions, but I think it established once and for all that there was never any political issue as between Left and Right, but both sides, of whom you and I are typical, were thinking exclusively in terms of the welfare of the theatre. Having established this, I do not think there's anything to stop us![42]

The Society of West End Theatre Managers soon managed to dampen this enthusiasm. Bronson Albery and Payne, at a meeting of the society, respectively proposed and seconded a resolution in favour of the retention of the Lord

---

[40] BLP, file 3/1. Summary of proceedings of British Theatre Conference, 6.
[41] Ibid. 9.   [42] Ibid., file 3/2. Letter from Levy to Smith, 11 Feb. 1948.

Chamberlain as censor. The resolution, to be forwarded to the Home Office, was published in *The Times* on 6 March 1948. Their main argument, already expressed by their fellow managers in 1909, was that 'if the censorship were abolished all concerned in the production of a play would be at the mercy of local watch committees'.[43] Neither the Government nor the managers would claim that the censorship exercised by the Lord Chamberlain was perfect, but it seemed to them preferable to the notion of censorship exercised at a local level.

The parliamentary interventions that followed after the Conference proved Levy's point that censorship was not a question of party politics. The Liberal MP for North Dorset, Frank Byers, was the first to tackle the issue. He asked the Home Secretary whether he would introduce legislation to abolish censorship. He received the much-used answer that Ede could not 'hold out any prospect of legislation on the subject'.[44] The draft presented to Ede for his written answer was a firm negation though it allowed that 'there may be arguments in favour of the abolition of censorship'. That part was struck through by Ede.[45]

Levy and Smith chose to approach the problem laterally by trying to address the known reservations of the theatre managers. Levy contacted the Solicitor-General, Frank Soskice, for legal advice while Smith pursued the same issue in the Commons. Levy wrote to Soskice on 26 February 1948, asking the following questions:

When a play is licensed by the Lord Chamberlain, this does not, of course, give it legal immunity from prosecution on the score of blasphemy, obscenity or sedition, although in practice it would naturally be a deterrent. But what are the rights of local Authorities or Chief Constables or Watch Committees

a) in re-censoring a play
b) in enforcing this re-censorship
c) in initiating a prosecution, and
d) what are the opportunities, rights and temptations to a common informer?[46]

In the meantime, Smith asked in the House of Commons: 'under what authority plays duly licensed by the Lord Chamberlain and of which the script, as licensed, has been strictly adhered to, may be compulsorily altered at the demand of a chief constable or a local watch committee?'[47] Smith's object was to spell out that theatre managers had no legal protection when taking a play on tour: the fact that a play had been licensed by the Lord Chamberlain did not prevent local watch committees from banning it or indeed threatening

---

[43] NA, HO 45/24954. Note by F. L. Haigh (Senior Executive Officer in the Home Office), 11 Mar. 1948.
[44] *Hansard* (Commons), 20 Feb. 1948, vol. 447, col. 275.
[45] NA, HO 45/24954, 19 Feb. 1948.   [46] Ibid. Letter from Levy to Soskice, 26 Feb. 1948.
[47] *Hansard* (Commons), 4 Mar. 1948, vol. 448, col. 529.

prosecution. This approach was meant to undermine the argument usually put forward by theatre managers that the Lord Chamberlain's approval of a play offered them security and protection from vexatious prosecution. Following consultations with the Lord Chamberlain's Office on this point, Home Office officials decided 'to minimise the fact that there is a possibility of overlapping jurisdiction in the censoring of plays, and to suggest that, if S of S [Secretary of State] is pressed on the point, he says difficulties are overcome by co-operation'.[48] Though a draft and supplementary answer were prepared, Ede curtailed further discussion in the House by replying: 'I will look into any particular cases if the Hon. Member will send me details.'[49] This adroitly cut short further consideration of a potentially awkward topic.

Smith and Levy worked in tandem. While Smith's intervention was dealt with in Parliament, Levy's letter was referred to the Home Office for a formal reply. This was sent on 30 March 1948:

The general position in these matters is that under the Theatres Act, 1843 the local licensing authority, which is now the County or County Borough Council with power to delegate to a committee, is required to make suitable rules for ensuring order and decency at the Theatres they license and, according to my information, these rules (e.g. those of the LCC [London County Council]) sometimes prohibit profanity or impropriety of language on the premises. It is however to the Lord Chamberlain that the Act gives the power to disallow any play or part thereof and to prohibit its acting or presentation. You will of course appreciate that in the event of any conflict, which happily does not seem to occur, only the Courts could settle the interpretation of the Act.

As regards enforcement of the rules Section 9 of the Act enables two Justices, where breach of the rules is proved on oath before them, to order closing of a theatre for such time as they think fit, and the licensing authority can, of course, take a breach into account when they come to consider application for the renewal of a licence.[50]

Though correct in theory, the legal procedure mentioned in the last paragraph was never carried out in practice. Levy's queries were intended to reveal the inevitable contradictions and inconsistencies in legislation that was now seriously out of date and irrelevant to modern circumstances. The Government was perfectly aware of the fact, but chose not to address the problem. Ede's reply to Levy carefully omitted the following passages (which had been drafted for his consideration):

It would appear that in such an area any person may lay an information alleging a breach of the rules, but if a prosecution ensues and a fine is imposed there is no

---

[48] NA, HO 45/24954. Note by J. I. Wall (Secretary in Home Office) to H. A. Strutt (Assistant Under-Secretary of State, Home Office), 3 Mar. 1948.

[49] *Hansard* (Commons), 4 Mar. 1948, vol. 448, col. 529.

[50] NA, HO 45/24954. Letter from Ede to Levy, 30 Mar. 1948.

question of the fine being payable to him . . . The only action which could be taken by a person who considers that the rules have been infringed would be to make representations to the licensing authority.

The question whether the rules can be used to enforce an alteration in the script of a play is, of course, a question which can only be decided by the Courts and so far as I am aware the point has not been raised before them. The HO [Home Office] has heard of only two or three cases, none of them recent, in which a local authority appears to have concerned itself with the script of a play, and difficulties which have occasionally arisen have been resolved by making representations to the Lord Chamberlain, who has powers under section 14 of the Act to prohibit performances of a play or any part thereof.[51]

This admission that prosecutions might be initiated against the production of a play licensed by the Lord Chamberlain was clearly deemed unfit for public consumption. In the event, the 'two or three cases' mentioned in the draft were replaced by the anodyne statement, 'in the event of any conflict, which happily does not seem to occur'.

The Home Office, under Ede's cautious and pedestrian leadership, was determined to avoid any change in the status quo. The resolution on theatre censorship carried at the British Theatre Conference was simply ignored, despite Cripps's assurance that any representative decision would be considered by the Government. Although the Government could claim that the statement issued by theatre managers proved that the abolition of censorship was not sought by the whole profession, evidence shows that the Home Office made very little use of the argument. The opinion of the Home Office was straightforward: 'it is . . . inconceivable that there should be no censorship of stage plays at all, and the only practicable alternative to the Lord Chamberlain's censorship would appear to be a censorship under the control of a Minister answerable to the House of Commons.'[52] As we shall see, this alternative was flatly rejected by the Government.

The policy of deliberate inertia pursued by the Home Office posed a real dilemma for the champions of reform. The parliamentary interventions of Levy and Smith had hitherto achieved very little by way of practical result. What was to be done? Levy listed the obstacles that stood in the way of reform when he replied to a letter from the manager and author H. M. Harwood:

No Government will act when even those most intimately concerned, namely the authors, continue divided on the matter. Many, including the President of the League, St John Ervine, that great champion of freedom and daring, have been frightened by the Managers' bogey—a police prosecution . . . we'd do better with the Authors'

---

[51] NA, HO 45/24954. Passages deleted from the undated draft letter from Ede to Levy.
[52] Ibid. Minute by Haigh, 6 Dec. 1946.

Society united behind us (I don't expect the Managers) even if it were possible (which it isn't these days) to introduce a Private Member's Bill. To raise it at Question Time or for a half hour's Adjournment Debate would only amount to a little academic ventilation. My own feeling is that this would do more harm than good unless it were part of a thorough and organised campaign of agitation. In other words it would merely tend further to stale an already rather dusty debating subject without involving any action.[53]

Despite the reservations about a Private Member's Bill expressed in this letter (and they were serious reservations, given the enormous legislative programme facing the Government), Smith and Levy decided to pursue this course of action. In January 1949, Levy proposed a Private Member's Bill entitled 'A Bill to exempt the theatre from any statutory restrictions on liberty of expression in excess of those applicable to other forms of literature'. Levy proved unlucky in the Ballot, but Smith was more fortunate. He was given leave to introduce a bill: 'to amend the laws relating to the censorship of plays and licensing of theatres so as to exempt the theatre from restriction upon freedom of expression in excess of those applicable to other forms of literature; and for purposes connected therewith'.[54] Smith's bill was supported by Levy, John Maude (Conservative MP for Exeter and son of actor Cyril Maude), John Lawson (Labour MP for Chester-le-Street), R. Hopkin Morris (Liberal MP for Carmarthen), Edward Keeling (Conservative MP for Twickenham), Reginald Paget (Labour MP for Northampton), Sir Wavell Wakefield (Conservative MP for St Marylebone), Kenneth Lindsay (Independent MP for English Universities), Sir William Darling (Conservative MP for South Edinburgh), Ralph Morley (one of two Labour MPs for Southampton), and Michael Foot (Labour MP for Plymouth Devonport). The First Reading of the bill on 28 February 1949 led Smith to write to Levy indicating that he expected a successful outcome:

I am assured of much support from my party. Wakefield and Darling insisted upon backing the Bill before it was read in dummy form . . . I think W. J. Brown will back it, too—which means every Party and some of no Party will be represented, that is, if you get Megan [Lloyd George]. We should spread the net as widely as we can.[55]

In contrast to 1909, contemporary dramatists failed to mount any kind of press campaign. Smith received a few scattered letters from individual play-wrights giving details of their difficulties with the Lord Chamberlain. However,

---

[53] BLP, file 5/2. Levy to Harwood, 13 Sept. 1948.

[54] *Hansard* (Commons), 28 Jan. 1949, vol. 460, col. 1242.

[55] BLP, file 5/2. Smith to Levy, 29 Jan. 1949. Brown was Independent MP for Rugby. Megan is Lady Megan Lloyd-George, the former Prime Minister's daughter, Liberal MP for Anglesea, and Vice-President of the Liberal Party.

no contemporary playwright of any distinction wrote in support. This is not entirely surprising. The best-known playwrights of the period were not socially committed authors. Christopher Fry, for instance, was an advocate of poetic drama; his latest play *The Lady's Not for Burning* (1948) was a romantic burlesque full of verbal brilliance and an ironic lightness of tone. Another distinguished exponent of poetic drama was the Anglo-American writer T. S. Eliot whose most recent work *The Cocktail Party* (1949) transported the concerns of Euripides' Alcestis to a modern London drawing-room. Rattigan wrote carefully crafted problem plays such as *The Winslow Boy* (1946) and *The Browning Version* (1948), both of which explored human dilemmas in a style reminiscent of the late nineteenth century. These were not the kind of playwrights who would engage in public confrontations with the Lord Chamberlain. Instead it was left to the veteran opponents of censorship, Housman and Shaw, to express their renewed opposition to the continued powers of the censor. Shaw, having previously failed to defeat censorship through logic, opted for studied irony: 'What is a censor of plays? He is an official of infinite wisdom, infallible judgment, and encyclopedic erudition, for whom time does not exist. That is, a fiction that can never come to life.'[56] Shaw's main point was that the principle of censorship, more than the practice, had to be fought.

Smith's bill attracted a good deal of attention before its First Reading. Elizabeth Barber, the secretary of the League of Dramatists and a lawyer, offered legal advice for the drafting of the bill.[57] The Haldane Society, an organization of socialist lawyers affiliated to the Labour Party, also proposed to help in the drafting of the bill. However, as the President of the Society was Cripps and Soskice was one of the Vice-Presidents, the offer was seen as problematic and was not taken up by Smith and Levy. The journalist and drama critic, Hannen Swaffer, though he was neutral prior to the debate, wrote an article in favour of the bill in the *Daily Herald*.

Levy and Smith received a significant boost before the Second Reading when the Attorney-General, Hartley Shawcross, sent them an encouraging letter in which he stated: 'expressing my purely personal view, which, of course, will not commit the Government in any way, I must say that I agree that there is a very strong case for the alteration of the present arrangements.'[58] David Maxwell Fyfe (National Conservative MP for Liverpool and previously Solicitor-General and Attorney-General) was in favour of the measure and Soskice was also sympathetic. More decisively, despite 'a good deal of obstruction inside his department', Levy felt that the Home Secretary was 'very favourable in

---

[56] 'Censorship of Plays. Mr Shaw's remedy', *The Times*, 7 Apr. 1949. In his letter to the editor, Housman still advocated the need for a court of appeal if censorship was not to be abolished.
[57] See BLP, file 5/2.   [58] Ibid. Shawcross to Levy, 10 Mar. 1949.

principle'.[59] Ede had met with Smith and Levy on more than one occasion and urged them 'to have the Bill printed and circulated <u>at once</u> as time is getting so short'.[60] Levy was fully aware that Ede's support was crucial, especially on matters of detail, and it could not be taken for granted.

The support of Members of Parliament from all parties and of prominent members of the Government seemed to offer real hope of success. Levy began to think that 'there may not even be a division'.[61] Yet, despite Ede's cautious optimism, the Government had not yet declared its formal position. Even before the Second Reading, Levy was concerned at the likelihood of the bill making slow progress during the Committee stage (given the crowded parliamentary agenda), which prompted him to ask his friend Bevan: 'What chance of the Government taking it over and providing time? It wouldn't need much.'[62]

Smith and Levy's initial plan of campaign was (as Smith outlined it) that 'we must go for complete abolition, and not any bastard compromise'.[63] However, just as support for the bill grew, so did opposition. Managerial organizations, which were opposed to any reform of the censorship system (notably the Society of West End Managers, the Theatrical Managers' Association, and the Theatres' National Committee), asked for a copy of the bill and an opportunity to discuss it. Smith and Levy foresaw that their arguments would be opposed by this branch of the industry and tried to meet the concerns of the managers in the drafting of the bill.

Moreover, the recent interventions in Parliament showed not only that the Government was reluctant to effect any change but also that the issue of the Royal Prerogative could prove to be an important stumbling block in the way of abolition. Smith therefore attempted to ascertain the constitutional and legal implications of his repeal bill by seeking the opinion of the Lord Chancellor, Jowitt, on 'an entirely non-Party matter':

It has been suggested to me that I must obtain His Majesty's permission to bring forward a measure curtailing the Royal Prerogative, which this Bill would unquestionably do . . . I cannot believe that this is true; but can you, as a personal friend,

(a) confirm it or otherwise;
(b) if you can, tell me the correct way to set about doing so?[64]

Jowitt's reply was strictly private and, he admitted, might be inaccurate:

As I understand the position, the broad principle is that the Royal Prerogative is from time to time invaded by Statute and where a matter is regulated by Statute the Royal

[59] Ibid. Levy to Smith, 14 Mar. 1949.   [60] Ibid. Smith to Levy, 16 Mar. 1949.
[61] Ibid., 18 Mar. 1949.   [62] Ibid., 19 Mar. 1949.
[63] Ibid. Smith to Levy, 29 Jan. 1949.
[64] NA, LCO 2/1186 (Lord Chancellor's Office). Letter from Smith to Jowitt, 3 Feb. 1949.

Prerogative ceases to apply. It seems to me that the matter with which you are dealing is regulated by Statute (see sections 14 and 15 of Theatres Act). I therefore think that you are wrong in stating . . . that this Bill would curtail the Royal Prerogative.

I think it more accurate to say that the Bill would alter the Act of 1843 which has now taken over what used to be and is no longer a subject-matter for the Royal Prerogative. I should have thought that if you had drafted your Bill so as to make it plain that what you are purporting to do was to alter the provisions of that Act no one could possibly argue that you were invading the Royal Prerogative.[65]

As the Cabinet member responsible for constitutional affairs and the judiciary, the Lord Chancellor's opinion in such a matter would obviously carry great weight. What is astonishing, however, is that this was seemingly the first occasion when any Member of Parliament or Government minister or Home Office official had sought the Lord Chancellor's opinion on the issue of theatre censorship and the Royal Prerogative. Jowitt's opinion differed markedly from the repeatedly expressed view of the Home Office that theatre censorship was exercised by the Lord Chamberlain under the Royal Prerogative. Despite his cautious disclaimer when responding to Smith, his advice regarding the Royal Prerogative in respect of theatre censorship was to prove to be legally correct, even though the issue was not clarified until the end of the parliamentary session.

By February 1949, Levy and Smith's Bill gave rise to growing concern over the representation of living persons on the stage. Although support for the bill was widespread across party boundaries, some Conservative Members of Parliament started to express reservations over the matter of living persons. Levy and Smith were in principle opposed to restrictive clauses. Yet, Smith judged it wiser to compromise in order to gain 'a lot of people over to our sides who would otherwise waver'.[66] While Smith was trying to reassure his Conservative colleagues, Levy's task was to draft the bill for its Second Reading. In approaching this task, he received the help of Members of Parliament and others who were qualified barristers, namely Paget (Labour MP for Northampton), Richard Mitchison (Labour MP for Kettering), and Gerald Gardiner (who was to become Lord Chancellor in Wilson's administration in 1964). His intention was to draft the bill in such a way as to meet the likely objections of theatre managers and to counter arguments that might be used by the Government to defeat the measure:

We'll never get the thing through unless we can show that the net result will be a freer theatre and not a less free theatre creeping along cautiously under the permanent threat

---

65 NA, LCO 2/1186 Letter from Jowitt to Smith, 4 Feb. 1949.
66 BLP, file 5/2. Letter from Smith to Levy, 3 Feb. 1949.

of petty prosecutions from Watch Committees, Vigilante Societies, Chief Constables, fanatical puritans and blackmailing libel litigants.[67]

Levy also had to take into account the mainly Conservative opposition to the bill on the issue of the representation of living persons, if only because Smith 'has half-promised [I. L.] Orr-Ewing and Herbert that he would do so'.[68] Both were potential supporters of the bill; the more important of the two was Herbert. Unfortunately Levy had opposed Herbert's suggested clause on entertainment duty during the debate on the 1947 Finance Bill, and had thereby prompted Dalton to reject the clause. Although Herbert and Smith were close allies, Herbert declared, at a meeting of Members of Parliament in favour of Smith's Theatre Censorship Bill: 'I'll be damned now if I vote for any Bill Benn Levy is interested in!'[69] Levy took the view that it would be better to avoid any compromise on the issue of living persons in the draft Bill:

for purely tactical reasons it might be smarter not to make them [concessions] all in advance, so to speak, but to wait until the Bill is debated and to make them then. They could be used as a valuable psychological gesture of conciliation. As a matter of fact, there is a second advantage in that, because . . . the drafting may present difficulties. . . If we accept the thing in principle, say, on Second Reading and invite those who might raise the matter to combine in drafting an amendment which might meet the case and be accepted, we could share the responsibility with them.[70]

Paget, who gave advice on the drafting of the bill, was equally opposed, though for different reasons, to offering any protection to living persons. He commented in a letter to Levy that he was 'opposed to protecting living people from caricature on the stage'. He went on to argue:

If people go into public life, by so doing they ask for comment. I can see no reason why they should not be caricatured on the stage as they are in newspapers. Indeed I think this would put a great deal of life into the theatre, and would be a great deal more straightforward than the sort of cracks which you find inserted into the average review.[71]

The first draft of the bill offered few, if any, concessions to the doubters. It was brief, to the point of terseness, and consisted of five short sections:

1. Sections 12, 13, 14 and 15 of the Theatres Act, 1843 (which provide that new plays shall be licensed by the Lord Chamberlain and impose certain penalties) are hereby repealed.

---

[67] Ibid. Levy to Paget, 4 Feb. 1949.   [68] Ibid.
[69] Ibid. Smith to Levy, 9 Mar. 1949.
[70] Ibid. Levy to Smith, 7 Feb. 1949.
[71] Ibid. Paget to Levy, 7 Feb. 1949.

2. Notwithstanding anything contained to the contrary in any public, local or private Act, no theatre licensing authority shall refuse to license any theatre and no existing licence shall be withdrawn from any theatre save upon one of the following grounds:—

   a) That the theatre is being conducted as a disorderly house

   b) That the structure of the theatre fails to comply with a regulation or bye-law providing for the safety or health of spectators and others in the said theatre

   c) That the management of the theatre have persistently failed to comply with regulations or bye-laws providing for the safety or health of spectators and others in the said theatre.

3. If any licensing authority refuses to license a theatre or revokes or suspends an existing licence the licensee or intending licensee shall have the right to appeal against such refusal, revocation or suspension to the Court of Quarter Sessions for the district in which the theatre is situate at the meeting next held after the expiration of 21 days from the date of notice of intention to appeal, such notice to be served by the licensee or intending licensee upon the licensing authority within 14 days of such refusal, revocation or suspension.

4. No criminal prosecution arising out of the performance of a play shall be commenced against any manager or owner of a theatre or dramatist or any other person directly or indirectly responsible for or associated with the production or performance of a play without the order of a Judge at Chambers being first had and obtained. Such application shall be made on notice to the person accused, who shall have the opportunity of being heard against such application.

5. This Act may be cited as the Censorship of Plays (Repeal) Act, 1949.[72]

The effect of the first section was to abolish not only the censorship of plays exercised by the Lord Chamberlain, but all theatre censorship. No safeguards for living persons were offered and no mention was made of any other laws to control the presentation of obscene or disturbing material. In contrast, no change was envisaged in the licensing of theatres. By implication (though not expressly stated) county councils were to continue to license theatres in London and other cities and towns, while the Lord Chamberlain was to remain responsible for Westminster and towns with a royal residence. Levy and Smith had planned to make the county councils responsible for the licensing of all theatres but the managers had expressed the wish to keep the present procedure unchanged. As this was unlikely to affect the main object of the bill, Levy and Smith yielded to the managers' request. The other sections provided for the protection of managers in respect of the licensing of theatres and the threat of legal proceedings arising out of specific performances. Levy was particularly keen to cover the point regarding the cases in which a licence

---

[72] The Censorship of Plays (Repeal) Bill, 1949.

could be withheld. He was adamant that local licensing authorities should not be able 'to use the withdrawal of a licence as a threat and a reprisal for productions of which they may disapprove'.[73] This, in effect, would be a form of censorship. Paget and Mitchison had been divided on the sanctioning authority that would allow legal proceedings to be initiated, arising out of a performance of a play. Paget had favoured a Judge at Chambers while Mitchison had thought the Attorney-General would prove a better and less expensive protection against petty prosecutions. Gardiner, who was drafting the bill, shared Paget's view, and this view had prevailed.

Levy and Smith had met with members of the Theatres' National Committee (Albery, Sir Charles B. Cochran, P. M. Selby, C. Egerton Killick, F. Carter, and J. Leslie Greene) on 11 February. They were anxious to find a formula that would be acceptable to the managers while ensuring freedom of theatrical expression. Smith was therefore eager to insert a clause making sure that the bill could only be amended by statute and not by local laws. Such provision would 'remove his people's [the Committee's] doubts and fears'.[74] Gardiner's proposed mechanism to prevent legal interference by local authorities was an addition to the beginning of section 2: 'Notwithstanding anything contained to the contrary in any public, local or private Act.' This decision was founded on the legal argument that 'it would require a very large Schedule to specify all the statutory powers to make bye-laws which require either repealing or amending'. It was also based on the political judgement that 'if you start interfering with local powers the local members will be stimulated into opposing the Bill'.[75] The managers were not convinced by the safeguards Smith and Levy had outlined. Instead they threatened them with the prospect of organizing a combined managerial censorship. This threat was assessed differently by Smith and Levy. While Levy feared the threat would be carried out, Smith was not impressed: 'As regards Bronnie's threat of a management censorship, this leaves me cold. Any manager can be his own censor today if he chooses. A combination would not worry me. They are far too disunited to abide by any such thing in a body.'[76] Once again, the dispute was settled by Gardiner's legal opinion. According to him, nothing could be inserted in the bill to prevent such an occurrence: 'I am sure that Equity is the answer to the informal management censorship, and in any case no clause preventing people combining to express a view against any particular play is a practical possibility.'[77]

[73] BLP, file 5/2. Letter from Levy to Paget, 8 Feb. 1949.
[74] Ibid. Smith to Levy, 22 Feb. 1949.
[75] Ibid. Gardiner to Levy, 25 Feb. 1949.
[76] Ibid. Smith to Levy, 22 Feb. 1949. Bronnie is Bronson Albery.
[77] Ibid. Gardiner to Levy, 25 Feb. 1949.

As part of his preparation for the Second Reading of the bill, Ede consulted the Lord Chamberlain on 'the need, or otherwise, for pre-production censorship'. Clarendon, in his reply, stated:

It is the Lord Chamberlain's experience that censorship of plays before production is necessary for the following reasons:—

1. It protects the public from excessive vulgarity, especially in pantomimes which are largely intended for children
2. It prevents the production of plays on perversion and other unsavoury subjects
3. It controls religious intolerance and blasphemy
4. It checks plays and passages which might give offence to foreign governments
5. It protects the individual or the family from hurtful publicity, which might arise from the personification of real people
6. It protects the managers, producers and employees from loss of contract and financial hardship.[78]

Clarendon's view was that dramatists should not enjoy the same degree of freedom as other literary authors because 'there is a considerable difference between reading, in private, certain types of books, and of sitting amongst strangers of both sexes and of all ages and watching a play . . . for the emotional and psychological effect of a stage play is recognised as being much greater than any other form of art.'[79] Similar arguments had been presented to the 1909 Joint Select Committee, which had solved the problem by recommending a voluntary system of censorship. Clarendon's final point was that 'the author of an ordinary decent play has nothing to fear from the censorship'.[80] This argument was immediately undermined by his admission that about 40 per cent of the plays he received in 1948 had to be censored in some way. It seems difficult to reconcile these two points of view. If four out of ten playwrights needed to accept some form of censorship, this seems to imply that a large number of playwrights were not writing 'ordinary decent' plays. Ede did not comment on the flawed reasoning underpinning the Lord Chamberlain's arguments.

On 7 March 1949, Levy and Smith left the draft of the bill with the Home Secretary for advice and comment. A Home Office official noted that 'they are willing to amend and would like advice'.[81] Two days later, the Theatres' National Committee forwarded to the Home Secretary their reasons why they wished the Lord Chamberlain to remain as censor. The one point which Home Office officials highlighted was the claim that the Committee 'will have no alternative but to set up its own Board to grant licences for the presentation of stage plays'.[82]

---

[78] NA, HO 45/24954. Memorandum from the Lord Chamberlain's Office to the Home Office, 3 Mar. 1949.
[79] Ibid.   [80] Ibid.   [81] NA, HO 45/24954.   [82] Ibid.

Following receipt of the Lord Chamberlain's views and the letter from the theatre managers, a draft was prepared in the Home Office for the memorandum Ede was to present to the Cabinet Legislation Committee. Ede acknowledged receipt of the draft on 13 March 1949. It recommended that:

the Government should decline to give any facilities for this Bill (which in any case stands no chance of passing into law) and that on 2nd Reading the Government should, if any statement is necessary, draw attention to the benefits to the public and the theatrical producer which result from censorship and the disadvantages which would result from the Bill, and advise the House against passing the Bill, which could only benefit the disreputable producers of revues who introduce or try to introduce objectionable matter.[83]

On 14 March, in a letter to Ede, Levy attempted to refute each of the managers' key arguments against abolition:

1. the abolition of a central censorship would expose the theatre to interminable frivolous prosecutions.

   This is covered by section 4 of the Bill, which is modelled on a Clause in the Newspaper Act of 1888 and which has proved a very adequate protection in a very analogous field.

2. local censorships would immediately proliferate to fill the vacuum.

   This is largely covered by our section 2. Incidentally, there are local censorships already, in spite of the Lord Chamberlain's office; and some very foolish and inconvenient things they have done from time to time. Under this Bill the position would be improved rather than otherwise.

3. (which is more a threat than an argument) the managers themselves might decide to establish a voluntary censorship.

   I very much doubt however whether this threat could be put into effect. Managers, after all, can only prevent the performance of a play if all the actors in England refuse to play in it. It is true that the Actors' Union (British Actors' Equity) is virtually a closed shop but, as they themselves are keenly in favour of the abolition of the censorship and indeed moved a Resolution at the British Theatre Conference last year which was supported by the League of Dramatists and unanimously passed, I think they could be relied on not to collaborate in any such threat to the freedom of the theatre.

[Our opponents] say, 'we agree that theoretically it is a wicked thing that freedom of speech should be denied to the dramatist alone in the community . . . But, shocking though all this is, somehow it works.' I can actually quote a round dozen of eminent authors who admit to having been deterred from writing for the theatre simply because

---

[83] Ibid. Unsigned draft for the Home Secretary.

they're not prepared to submit their time and property to the autocratic disposal of a fellow citizen.[84]

There is no record of any written reply to Levy. However, on the following day Kenneth Younger, Parliamentary Under-Secretary for the Home Office, prepared Ede's memorandum for the Cabinet Legislation Committee. His views were refreshingly different from those of most Home Office officials, but the conclusions he arrived at were remarkably similar:

The Government should adopt a neutral attitude . . . It may not be easy to limit one's remarks to the bald statement that the Theatres' National Committee are against it and that therefore the Government can do nothing but acquiesce in their views . . . I am quite satisfied that the present system is almost wholly indefensible. The only justification possible is that the big financial interests in the theatre require some protection . . . I think it would be most unfortunate if a Labour Government were to appear uninterested in the question of freedom of expression and concerned only with the protection of the owners' interests. The opinions of the Lord Chamberlain's Office, which are the basis of the present memorandum, seem to me pathetic in their irrelevance to the argument which we shall have to meet . . . My own view is that official pre-censorship of plays is objectionable in theory and that the practical need for it is not established . . . I suggest that I should admit its defects but indicate that, in the absence of a general consensus of opinion in the theatrical profession or any widespread demand for an alteration in the law, the Government does not feel able to give positive support to the present proposals, which will not have the effect of abolishing censorship but merely of giving rise to some other kind of censorship, the nature of which is as yet wholly undefined.[85]

The fatal flaw in the bill as drafted was that it had set out to repeal censorship without putting in place any legal alternative. Ede signed the memorandum and added that he 'had been intending to take this Bill myself on 2nd Reading'.[86]

On 22 March 1949, Ede sent his memorandum on the draft bill to the Cabinet Legislation Committee. He referred to the detailed views of the Lord Chamberlain and of the Theatres' National Committee. He then pointed out that 'offences would be left to the operation of the general law'. He had been advised that such an eventuality was inconvenient to the profession and inadequate for the protection of the public. He concluded:

In view of the expressed opposition of the theatrical producers I suggest that on Second Reading the Government spokesman should not argue the philosophical case for or against censorship, or discuss the present system or its alternatives, but should content himself with bringing to the notice of the House the considered views of

[84] Ibid. Letter from Levy to Ede, 14 Mar. 1949.
[85] Ibid. Memorandum from Younger to Ede, 15 Mar. 1949.
[86] Ibid. Handwritten reply from Ede to Younger, 15 Mar. 1949.

the Theatres' National Committee, the members of which would be the people most directly affected if the Bill were to be passed into law, and indicating that in the absence of any widespread demand for an alteration of the law the Government attitude is one of neutrality.[87]

His recommendation that the Government should adopt a pose of studied neutrality was yet another variant of the general policy, in respect of theatre censorship, of deliberate inertia. He admitted that 'censorship of plays is a controversial issue on which, on grounds of conscience, strong views are held and expressed'. This meant that the Government would be wise not to interfere or even take part in a philosophical debate on freedom of speech. Making a purely pragmatic assessment, Ede took the view that there was little chance the bill would ever become law as, 'if it reached the House of Lords, it would certainly be opposed there'.[88] Clearly, it was better that the Lords, rather than the Government, should be thought to be the obstacle that blocked the bill.

Three issues were discussed by the Cabinet Legislation Committee. Firstly, it was acknowledged that the censorship system was 'difficult to reconcile with democratic principles'. Secondly, 'the effect of the Bill would be to lead to different standards in different parts of the country' which meant that 'publicity would be focused on undesirable plays'. Thirdly, 'censorships were undesirable if they could be avoided'.[89] Despite the fact that censorship was unwelcome in principle, the committee agreed that the bill as drafted was open to serious objection. Its most likely and undesirable outcome would be local forms of censorship. It was decided that the question as to whether the Government should adopt an attitude of neutrality or of opposition was to be left to the Cabinet.

The response of the Government was soon agreed. For the meeting of the Cabinet on 24 March, 'a motion for the rejection of the Bill had been tabled',[90] even though the Cabinet Legislation Committee and the Home Secretary were 'opposed to censorship in principle'. The bluntly stated reason was pragmatism: 'the censorship of plays . . . had not in recent years given rise to any volume of public criticism; and in these circumstances it would be inexpedient for the Government to involve themselves in unnecessary controversy over this issue.'[91] The proposed bill would give rise to 'unnecessary controversy' both in the House and in the Government, as it was noted that ministers were divided on the subject. This fact was to be concealed from Members of Parliament to avoid provoking any attack on the Government

---

[87] NA, CAB 134/335. Memorandum by the Home Secretary, 18 Mar. 1949. [88] Ibid.
[89] NA, CAB 134/334. 11th Meeting of the Committee on Private Members' Bills, 22 Mar. 1949.
[90] NA, CAB 128/CM22(49). Minutes of the Cabinet meeting held on 24 Mar. 1949.
[91] Ibid.

for its cautious stance. Instead, the Home Secretary was to 'advise the House to reject this particular Bill on account of detailed defects in its structure'.[92] There was no reference in the minutes as to which defects the Government had found in the bill. Ede was merely counselled to avoid discussing censorship in general terms, particularly as he himself was not in favour of censorship.

Unfortunately for the Government, things did not go quite to plan. At the Second Reading, on 25 March 1949, there was a lively debate in Parliament and opinions were divided across party lines. The supporters of the bill emphasized the fact that only stage works were subject to censorship: no other form of literature was denied free expression. They also drew attention to the fact that the bill offered theatre managers protection from malicious prosecution. Some Members of Parliament defended the Lord Chamberlain's role as censor: others vigorously opposed the attempted neutral stance taken by the Home Secretary. Ede himself avoided discussing the issue of censorship in principle, as it could not be defended 'on the ground of logic'.[93] His attempt at criticizing the provisions of the bill was dull and unconvincing, and his views were effectively contradicted by Smith's followers. His inept presentation of the case against the bill failed to convey the fact that the Cabinet had decided to oppose the bill. His front-bench colleagues must have listened in consternation as he stated:

It is not a matter on which the Government feel that they ought to say to the House that a vote should be given one way or the other. After all, that in itself would be an attempt to impose in some ways a censorship on the House on this very delicate matter.[94]

Given Ede's personal opposition to censorship in principle, he was clearly uncomfortable at having to oppose the bill. Instead, he did his best to highlight the weaknesses of the bill as drafted:

I suggest that [the difficulties the bill will create] are at least as great as the difficulties which the present system creates, and I say quite frankly that I could not consent to the idea that a prosecution could only be undertaken if the consent of a judge in chambers had been obtained.[95]

In his concluding remarks, he once again stressed that the Government was not against the bill in principle, but considered that the bill was flawed:

The Government are neutral on the matter, and, so far as I am concerned, I regretfully think that, if the Bill goes to a Division, those difficulties which I have pointed out

---

[92] Ibid.
[93] *Hansard* (Commons), 25 Mar. 1949, vol. 463, col. 761.   [94] Ibid.
[95] Ibid., col. 765.

are so great that I should not be justified in voting for the Bill, but that is a personal opinion.[96]

This inept presentation, which was completely at odds with the instructions he had received in Cabinet, failed to convince the House. When the House divided, it was agreed by 76 votes to 37 that the bill should be given a Second Reading and then be sent to a Standing Committee for detailed consideration.

The Government's carefully prepared strategy had foundered. It is most unlikely that Ede, because of his personal dislike of censorship, had intended to galvanize support for the bill by failing to state the Government's view. The more likely explanation is that his performance on the floor of the House was yet another example of his general incompetence as Home Secretary. At the next Cabinet meeting held on 31 March, the Prime Minister expressed his disapproval of the way the Home Secretary had managed the debate in Parliament. In his view the Second Reading of the bill was a direct consequence of Ede's misleading claim that the Government was neutral whereas the Cabinet had 'understood that he would be prepared to advise the House to reject this particular Bill'.[97] Ede pleaded that he had misunderstood the Cabinet's wishes. To ensure no further 'misunderstandings', Attlee insisted that the Home Secretary 'take steps, in consultation with the Chief Whip, to ensure that the Censorship of Plays (Repeal) Bill should not be passed into law'.[98] This minute was quite unequivocal: Ede was to be assisted by an enforcer who would ensure that Cabinet instructions were carried out.

So what was it that made the Government so determined to reject the bill? In their haste to repeal all censorship provisions, the bill's sponsors had given too little thought as to what would happen to fill the vacuum left by the Lord Chamberlain. Hence, one of the key issues that concerned the Government was the prospect of the revival of the Royal Prerogative in respect of theatre censorship. At the Cabinet meeting held on 31 March, Cripps asked whether, 'if the provisions of the Theatres Act 1843 were repealed, the effect would be to revive the Prerogative Censorship'.[99] The Lord Chancellor repeated the opinion he had previously given to Smith, namely that 'the prerogative had gone when the Act of 1737 had been enacted'.[100] However, this left open the issue of what would happen if that statute, as amended in 1843, was repealed. The Prime Minister requested clear legal advice. A preliminary conclusion was

---

[96] Ibid., col. 767.
[97] NA, CAB 128/CM24(49). Minutes of the Cabinet meeting held on 31 Mar. 1949.
[98] Ibid.
[99] NA, HO 45/24954. Note by H. A. Strutt to L. S. Brass (Legal Adviser in Home Office), 31 Mar. 1949. Strutt mentioned Cripps's query because the Prime Minister had then asked the Home Secretary to provide an answer.
[100] Ibid.

reached on 8 April by H. Boggis-Rolfe, Legal Adviser in the Lord Chancellor's Office: 'the exercise of a Prerogative power is suspended by a statute covering the field of the power so long as the statute is in force.'[101] It therefore followed that 'if the relevant sections of the Act of 1843 were simply repealed, the Royal Prerogative would revive but so long as the Act of 1843 stands the Prerogative is . . . "abridged"'.[102] In other words, if the 1843 Theatres Act were simply amended, this would maintain the authority of the statute. In contrast, Smith's repeal bill would restore a Prerogative power that existed before 1737. As to the extent of that power, the Home Office knew too little about its exercise prior to 1737 to be comfortable with the possibility of its revival:

It seems from [some historical notes] that there is doubt whether the prerogative required the submission of plays for censorship in advance, or was merely a right to require the discontinuance of a play already in performance. The practice seems to have varied at different times.[103]

Though Boggis-Rolfe finally suggested that the Royal Prerogative 'would probably' be unenforceable if it were to be technically revived by the repeal of the statute, the Government might face a legal quandary if the bill became law. There were fluctuating opinions within the Home Office as to whether this point was of purely academic interest. At first, it was decided that there was no need for the Attorney-General to be consulted because 'the Bill is to be resisted by the Govt and is NOT likely to go further'.[104] But on 11 May 1949, Ede wrote to H. A. Strutt that 'it is, I fear, a rash assumption that this Bill will not be further discussed'.[105] In the following month the Home Office concluded that 'this Bill is last among Private Members' Bills & most unlikely to get beyond Committee stage'.[106] The reason the Home Office was confident that the bill would get no further was because Standing Committee E, which was to consider the bill, was not due to be set up until 23 November.

Smith and Levy had been aware of a likely delay at the Committee stage since March. In a letter written to Levy, Smith stated on 29 March:

I talked to Charlie McAndrew (Conservative MP for Bute) today about the Committee Stage. He has promised to appoint anybody we like to Standing Committee E when

[101] NA, LCO 2/4486. Memorandum on Censorship of Plays (Repeal) Bill, 1949, and Royal Prerogative sent by Boggis-Rolfe to the Lord Chancellor, 8 Apr. 1949.
[102] Ibid.
[103] Ibid. Memorandum sent by the Home Office, 16 Apr. 1949. As we have seen in earlier chapters, censorship exercised under the Royal Prerogative rarely involved pre-censorship of plays prior to production.
[104] NA, LCO 2/4486. Minute by Boggis-Rolfe after consultation with the Home Office, 29 Apr. 1949.
[105] NA, HO 45/24954. Note from Ede to Strutt, 11 May 1949.
[106] NA, LCO 2/4486. Minute by Boggis-Rolfe, 17 June 1949.

the time comes, so we must choose with care from all parties. But he went on to say, 'I must warn you that there is very little likelihood of its reaching the Committee Stage owing to the bottleneck.... I could put a little pressure on Aneurin [Bevan] (who is a personal friend of mine) to try to get him to persuade the Cabinet to adopt a similar measure on their own and introduce it in the normal way. But, of course, this is something only to be tried in the last resort.'[107]

This left very little time for the bill to be discussed in Committee and to be given a Third Reading before the end of the parliamentary session.

Although the likelihood of the bill becoming law seemed remote, through lack of parliamentary time, Shawcross, the Attorney-General, was consulted by the Lord Chancellor's Office in November. He agreed with the theoretical analysis provided by the Lord Chancellor's Office. On the practical issue of the revival of the Prerogative, however, his opinion was reassuring:

The matter is, however, somewhat academic since I do not see how, in existing circumstances, the Prerogative power could be enforced. It is possible that a prosecution might be brought as for a public mischief but I should have thought that there was little prospect of the Courts today entertaining legal proceedings to enforce the Prerogative.[108]

Though there seemed to be little prospect of the Royal Prerogative being revived in respect of censorship, it was more convenient for the Government to resist the bill than to face the legal vacuum that would be created if the 1843 Theatres Act were repealed. Ede followed the instructions he had been given in Cabinet and asked for a Home Office memorandum to be prepared on the inconsistencies of the bill. As Strutt noted: 'S of S told me that he did not want amendments put down: the Govt opposed the Bill in principle and would give it no facilities.'[109]

Now that the Government's intention was to oppose the bill on technicalities, Strutt had outlined a list of four inconsistencies for the Home Secretary to mention at the Standing Committee:

Firstly, Clause 2 would obliterate the provisions of sections 2 and 7 of the 1843 Act. Then, this power to suspend the licence of a licensed theatre would appear to be destroyed by Clause 2 unless the expression 'disorderly house' were defined in terms sufficiently wide to cover 'riot or misbehaviour'. The two Patent Theatres . . . continue, however, to be liable to be closed for 'riot or misbehaviour' under the Bill as it stands. Section 9 of the Theatres Act requires licensing authorities other than the Lord Chamberlain to make rules for ensuring order and decency at the theatres which

---

[107] BLP, file 5/2. Smith to Levy, 29 Mar. 1949.
[108] NA, LCO 2/4486. Memorandum entitled Censorship of Plays (Repeal) Bill signed by Sir Hartley Shawcross, 25 Nov. 1949.
[109] NA, HO 45/24954. Note by Strutt, 26 Nov. 1949.

they license. . . . Section 9 further provides that if a breach of the rules is proved before two Justices, the Justices may order the theatre to be closed for such time as they think fit. The existence of such rules seems incompatible with the intention of the Bill . . . and if the Bill made progress it would probably be thought necessary to incorporate in it a clause providing that any rules inconsistent with anything in the Bill shall be null and void. Section 11 of the Theatres Act provides for penalties on persons who act or present, or cause, permit or suffer the acting or presentation of a stage play in an unlicensed theatre. It would appear that under Clause 5 of the Bill as it stands an Order of a Judge at Chambers would be needed before proceedings could be taken under the Section, though this can hardly have been the intention of the promoters.[110]

When the Committee finally convened on 1 December 1949, it seemed at first that Ede was trying to avoid any detailed discussion of the bill by openly stating the Government's position: 'We regard it as a bad Bill. It raises more issues than it solves.'[111] He then queried whether the division of 25 March was truly representative of opinion in the House. After a skirmish with Levy on the issue of who was being disingenuous, Ede finally decided to bring up what he had called the inconsistencies of the bill.[112] These mainly dealt with the consequences of sections 2 and 5. He asserted that section 2 would destroy the discretion of 'the licensing authority to refuse a licence to a person whom they consider unsuitable'.[113] Levy's reply to the Home Secretary concluded with the comment: 'if my right hon. Friend had really believed for one moment that this proposal was tenable he would have seen fit to put down an Amendment.'[114] However, the Government was not prepared to consider amendments because it was opposed to the bill as a matter of principle. Following Levy's intervention, every section of the bill was ordered to stand as part of the bill. The Home Secretary remained silent for the rest of the sitting. The whole proceedings had taken less than an hour. The Leader of the House of Commons, Morrison, commented laconically:

I was told that members might learn something about drafting points in the course of considering this Bill, and that although those running it knew it was a complete waste of time, they rather liked the idea of meeting.[115]

By the time the bill reached the Standing Committee, its defects were all too apparent. Levy and Smith and their legal advisers, in drafting the bill,

---

[110] NA, HO 45/24954. Memorandum prepared by Strutt for Ede, 28 Nov. 1949.
[111] *Official Report of Standing Committee E*, 1 Dec. 1949, col. 1570.
[112] Ibid., cols. 1571 and 1573.
[113] NA, HO 45/24954. Memorandum prepared by Strutt for Ede, 28 Nov. 1949.
[114] *Official Report of Standing Committee E*, 1 Dec. 1949, col. 1574.
[115] *Hansard* (Commons), 24 Nov. 1949, vol. 470, col. 535.

had above all focused on their primary aim to ensure freedom of expression on stage. They had not considered the consequence of simply repealing parts of previous legislation without offering substantive new legislation to replace the Act as a whole. They had only specified minimal provisions to forestall local censorship and petty prosecutions. As a result they had created a bill which repealed parts of the 1843 Theatres Act but had failed to note how different sections of the Act related one to another. Furthermore, by repealing only those parts of the 1843 Theatres Act concerned with the theatre censorship exercised by the Lord Chamberlain, one unforeseen consequence of the bill would have been, at least in theory, to revive the Royal Prerogative in respect of theatre censorship. This prerogative power, if revived, would almost certainly have been devolved on a day-to-day, operational basis to the Home Office, which would then have been burdened with the direct responsibility for stage censorship. This was a prospect that the Home Office had already rejected out of hand. In drafting the bill, Gardiner had based his approach on the mistaken assumption that 'a private Bill like this does not stand much chance unless its objective is short and simple, and the Bill itself is kept free from complications'.[116]

On 8 December, Morrison, then Lord President of the Council, stated the obvious: 'I do not see much prospect of our being able to afford time for that Bill this Session.'[117] The fate of the bill was in fact decided in May, when the Chief Whip explained to the Cabinet Legislation Committee that 'Bills which were through Committee by 30th June could be considered on the last Friday set apart for Reports and Third Readings . . . Later Bills to be considered included the War Damage (Amendment) Bill and Censorship of Plays (Repeal) Bill, which the Government did not wish to see passed.'[118] The legislative programme was so impossibly crowded that the Cabinet agreed in the same month that 'time should not be made available in the 1950 Session for Private Members' Bills'.[119]

With the advantage of hindsight, it is clear that the bill fell for a number of disparate reasons. Above all, the legal implications of the bill had not been properly thought through by its sponsors. Then, the theatrical profession was hopelessly divided in its opinions and was therefore unable to provide clear guidance for the Government. Next, the legislative programme already agreed by the Labour Government was far too crowded to allow for a Private Member's Bill which was poorly drafted and which lacked unanimous support.

[116] BLP, file 5/2. Gardiner to Levy, 25 Feb. 1949.
[117] *Hansard* (Commons), 8 Dec. 1949, vol. 470, col. 2093.
[118] NA, CAB 134/334. 14th Meeting of the Cabinet Legislation Committee, 3 May 1949.
[119] NA, CAB 128/CM35(49). Minutes of the Cabinet meeting held on 16 May 1949.

Finally, the Home Secretary lacked any firm commitment to reforming legislation: indeed he seems to have lacked any social vision at all. The upshot was that the socially conservative Government led by Attlee was not prepared to waste parliamentary time on reforming legislation whose outcomes were likely to be contentious. No further attempt at abolishing or modifying the system of theatre censorship was made before 1956. None succeeded before 1968.

6

Further Attempts to end Statutory Theatre
Censorship

THE 1950s AND EARLY 1960s: THE CULTURAL
AND POLITICAL BACKGROUND

After the gloom and austerity of the immediate post-war years, the 1950s opened with the prospect of a new and brighter future for Britain. In particular, the Festival of Britain in 1951 brought a celebration of modern achievement and a reassertion of national pride: its lasting legacy was the (Royal) Festival Hall on the South Bank which embodied a spirit of cutting-edge innovation for the performance of modern classical music. Composers such as Benjamin Britten and Ralph Vaughan Williams wrote outstanding operas, choral, and orchestral works for contemporary audiences. 1951 saw premières of Vaughan Williams's music drama, *Pilgrim's Progress* and Britten's *Billy Budd* at Covent Garden. The accession of Queen Elizabeth II in 1952 inspired Britten to write his homage to the Queen entitled *Gloriana* for the Coronation year of 1953. Amongst the many splendid choral works written by Vaughan Williams was his Christmas cantata *Hodie*, which was given its première at the Festival Hall in 1954. This ferment of activity in the music scene involved a celebration of all that was new and innovative in the Performing Arts and helped to create a sense of real excitement in the London Arts world.

In contrast, London's commercial theatres seemed pedestrian and out of touch with this brave new world. The intrusive censorship exercised by the Lord Chamberlain ensured that innovative plays written by foreign authors (in particular Samuel Beckett, Arthur Miller, and Tennessee Williams) could only be viewed in club theatres, and innovative plays by British writers were few and far between. Christopher Fry continued to write thoughtful verse plays for the London theatre, including *Venus Observed* (1950), *A Sleep of Prisoners* (1951), and *The Dark is Light Enough* (1954). John Whiting's play *Saints Day* won first prize at the Festival of Britain play competition at the Arts Theatre in 1951, but it baffled contemporary critics and audiences, and has since been only rarely revived. Even his more light-hearted piece, *A Penny for a Song* (1949/50), had mixed reviews when it was first directed by Peter Brook at the Haymarket Theatre in 1951. It was not until May 1956, when John Osborne's play *Look Back in Anger* was performed at the Royal Court Theatre, that a new era began for the British theatre. Thereafter, Osborne himself and other young playwrights began to produce work that seemed both exciting and innovative to contemporary audiences. The output of these writers would involve a constant process of argument and disagreement with the Lord Chamberlain, which would by the late 1960s culminate in the abolition of theatre censorship. During the 1950s, however, the attempts to challenge the authority of the Lord Chamberlain were largely unsuccessful.

The fact was that during the 1950s and early 1960s the political scene was consistently unpromising for those interested in challenging theatre censorship (or, indeed, in raising other controversial domestic issues). First, the 1950s saw the dispiriting final days of Attlee's Labour Government. Re-elected in February 1950 with only a wafer-thin majority, a tired and divided team of ministers limped on until they lost the election of October 1951. The new Conservative Government, however, was scarcely more enterprising on the domestic front. It was led by a visibly deteriorating Churchill who, on his return to Downing Street, was already 77 years of age. It was widely assumed that he would quickly make way for his impatient heir apparent, Anthony Eden. But, despite suffering a serious stroke in 1953, he stubbornly clung on to office until past his eightieth birthday, finally stepping down with great reluctance in March 1955. It cannot be said that he made much use of his three-and-a-half years back in power. True, on the domestic front he presided over the end of rationing, a measure that was almost universally popular. But otherwise his administration was almost paralysed by fear of provoking controversy and of granting the Labour Party any chance of convincingly accusing the Conservatives of wishing to return to the 'Hungry Thirties'. In any case, Churchill himself had not been centrally interested in domestic affairs since he ceased to be Chancellor of the Exchequer as long ago as 1929. His wish, in short, was to play a major part, as during the Second World War, in shaping the destiny of the world. But to his chagrin, the United States was rarely willing to dance to his tune.

It was assumed by some that years of inertia in domestic matters, which had been made no less dreary by Attlee's decision to remain as Labour Leader, would give way to something much more dynamic once Eden, still in his fifties, succeeded as Prime Minister. He had a reputation for being a liberal-minded politician eager to embrace what later came to be called one-nation Toryism. But these hopes were dashed. By the time he got to Number Ten Eden was in desperately poor health, following a botched operation. All too soon it became apparent that he was in any case singularly ill-equipped to direct economic and social policy, mainly as a consequence of his lack of previous ministerial experience in these fields. His abiding interest was in foreign affairs. He had served as Foreign Secretary in three separate spells, but ironically this was the field that proved to be his undoing as Prime Minister.[1] He became unhealthily obsessed with the threat that Egypt's Gamal Nasser posed to British interests; and he did not have colleagues willing and able to challenge his 'silencing authority'. The upshot was the Suez fiasco of 1956 that saw the United States use economic sanctions to force Great Britain, France, and Israel to abort their ill-judged attack on Egypt.[2] Eden subsequently resigned, citing ill health, at the beginning of 1957.

Harold Macmillan, the new Prime Minister, now faced a daunting series of interconnected hard choices concerning the country's future international policies that left little time for him and his colleagues to reflect on domestic and social questions.[3] A first need for the country was to decide whether to re-establish the fractured 'special relationship' with the United States that could now only be resumed on the unambiguous basis of being a subaltern and not an equal. There was also a longer-term loss of British self-confidence in many quarters that Macmillan was certainly unable to overcome. As Margaret Thatcher wrote in her memoirs:

Harold Macmillan's great and lasting achievement was to repair the relationship with the United States. This was the essential condition for Britain to restore her reputation and standing. Unfortunately, he was unable to repair the damage inflicted by Suez on the morale of the British political class—a veritable 'Suez syndrome'. They went from believing that Britain could do anything to an almost neurotic belief that Britain could do nothing.[4]

Meanwhile another post-Suez trauma faced the British political class. Could they any longer continue to afford to run a large empire, formal and informal, in the face of growing insurgencies partly encouraged by Eden's humiliation? To the great dismay of many of his followers Macmillan decided on rapid retreat. Unsurprisingly, therefore, many agreed when Dean Acheson, the former US Secretary of State, claimed in 1962 that 'Great Britain has lost an empire but has not yet found a role'.

---

[1] For biographies of Eden see David Carlton, *Anthony Eden: A Biography* (London: Allen Lane, 1981); Robert Rhodes James, *Anthony Eden* (London: Weidenfeld and Nicolson, 1986); and D. R. Thorpe, *Eden: The Life and Times of Anthony Eden, First Earl of Avon, 1897–1977* (London: Chatto and Windus, 2003).

[2] On the Suez Crisis see Keith Kyle, *Suez* (London: Weidenfeld and Nicolson, 1991).

[3] On Macmillan see Richard Lamb, *The Macmillan Years, 1957–1963: The Emerging Truth* (London: John Murray, 1995).

[4] Margaret Thatcher, *The Path to Power* (London: HarperCollins, 1995), 91.

Though the British had entered the new decade with no very obvious grand strategy, Macmillan soon thought he had found one: the country should join the European Economic Community, a body that Eden's government had rebuffed in 1956, citing principled loyalty to the Commonwealth. After bitter battles within and between the major British political parties, the Prime Minister was authorized to apply for membership. In 1963, however, France, already distancing itself from NATO and the United States and committed to building at great expense a wholly independent nuclear arsenal, brutally vetoed the application. President Charles de Gaulle clearly thought that Great Britain, having opted to be a subaltern of the United States, was unworthy of a place at Western Europe's top table. In its own way this was a humiliation for much of the British political class no less wounding than the outcome of the Suez Crisis.

Against this tumultuous background during the premierships of Eden and Macmillan few British politicians chose to give priority to legislating on social questions, least of all one as peripheral to the day-to-day concerns of government as theatre censorship. In addition, the men who occupied the role of Home Secretary from the mid-1950s until the early 1960s showed little or no interest in cultural matters. Throughout Eden's premiership, the Home Secretary was Gwilym Lloyd George, son of the former Prime Minister. During the three years he served as Home Secretary (1954–7), he showed no inclination to favour any kind of socially reforming agenda at all. Lloyd George was succeeded as Home Secretary by R. A. (Rab) Butler who was given the post as a consolation prize for having failed to be appointed Prime Minister. He served as Home Secretary until 1962 and managed to pursue a reforming agenda in terms of a new Criminal Justice Act which became law in his final year of office. Although a distinguished reformer on issues such as education and justice, he had no particular interest in the theatre, but was at least initially willing to contemplate the need for some reform in this area. This was the unpromising political context in which renewed attempts were made to raise the issue of theatre censorship, both in the press and in Parliament, during the late 1950s and early 1960s.

CENSORSHIP, THEATRE CLUBS, AND PARLIAMENTARY QUESTIONS IN THE 1950s

The Earl of Scarbrough, Lord Chamberlain between 1952 and 1963, was a more liberal censor than his predecessors and preferred to compromise than to ban plays outright. This can be seen from his tendency to put plays in the 'waiting box' list (i.e. subject to negotiation) rather than in the 'licence refused' category. Despite this more cautious approach, many of Scarbrough's censorship decisions were subject to critical comment in the press.[5] In particular, a number of foreign plays of outstanding artistic merit were banned during Scarbrough's period of office as Lord Chamberlain. These included Robert Anderson's *Tea and Sympathy* (1954); Williams's *Cat on a Hot Tin Roof* (1955); Miller's *A View from the Bridge* (1956); and Beckett's *Endgame* (1958). All these, and other plays, had to be presented privately to theatre club audiences in London. As we have seen, the status of theatre clubs had not been resolved during the inter-war years. But they were generally tolerated under the guidelines drawn up in 1926 for theatre societies. The key issue in both cases was that any private production had to be for members only and therefore not 'for Hire'. Initially theatre clubs had catered for a minority audience. In the 1950s their membership grew significantly, which inevitably began to undermine the fragile system of toleration that had been in place for decades. Private productions had been tolerated because they were viewed as a safety valve for a minority. If private productions were no longer performed for a minority, they might be seen as undermining the whole concept of censorship practice.

Two theatre clubs in particular acquired a very large membership base during the 1950s. In 1956, the Comedy Theatre reopened as a club theatre run by the New Watergate Theatre Club (whose premises in Buckingham Street were scheduled for demolition). The Comedy Theatre was a much bigger venue and allowed for a membership that grew to 68,000 people. This extraordinary growth in membership can be attributed to the quality of the repertoire. Most of the plays presented by the club had been banned by the censor. The first production, directed by Peter Brook in 1956, was Miller's *A View from the Bridge*. For this production, it was announced, as a publicity stunt, that Marilyn Monroe had become the first club member.[6] Following productions included Anderson's *Tea and Sympathy* and Williams's *Cat on a Hot Tin Roof*. All three plays had been banned because they touched on the theme of homosexuality. The Arts, with a total membership of around 30,000, presented Peter Hall's production of *Waiting for Godot* in 1955, one of many plays banned by the Lord Chamberlain.

Inevitably, the banning of plays of outstanding artistic merit was bound to attract the attention of Members of Parliament. The first to raise the issue of

[5] See for instance the following articles in *The Times*: 'Samuel Beckett Play refused licence', 10 Feb. 1958; 'Censorship cuts in Play absurd', 3 Nov. 1958 (an adaptation of *Ulysses* at Oxford University); '15 cuts ordered in Play' (*Fings Ain't Wot They Used T'Be*), 13 Feb. 1961; 'Plea to drop Ban on Revue Items', 21 July 1962 (five sketches about President Kennedy and his family).
[6] 'Mr. Brook to Produce at Comedy', *The Times*, 10 Sept. 1956.

censorship in Parliament during the 1950s was Denis Keegan (Conservative MP for Nottingham South), supported by George Strauss (Labour MP for Vauxhall). After representations from Equity, Keegan asked the Home Secretary (Lloyd-George) in November 1956 whether he would consider abolishing or, at least, modifying the antiquated system of censorship in the theatre. Lloyd-George was unwilling to acknowledge that the Lord Chamberlain's practice was causing any anomalies which would necessitate amending the 1843 Theatres Act.[7] The following year Butler gave the same answer to Marcus Lipton (Labour MP for Brixton) when he asked for the abolition of censorship. Lipton drew attention to the way theatre clubs were proliferating in order to circumvent theatre censorship legislation:

Is not the Home Secretary aware that, for the small sum of 5s, anyone joining a club can evade this ridiculous, outdated censorship exercised by the Lord Chamberlain? Does he not realise that if the Government surrender on this issue they will get very much more public support than on other surrenders that are likely to take place in the not too distant future?[8]

This was a direct reference to the activities of the New Watergate Theatre Club where membership was a mere 5 shillings.

In 1958, the need for an amendment of the Theatres Act was suggested in the House of Lords, when the Viscount Massereene and Ferrard asked whether Her Majesty's Government 'will consider amending the law relating to the censorship of plays, in view of the fact that any member of the public can, on paying a subscription of a few shillings, see a banned play by joining one of the organisations which specialise in producing such plays for the theatre'.[9] Other members of the House of Lords, including Lord Wilmot of Selmeston and the Earl of Swinton, concurred that an inquiry was necessary into 'this picturesque survival of the past'.

Lipton's Parliamentary Question and the increasingly provocative behaviour of theatre clubs began to cause concern to the Lord Chamberlain. As a result, he decided to consult the Home Secretary to discuss 'a position in which the law and the censorship was becoming rather farcical'.[10] In preparation for this meeting, Strutt, still a senior official in the Home Office, drafted briefing notes for the Home Secretary on the legal position of club performances. Strutt's view was that 'logic would demand either—(a) the abolition of the censorship (which has been advocated in two recent Parliamentary questions

---

[7] *Hansard* (Commons), 1 Nov. 1956, vol. 558, col. 1614.

[8] Ibid., 13 May 1957, vol. 570, col. 34.

[9] *Hansard* (Lords), 6 Mar. 1958, vol. 207, col. 1197.

[10] NA, HO 300/12. Report by Lord Scarbrough on his meeting with the Home Secretary, 4 June 1957.

and in articles in some newspapers recently), or (b) the extension of the censorship to private performances'.[11] On balance, he was opposed to any legal action against theatre clubs because 'it would be a mistake to launch a prosecution at the present time. If it were to be unsuccessful, it would result in the authorities being branded by the popular Press as being Philistines; if it were successful, it would lead to a demand to relax or abolish the censorship, or to substitute a censorship by local authorities.'[12] Once again the preferred response of Home Office officials was to choose to do nothing (namely, to engage in a deliberate policy of inertia) rather than contemplate amending an Act which they themselves described as obscure and legally intricate.

Scarbrough's request for a meeting with the Home Secretary was prompted by a desire to reform current censorship practice, in order to prevent further criticism of his work. He suggested firstly the creation of a certificate which would allow only adults to certain performances and secondly a relaxation of the policy regarding homosexuality. These two proposals were linked together as criticism had sprung from the banning of *Tea and Sympathy* and *A View from the Bridge*: both plays had been performed privately at the Comedy Theatre by the New Watergate Theatre Club. Butler commented on the first point that 'this relatively minor amendment of the 1843 Act might form a suitable subject for legislation by a Private member and if this is agreed the subject might be added to the Chief Whip's list of such subjects'.[13] A draft memorandum on the amendment of the Theatres Act was prepared in August. However, technical considerations, mainly connected with the effect of the amendment in Scotland, resulted in the postponement of the initiative. In February 1958, however, Butler prepared a draft memorandum on the topic for discussion at Cabinet:

I agree with the Lord Chamberlain that there is a case for amendment of the law to enable him to pass plays on condition that children are excluded from the audience. The suggested age of admission for this purpose is 18 . . . This could be most simply achieved by a short Bill to (a) confer on the Lord Chamberlain power to declare a play unsuitable for children and (b) make it an offence by the licensee if a child is admitted to the public performance of a play declared to be unsuitable for children. Such a Bill might stir up controversy in as much as it would bring the whole question of censorship under discussion; but in itself the scheme seems likely to be widely welcomed as a sensible reform.

I see no prospect at present of Government time being found for such a Bill, but it seems a very suitable subject for a Private Member's Bill. I accordingly ask authority

---

[11] Ibid. Note from Strutt to the Secretary of State, 3 June 1957.   [12] Ibid.
[13] Ibid. Note for record, 4 June 1957.

for a Bill to be drafted on the lines suggested above, with a view to its introduction by a Private member.[14]

In the event, the memorandum was not submitted to the Cabinet and the suggested amendment was dropped. Why was this? First, the New Watergate Theatre Club closed in the same year, which effectively terminated Scarbrough's main cause for concern. Secondly, as a result of the Wolfenden Report on homosexuality, Scarbrough yielded to pressure and decided to relax his strict policy on the treatment of homosexuality on the stage. This change of policy was announced in a letter to the Theatres' National Committee published in *The Times*:

This subject is now so widely debated, written about and talked of that its complete exclusion from the stage can no longer be regarded as justifiable. In future, therefore, plays on this subject which are sincere and serious will be admitted, as will references to the subject which are necessary to the plot and dialogue, and which are not salacious or offensive.[15]

The need for a change of policy was already clear by the end of 1957, when *A View from the Bridge* was the opening production of the New Shakespeare Theatre Club, Liverpool. It attracted a private audience of 20,000. This was followed by a production of *Tea and Sympathy*, which was equally well attended. The Lord Chamberlain's change of policy would in future permit productions of similar plays of artistic merit dealing with the topic of homosexuality. However this did not imply that all plays that touched on homosexual themes would from then on be licensed. The new guidelines were as follows:

(i) Every play will continue to be judged on its merits. The difference will be that plays will be passed that deal seriously with the subject.

(ii) Plays violently homosexual will not be passed.

(iii) Homosexual characters will not be allowed if their inclusion in the piece is unnecessary.

(iv) Embraces or practical demonstrations of love between homosexuals will not be allowed.

(v) Criticism of the present homosexual laws will be allowed, though plays obviously written for propaganda purposes will be judged on their merits.

(vi) Embarrassing displays by male prostitutes will not be allowed.[16]

---

[14] NA, HO 330/12. Unsigned draft of memorandum by the Secretary of State for the Home Department and Lord Privy Seal on Amendment of The Theatres Act, Feb. 1958.

[15] 'Homosexuality on the Stage. Censorship Policy Changed', *The Times*, 7 Nov. 1958.

[16] These new guidelines were presented as evidence in the Report of the Joint Select Committee on Censorship of the Theatre, 1968, Appendix 22, 184.

Scarbrough's decision came belatedly and as a result of cumulative pressure. His authority had been undermined by club productions; at the same time changing social attitudes, as exemplified in the Wolfenden Report, were helping to modify public opinion.

Interestingly, it was not a private production that sparked off the next wave of opposition to the censor. Instead, it was a public production of Henry Chapman's *You Won't Always be on Top* by Theatre Workshop (9 October to 2 November 1957). Departures from the licensed script in performance provoked the Lord Chamberlain into initiating legal proceedings against Theatre Workshop in January 1958. On 16 April 1958, five members of Theatre Workshop were instructed to appear in court: Chapman (author and bit-part actor), Joan Littlewood (producer), Gerald Raffles (manager of Theatre Workshop), John Bury (licensee), and Richard Harris (the actor playing Nick). The summons, delivered in January 1958, was brought under section 15 of the 1843 Theatres Act. The named individuals were charged with presenting parts of a play that had not been allowed by the Lord Chamberlain. Wayland Young (drama critic of *Tribune*) opened a defence fund which reached £150 to pay for a good defence lawyer: he had Gardiner in mind. His appeal for financial support was signed by prominent theatrical personalities, including Lord Harewood, George Devine, Wolf Mankowitz, Richard Findlater, Henry Sherek, Peter Hall, and Kenneth Tynan. Sir Alec Guinness and Michael Redgrave sent messages of support in favour of Theatre Workshop. Gardiner and his co-counsel Harold Lever (Labour MP for Manchester Cheetham) waived any charges for their services.

For Theatre Workshop the problem was that improvisation was central to Littlewood's approach to directing. Ian Smith argued for the prosecution that there was a significant divergence between the script as licensed and the script as witnessed on 31 October and 1 November by representatives of the Lord Chamberlain's Office: 'In the second act something like 25 or 30% of the matter was in a form never submitted to the Lord Chamberlain. The third act was almost completely new—something like 80 to 90%.'[17] He went on to state that the alterations had rendered passages 'vulgar or not in good taste'. This meant that the V-sign had allegedly been made on stage. In particular, he also contended that Churchill had been satirized in an unbecoming manner. He referred to a scene outside a building labelled 'Gentlemen' during which a character called Nick made a speech in which he appeared to be opening the building. As he spoke he altered his voice to imitate that of Churchill. He went on to give his version of

---

[17] 'Lines not approved by Lord Chamberlain', *Manchester Guardian*, 17 Apr. 1958.

what Churchill would have said had he been called upon to open a public lavatory.[18]

Gardiner advised the defendants to plead guilty to what was a trivial accusation. He pointed out for the defence that 'if there had been any charge of obscenity the issue would have been contested'.[19] The defendants were duly fined but the case, reported in every national newspaper, reflected badly on the Lord Chamberlain. The fines themselves were nominal: Chapman and Harris were given conditional discharges on payment of 11*s*. 6*d*. each; Joan Littlewood was fined £2; John Bury £5 and Gerry Raffles £5, with £2. 19*s*. 11*d*. costs. In Littlewood's own words: 'We got off scot-free, cautioned not to commit the same offence again.'[20] Young then decided 'to divide the residue of the fund, after the payment of such expenses as there have been, fifty-fifty between the general purposes of Theatre Workshop and a new fund now being set up, with the self-explanatory title of "Censorship Reform" '.[21] The net outcome of this ill-advised attempt at prosecution was that censorship legislation had been defied openly and with impunity. The derisory fines levied were a clear sign that the matter should never have been brought to court. In addition, the case initiated by the Lord Chamberlain helped to kick start the formation of a committee dedicated to the abolition of theatre censorship.

THE THEATRE CENSORSHIP REFORM COMMITTEE

The Theatre Censorship Reform Committee was officially formed at a meeting organized by the English Stage Society at the Royal Court Theatre on 20 April 1958. Young stated that 'its provisional charter would be to press for the liberalisation of the theatre censorship'.[22] While Maurice Edelman (Labour MP for Coventry North and a novelist) hoped for the end of the 'Court flunkey, answerable to nobody democratically', Dingle Foot (Labour MP for Ipswich) announced that he would ask the Government to legislate. The initial list of supporters of the committee, chaired by the journalist Sir Gerald Barry, included other journalists, politicians, playwrights, theatre professionals, and academics. This list included: Noel Annan, Anthony Asquith, Frith Banbury, Neville Coghill, Ronald Duncan, Edelman, George Fearon, Richard Findlater,

---

[18] 'Divergence from permitted script of Play. Fines after Theatre Workshop Performances', *The Times*, 17 Apr. 1958.
[19] 'Lines not approved by Lord Chamberlain', *Manchester Guardian*, 17 Apr. 1958.
[20] Joan Littlewood, *Joan's Book* (London: Methuen, 1994), 511.
[21] 'Theatre Workshop', *Observer*, 20 Apr. 1958.
[22] 'Plea for Stage Freedom', *The Times*, 21 Apr. 1958.

Charles Fletcher-Cooke, Dingle Foot, Clive Goodwin, Alec Guinness, Roy Jenkins, Levy, Wolf Mankowitz, Norman Marshall, Tina Murdoch, Sean O'Casey, Osborne, Edward Percy, Robert S. W. Pollard, Robert Sharrow, Kenneth Tynan, and Young.[23] Some, notably Annan and Jenkins, were in the following decade to play a key role in the eventual abolition of theatre censorship. Not surprisingly, Levy was also a member.

Soon after the prosecution against Theatre Workshop, and the announcement in the press that the Government was considering the question of censorship, Levy tried to arrange a meeting with the Home Secretary. Earlier that year, Levy had already prepared, in consultation with Harewood and Ronald Duncan, a memorandum which he considered as 'a spring-board for discussion with Scarbrough and his colleagues'. The aim of his proposals was to effect reform rather than complete abolition of the censorship system. What he envisaged was:

That the Censor's office should be empowered to issue two categories of certificate for plays, i.e. those fit for adult audiences and those fit for universal audiences. This would replace the existing system whereby the Censor is faced with the alternative of passing a play in toto, or of mutilating it, or of banning it.[24]

This would restore to dramatists the same freedom as any other citizen under the law with the proviso that frivolous prosecutions should be avoided by requiring the approval of a Judge in Chambers for any prosecution to be brought. These were presumably the ideas Levy wished to discuss with Butler. In the event, it was Butler's Joint Parliamentary Under-Secretary, David Renton (Conservative MP for Huntingdonshire), who met with Levy and explained: 'Neither he nor the Civil Servant were at all hostile to the idea and assured me that such announcements as had been made on the line of "active consideration" did not at all mean that Government ideas had crystallized on the subject.'[25] Levy concluded from his discussion with Renton that 'consideration was not yet active at all except in the abused parliamentary sense of the word'.[26] Given that the amendment to the 1843 Theatres Act prepared by Butler in February had not been forwarded to the Cabinet, Levy's comment on the Government's intentions was probably correct.

While Levy had attempted to exert some pressure behind the scenes, the creation of the Theatre Censorship Reform Committee was intended as a means of exerting concerted public pressure on the Government. The first meeting was held on 5 June 1958; the last one on 3 July 1959. The initial

---

[23] See 'Sir G. Barry Chairman of new committee', *The Times*, 2 May 1958.
[24] BLP, file 1/10. Levy to Duncan, 27 Jan. 1958.
[25] Ibid. Levy to Duncan and Harewood, 13 May 1958.   [26] Ibid.

decision taken by the committee was to gather information on current attitudes to censorship and current censorship practice, as such information was not readily available in the public domain. The committee wrote to the various interest groups involved and to the Lord Chamberlain's Office. In response, Equity and the League of Dramatists confirmed their support for the abolition of censorship. The Lord Chamberlain's Office, however, refused to forward details of banned plays and prosecutions to an organization of 'unofficial character'.[27]

A working committee which included Eric Falk, Fletcher-Cooke, Hugh Jenkins (General Secretary of Equity),[28] Levy, Tynan, and Young was then constituted to prepare a draft bill. Though it followed the broad aims of the 1949 repeal bill, the new bill entitled 'Theatres Act 1958' sought to repeal the whole, rather than a part, of the 1843 statute. The first section of the bill dealt in five clauses with the theatres. The clauses preventing the withholding of theatre licences by local authorities were similar to Levy's bill. Section 2 concentrated on stage plays. After much discussion, it was decided not to include any prohibition against the representation of living persons on stage. With respect to the sovereign, the committee thought the law of sedition was ample protection. Clause 9 was designed to protect further the interests of the managers against frivolous prosecutions:

No criminal prosecution arising out of the performance of any stage play shall be commenced against any manager, owner, or lessee of a theatre, or any dramatist, or any person directly or indirectly responsible for or associated with the production or performance of such play, without the order of a Judge in Chambers.

PROVIDED that the prosecution shall give forty eight hours' notice to the said manager, owner, lessee, dramatist, or other person that application for such an order is to be made to a Judge in Chambers, and provided also that they or any of them shall have the right to be heard against such application.[29]

This provision once more echoed Levy's 1949 bill, but with the addition of a two-day notice for any prosecution. Tynan, however, pointed out that 'this clause would put managers in such an exposed position, particularly on tour, that they might be expected to become more timid than they are now'.[30]

The problem of having to close down a play before a court hearing, which might involve a delay of several weeks, was another issue that needed careful consideration. Such an eventuality was bound to affect the managers' willingness to present plays that might prove controversial. West End theatre

---

[27] Ibid., file 1/11. Confidential letter from Sir Norman Gwatkin (Lord Chamberlain's Office) to Young, 16 June 1958.
[28] Jenkins was to become one of the members of the 1966 Joint Select Committee.
[29] BLP, file 1/11, 'Theatres Act 1958'.   [30] Ibid. Meeting report, 28 Oct. 1958.

managers were already cautious in their response to new work. Generally they waited for successful productions of new plays in theatre clubs before considering a transfer to the West End. The committee was well aware that, if the bill was to be accepted by the managers, they needed a tight legal framework to protect them from prosecution and from censorship by local authorities. On previous occasions when reform had been attempted, the Government had been able to state that not all sectors of the theatrical profession were in favour of the abolition of censorship: the support of the managers was therefore crucial.

In view of Tynan's objections and with no immediate alternative in view, Levy expressed doubts about the draft provisions of the bill. Other members followed his lead. As a result, another bill was drafted in December 1958. Instead of requiring total abolition of the 1843 Theatres Act, the new draft bill (Licensing of Plays Amendment Act) repealed sections 12, 14, 15, and 16 of the 1843 Theatres Act. Censorship was still to be exercised by the Lord Chamberlain, but the licence was to be replaced by a certificate. The two main clauses dealt with the protection of managers. On this topic, the only change from the previous draft was the involvement of the Director of Public Prosecutions: 'No prosecution arising out of the presentation or performance of any play shall be commenced without the order of a Judge in Chambers made upon application only by the Director of Public Prosecutions.'[31] A plan of action was drawn up to hand the bill to the Government and to postpone any publicity campaign until the bill was published. Once again, however, Levy opposed the new draft bill.

In Levy's view, the bill was unclear. Its aim was twofold: to initiate a system of voluntary censorship, so that submitting plays to the Lord Chamberlain would be optional, and to replace the Lord Chamberlain's licence or ban by a certificate. The notion of a voluntary system of censorship had already been recommended by the 1909 Joint Select Committee, and it had not met with widespread approval. As for certification, it was not made clear whether the committee contemplated a system of certification similar to that used by the British Board of Film Censors. If the Lord Chamberlain were to remain the censor, any play of which he disapproved or which he had not certified would still be suspect in the eyes of the theatre managers. If a manager was courageous enough to present a play without the censor's certificate (which would be a perfectly legal thing to do), and if a prosecution ensued, then it would be likely that the lack of a certificate would prejudice the court. It was probable that only plays without a certificate would be prosecuted. Levy was not convinced that this new bill was sufficiently clear to succeed; there were

---

[31] Ibid., 'Licensing of Plays Amendment Act'.

still too many flaws that recalled his own ill-fated attempt to introduce a bill in 1949. Meanwhile, he wrote to the chairman of the committee explaining that the best course of action for the moment was to maintain the kind of parliamentary pressure that had already led to reforms of censorship practice on the part of the Lord Chamberlain:

If it is true that the Lord Chamberlain is beginning to help safeguard the serious author instead of harassing him, then this crossing of the line is partly due to those who have continued to raise their protesting voices in the Press, Parliament and elsewhere. I don't doubt that this Committee, for example, with its 'high-powered' membership has had its effect, and it might be a very good thing if we were to stay in being as a permanent Vigilance Committee, calling meetings ad hoc whenever abuses were brought to our attention. The mere fact of our existence would be salutary.[32]

The draft amendment bill was eventually rejected by the committee because it would create additional legal problems for managers. Both the Lord Chamberlain and the Director of Public Prosecutions would be involved in any court case: a possible clash between these two authorities seemed undesirable. Despite the lawyers' conclusion that 'evidence of the withholding of a Lord Chamberlain's certificate would not be admissible',[33] Levy was concerned about this crucial argument:

The Director is unlikely to prosecute what the Lord Chamberlain has passed simply on the grounds of bureaucratic freemasonry. But if this is so, isn't the Home Office correspondingly unlikely to accept this draft Bill, since its result must be to invite perpetual anomalous comparison between the judgments of the Courts and the judgments of St James's Palace?[34]

He went on to draw attention to the likely embarrassment that might be caused to the Arts Council by the draft bill:

The Arts Council . . . would be in a hell of a predicament if it could be shot at for subsidising with public funds, plays that bypass the Lord Chamberlain or were banned by him. A nice brouhaha there would be if a play supported by Arts Council money were successfully prosecuted![35]

Failures of past attempts to repeal the 1843 Theatres Act and to abolish censorship explain Levy's legal and political objections. Despite his prominent role in the committee, his opposition to new draft legislation was deeply regretted by Young, who was eager to proceed with a bill in view of the obvious defects of censorship:

---

[32] Ibid., file 1/10. Levy to Young and Barry, 21 Jan. 1959.
[33] Ibid., file 1/11. Meeting report, 2 Mar. 1959.
[34] Ibid., file 1/10. Levy to Falk, 3 Feb. 1959.   [35] Ibid.

[W]e should have clear between us now which direction we are both going in! . . . What it really comes to, is that I think you ought either to support something, or else let those that do go ahead! We adopted your own 1949 bill, revised it, and you and Ken made us drop it. Then I injected the compromise bill, we revised it in the drafting subcommittee, and then you made us drop it.[36]

This not entirely amicable division of opinion was reported at the meeting of 2 March, when a decision had to be made as to the future role of the committee. The alternatives facing the committee were summarized as follows:

For proceeding now: —

1) The Lord Chamberlain still in fact making arbitrary decisions and could reverse recent liberalisation

2) Playwrights discouraged from spending time on some subjects in fear of censorship difficulties

3) Censorship of plays on political and religious subjects, and about historical characters still unaffected by liberalisation

4) The Lord Chamberlain now yielding under pressure and this was the time to finish the system altogether

5) It would in practice be some time before the Bill could be presented to Parliament, and much more work could be done in mustering support in the meantime.

Against proceeding now: —

1) This is a bad time tactically to muster support, the recent relaxation and announcement of policy having removed many of the strongest arguments for abolition

2) At the moment more adventurous plays were being presented with The Lord Chamberlain's certificate than managements would dare to put on without it. Thus the censorship system was at the moment more an encouragement than otherwise

3) In time, public opinion would become accustomed to the more liberal theatre resulting from the above; managers would then not need to fear prosecution by offended minorities if the present system of censorship were abolished.[37]

This attempt to define the future strategy of the committee was prompted by a proposal from Lord Huntingdon to open a debate on censorship in the Lords, which was seen as an opportunity to test public opinion. However, influenced by Levy's arguments, Huntingdon abandoned his Lords' Motion. The drive to take clear policy decisions was further diminished when Sir Frank Soskice (Labour MP for Newport and Opposition spokesman on legal affairs) was invited to a meeting of the committee. Like Levy, he doubted 'the wisdom of disturbing the present situation on the grounds that the present climate

---

[36] Ibid. Young to Levy, 29 Mar. 1959.   [37] Ibid., file 1/11. Meeting report, 2 Mar. 1959.

allowed for a considerable degree of lenience in licensing'.[38] The committee was still hoping to bring forward proposals for new legislation and suggested two new schemes: revert to the total abolition bill and add a right of appeal, or give the Lord Chamberlain an Advisory Board (the Board created in 1910 had been dormant since the 1930s) which would have power to overrule the censor's decisions. Soskice's political opinion, not surprisingly, was that 'any Government would prefer either of these to either of the Committee's draft Bills'.[39] By the time of its last meeting in July 1959, the committee had failed to draft any new bill as it was felt that the likely outcome of the forthcoming election would not favour new legislation. As expected, Macmillan was re-elected and there was no prospect that his Conservative Government would change its view on theatre censorship. The committee therefore settled for a watching brief.

In order to stifle calls for the complete abolition of censorship, Scarbrough had made a few concessions to public taste in the way censorship was exercised. But for the most part, censorship practice (apart from a more tolerant view of homosexual material) remained unchanged. The real reason that no action was taken in Parliament was lack of unanimity on the part of those who wanted the abolition of theatre censorship. And this time theatre managers (the traditional opponents of change) had not even been implicated. The legal and political difficulties involved in abolishing or amending censorship legislation suggested that only the Government would be able to decide on the fate of censorship when it was ready to draft its own bill. But the fact of the committee's existence may have been instrumental in persuading the Lord Chamberlain to take account of public opinion. The committee may also for a brief period have served to keep the issue of censorship alive in the minds of the Government and of theatre practitioners. But its lifespan was too short to have any long-term effects.

Two further attempts by Members of Parliament to ask for theatre censorship to be investigated or abolished were opposed by the Home Secretary. In 1958, following the Theatre Workshop court case, Butler had been careful to acknowledge the difficulties inherent in the censorship system when Dingle Foot made a plea for abolition.[40] By 1960, however, when all formal campaigning for the abolition of theatre censorship had ceased, he reverted to the usual Home Office response when asked for an enquiry into censorship by Stephen Swingler (Labour MP for Newcastle under Lyme).[41]

---

[38] Ibid. Meeting report, 19 Mar. 1959.   [39] Ibid.

[40] *Hansard* (Commons), 8 May 1958, vol. 587, col. 1414.

[41] Ibid., 14 July 1960, vol. 626, col. 1569.

In 1962, Dingle Foot, under the Ten Minute Rule, was permitted to move 'that leave be given to bring in a Bill to make it optional to submit a play to the Lord Chamberlain for licence, and legal to perform an unlicensed play whether it has been submitted or not'.[42] Bills introduced under the Ten Minute Rule have little chance of finding their way on to the statute book, but they offer an opportunity for a Member of Parliament to draw attention to an issue and to test Parliament's opinion. Foot gave a concise summary of the history of censorship since the 1737 Licensing Act and pointed to some of the absurdities to which it gave rise, notably in those cases when plays relied on improvisation. He concluded his argument by asserting that 'it is astonishing that we have put up with this essentially silly form of restriction for two-and-a-quarter centuries'.[43] His motion was opposed by W. R. Rees-Davies (Conservative MP for the Isle of Thanet) who asserted that there was an unbroken line of censorship activity stretching back to Henry VIII. Rees-Davies, with deliberate disingenuousness, ignored the distinction between censorship exercised under the Royal Prerogative and censorship defined in statute law. He also quoted partial and therefore completely misleading passages from the 1909 Joint Select Committee report. When the House divided, Foot's motion was lost by 77 votes to 134. This was the last attempt to raise the issue of theatre censorship during Macmillan's administration.

It was only when the Labour Party came to power under Wilson's premiership in 1964 that theatre censorship legislation would be finally repealed. The various previous attempts to seek reform or abolition of the 1843 Theatres Act had all foundered because of divisions within the theatrical profession (immediately exploited by Home Office officials or spokesmen) or because of drafting errors in the preparation of bills to replace the 1843 Theatres Act. It was not until Wilson's administration that those who were keen to see the abolition of theatre censorship were finally given government assistance to prepare a draft bill that would satisfy all parties within the theatrical profession and close all the legal loopholes that had previously baffled those in Parliament who advocated or supported reform. It required further battles with the censor, an articulate new generation of playwrights, a significant shift of public opinion, and the intervention of a reforming Home Secretary, to persuade even Wilson's Cabinet to offer the necessary support to those advocating reform. But as soon as the Government agreed to give drafting assistance to the reformers, the way was finally open to effect a lasting change to the statutes of 1737 and 1843 that had for so long prevented freedom of expression on the stage.

---

[42] Ibid., 5 Dec. 1962, vol, 668, col. 1321.   [43] Ibid., col. 1326.

7

The 1960s and the 1968 Theatres Act

THE EARLY WILSON ERA

In October 1964, after thirteen years in the wilderness, the Labour Party, led by Harold Wilson, returned to office with an overall majority in the House of Commons of just three. It was obvious that another general election could not be long delayed. In March 1966 the electorate was in effect asked whether Labour had made a sufficiently good impression to merit confirmation in power. The verdict was positive and the Labour Party entered upon a four-year period with a majority of around one hundred seats: only the second occasion on which Labour had ever been accorded a clear working majority.

Among Labour Party activists, and in much of the population generally, hopes were high that the Wilson Government would go down in history as one with a reforming record comparable to those of the Edwardian Liberals and of Attlee. But Wilson and his Cabinet quickly lost their way. They began to suffer by-election defeats with huge adverse swings that were unprecedented; and in 1970 they were to go down to ignominious defeat at the hands of Edward Heath and the Conservatives. At the time and subsequently, even Labour zealots concluded that the party's record in office between 1966 and 1970 was not one in which to take much pride.

Only two Government ministries appear to have avoided the generally negative verdict among party activists in respect of Wilson's administration. These were Education and the Home Office. In the case of Education the late 1960s saw Labour introducing major innovations. This was perhaps all the more striking in view of the party's unimpressive record in this field under the premierships of MacDonald and Attlee. The death-knell was sounded for the eleven-plus examination and the country put firmly on the road to comprehensive secondary education. The expansion of higher education was accelerated by the Secretary of State, Anthony Crosland, who introduced the so-called polytechnics, which were meant to favour technological and vocational subjects. Finally, the Minister of State with responsibility for the Arts, Jennie Lee (Bevan's widow), launched the Open University, which was to be the world's first major experiment in distance learning for mainly mature people. Significantly, Wilson later came to regard the founding of the Open University as the major achievement of his term of office.[1]

The Home Office's principal achievement was to preside over radical changes in legislation governing social and personal behaviour. Capital punishment was first suspended in 1965 and then permanently ended in 1969. Abortion was made legally available in 1967. Homosexual acts between consenting males in private were decriminalized in 1967. The Divorce Reform Act of 1969 introduced the irretrievable breakdown of marriage as one of the grounds for divorce. This meant that divorce was for the first time made possible on the basis of mutual consent (after a separation of two years) rather than requiring proof of a matrimonial offence.[2] Finally, and of central interest for our present enquiry, the antiquated system of theatre censorship, introduced by Walpole in 1737, was at last abolished in 1968.

Generally, in such matters the traditional line was that Members of Parliament could exercise their individual judgements according to their consciences and that party whips should play no part. This was to be the case again in the late 1960s. Even so, successive Home Secretaries, Soskice, Jenkins, and James Callaghan, as well as the Prime Minister, the Cabinet, and the Government's business managers, had roles of determining importance. For, as happened in 1949 with the failed attempt to abolish theatre censorship, they could in practice deny backbenchers the necessary time to enable Private Members' Bills, however popular, to become law. In the late 1960s there was not only a clear majority in the Commons (by no means involving only Labour Members of Parliament) in favour of these social changes but also an administration, which, despite some hesitation and wavering, was willing to assist. The result was that the Labour Government as a whole, and Jenkins in particular, were able in later years, not unfairly, to claim that their Home Office record was outstanding and contrasted very favourably with the otherwise largely poor performance of the Wilson Government.

Why, then, was the broad picture with respect to the 1966–70 period so dismal? At the heart of most of the difficulties was the Wilson Cabinet's handling of the economy.[3] Arguably the most damaging event was the sterling crisis of November 1967 when devaluation was visibly forced by

---

[1] On Crosland see Susan Crosland, *Tony Crosland* (London: Jonathan Cape, 1982); and Kevin Jefferys, *Anthony Crosland* (London: Richard Cohen Books, 1999). On Lee see Patricia Hollis, *Jennie Lee: A Life* (Oxford: Oxford University Press, 1997).

[2] The playwright George Farquhar had pleaded for divorce by consent in his comedy, *The Beaux Stratagem*, written in 1707. It took even longer to achieve this change in legislation than it did to abolish the statute on theatre censorship introduced in 1737.

[3] For an early work on Labour's handling of the economy see Wilfred Beckerman (ed.), *The Labour Government's Economic Record* (London: Duckworth, 1972). For a more recent

market pressure on a reluctant Cabinet. This turned out to be the disastrous defining moment for the Wilson Government, which cost Callaghan his position as Chancellor and saw him moved sideways to Home Secretary. While devaluation was not in itself ruinous, far from it, it was inevitably seen, because of the uncompromising language used by ministers in earlier years, as an unwanted defeat for the country rather than as an opportunity to break out of a straitjacket. Secondly, Wilson personally blundered in telling the nation in a television broadcast that the 'pound in your pocket' had not been devalued. To many these words seemed patronizing or even seriously misleading. Connected to the Labour Government's economic woes was a gradual worsening in industrial relations. Wilson found himself faced by a drift towards extremism in the trades unions, and especially so after the collapse of the Government's broad economic strategy symbolized by devaluation and the accompanying deflation.

In addition to these domestic issues, a series of setbacks that occurred on the international front contributed to the general feeling of malaise afflicting the Labour Government. A serious humiliation for Wilson and his Cabinet was occasioned by the decision of Ian Smith and his colleagues in Southern Rhodesia (now Zimbabwe) to end notional British colonial status by making a Unilateral Declaration of Independence (UDI) on 11 November 1965. The White House was angry with London because of Britain's lukewarm support over Vietnam. The Kremlin continued to resist any serious moves towards détente. Meanwhile, the Wilson Cabinet decided in May 1967 to try and build new links with Europe. The first step was to seek to remove President Charles de Gaulle's veto of British membership of the European Economic Community, which he had first exercised, to the glee of many in the Labour Party, against Macmillan's Government in January 1963. Eventually Wilson got the same negative answer in November 1967. But the Labour Cabinet's public preparations to make a new formal application proved divisive throughout the Labour Movement. Once again, therefore, many Labour backbenchers were reinforced in their determination to have their way on social issues that were supposedly a matter for their individual consciences.

The backbenchers in question were as a collective group significantly different from their predecessors in the Attlee era. They were certainly less likely to be from a working-class, trades union background. Many of those elected for the first time in 1964 and 1966 were well-educated lawyers, lecturers, and teachers. Moreover, some represented constituencies which had

analysis see Edmund Dell, *A Strange Eventful History: Democratic Socialism in Britain* (London: HarperCollins, 2000). Dell was a junior minister during the late 1960s, but his account is far from flattering to his senior colleagues.

never previously had Labour Members of Parliament. The Labour Cabinet in the 1960s was also very different in character from those headed by MacDonald and Attlee. Many appointed by Wilson had university degrees. Indeed, graduates of Oxford University who served in the Cabinet during this period included the following: Wilson himself, Jenkins, Barbara Castle, Patrick Gordon Walker, Crosland, Soskice, Michael Stewart, Denis Healey, Anthony Greenwood, Richard Crossman, Anthony Wedgwood Benn (as he was then known), and Lord Longford. These people were by no means, however, all from the same mould. For they had not all held similar views even when at Oxford. For example, during the late 1930s Wilson had been mainly non-political; Healey had been a member of the Communist Party; and Jenkins and Crosland had been democratic socialists committed to trying to break the grip of the Communists on the Oxford Labour Club.

Non-graduates were thus the exception rather than the rule in Wilson's Cabinet. However, they included two with real weight, namely Callaghan and George Brown, who had served as trades union officials before entering Parliament. Both, because of their positions in government, were to play an important role in the matter of theatre censorship. Given that both were socially conservative, it might come as a surprise that they helped the progressive cause; though in both cases personal hostility to Wilson may have been a factor in their calculations.[4] In fact, Wilson himself, despite his background as a graduate and a don at Oxford and as a reputed Bevanite in the 1950s, was, as will be seen, to be no 'knee-jerk progressive' on social issues during the 1960s. The fact was that he had lower middle-class roots in West Yorkshire that left him with at least some strong traits that Oxford could not or at least did not succeed in eliminating.[5] He was a nonconformist Christian by upbringing, married to the daughter of a Congregationalist Minister. He was personally a puritan in many different respects: he dressed soberly, rarely used profanities, discouraged adultery among his ministers, and claimed to prefer tinned to smoked salmon. Certainly in the street in which he lived as a boy few people would have thought they needed access to easier divorce or abortion or pornography, and few would have been opposed to theatre censorship.

Wilson was also something of a philistine. He rarely visited the theatre or the opera, occasional exposure to Gilbert and Sullivan or *The Messiah* being

---

[4] On Callaghan see James Callaghan, *Time and Chance* (London: William Collins, 1987); and Kenneth O. Morgan, *Callaghan: A Life* (Oxford: Oxford University Press, 1997).

[5] For information on Wilson see Philip Ziegler, *Wilson: The Authorised Life* (London: Weidenfeld and Nicolson, 1993); and Ben Pimlott, *Harold Wilson* (London: HarperCollins, 1992).

rather more to his taste. Indeed, Philip Ziegler, his authorized biographer, tells a revealing story about his ignorance of theatrical matters:

Once, at a gala evening, he was forced to sit through extracts from a number of plays: *The Rivals, Henry V, The Importance of being Earnest.* In the interval he was heard to ask—it seems guilelessly—'Do you think anyone has seen any of these plays all through?'[6]

He was from boyhood a supporter of Huddersfield Town Football Club and had no time for such pastimes as Rugby Union or hunting, the preserve in his eyes of 'toffs'. Yet, perhaps unsurprisingly, his social conservatism made him paradoxically somewhat deferential towards the British royal family. Getting on well with Elizabeth II (with whom as Prime Minister he was required to have a weekly meeting), he would naturally have been troubled by any developments likely to cause her distress. So it may be that Wilson's deferential instincts led him to exercise extreme caution with respect to the one social reform that touched on the role of the Royal Household, namely theatre censorship.

Another Oxonian had a more confident and robust approach to social reform generally and to the monarchy in particular: this was Jenkins.[7] He too, however, had lower middle-class, provincial origins that might superficially have seemed likely to imbue him with similar inhibitions to Wilson's. But in Jenkins's case, the reverse was true. He emerged from Oxford as someone with no trace of a regional accent and with a taste for good living that led his critics in later years to speak of him looking at the world through claret-splashed spectacles. True, he was glad to follow his father into the House of Commons in the Labour interest but he did not, perhaps fortunately, succeed in obtaining a seat in his native South Wales, being rejected, for example, in Ogmore in favour of a trades union official. He did manage, however, to represent first Central Southwark in 1948 and then Birmingham Stechford from 1950 onwards. These constituencies in the country's two largest cities were convenient for his urbane lifestyle and enabled him effectively to cut any remaining political ties with provincial backwaters. Wilson, by contrast, was to represent Huyton in Lancashire, which had a large Roman Catholic element, probably a constraint on him when issues like abortion, divorce, and homosexuality were on the political agenda.[8]

---

[6] Ziegler, *Wilson*, 47.

[7] On Jenkins see John Campbell, *Roy Jenkins: A Life* (London: Weidenfeld and Nicolson, 1983); and Roy Jenkins, *A Life at the Centre* (London: Macmillan, 1991).

[8] For example, one writer has claimed that 'Wilson was worried by the number of Catholics in his constituency of Huyton' when David Steel was promoting his bill concerning abortion. See Clive Ponting, *Breach of Promise: Labour in Power* (London: Hamish Hamilton, 1989), 266.

Jenkins was never to be sponsored by a trades union. He associated himself with the right-leaning former Economics don Hugh Gaitskell, and he was to favour throughout his career ever-closer British involvement with continental Europe. He also wrote several academically respectable books on themes connected with late Victorian and Edwardian Liberalism, suggesting to some that he would have felt more politically at home in that era rather than in a mid-twentieth-century political party that paid at least lip-service to socialism.[9] Clearly he was no populist, and, probably rather to his credit, his trades unionist father was seldom invoked in his speeches even to the Labour Movement. So we can safely say that Labour traditionalism held no appeal for Jenkins. On the other hand, his commitment to social reform was clearly signalled long before he became Home Secretary. In August 1959, for example, he wrote in the *Spectator*:

On the whole range of issues where much progress remains to be made—hanging, Wolfenden [homosexuality and prostitution], the licensing laws, betting reform, Sunday observance, divorce, theatre censorship, police control, the abortion laws— there is immensely more to be hoped for from a Labour Home Secretary than from the most liberal Conservative Minister.[10]

In this same period, with Labour in Opposition, he was able to play a major role in promoting a Private Member's Bill that led to the reform of the law governing obscene publications.[11] Such then was the Home Secretary who played the leading role in the Cabinet in facilitating a legislative transformation in the direction, as he saw it, of tolerance, humanity, and a civilized society. But in the Cabinet he had fewer natural allies than might have been expected given the presence of so many supposedly civilized Oxonians.

What finally can we say about the general *Zeitgeist* in which politicians debated the merits and demerits of permissive legislation during the 1960s? This was, after all, an era of great social upheaval throughout the West. Britain would therefore have changed greatly even if Westminster legislators had adhered to a reactionary outlook. These were the years of, for example, *That Was The Week That Was*, of *Oh! What A Lovely War*, of the first publication in Great Britain of *Lady Chatterley's Lover*, of the emergence of The Rolling Stones, of miniskirts, of the occupation of university and college campuses by students in revolt, of the widespread recreational use for the first time of cannabis, of the siege of the US Embassy in Grosvenor Square by anti-Vietnam protestors, and, perhaps most significantly, of the general availability to women of the contraceptive pill. Linking this wider ferment of sexual

[9] His historical books published before he held high office included *Mr. Balfour's Poodle* (1958) and *Asquith* (1964). See notes to Chapter 4.
[10] Quoted from Campbell, *Roy Jenkins*, 55.   [11] Ibid. 53–4.

libertarianism and general iconoclasm to the conduct of mostly middle-aged and elderly politicians at Westminster is not particularly easy. Indeed, there is not much evidence that the passing of a wide range of liberal legislation was in any way the product of external pressure. Rather it would seem that had committed puritans held the Home Office throughout Wilson's premierships and had Jenkins been sent, say, to Washington as British Ambassador in 1964, the progressive backbenchers could easily have been frustrated just as they had been in Attlee's time. However, under the guiding hand of Jenkins, a reforming Home Secretary, the Wilson Government distinguished itself by facilitating a swathe of socially reforming legislation that was to alter radically people's personal, social, and cultural freedoms. Looking back on the sixties shortly before his death in 2002, Jenkins claimed modestly to have found a 'liberal hour', which facilitated his reforming agenda. In a letter to one of the co-authors of the present volume, he commented:

As to why it worked then and not previously I think the answer is that I was determined to clear a lot of cobwebs out of the Home Office and was lucky enough to strike 'a liberal hour'. Homosexual liberalisation, abortion etc created a momentum which carried through into theatre censorship.[12]

THE THEATRICAL BUILD-UP TO THE 1968 THEATRES ACT

In the 1960s, as in 1909, the demand for reform in theatre legislation was spearheaded by a new generation of articulate and outspoken dramatists. What gave added impetus to their campaign to abolish theatre censorship was the fact that they were the first generation of playwrights to come from largely working-class backgrounds. They had benefited from Butler's 1944 Education Act, which, for the first time in English social history, opened up the possibility of free secondary education to the country's underprivileged working classes. These young writers emerged from their education, not conformist and cowed, but articulate, intellectually trained, and angry at the antiquated social structures and codes of conduct of their contemporary world. They felt nothing but contempt for the elite classes who had for so long ruled at home and abroad, as they saw it, with a lethal combination of arrogance, stupidity, and stubbornness. They despised the outdated class system which had condemned untold numbers of the working classes to lives

---

[12] Letter from Lord Jenkins of Hillhead to David Thomas, 13 Mar. 2002.

of social and cultural deprivation. It was not fortuitous that the first play to give voice to the concerns of this new generation was called *Look Back in Anger* (1956). Osborne's play, masquerading under the guise of a piece about marital breakdown, was in fact a merciless depiction of class antagonism: the main characters Jimmy Porter and his wife Alison struggle with each other across the chasm of widely divergent social backgrounds. It was also an outspoken expression of the frustration experienced by young working-class intellectuals who deeply resented the way the path to power and preferment seemed to be based on class rather than merit.

Osborne's first major clash with the censor occurred in respect of his play *A Patriot for Me*, which was refused a licence by the Lord Chamberlain in August 1964 because of its homosexual drag ball sequence involving Albert Redl, an officer in the Imperial Austrian army. The play was subsequently staged as a 'private performance' by the English Stage Society at the Royal Court Theatre. Osborne explained that 'in eight weeks 25,000 or 30,000 people saw *A Patriot for Me* and they went through this elaborate farce of becoming members'.[13] As the play was unlicensed, it could not be transferred to the West End. This meant that Osborne and the Royal Court had to bear part of the expensive production costs despite the fact that the fifty-three performances had played to 95 per cent of the theatre's capacity. The Lord Chamberlain, Lord Cobbold,[14] was sufficiently irritated at the widely publicized production of a play he had banned to explore whether legal action might be taken against the Royal Court. His Assistant Comptroller prepared a draft letter to the Director of Public Prosecutions dated 2 July 1965:

On the information at present available to him, it appears to the Lord Chamberlain:

(a) that no genuine club facilities exist, that the Society is no more in this regard than a public booking agency charging a small registration fee, and that the arrangements are capable of being so widespread and general as to render the Royal Court Theatre a place of public resort.

(b) That the membership fee, particularly for associate membership is so slight as to offer no significant support for the maintenance of any company of actors associated with the enterprise, and it is therefore a mere pretence; the support of the company and of play production depending for all practical purposes on the sale of tickets. This is confirmed by the disparity between the cost of tickets and the cost of 'membership', and there would appear to be direct payment for admission to the theatre to see a stage play.

---

[13] Minutes of the 1966 Joint Select Committee. Question 109, 22.
[14] Lord Cobbold was to be the last Lord Chamberlain to exercise the role of theatre censor. Having married Lady Hermione Bulwer-Lytton in 1930, he was related by marriage to Edward Bulwer who had made the first attempt to abolish theatre censorship in 1832.

These facts led the Lord Chamberlain to believe that the performances of the stage play A Patriot for Me are to be given 'for hire' in a theatre . . . without his approval and thus contrary to sections 12 and 15 of the Theatres Act 1843.

The Lord Chamberlain's views on this subject were given verbally in general terms to Mr. George Devine [Artistic Director of the Royal Court Theatre] on 6 November 1964.

I am now to ask that the Director [Director of Public Prosecutions] should consider this position.[15]

On 9 July Cobbold had a long meeting with Norman Skelhorn, Director of Public Prosecutions. Both agreed that in the case of *A Patriot for Me* the club arrangements were obviously a subterfuge. On the other hand, the Lord Chamberlain claimed that he had no desire to prevent legitimate club performances. The problem was, as he saw it, that if no action were taken on this occasion, then it would be difficult to take action at a later date if there were even more bogus attempts at club performances. This would bring the law into disrepute. Skelhorn promised to investigate the matter but he commented that he would only start proceedings if he felt there was a reasonable chance that a court would uphold his view. He also promised to consult the Attorney-General.[16] After this process of consultation, the agreed view of the Law Officers was that no action should be taken. Cobbold was informed on 27 July 1965 that:

The Law Officers agree that the way in which this play is being presented at the Royal Court Theatre constitutes a 'public performance' and that a prosecution under section 15 of the Theatres Act 1843 would stand a good chance of success. They are, however, strongly of the opinion that it would be inexpedient to institute such a prosecution in connection with the performance of this play which has attracted a great deal of public interest and a good deal of support and which has been running for some time. Having regard to this view I would accordingly not propose to take any further action.

The Attorney-General [Sir Elwyn Jones] desires that I should make it clear that the Parliamentary Questions, which you no doubt saw were recently asked of the Prime Minister concerning the licensing of plays and the answers thereto, were not in any way connected with, or inspired by, my reference of this case to the Law Officers.[17]

Cobbold was vexed at this response. The Law Officers had failed to support him, when clearly the Royal Court did have a case to answer. In addition, as is implied by the Attorney-General's reassurance to the contrary, he seems to have suspected that someone in the Law Officers' Department had engineered recent questions in Parliament about censorship and the licensing of plays. In

---

[15] BL, LR Corr. 1964/1, *A Patriot for Me*. Draft letter from Assistant Comptroller to Director of Public Prosecutions, 2 July 1965.

[16] Ibid. Note for file by Lord Chamberlain re: long talk with DPP on 9 July, 12 July 1965.

[17] Ibid. Skelhorn (DPP) to Cobbold (delivered by hand), 27 July 1965.

addition, he was doubtless well aware that the Solicitor-General, Sir Dingle Foot, favoured the abolition of censorship and had presented a Private Member's Bill under the Ten Minute Rule to reform theatre censorship in 1962. With some justification, Cobbold must have felt that his views were being disregarded. In view of this, he made it clear in his reply to the DPP that he would not let matters rest and would 'take similar action if there should be a more flagrant case of this nature in the future'.[18]

Matters soon came to a head. Once again, the issue crystallized around the banning of a new play: on this occasion the play was called *Saved*, and was written by the dramatist Edward Bond. As in the case of Osborne's play, *Saved*, immediately after it was banned, was produced privately at the Royal Court. This time Cobbold was out for blood. The initial report on the play, written on 30 June 1965 by his Reader C. D. Heriot, was scathing:

A revolting amateur play by one of those dramatists who write as it comes to them out of a heightened image of their experience. It is about a bunch of brainless, ape-like yobs with so little individuality that it is difficult to distinguish between them. They speak a kind of stylised cockney but behave in an unreal way, not because what they do is false, but that their motivation is not sufficiently indicated.

... They are all moral imbeciles ... The writing is vile and the language and conception worse. Whether this could ever be considered a work of art is a matter of opinion—but it does seem that the taste of Messrs Devine and Richardson [George Devine and Tony Richardson, Directors of the Royal Court] has gone rancid—though with all the public money at their disposal, I don't suppose anybody cares.[19]

This initial report was enough to set alarm bells ringing in the Lord Chamberlain's Office. But his colleagues and officers from the DPP's office were at a loss to find grounds for banning the play outright, as it was not blasphemous, did not contain any reference to homosexuality, and was not likely to cause a breach of the peace.[20] The Comptroller, Eric Penn, therefore wrote to the Lord Chamberlain on 27 July 1965:

This is a disgusting play and I can see no skill or pleasure in it. I cannot think why Devine has even submitted it unless it is a trick to use to his advantage, in publicity, whatever the Lord Chamberlain's decisions may be. I suppose this wretched play can be claimed to represent the most sordid and shabby.

Tim [Nugent] has talked to me about it and I believe it may be right to cut it to ribbons rather than ban it, as the latter may give Devine the greater advantage.[21]

---

[18] Ibid. Lord Chamberlain to DPP, 28 July 1965.
[19] BL, LR Corr. 1965/2, *Saved*. Report by Heriot, 30 June 1965.
[20] Ibid. Memorandum from Tim Nugent (DPP's office) to Eric Penn (Comptroller) , 25 July 1965.
[21] Ibid. Comptroller to Lord Chamberlain, 27 July 1965.

Deceptively icy in tone, *Saved* was written with restrained fury. It offered an alarming exploration of the effects of social and cultural deprivation on a group of barely articulate young people living in South London. The action culminated in the wanton stoning to death of a baby, left in its pram in a park, a terrifying scene in which the atavistic rage and frustration of the youngsters were unleashed on a completely innocent victim. In an author's note to the published edition, Bond wrote of this key scene in his play:

Clearly the stoning to death of a baby in a London park is a typical English understatement. Compared to the 'strategic' bombing of German towns it is a negligible atrocity, compared to the cultural and emotional deprivation of most of our children its consequences are insignificant.[22]

One only has to compare the derisive comments made in the Lord Chamberlain's Office with those of Bond himself to realize that these differing responses to the play embodied a profound clash of cultures. England's young playwrights no longer spoke the same language as those charged with controlling their output through censorship; and their divergent views of reality and life were so extreme as to admit of no compromise. Bond refused to have his play 'cut to ribbons', and the Royal Court had no option but to mount a club performance of *Saved*.

In Cobbold's view, this was now a test case that would require the DPP to take action. Quite rightly, he foresaw that, as with *A Patriot for Me*, the presentation of the play as a club performance would be no more than a subterfuge to circumvent his powers of censorship and would inevitably be in breach of the 1843 Theatres Act. This time he was not prepared to be brushed aside with lame excuses as happened in respect of Osborne's play a few months earlier. He therefore began a pre-emptive campaign even before the play was in production. He wrote to Skelhorn on 6 October 1965:

May I refer to our conversation and correspondence in July about the performance of *A Patriot for Me* at the Royal Court Theatre . . . I think I must now ask you to consider the position which will arise when the new play is produced on the same basis as to club membership but without, perhaps, the same reasons for inaction on grounds of expediency.

I assume that you will probably wish to consult the Law Officers. If so, I should be grateful if you would emphasise that I am not at all moved by any hostility to theatre clubs; on the contrary I think that genuine theatre clubs make a valuable contribution. Nor have I any desire to wage war on the Royal Court Theatre.

What does concern me is that if the move away from genuine theatre clubs to disguised public performance is allowed to go unchallenged, it is bound to spread and, as I see it, to bring the law into disrepute. I think that any Lord Chamberlain would

----

[22] Edward Bond, *Saved* (London: Methuen, 1969), 6.

find difficulties in attempting to administer the present Theatres Act indefinitely if it became clear that it could be flouted with impunity. At the risk of impertinence I still wonder whether some form of investigation and warning might not serve to mark the point of principle and hold the line.[23]

Skelhorn replied on 12 October that nothing could be done until the production actually opened in November.[24] He also reminded the Lord Chamberlain of an earlier letter from the DPP's office where he was advised to send one of his staff to witness a performance at the first opportunity and to gather evidence of the terms on which admission was obtained and the extent to which the society might be considered to be a bona fide theatre club.[25]

The Lord Chamberlain followed this advice and duly sent one of his staff to report on the second-night performance of *Saved* on 4 November.[26] A few days later, the Lord Chamberlain was told that a police officer had gone to the theatre and was able to gain admission without producing a membership card. A month later, the DPP's office took the decision to institute proceedings against Alfred Esdaile (the licensee of the Royal Court), William Gaskill (the director of the production), and the English Stage Society. The case was heard at Marlborough Street Magistrates Court on 14 February 1966. The defendants were found guilty but were given a conditional discharge for 12 months, subject in the case of the English Stage Society to costs of 50 guineas:[27] these punishments were nominal. In giving judgement in April 1966, the magistrate Leo Gradwell declared: 'I am sitting on the rock of the statute and inviting you as Perseus to come and rescue me.'[28] Gradwell explained what he meant by this. On the one hand, the English Stage Society 'was as careful as they could reasonably be expected to be, and that everybody connected with the Stage Society was "perfectly splendid" '.[29] On the other hand, the statute made it clear that 'everybody who showed for hire a play unlicensed by the Lord Chamberlain was liable under the Act'.[30] He went on to assert that in his view even 'a rich man who hired actors to perform an uncensored play for himself alone would bring himself within the statute'.[31] Whether the society was a bona fide club and the performances were genuinely private, which was the case for the defence, was in fact not questioned by the magistrate. His interpretation of the 1843 statute meant that all private performances by theatre clubs were illegal under the terms of the 1843 Theatres Act: 'He went

[23] BL, LR Corr. 1965/2, *Saved*. Letter from Cobbold to DPP, 6 Oct. 1965.
[24] Ibid. DPP to Cobbold, 12 Oct. 1965.
[25] Ibid. J. F. Claxton (DPP's office) to assistant comptroller, 6 Oct. 1965.
[26] Ibid. Report on performance of *Saved*, 5 Nov. 1965.
[27] Ibid. Note on the trial, 4 Apr. 1966.
[28] William Gaskill, *A Sense of Direction* (London: Faber, 1988), 69.
[29] 'Magistrate finds law broken over the play *Saved*', *The Times*, 2 Apr. 1966.
[30] Ibid.   [31] Ibid.

so far as to say that the law as he saw it was that no one could present an unlicensed play unless the public or audience went in free of charge and the bar was closed.'[32] This verdict effectively swept away the whole basis for the Lord Chamberlain's toleration of theatre clubs. The Lord Chamberlain's colleague, R. J. Hill, concluded ruefully: 'This is an unusual view, and I am more than a little afraid that it may be upset on appeal.'[33] Both the Lord Chamberlain and the DPP agreed that the verdict was most unfortunate, but it had already been overtaken by events on the political scene.[34]

THE POLITICAL BUILD-UP TO THE 1968 THEATRES ACT

Confronted by the increasingly challenging nature of the new plays given club performances at the Royal Court in the mid-1960s, the Wilson Government faced a real dilemma. Not to prosecute the English Stage Society would bring the Law into disrepute: to prosecute would open up for public debate the whole issue of theatre censorship. The problem was outlined to the Lord Chamberlain by the Solicitor-General, Dingle Foot, when they met for lunch on 9 November 1965. Foot explained that the Law Officers were in something of a quandary over the production of *Saved*: 'They had little doubt that the production was illegal and that a prosecution would be successful. But they thought that this would bring up the whole question of stage censorship, and were not sure whether or not this would be desirable.'[35] Cobbold took the view that if he was expected to administer a law that was constantly being broken, then the situation would need to be clarified in public. Foot concluded that, 'if they decided to prosecute, it would be wise to set up some "new look" enquiry into the censorship'.[36] Cobbold made it clear that he would welcome an enquiry as long as it was not an inquest.[37] Pressure to move in that direction was already coming from Parliament.

In July 1965, William Hamling (Labour MP for Woolwich West) asked the Prime Minister, in a Parliamentary Question, what his policy was 'with regard to the introduction of legislation to abolish the Lord Chamberlain's function relating to censorship'. There is no previous record of any interest on the part of Hamling in theatre censorship. This suggests that his question may well have been planted by one or other of the Government's Law Officers. Wilson

---

[32] BL, LR Corr. 1965/2, *Saved*. Note on the trial, 4 Apr. 1966.   [33] Ibid.
[34] Ibid. DPP to Cobbold, 3 May 1966; and Cobbold to DPP, 6 May 1966.
[35] Ibid. Confidential note from Cobbold to staff, 9 Nov. 1965.
[36] Ibid.   [37] Ibid.

responded by stating that he had 'no proposals for legislation on this subject at this stage'. Pressed with a further question by Jeremy Thorpe (Liberal MP for North Devon), he added: 'I think we had better leave this matter in the hands of the Lord Chancellor, with the law reform facilities which he has, to consider whether this aspect of our law and practice should be modernised.'[38] Wilson's off-the-cuff response, which must have taken the Lord Chancellor by surprise, was clearly intended to stall any further probing questions from the floor of the House. However, the contentious issue of private club performances of plays that had been refused a licence altered the nature and timing of what might otherwise have been a leisurely and inconclusive enquiry by the Office of the Lord Chancellor.

Because of the Lord Chamberlain's determination to obtain a prosecution against those responsible for the production of *Saved*, the DPP consulted the Attorney-General. He in turn kept the Home Secretary informed of his views. In a letter (dated 22 October 1965) written to the then Home Secretary, Soskice, Jones expressed some sympathy for the Lord Chamberlain's point of view. He went on to disagree with the Prime Minister's view that this matter could be left to the Lord Chancellor and hence to the Law Commissioners. It was clearly a question of policy and not 'lawyers [*sic*] law'. He concluded by summing up, with admirable clarity, the dilemma facing the Government and the inevitable consequence that followed from this dilemma:

At the present time the law is being systematically evaded and thereby brought into disrepute. On the other hand, a prosecution under Section 15 of the Theatres Act 1843 would spotlight the manifest absurdities of the present system. In these circumstances I suggest that the time has come for a fresh enquiry.[39]

This letter brought matters to a head for ministers and officials in the Home Office. The copy of the letter in the National Archives is annotated with Soskice's comment: 'Probably the answer is some kind of inquiry. It is of course a matter entirely for him [the Attorney-General]; but I should have thought it was quite impossible for this A.G. [Attorney- General] to watch the criminal law being continually flouted without taking action.'[40]

A draft letter, written on 28 October 1965 by a Home Office official, K. P. Witney, confirms that Home Office policy over the years on the question of theatre censorship had been 'to let sleeping dogs lie'.[41] The reasoning behind this policy of deliberate inertia was that, though the system of theatre

---

[38] *Hansard* (Commons), 20 July 1965, vol. 716, cols. 1335–6.
[39] NA, HO 300/56. Letter from the Attorney-General to the Home Secretary, 22 Oct. 1965.
[40] Ibid.
[41] NA, HO 300/56. Draft letter written by K. P. Witney (Assistant Under-Secretary of State in the Home Office).

censorship might be anachronistic, it had worked 'well enough in practice'. Hitherto, Witney argued, a public campaign against censorship had been avoided by the outlet provided by so-called clubs. If this outlet were closed off, it would clearly precipitate demands for an enquiry. Because of this, Witney acknowledged that it was unlikely that the Home Office could maintain its traditional position in future. The Department's attention should now focus on what kind of enquiry should be recommended. In a handwritten marginal note on Witney's draft, the Home Secretary commented that the draft exactly expressed his own views and that he would write as proposed. However, he feared that the present arrangements might be replaced by something worse.[42]

Slowly but surely, the wheels of government were beginning to turn. At a formal meeting between the Home Secretary, the Lord Chancellor, and the Solicitor-General on 19 November 1965, it was agreed that the present system of censorship was no longer viable. The Home Secretary, Soskice, had begun the meeting by stating that he had grave doubts about disturbing the present arrangements. In contrast, the Solicitor-General, Foot, argued that the present system had many absurdities. The Lord Chamberlain's powers extended only to plays presented on the live stage and not to ones on television. In addition, some of his rules could make for anomalies. The Lord Chancellor, Gardiner, was even more forthright in condemning the present system of censorship:

The last examination of the censorship had been in 1909 and the position, if anything, had got more ridiculous. The anomalies were becoming increasingly absurd, particularly when it was borne in mind that the Lord Chamberlain's insistence on seeing scripts in advance which could not be changed virtually ruled out a whole school of modern acting which relied entirely on a completely spontaneous performance by actors reacting to given situations.[43]

The meeting concluded that the Home Secretary should recommend to the Home Affairs Committee of the Cabinet that a Departmental Committee should be established to examine the problem.[44]

The views of the Lord Chancellor and the Solicitor-General, as expressed in their meeting of 19 November, were communicated to the Lord Chamberlain in a meeting held at the Home Office on 22 November. The Home Secretary explained that the Law Officers had felt particularly strongly that 'some public enquiry should be set up since there would probably be a considerable furore

---

[42] Ibid.
[43] Ibid. Record of a meeting between the Secretary of State for the Home Department, the Lord Chancellor, and the Solicitor-General on 19 Nov. 1965.
[44] Ibid.

over any prosecution of "Saved" '.[45] The Lord Chamberlain, for his part, made it clear that if there was no prosecution of *Saved*, because the Law Officers thought that it was not in the public interest, then he would feel compelled 'somehow to represent to Parliament that it was impossible for him to carry out his duties as theatre censor under the Theatres Act, 1843'.[46] After this threat, the discussion turned to what kind of enquiry might be set up. The Lord Chamberlain made it clear that he welcomed the idea of an enquiry. In his view the Theatres Act of 1843 had become out of date. He also felt that any enquiry should be extended to cover films and television.[47] Finally, he wanted any enquiry handled so that the Crown was not in any way involved.

When informed of the outcome of these meetings, the Prime Minister was seemingly not averse to an enquiry, but he did not share the view that this should be left to a Departmental Committee. On 26 November 1965, he instructed Peter le Cheminant, his Principal Private Secretary at Downing Street, to write to his opposite number at the Home Office, Ralph Shuffrey, as follows: 'The Prime Minister has commented: "Our reliance on Departmental Committees and Royal Commissions is becoming a joke. Why shouldn't we give M.P.s a job to do for a change?" '[48]

Soskice now prepared a memorandum on theatre censorship for the next meeting of the Cabinet Home Affairs Committee, scheduled for 3 December 1965. It was measured in tone and thorough in content. Soskice began by outlining both the case for a change in the present law and the arguments in favour of leaving things as they stood. He went on to report that, after discussing the matter with the Law Officers, they were all agreed that there was a good case for amending legislation. As there had been no enquiry into theatre censorship since 1909, a fresh enquiry was required with the following suggested terms of reference: 'to review the law relating to the censorship of stage plays and to make recommendations.'[49] Soskice went on to explain that the main argument against extending the terms of reference to films and television was that there had been no change in legislation affecting stage plays for over 120 years whereas the arrangements for the censorship of films were of relatively recent introduction and 'in the case of broadcasting the

---

[45] Ibid. Record of a meeting between the Secretary of State for the Home Department and the Lord Chamberlain on 22 Nov. 1965.

[46] Ibid.

[47] John Trevelyan, Secretary of the British Board of Film Censors, was asked for his views two days later. He did not object to a wide-ranging enquiry, but thought that from a practical point of view there was much to be said for limiting any enquiry to stage plays. See NA, HO 300/56.

[48] Ibid. Note from Peter le Cheminant to Ralph Shuffrey, 26 Nov. 1965.

[49] NA, CAB 134/2001 (Miscellaneous Cabinet Committees). There is an undated draft of the memo in NA, HO 300/56. Memorandum from the Secretary of State to the Home Affairs Committee, 1 Dec. 1965.

requirements placed upon the B.B.C. and I.T.V. to ensure proper standards make any more formal censorship unnecessary'.[50] He concluded by outlining the cases for a Select Committee and a departmental enquiry.

The Committee's discussion of Soskice's memorandum was distinctly unfocused. His lucid outline set before them was soon submerged in concerns of how best to deal with theatre practice; how to cope with broadcasts of plays banned from the stage; how to extend a form of liberal censorship to television; and how to avoid pressure groups such as the National Listeners' and Viewers' Association from imposing a more severe form of censorship. Unable to reach satisfactory conclusions on these various topics, the Committee resolved that: 'It might . . . be better, before deciding to set up an inquiry, to arrange a debate in the House of Lords in the New Year which would afford an opportunity for liberal opinion to express itself and for public reaction to be judged.'[51]

On 7 January 1966, a meeting was called by the Lord Chancellor to discuss how best to implement the decision of the Home Affairs Committee. It was attended by Lord Stonham (Minister of State at the Home Office), officials from the Home Office, and Lord Annan (for the second part of the meeting). The Lord Chancellor began by explaining that he had arranged for Annan (Provost of King's College, Cambridge) to propose a motion to the House of Lords on 17 February: 'to draw attention to the problem of censorship in the theatre; and to move for papers.'[52] This was to allow the Government to test opinion before deciding whether to set up an enquiry. The minutes note tersely that there had been some disagreement at Home Affairs Committee about the form and terms of reference of any enquiry. Stonham took the view that the terms of reference of any enquiry should limit its scope to the theatre. It was then made clear to the meeting that Jenkins, who had replaced Soskice as Home Secretary in December 1965, favoured a Select Committee.

After this rapid progress, the meeting went on to consider the form and function of Annan's motion:

In view of the pressure which would be provoked by the Royal Court prosecution and the fact that the Home Secretary and the Lord Chancellor were now in agreement about the form and scope of the proposed enquiry there would be every advantage in announcing it during the Debate on Lord Annan's motion. It could then appear as a Government initiative rather than a belated response to pressure.[53]

This was an unusually frank minute recording a deliberate decision to deceive the House of Lords about the Government's policy hitherto. When Annan was

[50] NA, CAB 134/2001 (Miscellaneous Cabinet Committees).
[51] NA, CAB 134/1997. Minutes of the Home Affairs Committee of the Cabinet, 3 Dec. 1965.
[52] NA, HO 300/56. Report of a meeting between Lord Chancellor, Stonham, Annan, and Home Office officials on 7 Jan. 1966. Report written on 10 Jan. 1966.
[53] Ibid.

ushered into the meeting, he expressed his willingness to amend his motion to call for an enquiry if he were told informally that the Government intended to set one up. At the end of the meeting, it was resolved that Annan would be informed of the Government's decision on the matter and would change the terms of his motion accordingly. In addition, he agreed to let the Lord Chancellor see a copy of his speech before the debate. Finally, it was agreed that Stonham would announce the decision to set up a Select Committee in the course of winding up the debate. This was a good example of how the hidden levers of government can be used to cope with even the most controversial topics.

Meanwhile, on 13 December Cobbold, prior to this crucial meeting, received a note from the Home Secretary informing him that the Government had decided to have a debate in the House of Lords to test public reactions before taking a decision on how best to investigate the issue of theatre censorship. Although the Lord Chamberlain agreed with this suggestion, he immediately began to consider how he too might contribute to this debate. On 7 January 1966, Cobbold called on the Prime Minister to outline his views. A letter from Wilson's Private Secretary to the Home Office makes it clear that Cobbold had discussed the matter with the Queen and that he had her personal authority to speak in the House of Lords debate:

When Lord Cobbold came to see the Prime Minister on another matter this morning he mentioned the question of stage censorship. He said that he had discussed with Sir Frank Soskice the possibility that he might unload his present personal responsibility on to a Board of Censors on the lines of the British Board of Film Censors. One question was how to obtain Parliamentary approval for such a course. Here he had in mind a Debate in the Lords, *in which he had The Queen's authority to speak.*[54]

This intervention, with the confirmed support of the Queen, caused some consternation to staff in the Home Office, who were at a loss as to how to respond to it. They decided to discuss it with the Secretary of State, as, that same day, Cobbold made an appointment to see Jenkins to discuss his suggestion in more detail.

Further pressure on the issue was exerted from 10 Downing Street. On 17 January 1966, Le Cheminant wrote to his opposite numbers in the Home Office and the Office of the Lord Chancellor asking for a note for the Prime Minister on the practicability of Cobbold's suggestion. The response from Gardiner's office amounted to a magisterial put-down for the Lord Chamberlain. The Lord Chancellor's Private Secretary replied on 19 January 1966:

---

[54] Ibid. Letter from the Prime Minister's Private Secretary to the Home Office, 7 Jan. 1966. Italics supplied.

With reference to your minute of 17th January the Lord Chancellor is of the opinion that, from the point of view of those interested in the free expression of ideas in the theatre, a Board of Theatre Censors should be as objectionable as the present censorship. What the Lord Chancellor actually said was: 'Over my dead body'.[55]

The British Board of Film Censors had been set up in 1912. In practice it had operated as a paternalistic barometer of public taste and had sought to prevent any scene being presented in a film that might give moral or political offence. It signally failed to protect filmmakers from local authority interference as local authorities could still ban the showing of films given a certificate by the Board or conversely agree to show films refused a licence. Setting up a new Board of Theatre Censors with a similarly diffuse, paternalistic role clearly did not appeal to the Law Officers of the Wilson Government.

In the early stages of discussion, the Prime Minister took a neutral view on the issue of theatre censorship. Initially, as we have seen in his response to a Parliamentary Question, he was reluctant to envisage any change to the status quo. When it became apparent, however, that demands for change would be inevitable following legal action over the production of *Saved*, he supported the view of his Law Officers and the Home Secretary that the Government should anticipate demands for an enquiry and should make appropriate forward plans. As we have seen, he resisted initial Home Office pressure for a departmental enquiry, and encouraged the setting up a Joint Select Committee which would be suggested in the debate in the House of Lords.

The actual decision to set up a Joint Select Committee was taken at the meeting of the Home Affairs Committee of the Cabinet held on 26 January 1966. Jenkins had prepared a carefully argued memorandum for the meeting, in which he invited his colleagues to agree that, in the debate arranged for 17 February in the House of Lords, Annan should be invited to propose a motion calling for the appointment of a Joint Select Committee to review the law and practice relating to the censorship of stage plays.[56] The Home Affairs Committee duly accepted Jenkins's advice and also agreed that 'the Government spokesman in the debate to advise the House to accept the Motion'.[57] The following day, Wilson concurred that the proposal for a Joint Select Committee could be approved without coming to Cabinet.[58]

---

[55] NA, HO 300/56. Note from Thomas Legg (the Lord Chancellor's Private Secretary), 19 Jan. 1966 in response to Le Cheminant's note, 17 Jan. 1966.
[56] NA, CAB 134/2852. Theatre Censorship. Memorandum by the Secretary of State for the Home Department, 21 Jan. 1966.
[57] NA, CAB 134/2851. Minutes of the Cabinet Home Affairs Committee, 26 Jan. 1966.
[58] NA, PREM 13/2152 (Office of the Prime Minister). Handwritten comment by Wilson on a note from the Office of the Duchy of Lancaster, 27 Jan. 1966.

The lengthy debate in the House of Lords on 17 February 1966 was a memorable occasion. In proposing the motion to set up a Joint Select Committee 'to review the law and practice relating to the censorship of stage plays', Annan gave an impressive summary of the reasons for the introduction of theatre censorship and of the subsequent attempts to abolish it. He managed with feline grace, on the one hand, to compliment the Lord Chamberlain for the polite and thoughtful way he exercised his office as censor and, on the other, to criticize with deft precision some of the more unfortunate decisions taken by him. He frankly acknowledged the difficulties involved in finding a viable alternative to pre-censorship. But he concluded his introduction by reminding the House that: 'When we are dust we shall be remembered less for the deeds we did than for the few good plays and other works of art which we witnessed and which survive from our generation. I hope it will be said that we succoured and not strangled them.'[59]

His remarkable speech was followed by some equally trenchant contributions from men of distinction in the Arts and in Law. The Lord Chancellor repeated the view he had already expressed to his Private Secretary that any board of play censors or any committee of experts would be much worse than the present system of censorship.[60] Lord Harlech, who had recently taken over as President of the British Board of Film Censors, gave a detailed account of the shortcomings of this system of censorship. Given its inadequacies (it had no statutory powers and its decisions could be overruled by any local authority), he doubted that it would provide an effective blueprint for 'any method of dealing with censorship in the theatre'.[61] Lord Goodman, who was Chairman of the Arts Council, made the telling point that many contemporary playwrights saw the Lord Chamberlain as a goad and did their best to provoke him in what they wrote. Instead of censorship protecting the public, it therefore did serious damage.[62] Lord Willis (the popular playwright Ted Willis who wrote the hugely successful television series *Dixon of Dock Green*) made a passionate plea for freedom of speech in the theatre. He also pointed out that the current system of censorship 'puts one man in the position of immense political power; and this point has to some extent been overlooked because of the concentration on sex, violence and pornography in the theatre'.[63] At the end of his speech, he concluded that theatre censorship may seem unimportant when compared to events on the larger political scene. But he went on to argue that it was not:

No issue of artistic freedom is ever small or unimportant. Do not let us muddle on any longer with this; do not let us say that because it works in a liberal fashion, therefore we shall tolerate it. It is an affront to the freedom of artists. It must be abolished.

---

[59] *Hansard* (Lords), 17 Feb. 1966, vol. 272, col. 1162.   [60] Ibid., col. 1179.
[61] Ibid., col. 1184.   [62] Ibid., col. 1196.   [63] Ibid., col. 1210.

In present hands it may operate in a liberal way; in other hands it may not. As an institution it is wrong. As an institution it is false and it must go.[64]

Despite the polite words of praise for his work as censor, the Lord Chamberlain did not take kindly to the detailed criticisms of his censorship decisions that were frequently expressed in the debate. In particular, he was plainly irritated by Goodman's criticism of his decision to ban *A Patriot for Me*. In responding to Goodman, he commented with some petulance: 'So long as the present Act remains on the Statute Book whatever may be the outcome of this debate and of deliberations in the next few months, I shall see it as my duty to Parliament to do my best both to administer the Act and to see that it is enforced.'[65] As expected, he went on to express the view that some form of censorship should be retained. He argued that the primary object of censorship throughout the centuries was 'to prevent offence being given'.[66] In his view it was still the function of censorship to prevent offence being given 'to individuals, to sections of the community or to the community at large'.[67] Despite the critical account given of the British Board of Film Censors by Harlech, this was still the Lord Chamberlain's preferred alternative. In his view, a board of censors would be required in future to prevent the depiction of extreme violence on stage, to protect the treatment of Christianity on stage and to guard against 'offensive representation of living personalities, from the Royal Family and foreign Heads of State downwards'.[68] At the conclusion of the debate, Stonham, speaking on behalf of the Government, stated that the Government favoured the setting up of a Joint Select Committee and invited the House to support Annan's motion. This was duly agreed and was sent to the House of Commons. Although the whole occasion had been stage-managed by the Lord Chancellor and Stonham, the debate itself marked something of a watershed in British cultural history. Instead of resorting to platitudes and obfuscation, with opinion split on party lines, the House of Lords for the first time ever gave mature and measured consideration to the crucial issue of the right to free speech for playwrights. It had, however, taken some 230 years since the passing of Walpole's Licensing Act to achieve this. Both Houses finally approved the motion to set up a Joint Select Committee in May 1966.

The membership of the Joint Select Committee was finalized in July 1966. The eight representatives of the House of Lords appointed on 19 July were Scarbrough (who had served as Lord Chamberlain), the Earl of Kilmuir, Viscount Norwich, Lord Tweedsmuir, Baroness Gaitskell, Lord Lloyd of Hampstead, Annan, and Goodman. The eight Commoners appointed on 21

---

[64] Ibid., col. 1214.   [65] Ibid., col. 1234.
[66] Ibid., col. 1236.   [67] Ibid.   [68] Ibid., col. 1238.

July were Andrew Faulds (Labour MP for Warley East), Michael Foot (Labour MP for Ebbw Vale), Emlyn Hooson (Liberal MP for Montgomeryshire), Hugh Jenkins (Labour MP for Wandsworth, Putney and future Minister for the Arts), Sir David Renton (Conservative MP for Huntingdonshire), Norman St John Stevas (Conservative MP for Chelmsford and future Minister for the Arts), George Strauss (Labour MP for Lambeth, Vauxhall), and William Wilson (Labour MP for Coventry South). The Committee appointed Strauss as chairman and deliberated throughout the autumn of 1966 and the winter months of 1967. It held sixteen meetings and took advice from nine witnesses and other interested parties. The witnesses were Cobbold, Dingle Foot, John Mortimer (League of Dramatists), Osborne (playwright), Levy (former Member of Parliament and co-sponsor of the 1949 bill to abolish theatre censorship), Peter Hall (Director, RSC), Tynan (Literary Manager, National Theatre), Emile Littler (Society of West End Theatre Managers), and Peter Saunders (theatre manager). In its report, the Committee summarized the nature of the problem before it:

> The question . . . which the Committee have had to consider is whether or not the freedom of expression which the playwright, as a creative artist, naturally desires is in certain circumstances so likely to offend or deprave or corrupt the members of the public who have paid to attend the performance that their freedom to enjoy the theatre needs to be protected by some special form of censorship, over and above the protection inherent in the law that applies to other forms of artistic production generally.[69]

It then went on to outline the four options before it: viz. to recommend a continuation of the present system; the transfer of the present powers of the Lord Chamberlain to some other pre-censorship body; some form of voluntary censorship; or the complete abolition of censorship. It dealt with all four options in a clear and concise manner. What emerges from its account is that, as on previous occasions, only the West End theatre managers were in favour of retaining censorship exercised by the Lord Chamberlain. The only other witness in favour of retaining censorship was the Lord Chamberlain himself. Yet again, Cobbold argued for the retention of some form of pre-censorship (exercised this time not by a Board of Theatre Censors but by the Arts Council) in order to protect the royal family and other distinguished living persons from offensive attacks on stage.[70] The Lord Chamberlain's interventions made it clear that his primary motive for wishing to retain theatre censorship in 1967 was the same as led to its introduction in 1737, namely the desire to protect those in authority, and especially the royal family,

[69] Report of the Joint Committee on Censorship of the Theatre, 1967, p. ix.
[70] Ibid. 36–8.

from satirical or malicious attacks on stage. Despite his endless disputes with playwrights over sex, violence, and bad language, what really concerned him was the status and authority of the Queen and her government. The Joint Select Committee did not share his view. Its conclusions were unambiguous: all forms of pre-censorship should cease and the theatre should enjoy the same freedom of speech, subject only to the constraints of the criminal law, which generally apply to other art forms. No special protection should be offered to living persons or a person recently dead. In order to prevent frivolous prosecutions, the Attorney-General would have to give permission for any prosecution to be brought. Obscene productions should be dealt with by the same provisions as in the Obscene Publications Act. In order to ensure uniform application of the law the Committee recommended that the licensing functions of local authorities should be confined to such matters as the design and structure of theatre premises and should not be capable of being used as a means of censorship. Its conclusions were summarized in one remarkable paragraph:

> The effect of the recommendations of the Committee will be to allow freedom of speech in the theatre subject to the overriding requirements of the criminal law which generally speaking applies to other forms of art in this country. The anachronistic licensing powers of the Lord Chamberlain will be abolished and will not be replaced by any other form of pre-censorship, national or local. The theatre will be subjected to the general law of the land, and those presenting plays which break the law will be subjected to prosecution under the relevant procedure. The penalties for offences will be realistically severe, but the author and producer will have the right to defend themselves before a jury and to plead the defence of artistic merit. *Political censorship of any kind will cease.*[71]

After the publication of the Committee's report on 19 June 1967, events began to move swiftly. At a meeting of the Cabinet's Home Affairs Committee held on the same day, Jenkins proposed that the main recommendations of the Joint Select Committee should be accepted and that an announcement should be made to this effect before the parliamentary recess. The Committee was aware that this decision might place the Lord Chamberlain in a difficult position during the interim period before legislation was enacted. In addition, the Committee noted that it might be unfortunate if the Lord Chamberlain chose to advocate the setting up of an alternative method of censorship, of the kind he had suggested to the Joint Select Committee. In discussion, it was suggested, given the increasing popularity of satire, that it might be wise to safeguard against the depiction of a living person on stage, or a person whose death had occurred within the preceding ten years. The minutes of

---

[71] Report of the Joint Committee on Censorship of the Theatre, p. xix, §55. Italics supplied.

the meeting do not make it clear who raised this point, but other evidence suggests that it was George Wigg (Paymaster-General) acting as an emissary for the Prime Minister.[72] This view did not commend itself to the Committee. The Committee concluded by agreeing to 'accept the main recommendation of the Joint Select Committee that the Lord Chamberlain's censorship powers should be abolished and not be replaced by any other pre-censorship provisions'.[73] Following this meeting, Jenkins, on 25 July, prepared a memorandum for the Cabinet meeting to be held on 27 July 1967. In it, he asked the Cabinet to endorse the decision of the Home Affairs Committee that 'the broad principle of the main recommendations of the Joint Select Committee should be accepted and that this decision should be announced in Parliament before the recess'.[74]

Sir Burke Trend, the Cabinet Secretary, prepared a detailed note for the Prime Minister on 26 July in which he drew particular attention to the issue of safeguards against the presentation of living persons. Should the Home Secretary make reference to this, perhaps in response to 'an inspired supplementary'? Trend could see 'no obvious reason why the Home Secretary should declare before the Recess—as he wishes to—that the Government accept even the broad principle of the Select Committee's recommendations'.[75] The Prime Minister did not accept Trend's advice on delaying an announcement, but he was swift to follow the line suggested by Trend on the representation of living persons. At Cabinet, Jenkins found himself, without prior warning, obstructed by the Prime Minister. The minutes of the Cabinet meeting give an unusually full account of the Prime Minister's concern which was that 'the portrayal of the Sovereign or of heads of foreign States might cause offence in this country and abroad; and, while no exception could be taken to political satire as such, plays portraying public men for purposes of political advantage or private malice might well do harm to the public interest.'[76] In summing up the discussion, the Prime Minister said that the Cabinet in general supported the Joint Select Committee's main recommendations, but that it was important that a solution should be found to the problem of the portrayal of living persons (in particular, important living persons) on the stage. Jenkins was given permission to announce, in response to a pre-arranged Parliamentary Question from Strauss, that the Government accepted the general principle

[72] See Richard Crossman, *The Diaries of a Cabinet Minister* (London: Hamish Hamilton and Jonathan Cape, 1976), ii. 442

[73] NA, CAB 134/2854. Minutes of the Home Affairs Committee of the Cabinet held on 19 July 1967.

[74] NA, CAB 129/133 (Cabinet Memoranda). Memorandum from the Secretary of State for the Home Department, 25 July 1967.

[75] NA, PREM 13/2152. Note from Cabinet Secretary for the Prime Minister, 26 July 1967.

[76] NA, CAB 128/42 (Cabinet Minutes). Minutes of the Cabinet, 27 July 1967.

of the recommendations of the Joint Select Committee. However, he was also invited 'to consider how provision could be made to deal with the problems of the presentation of living persons on the stage and to bring proposals before the Home Affairs Committee'.[77]

In making this intervention, Wilson abandoned his earlier studied neutrality on the issue of stage censorship and adopted a position that was now identical to that of the Lord Chamberlain. This new position was also patently at odds with the views of his Law Officers, his Home Secretary, the members of the Home Affairs Committee of the Cabinet and the recommendations of the Joint Select Committee. Clearly, a seismic shift of this nature did not happen of its own accord. Something must have been said or done to cause Wilson to change his mind so drastically. Evidence pointing to the reason for this shift can be found in Crossman's diaries. In his published diaries, Crossman (who was at the time Lord President of the Council and Leader of the House of Commons) records the minutiae of his dealings with Wilson and other Cabinet colleagues with refreshing indiscretion. On the issue of theatre censorship, he spells out Wilson's private reasons for changing his position:

The only subject the P.M. wanted to talk about was theatre censorship. There had just been published a report from a very representative committee which unanimously recommended the abolition of the functions of the Lord Chamberlain as censor of the living drama. This Roy Jenkins had very much wanted to accept but the P.M. told John [John Silkin: Chief Whip] and me this would be a terrible mistake and he also let us know that he'd sent George Wigg to the Home Affairs Committee to warn them against accepting it. I had had to leave the Committee just when George Wigg was starting to speak and hadn't realized that he was the P.M.'s emissary: indeed, I thought he'd gone there with a brief from Arnold Goodman, who was a member of the original departmental committee. Harold's explanation was very elaborate, I think because he was a little embarrassed. 'I've received representations from the Palace', he said. 'They don't want to ban all plays about live persons but they want to make sure that there's somebody who'd stop the kind of play about Prince Philip which would be painful to the Queen. Of course,' he hurriedly added, 'they're not denying that there should be freedom to write satirical plays, take-offs, caricatures: what they want to be able to ban are plays devoted to character assassination and they mention, as an example, "Mrs Wilson's Diary".'[78]

Crossman continued: 'It was obvious from the way he talked that he wanted the censorship as much as the Queen. Indeed he wanted it so much that he'd put it on Thursday's Cabinet agenda.'[79] Crossman's account of the Cabinet meeting runs as follows:

---

[77] Ibid.
[78] Crossman, *Diaries*, ii. 442.   [79] Ibid. 442–3.

Cabinet once again—three Cabinets running in a week. Theatre censorship, as Harold promised, was the first item on the agenda. Despite George Wigg, the Home Affairs Committee had recommended acceptance of the committee's report. One of its main arguments was that one could hardly forbid the portrayal of living persons in the live theatre when it was not prohibited on television. Here Harold had equipped himself with an effective reply, namely an assurance from Charlie Hill that the powers vested in the Governors of the B.B.C. were quite adequate to ensure that character assassination was altogether forbidden.

I had been expecting a great confrontation between Harold and the man he detests and whose influence he really hates in the Cabinet. Faced with the P.M.'s unexpected coup Roy was quite firm, cool and collected. He said of course he would consider this and the matter must certainly go back to Home Affairs for reconsideration. But he added that it would be extremely difficult to evolve any way of controlling the live theatre which didn't mean the reintroduction of censorship and more discrimination against it in comparison with television and radio. The Prime Minister seemed content with this and when I intervened to suggest that we needn't rush the Bill he indicated that it should be given high priority and he hoped that Roy would be able to satisfy him on this point. The agreement reached, as recorded in the Cabinet minutes, runs: 'In neither medium would ordinary political satire be forbidden but there should be safeguards against the theatre being used deliberately to discredit or create political hostility towards public political figures.'[80]

In the published version of his diary, Crossman recorded with great brevity the ensuing conflict between Wilson and Jenkins. In the manuscript version of the diary, held in the Modern Records Centre at the University of Warwick, Crossman gave a more detailed account of his attempt to explain Wilson's position to Jenkins and of his plea to Jenkins to take a more conciliatory line.[81] Crossman repeatedly asserted to Jenkins that Wilson had been pressed by the Palace to ensure that there would be protection for living persons if theatre censorship were to be abolished. Wilson's behaviour in Cabinet is entirely consistent with this explanation. Jenkins, however, refused to give ground and threatened to resign if he was forced to compromise on the issue.

Before the issue of censorship came back to the Home Affairs Committee on 24 November 1967, Jenkins prepared a memorandum for the Committee on 21 November. He began by pointing out that Strauss, who had chaired the Select Committee, had secured tenth place in the ballot for Private Members' Bills and proposed to introduce a bill to abolish theatre censorship. Jenkins concluded: 'I think that, rather than to try and persuade him to yield

---

[80] Ibid. 445–6.
[81] See Crossman Diary Manuscript (Modern Records Centre, University of Warwick), MSS/154/8/100, 91–2.

place to a Government Bill, the right course would be to give him drafting assistance.'[82] On the issue of the representation of living persons on stage, Jenkins made it clear that he had found it impossible to devise a solution that would satisfactorily deal with the problem. In particular, he did not agree with Goodman's suggestion of distinguishing between people in their private as opposed to their public lives. He therefore concluded that it was better to see the reaction of Members of Parliament to a bill without any such provision and to make amendments at the Committee stage if necessary. Paragraph 12 of his memorandum spelt out the political implications of his recommendation:

The Select Committee attached importance to placing the theatre on the same footing as other media, and to prohibit the characterization of living persons would be criticised as substituting one form of political censorship for another. The prevalence of political satire was one of the main causes of the original Licensing Act of 1737.[83]

On the same day that he prepared his memorandum, Jenkins sent a note to the Prime Minister, outlining in greater detail the reasons for his recommendation. He explained that the problem of living persons had been looked at from all angles, but no satisfactory method of dealing with it had so far been found. He gave some detailed illustrations of the practical problems, and then reiterated the objection of principle spelt out in his formal memorandum to the Home Affairs Committee. He made it clear that he would be strongly opposed to making it a condition of the Government's offering drafting assistance to Strauss that some provision should be included. But he concluded his note by stating: 'I think we should be prepared to take account of views expressed in Parliament on the point.'[84]

The Home Affairs Committee agreed with Jenkins, noting that a special case could be made for 'affording protection to the Sovereign, but the practical problems remained'.[85] Michael Stewart (First Secretary of State), who chaired the meeting, summed up the discussion as follows:

The Committee approved the main provisions which it was proposed to include in the Bill, and considered it desirable that drafting assistance should be given. They agreed with the Home Secretary in thinking that there was no means of effectively prohibiting the presentation of living persons, and that the Bill should therefore follow the recommendations of the Select Committee in making defamation in a stage play a ground for an action for libel. Since, however, the Cabinet had remitted this problem

---

[82] NA, CAB 134/2858. Theatres. Memorandum by the Secretary of State for the Home Department, 21 Nov. 1967.

[83] Ibid.

[84] NA, PREM 13/2152. Note from RHJ [Jenkins] to Prime Minister on Theatres: representation of living persons, 21 Nov. 1967.

[85] NA, CAB 134/2854. Minutes of the Home Affairs Committee of the Cabinet, 24 Nov. 1967.

for further consideration, the Home Secretary's conclusions should be reported to the Cabinet in the following week. In the meantime, Mr. Strauss should be offered drafting assistance and given a long title to put down on 29th November.[86]

These recommendations now had to come back to Cabinet. On 28 November, Jenkins prepared a memorandum for the Cabinet setting out the decision taken by the Home Affairs Committee and the reasons for it:

On 24th November the Home Affairs Committee agreed unanimously to the proposal in my memorandum on theatres that there is no means of effectively prohibiting the presentation of living persons, and that the Theatres Bill should therefore follow the recommendations of the Select Committee on Theatre Censorship in making defamation in a stage play a ground for an action for libel.[87]

Jenkins concluded his memorandum by inviting the Cabinet to endorse the decision of the Home Affairs Committee on this point. A major confrontation between Jenkins and Wilson at the next meeting of the Cabinet now seemed a distinct possibility.

Fortunately for the Cabinet, a head-on clash between the Home Secretary and the Prime Minister was avoided by a sequence of unforeseen 'events' (as Harold Macmillan once so famously called them) that so often seem to determine the course of history. The main 'event' was the devaluation crisis in November, which, as we have seen, saw Callaghan forced to relinquish his position as Chancellor of the Exchequer. On 30 November, he was replaced as Chancellor by Jenkins and Callaghan found himself moved sideways to Jenkins's previous position of Home Secretary. One of the first tasks undertaken by Callaghan was to revisit the issue of whether the Theatres Bill should prohibit the representation of living persons on the stage. On 15 December, he prepared a memorandum for Cabinet in which he went through the various possibilities now facing him. He reported that he had discussed the issue with the Lord Chamberlain, who would like to see a general protection in the bill, 'but not one limited to The Queen and the Royal Family'.[88] He went on to deal with Goodman's suggestion for differentiating between the representation of a person's public and private life, concluding that this did not solve the difficulty. In the final paragraph, he found himself coming to the same conclusions as his predecessor, Jenkins, and supported Jenkins's suggestion that the Government might wish to take note of responses in the House:

[86] Ibid.
[87] NA, CAB 129/134. Theatres. Memorandum by the Secretary of State for the Home Department, 28 Nov. 1967.
[88] NA, CAB 129/134 pt. 2. Theatres. Memorandum by the Secretary of State for the Home Department, 15 Dec. 1967.

I have reached the conclusion that the difficulties of a provision prohibiting the representation of living persons are such that we should not try to persuade Mr. Strauss to accept one in the Bill as introduced. (He would not do it anyway.) We should, however, take into account the reactions of the House on Second Reading and if there is a general desire to include some provision to protect living persons we can consider the matter again. For the present the Bill would simply make defamation in plays a ground of action for libel. But Mr. Strauss will understand that there is likely to be pressure for the adoption of some prohibition of the representation of living persons, and he would be told that the Government are not to be taken as committed to rejecting this course or some other means of dealing with the matter at a later stage of the Bill.[89]

The next 'event' that prevented a showdown in Cabinet over theatre censorship was the fact that Wilson had to leave the country on 20 December for an official visit to Australia. George Brown, the Foreign Secretary, in his absence, therefore chaired the crucial meeting of the Cabinet on 21 December, which received the latest recommendations of the Home Affairs Committee and the two memoranda written, respectively, by Jenkins on 28 November and Callaghan on 15 December. A briefing paper prepared for Brown by Trend, the Cabinet Secretary, set out the issues clearly for him. On the vexed question of protection for living persons, Brown was advised as follows:

Since it is now clear that Mr. Strauss will not introduce a Bill going further than this [defamation in a play as grounds for a civil action] towards restricting the representation of living persons, the immediate question is whether the Government should provide him with the draft of a Bill on these lines, while making it clear that they reserve the right to seek, later on, to have it amended by the inclusion of some specific provision on living persons. If this is agreed, the Cabinet can consider after Christmas, when the agenda may be less heavy, whether any provision, and, if so what, should be prepared, with a view to deciding, in the light of the Second Reading debate, whether to attempt to get it introduced in Committee.[90]

When the Cabinet considered the latest report of the Home Affairs Committee as part of a very crowded agenda, Crossman reminded the meeting what the real issue was, namely the concern of Wilson and the Queen with the representation of live personages in the theatre.[91] The Cabinet duly recorded its continuing concern over the issue of protecting living persons from attack on stage, but followed the line taken by Callaghan in his memorandum. It was agreed that 'The Cabinet could consider the matter again in the light of the views expressed in the House of Commons in the debate on the Second

[89] Ibid.
[90] NA, PREM 13/2152. Briefing note on Theatres for the Foreign Secretary, 20 Dec. 1967.
[91] See Crossman Diary Manuscript, MSS/154/8/104, 50.

Reading of the Bill.'[92] In the meantime the Cabinet approved the proposal to hand Strauss a bill on the terms outlined in the report of the Home Affairs Committee. In the published version of his diary, Crossman commented laconically:

This was round three of the row between Roy Jenkins and the Prime Minister about the Select Committee report recommending that the whole of the Lord Chamberlain's censorship of the theatre should be abolished.

Harold Wilson had held this up last July on the grounds that he and the Queen were worried about the presentation of live personages in the theatre . . . Last July Harold was in a powerful enough position to threaten Roy and say he just couldn't do it. Roy played it cool, he did nothing about it . . . I often asked him to go back and talk to Harold but he was too proud to and now he has ceased to be Home Secretary. James Callaghan presented exactly the same Bill and in Harold's absence the Queen's objections lapsed. In a small way this shows what a decline there has been in Prime Ministerial government.[93]

THE 1968 THEATRES ACT

The Second Reading of the Theatres Bill took place in the House of Commons on 23 February 1968. Strauss, who had chaired the Joint Select Committee, moved the Second Reading, and his speech gave a succinct résumé of the Committee's deliberations. He pointed out that the Committee, despite its disparate membership with widely differing views, came to a unanimous conclusion and it did so 'because the evidence and the argument put before us led to the inescapable conclusion that the pre-censorship of plays by the Lord Chamberlain should cease and be replaced by the application of the laws of the land'.[94] He went on to remind the House that, since the Acts of 1737 and 1843, every author with original ideas on social or political issues had had his plays censored: these authors included Ibsen, Shaw, and Luigi Pirandello. He stressed the political nature of the censorship exercised by the Lord Chamberlain, which meant, for instance, that plays portraying Communist leaders in an unfavourable light were permitted whereas works critical of the United States, such as *Us* and *Macbird*, were censored. He pointed out that the Lord Chamberlain himself felt that the power of censorship should no longer be vested in a court official. However, the Lord Chamberlain's preferred alternative caused some consternation to the Committee:

[92] NA, CAB 128/42 pt. 3. Minutes of the Cabinet meeting held on 21 Dec. 1967.
[93] Crossman, *Diaries*, ii. 617–18.
[94] *Hansard* (Commons), 23 Feb. 1968, vol. 759, cols. 825–6.

Lord Cobbold, to our surprise and to the horror of the Chairman of the Arts Council, Lord Goodman, suggested that the Arts Council should take on that responsibility. Obviously no body can simultaneously discharge the duty of fostering and fettering the art of the theatre. In fact, the Arts Council has come down firmly in favour of the abolition of a pre-censorship of plays.[95]

Strauss then gave the House a detailed summary of what were, in his view, the more important features of the proposed Bill. He explained that Clause 1 not only abolished the censorship powers of the Lord Chamberlain over plays, it also addressed the vexed issue of the Royal Prerogative which had surfaced repeatedly throughout the twentieth century. As Strauss commented: 'We are doubtful whether there is a Royal Prerogative and that the Sovereign is entitled to stop or to censor plays, but we were advised that that may be so and that it was necessary to make the position clear.'[96] Clause 1 therefore abolished the Royal Prerogative in respect of stage censorship: 'The Theatres Act 1843 is hereby repealed; and none of the powers which were exercisable thereunder by the Lord Chamberlain of Her Majesty's Household shall be exercisable by or on behalf of Her Majesty by virtue of Her royal prerogative.'[97] Clause 1 also established that theatre licensing authorities (namely local authorities) should not have any censorship powers: 'the licensing authority shall not have power to impose any term, condition or restriction as to the nature of the plays which may be performed under the licence or as to the manner of performing plays thereunder.'[98]

Strauss went on to explain that Clause 2 of the Bill applied the provisions of the Obscene Publications Act to the theatre so that: 'a performance of a play shall be deemed to be obscene if, taken as a whole, its effect was such as to tend to deprave and corrupt persons who were likely, having regard to all relevant circumstances, to attend it.'[99] However, as specified in Clause 3, the same grounds for defence were permitted as in the Obscene Publications Act, namely that a work was in the public good on the grounds that it was 'in the interests of drama, opera, ballet or any other art, or of literature or learning'.[100] Strauss explained that Clause 4 permitted anyone slandered on the stage to bring an action under the laws of libel:

For the purposes of the law of libel and slander (including the law of criminal libel so far as it relates to the publication of defamatory matter) the publication of words in the course of a performance of a play shall . . . be treated as publication in permanent form. . . . In this section 'words' includes pictures, visual images, gestures and other methods of signifying meaning.[101]

---

[95] Ibid., col. 828.   [96] Ibid., col. 829.
[97] Theatres Act 1968 (c. 54), Clause 1.   [98] Ibid.   [99] Ibid., Clause 2.
[100] Ibid., Clause 3.   [101] Ibid., Clause 4.

Strauss then moved on to Clause 11 and the following clauses which dealt with the licensing of theatres: in effect they applied the licensing provisions of the London Government Act of 1963 to the remainder of the country.

Finally, Strauss explained to the House that the Committee had spent some time considering the issue of whether the representation of living persons should be permitted on stage. The Committee had concluded that it would be 'impossible to draft an Amendment to the Bill which would protect living individuals from presentation on the stage without at the same time banning justifiable satire'.[102] The Committee had considered at some length whether any special protection should be offered to the Sovereign, but concluded that it would be difficult to draft acceptable words to achieve this. It also seemed illogical to ban any contemptuous references to the Sovereign when no such ban exists for newspapers, magazines, and books. Finally, the Committee was persuaded that the public would not tolerate offensive references to the Sovereign on stage any more than they would in the press.

The debate was very poorly attended. At one point, a count was taken to ensure that the House was quorate; it was, but only just, with the minimum number of forty Members present in the Chamber. Many of those who spoke in the debate were members of the Joint Select Committee. All praised the diplomatic skills of Strauss who had successfully steered the Committee to its unanimous conclusion. Some, notably St John Stevas (member of the Joint Select Committee), were still concerned about the issue of the representation of living persons on the stage. Others raised issues in clauses which Strauss had not mentioned in his introduction. Ronald Bell (Conservative MP for Buckinghamshire South) was concerned at Clause 5, which was designed to prohibit material that would inflame racial hatred and included wording taken directly from the Race Relations Act:

if there is given a public performance of a play involving the use of threatening, abusive or insulting words, any person who (whether for gain or not) presented or directed that performance shall be guilty of an offence under this section if—

(a) he did so with intent to stir up hatred against any section of the public in Great Britain distinguished by colour, race or ethnic or national origins; and

(b) that performance, taken as a whole, is likely to stir up hatred against that section on grounds of colour, race or ethnic or national origins.[103]

He was also concerned at Clause 6, which was designed to bar material likely or intended to cause a breach of the peace:

---

[102] *Hansard* (Commons), 23 Feb. 1968, vol. 759, col. 831.
[103] Theatres Act 1968 (c. 54), Clause 5.

if there is given a public performance of a play involving the use of threatening, abusive or insulting words, any person who (whether for gain or not) presented or directed that performance shall be guilty of an offence under this section if—

(a) he did so with intent to provoke a breach of the peace; or

(b) the performance, taken as a whole, was likely to occasion a breach of the peace.[104]

Having always been opposed to censorship, Bell queried whether these two clauses would in effect impose a new form of repressive pressure on playwrights.

Sir Stephen McAdden (Conservative MP for Southend) expressed concern at Clause 8 which stated that no legal proceedings may be instituted except with the consent of the Attorney-General:

Proceedings for an offence under section 2, 5 or 6 of this Act or an offence at common law committed by the publication of defamatory matter in the course of a performance of a play shall not be instituted in England and Wales except by or with the consent of the Attorney-General.[105]

In his view, this placed too much power in the hands of one man.

These were all important matters that needed to be carefully considered by Members of Parliament. It is, however, remarkable that a further key issue in the bill was passed over in silence: namely the extensive powers given to the police to bring a prosecution under Clauses 2, 5, or 6. Clause 10 of the Act gives powers to the police (specifically a police officer above the rank of superintendent) to make an order in writing relating to a person and a performance if he has reasonable grounds for suspecting that an offence has or is likely to be committed in respect of obscenity, racial hatred, or a breach of the peace. The police officer may also require the named person to furnish an actual script on which the performance has or will be based. (This provision explains the presence of police officers at rehearsals after 1968 whenever a play faced the threat of prosecution under Clauses 2, 5, or 6 of the Act.)

In contrast to those Members of Parliament expressing detailed concerns, Michael Foot (member of the Joint Select Committee) stressed the political intentions of censorship:

People have forgotten that politics have been the main cause of censorship. From the way in which the matter is sometimes discussed it might be thought that alleged obscenity was the great danger against which the censor was supposed to guard, but the evidence presented to us, and in particular the evidence by the Lord Chamberlain, underlined that it was political fears which have sustained the censorship. It was

---

[104] Ibid., Clause 6.   [105] Ibid., Clause 8.

political fears which persuaded the original introduction of the censorship and it has very largely been political fears which have sustained it ever since. Whenever an effort has been made to get rid of it by one means or another, in the House or elsewhere, political fears have stopped the change.[106]

In responding to the debate for the Government, Dick Taverne, Under-Secretary of State for the Home Department, began by reminding the House that, when the report of the Joint Select Committee was published, the then Home Secretary, Jenkins, had stated (in response to a Parliamentary Question) that the Government accepted the general principle of the Committee's report and would introduce legislation when a suitable opportunity occurred. Because a Government Bill could not be introduced this session, it was decided to give drafting assistance to Strauss for his Private Member's Bill. Taverne went on to state unequivocally that the 'Bill certainly has the Government's support'.[107] Taverne then responded to key issues raised in the debate. On the question of requiring the agreement of the Attorney-General before any legal proceedings may be initiated, Taverne commented that this was not censorship by one man under another guise. The intention was to prevent vexatious or frivolous prosecutions. Furthermore, the Attorney-General, unlike the Lord Chamberlain, is answerable to the House. On the issue of the representation of living persons, Taverne was firmly supportive of the Committee's conclusions and commented that he could see 'formidable difficulties and objections in the way of any kind of ban or limitation on the representation of living persons'.[108] Given the known concerns of the Prime Minister on this issue, as expressed in Cabinet, this was a surprisingly forthright comment. Taverne finally responded to concerns expressed over Clauses 5 and 6. Clause 5, in his view, was necessary and could not simply be left to a new Race Relations Bill. Things that affected the theatre should be in one self-contained bill. Clause 6 was included as it embodied a form of restraint at present exercised by the Lord Chamberlain. The requirement that performances should not be designed or likely to cause a breach of the peace was an important provision for what was a public occasion. Taverne concluded by observing that this was an important and historic bill and on behalf of the Government, he commended it to the House. The Second Reading was agreed without a division and the bill was sent for more detailed consideration to a Standing Committee.

It was reported to the Home Affairs Committee of Cabinet, at its meeting held on 26 April 1968, that three amendments had been tabled at the Standing Committee by Opposition Members to prohibit the representation of, respectively, the royal family, any head of state, and any living person.

---

[106] *Hansard* (Commons), 23 Feb. 1968, vol. 759, col. 854.　　　[107] Ibid., col. 863.
[108] Ibid., col. 868.

The Home Affairs Committee, chaired by Crossman, began its deliberations by noting that the Cabinet had expressed some misgivings about abolishing censorship without finding a means to prevent 'objectionable presentation of living persons'.[109] It was further noted that the Second Reading Debate had been 'too sparsely attended to be a reliable test of opinion'.[110] In view of the amendments that had been tabled at the Standing Committee, the Home Affairs Committee needed to determine the line to be taken by the Home Office spokesman on the Standing Committee. In discussion, it was agreed to oppose the amendments so far put forward but to explore a suggestion made by Lord Stow Hill (formerly Soskice, the Home Secretary) to Strauss that a person should be given the right to obtain an injunction prohibiting the repetition of offensive references in a play. In particular: 'It should be considered . . . whether scurrilous, abusive or indecent references falling short of libel ought to be the subject of action.'[111] Summing up the discussion, Crossman noted that the Government had not so far been prepared to amend the bill to offer protection for living persons 'because no method of doing so had been put forward which would not run contrary to the principle of abolition of pre-censorship, which was the essential feature of the Bill'.[112] He wanted the Government to give further consideration to the problem of living persons before the bill reached the Lords. Meanwhile, the Government spokesman on the Standing Committee should oppose the amendments so far proposed but should make it clear that the Government was still willing to consider any practicable proposal to offer safeguards to living persons without destroying the principle of the bill.

Immediately after this meeting, Parliamentary Counsel were given the task of drafting amendments to the bill so that individuals might have the right to obtain an injunction prohibiting offensive references in a play. These drafts[113] were shortly afterwards considered and rejected at a meeting attended by Stonham, the Lord Chancellor, and the Attorney-General. Stonham explained the sequence of events in a memorandum written on 6 May 1968 for the Home Affairs Committee. The drafts prepared for Stonham and the Government's Law Officers were an attempt to explore whether a viable option for protection could be based on Stow Hill's proposals:

Our conclusion was that Lord Stow Hill's proposal constituted too great an encroachment on freedom of expression. We considered two possible alternative clauses prepared by Parliamentary Counsel designed simply to deal with offensive references

---

[109] NA, CAB 134/2859. Theatres Bill: Living Persons. Minutes of the Home Affairs Committee of the Cabinet, 26 Apr. 1968.
[110] Ibid.   [111] Ibid.   [112] Ibid.
[113] NA, HO 300/77. Theatres Bill. Draft new clauses.

to living persons made in an inexcusably coarse and indecent manner. We rejected one, which would have empowered the Attorney-General to move in the public interest for an injunction to prohibit references to living persons made in a manner that were [*sic*] grossly offensive to public taste, on the ground that this would almost saddle the Attorney-General with the very responsibility for acting as an arbiter of public taste which the Bill was designed to take away from the Lord Chamberlain. We rejected the other, which would have enabled the victim of a reference made in an offensively indecent manner to secure an injunction, because the substance of the complaint was likely to be too elusive to serve as a basis for judicial proceedings. In general we concluded that no satisfactory provision could be founded on this basis; and that in any event the law of defamation, together with the provision in clause 6 of the Bill making it an offence to present or direct a performance involving the use of threatening, abusive or insulting words or behaviour with intent to provoke a breach of the peace or that was likely to occasion a breach of the peace, afforded the correct degree of protection to living persons.[114]

Stonham's memorandum was considered at the next meeting of the Home Affairs Committee held on the morning of 10 May 1968, which was chaired by the Lord Chancellor and attended by the Attorney-General. The Committee resolved that 'no amendment to the Bill to protect living persons was necessary or practicable and that the Government should support Mr. Strauss in resisting amendments for this purpose'.[115]

After many months of fruitless deliberation, the Home Affairs Committee of Cabinet finally reached the same conclusion that Jenkins had first arrived at almost a year earlier in July 1967 and had subsequently confirmed in his memorandum for the Cabinet written in November 1967. The attempt to find some form of protection for living persons on stage had initially been insisted on by Wilson, allegedly at the request of the Queen. It was subsequently pursued by St John Stevas during the Second Reading and in the Standing Committee. Now, having exhausted all legal possibilities, the Home Affairs Committee of Cabinet agreed that the Government spokesman on the Standing Committee should support Strauss in resisting any further 'amendments designed to prohibit references to living persons or their representation on the stage'.[116]

Later that same morning of 10 May, the Theatres Bill was given an unopposed Third Reading in the Commons. As before, there was widespread congratulation for Strauss for so adroitly piloting his bill to a successful conclusion. Strauss thanked the Government for their warm support and for

---

[114] NA, CAB 134/2861. Record of a meeting between Stonham, the Lord Chancellor, and the Attorney-General, 3 May 1968.
[115] NA, CAB 134/2859. Theatres Bill: Living Persons. Minutes of the Home Affairs Committee of the Cabinet, 10 May 1968.
[116] Ibid.

their help in drafting the bill so as to implement fully the recommendations of the Joint Select Committee. He also expressed a personal sense of gratification that the bill had made such swift and smooth progress:

I expected a long and bitter battle over the Bill and that we should have strenuous opposition from those elements in the House that are always fearful of libertarian advances and resist them. That has not happened. I think the reason is that the Report of the Joint Select Committee which considered the matter was unanimous and . . . that the Report was exceedingly well argued and presented an irresistible case.[117]

The Theatres Bill was given an unopposed Second Reading in the House of Lords on 28 May. In a unique break with precedent, however, the Lord Chamberlain had previously signalled his wish to the Home Secretary, Callaghan, to express his reservations about this bill, a bill which, at that juncture, had clear Government support. In a letter sent on 15 May he explained that he would like to express his continuing unease on the issue of living persons. Aware of the constitutional minefield into which he was about to proceed, Cobbold wrote:

I shall, of course, be prepared to support the Second Reading, but I must in conscience repeat reservations I have made on certain points, particularly the treatment of 'living persons', and express the hope that the Bill could be suitably amended in Committee. May I assume that this would not be regarded by the Prime Minister or yourself as in any way contravening the understanding that the Lord Chamberlain does not speak against the Government, bearing in mind both that this is a Private Member's Bill and that Mr Morgan said, when dealing with the St John-Stevas amendments: 'The Government are not committed to opposing every amendment and if a practicable proposal were put forward at a later stage we should be prepared to examine it'? I have had a brief word with Lord Beswick about arrangements, and propose to have a talk with Lord Stonham, who will, I assume, be speaking for the Government.[118]

A formal reply was drafted in the Prime Minister's office for Callaghan to sign as Home Secretary. The reply made it clear that the Government, after full consideration of the matter, would not support an amendment to give specific additional protection to living persons. Furthermore, any intervention by the Lord Chamberlain, along the lines he had suggested would cause considerable embarrassment to the Government:

As to your speaking in the House of Lords, I find myself in great difficulty. As you will see, you would be urging on the Government a course of action which they have considered and decided not to adopt. But there is a further consideration. In your theatre licensing capacity you must have more than most people to contribute by way

---

[117] *Hansard* (Commons), 10 May 1968, vol. 764, col. 771.
[118] NA, PREM 13/2152. Letter from Cobbold to Callaghan, 15 May 1968.

of practical experience of the kind of material that managers want to put on, and this experience would clearly be invaluable to the House. On the other hand, will it be possible in your position in The Queen's Household to avoid creating the impression that you are conveying Her Majesty's own views?[119]

Because a meeting was arranged between Cobbold and Stonham on 22 May, the draft reply was never sent. Callaghan's Private Secretary, Geoffrey de Deney, informed Wilson's Private Secretary, Le Cheminant, of the sequence of events:

I enclose a copy of a letter from the Lord Chamberlain to the Home Secretary . . . Departmentally, we saw considerable difficulty in this and had prepared a reply for the Home Secretary to send, a copy of which I enclose. Since that reply was drafted, Lord Stonham met Lord Cobbold; I enclose a copy of the note of the meeting, together with a copy of the draft extract from Lord Cobbold's speech referred to in the note. We have not yet had an opportunity of examining Lord Cobbold's alternative proposal in detail but at first sight it appears to resemble one of the alternatives considered at the 13th meeting of Home Affairs [held on 26 April] and rejected.

As you will see, Lord Cobbold's view is that any opinions expressed would not be likely to be regarded as being those of the Queen. However, there remains the question whether, supposing Lord Cobbold's views do prove to conflict with Government policy, the conventions point to advising him against speaking. If the answer is yes, Lord Cobbold has asked to be given an opportunity to discuss the matter with both the Prime Minister and the Home Secretary . . . I should be glad to have your views.[120]

In addition to sending this note, De Deney telephoned Le Cheminant. The latter kept a record of their conversation:

The Home Office provisional view was to tell Lord Cobbold that the Government could not accept the amendment on the lines of that proposed by Lord Stow Hill and to hint delicately that intervention by Lord Cobbold might be misinterpreted as a plea from the Palace.

I said that we could not properly seek the Prime Minister's advice without a sight of the papers and De Deney promised to supply these urgently. I pointed out also that the conclusions of the Home Affairs meeting of April 26 did not amount to an outright rejection of Lord Stow Hill's amendment in the form that it then took but had invited the Home Office to consult further with the Attorney-General to see whether it could be amended in some acceptable manner. The Committee had also decided that the Government should let it be known that they would be perfectly prepared to consider any practical proposals put forward in the course of the debates to afford a measure of protection to living persons provided they did not run counter to the basic principle of the abolition of pre-censorship. In the light of this it seemed to me that Lord Stonham

---

[119] Ibid. Letter to Cobbold drafted for signature by Secretary of State.
[120] Ibid. Letter from De Deney (Home Office) to Le Cheminant (Prime Minister's Office), 22 May 1968.

could only stall when he met Lord Cobbold, though he could no doubt repeat once again that the Government would be prepared to consider any practical proposal and point out the dangers of possible misinterpretation of a speech by Lord Cobbold.[121]

According to a formal record made by Le Cheminant, in the meeting between Stonham and Cobbold, Stonham reiterated the concern already expressed in the draft note prepared for Callaghan (but not sent), namely that it would be 'difficult not to create the impression that, in view of his position in the Queen's Household, he was conveying Her Majesty's own views'.[122] Furthermore, any intervention of the kind planned by the Lord Chamberlain would be seen as urging a course of action which the Government found itself unable to adopt.[123] He also made it clear that everything he said was subject to the final decision of the Prime Minister. Cobbold argued that he was not seeking to oppose the Government but simply to respond positively, on the issue of living persons, to the statement made by the Government spokesman at the Standing Committee, namely that the Government still had an open mind on the issue. He also made it clear that he would make no reference to Her Majesty. Stonham pointed out that Morgan's statement in Standing Committee reflected the Government's position at the time, but the Government 'would not now feel able to support an amendment to give specific additional protection to living persons'.[124]

Cobbold commented that he had given further thought to this and had a new suggestion to make. He handed Stonham a draft of the speech he intended to make in the Lords in which he stressed his concern at the lack of protection for the Sovereign.[125] He went on to suggest the use of a form of words found in the Television Act of 1964. In that Act television authorities are required to satisfy themselves that 'nothing is included in the programmes which offends against good taste or decency or is likely to encourage or to incite to crime or to lead to disorder or to be offensive to public feeling'.[126] He wanted to see the same form of words used to offer protection to living persons. In making this suggestion, Cobbold glossed over an essential difference between television and the theatre. In the case of television, the form of words used is a duty laid upon the television authorities: in the case of the theatre, it would be legitimate grounds for criminal proceedings.

Cobbold concluded his discussion with Stonham by stating that he would not table any amendment himself but simply hope that the Government would explore his suggestion. Stonham stated that the Home Secretary would write

---

[121] Ibid. Le Cheminant. Note for record, 22 May 1968.
[122] Ibid.   [123] Ibid.
[124] Ibid. Dafydd Elystan Morgan was a junior minister in the Home Office.
[125] Ibid. Draft of Lord Cobbold's proposed speech to the House of Lords.
[126] Ibid.

to Cobbold as soon as the Prime Minister's decision was received (namely as to whether it was constitutionally feasible for the Lord Chamberlain to speak against a bill supported by Her Majesty's Government). This constitutional impasse was resolved the very next day when the Prime Minister finally agreed that Cobbold should have permission to speak in the House of Lords debate. Le Cheminant wrote to De Deney on 23 May 1968 and stated that, in the Prime Minister's view, a speech from the Lord Chamberlain, given his deep knowledge of the subject, was to be welcomed. He would also be very content for Cobbold to make his points about 'living persons' even though the chances of a workable solution were 'now so slim'.[127] This indeed proved to be the case.

As outlined in his draft, Cobbold intervened in the Lords debate to urge that some protection be given in Law, based on the wording of the Television Act, to prevent offensive depictions of the Sovereign and the royal family on stage. He carefully followed the wording in his draft and then went on to argue:

I suggest, my Lords, that at least so far as representation of and reference to living people is concerned, the theatre is far more akin to television than to the written word and that it would be eminently reasonable for a similar degree of protection to be afforded in both media, stage and television. No one would wish to restrict genuine political satire, and indeed it could never be held to be offensive to public feeling. But a clause making it an offence to represent or refer to living persons and those recently dead in a way calculated to offend public feeling would bring the standard that applies on the stage into line with that for plays on television and would afford, in my judgment, much needed protection to certain categories of people.

I suggest for your Lordships' consideration that some amendment on these lines would improve the Bill without damaging its general concept, and would allay what I believe to be widespread concern on this matter.[128]

Cobbold's suggestion was vigorously opposed by Stonham on behalf of the Government. Stonham's speech was drafted by the Home Office. In these 'Notes for the Speech for Minister of State',[129] Stonham was required to spell out the Government's position on the issue of protection for living persons. He did so in the Lords debate, following the prepared notes very closely:

My Lords, I come now to the major point, if there be a major point, which is at issue in this debate. It has been suggested that an exception ought to be made in respect of the representation of living persons in a stage performance . . . The Government have had this problem very much in mind, not over the last few days or weeks, but for months, and it seems right at this stage I should indicate the conclusions which the Government have reached about it.

---

[127] Ibid. Note from Le Cheminant to De Deney, 23 May 1968.

[128] *Hansard* (Lords), 28 May 1968, vol. 292, cols. 1059–60.

[129] NA, HO 300/78. Theatres Bill. Second Reading: Lords. Notes for Speech for Minister of State.

To put it quite bluntly, our conclusion is that the Bill is right as it stands, and that the protection provided by Clause 8 which makes defamation in a stage performance of a play count as libel instead of slander, is as much as it would be right to provide. The right of free speech is one of the most cherished traditions in this country; and rightly so. It is not something which we should lightly jeopardise or erode, even in a small way, except for the most compelling reasons. It is only right therefore to make clear here and now that the kind of protection that seems to be envisaged, or has been envisaged, by some noble Lords, can scarcely be secured except by what would amount to substantial inroads on the principle of free speech . . .

The noble Lord, Lord Cobbold, suggested a possible solution to the problem posed by the portrayal of living persons. He suggested a provision making it an offence to portray on the stage living people, or people who had recently died, in a manner offensive to public feeling. This would be similar to the terms under which the I.T.A. operate . . . This kind of criterion for what should not be allowed on the stage was one which was considered in the general examination by the Government of the whole problem of whether living people should be protected from portrayal in plays. The inescapable conclusion we reached was that it would not be a suitable, or even practicable, formula on which to found a criminal offence. It was too elusive a criterion to serve as a proper basis for criminal proceedings.[130]

Having swept aside Cobbold's attempt to retain some form of protection for the royal family, Stonham concluded by commending the bill to the House. It was given an unopposed Second Reading. Thereafter the progress of the bill was uneventful. It was passed by both Houses of Parliament in July and received the Royal Assent on 26 July 1968.

OPPOSITION TO THE THEATRES ACT BY THE ROYAL HOUSEHOLD

The sequence of events outlined in this chapter suggests that there was deep unhappiness in the Royal Household at the prospect of a theatre unfettered by censorship. According to Crossman, the Prime Minister was enlisted in the Palace's campaign against the abolition of theatre censorship at an early juncture in the controversy. As the chief officer of the Sovereign's Household, the Lord Chamberlain acted throughout as the main conduit for expressing the views of the Palace. We have also seen how Crossman, who shared the concerns of Buckingham Palace (and was therefore not writing with any mischievous intent), stressed repeatedly in his diary that the worries of the Queen over the presentation of living persons on stage were the real problem.

---

[130] *Hansard* (Lords), 28 May 1968, vol. 292, cols. 1098–1100.

One can only guess at what caused the Palace to react so vigorously against the notion of a theatre free from the shackles of censorship. It may be, as Crossman suggested, that initially the Queen was concerned how the Duke of Edinburgh might be depicted on stage. There is no other evidence to corroborate Crossman's view. However, as we shall see, there is evidence to suggest that the most plausible explanation for the growing opposition of the Royal Household to the Theatres Bill may be found in the text of Bond's play, *Early Morning*, written in 1967.

Early Morning was a savage, surreal farce in which Bond showed a nightmarish vision of Victorian England, tearing itself to tatters. The play opens with Disraeli plotting with Prince Albert to kill Queen Victoria. She, meanwhile, is shown as the mother of Siamese twins, George and Arthur. Having married off one of her twin sons, George, to Florence Nightingale, Queen Victoria then proceeds to rape Florence and have a lesbian love affair with her. She persuades Florence to poison Albert whom she then strangles with his own garter sash. Disraeli, the plotter, is shot by his own men. Gladstone, a would-be revolutionary, talks like a manic trades union official and dies of a heart attack. The Lord Chamberlain bobs in and out of the action as a vacuous buffoon who wants to know what John Brown has under his kilt (in fact it is Florence in drag). George dies twice and slowly rots away, while still attached to his brother, Arthur. In despair at the total absurdity of this mad world, Arthur engineers a murderous tug-of-war on Beachy Head which kills his own and Queen Victoria's men. After a life of homicidal conflict, they all end up in Heaven which is shown as a mirror image of the mad world they have just left, only worse. The various characters who have plotted against each other on earth now pass the time by eating each other in grotesque acts of cannibalism. As they are in Heaven, no lasting harm is done and the murdered corpses grow again so that the process can recommence afresh. Arthur emerges as a reluctant rebel, which leads him to a process of resurrection after his mother has attempted to stuff him into a coffin. Against all the odds, Arthur pursues the path of personal freedom in a world and a Heaven that are shown to be completely insane. Underneath the horror-film events shown in the action, and the often grotesquely obscene dialogue, there was, according to Bond, a deeply serious (evidently existentialist) purpose underpinning the play which he defined as follows:

I say that freedom is a possibility for human beings and that the negative social situation is not predicated by faults in the individual. So that it's a freedom play in that way, that . . . whatever happens, whatever comes, it is possible for the individual to be free.[131]

---

[131] Quoted from Malcolm Hay and Philip Roberts, *Bond, a Study of His Plays* (London: Methuen, 1980), 76.

As in the case of *Saved*, only more so, there was an unbridgeable gulf between Bond's social and philosophical consciousness and that of the Lord Chamberlain and his Readers. *Early Morning* caused real offence in the Lord Chamberlain's office and led to a final major confrontation between the censor and the Royal Court Theatre. The text of the play was submitted to the Lord Chamberlain in October 1967. It was banned outright (the only play submitted by the Royal Court to have been completely banned) on 8 November 1967. The initial Reader's report stated:

There may be some dramatic truth in this nightmarish plot and distorted characterisation but it is not a normal vision. It is possible to see this play as a weird phantasmagoria, making a strong, sour statement about power and politics in the Victorian age. But the defamatory treatment of the chief characters apart, the play appears to this reader to be the product of a diseased imagination; cannibalism and lesbianism may be legitimate themes for dramatisation, but not in this context.[132]

This initial response to the play was confirmed by John Johnston, the Assistant Comptroller, who wrote to the Lord Chamberlain on 5 November 1967:

I am quite sure it should not be licensed. The plot is difficult to follow and gets more and more meaningless. The author must have a very sick mind, and I cannot conceive that anyone would want to see the play, except possibly in anticipation of the Zany treatment of Queen Victoria and her relationship with Florence Nightingale.

It is a weird mixture of supposed history and modern trappings of the cinema, TV, radio, etc . . . To me the cannibalism of the third act is disgusting, even if it were to be played as farce.

When I began to read the play I hoped in a way that I might be able to disagree with both readers and recommend a licence in some form, but with the best will in the world this just does not seem possible.[133]

Gaskill, who was directing the play for the Royal Court Theatre, was clearly exasperated by the decision to ban the play without giving any reason. He wrote at some length to Johnston on 15 January 1968 enquiring what had led to the ban. Was it the theme of lesbianism, or cannibalism? Was it the comic treatment of the Lord Chamberlain? Or was it the treatment of royalty, in this case Queen Victoria, which was not wholly sympathetic? Gaskill continued:

I cannot help thinking that it is the last point which may have produced the total ban. I hope you have not been misled by the author's statement on the title page: 'the events of this play are true.'

The play is an intensely subjective, poetic fantasy about the author's own experience of the world today. It is not intended to have any historical truth whatsoever, and the

---

[132] BL, LR 1968/4 *Early Morning*. Reader's report: play refused, 25 Oct. 1967.
[133] Ibid. Note from Johnston to Cobbold, 5 Nov. 1967.

work it most resembles is probably *Alice in Wonderland*. Queen Victoria is a symbolic figure like the Queen of Hearts, always shouting: 'Off with her head'. Gladstone, for instance, is a typical Trades Union leader of today and bears no resemblance to his historical counterpart. The very fact of Victoria having Siamese twins shows immediately there is no historical basis for the play, and that it is meant to be seen as a fantasy. In every other way, I would consider it to be a much less disturbing play than *Saved* and certainly contains no scene as violent as the stoning of the baby.[134]

Gaskill concluded his note by stating that it would be helpful to have a clear indication of the reasons for the ban and to be given some reassurance that, in view of the court case over *Saved*, there was no undue sensitivity to Bond's work or to plays submitted from the Royal Court Theatre.

Johnston discussed Gaskill's letter with the Lord Chamberlain and sent a detailed reply on 18 January 1968: it is very revealing. As far as the Lord Chamberlain was concerned, *Early Morning* had clearly touched a raw and sensitive nerve. It obviously demonstrated in his eyes all the dangers he was trying to warn against in respect of the offensive representation on stage of living persons or the recent dead. Queen Victoria might not easily be seen to fall into either of these two categories, but the way she was treated in this play could be used as a template for the treatment of 'living persons'. Johnston wrote:

The Lord Chamberlain wishes me to say that whilst he understands the play to be a fantasy, that fact does not absolve it from being required to conform to the general criteria upon which plays are to be judged.

The play *Early Morning* comprises mainly historical characters, who are subjected throughout to highly offensive . . . and untrue accusations of gross indecency. They are selected for insult apparently as being nationally respected figures with long records of devoted service to their country and fellow citizens.

Whilst lesbianism, hetero-sexual perversion, cannibalism and false accusations of murder may be legitimate subjects for some plays, the Lord Chamberlain does not agree that they should be falsely attributed to historical personages of recent date. If allegory is required then the characters should be allegorical.

Since the Lord Chamberlain's disallowances are of so fundamental a kind it is, I am afraid, beside the point to detail phrases which give particular offence.[135]

Johnston's reply was clearly intended to foreclose any further correspondence on the issue. Gaskill was, however, not so easily deterred. He replied to Johnston on 30 January 1968 and directed some pointed questions on the key issues set out in Johnston's letter. Does the Lord Chamberlain mean that all plays insulting historical personages of recent date should be banned? Would

---

[134] Ibid. Letter from Gaskill to Johnston, 15 Jan. 1968.
[135] Ibid. Letter from Johnston to Gaskill, 18 Jan. 1968.

this apply to plays about Lenin and Trotsky? How recent does the date have to be? Would a play about Queen Anne, rather than Queen Victoria, be acceptable? Would the play be licensed if the characters were non-historical? Gaskill explained that he needed answers to these questions before approaching the author to see if any changes might be made. He concluded his note by stating that if 'His Lordship' were not prepared to discuss the matter further, then the play would have to be presented as a club performance. Would 'His Lordship' have any objection to such club performances?[136]

On 9 February, Johnston met with Gaskill to discuss whether any changes might be made to the script, for instance by removing the action from a specific historical context. He reported to the Lord Chamberlain that Gaskill was not convinced that Bond would be prepared to compromise. He also reported that he had 'fired a warning shot' on club performances by stating that the Lord Chamberlain only intervenes when banned plays are put on in public under 'some transparent evasion'.[137] Responding to Johnston that same day, the Lord Chamberlain commented that he would look at the play in a new light if the play were re-submitted with allegorical and non-historical characters. He would probably ask for a few, but not very many alterations. On the question of a club performance, Cobbold wrote:

As at present advised and assuming that the 'Club' arrangements were the same as those ruling at the time of the Magistrate's decision in the *Saved* case, I should feel bound to pass the papers to the D.P.P. The decision as to whether proceedings would be instituted would not be for me, but my personal view is that the Royal Court would be unwise to assume that action would not be taken.[138]

On 16 February Gaskill reported to Johnston that Bond was unwilling to remove all sense of historical personages from his play as this would weaken its impact. He therefore asked whether the Lord Chamberlain would be prepared to allow genuine club performances for between one and three weeks.[139] Johnston was instructed to inform Gaskill that the Lord Chamberlain would not speculate on any future action he might take, but if there were a club performance today, he would feel bound to pass the papers to the DPP.[140]

The original intention, as reported by *The Times* on 21 March 1968, was for *Early Morning* to have been given a three-week season of club performances at the Royal Court opening on 23 January. This had to be postponed because Gaskill was taken ill with pneumonia. However, *The Times* now reported that

    136 Ibid. Letter from Gaskill to Johnston, 30 Jan. 1968.
    137 Ibid. Note from Johnston to Cobbold, 9 Feb. 1968.
    138 Ibid. Note from Cobbold to Johnston, 9 Feb. 1968.
    139 Ibid. Letter from Gaskill to Johnston, 16 Feb. 1968.
    140 Ibid. Note from Cobbold to Johnston, 20 Feb. 1968. Letter from Johnston to Gaskill, 21 Feb. 1968.

the play would be performed at the Royal Court on Sunday, 31 March, and Sunday, 7 April. The immediate response of the Lord Chamberlain was to ask Johnston to discuss with the DPP's office what action might be taken. Johnston had a meeting with Nugent at the DPP's office on 25 March. During the course of this meeting, Johnston outlined the fact that the Lord Chamberlain had 'very strong views about the undesirability of this play'.[141] Nugent, representing the DPP, appears to have taken a less than supportive line. He explained that he 'felt diffident in proceeding in circumstances that had been "connived at" by successive Lord Chamberlains for many years'.[142] He also made the point that successful proceedings against the Royal Court for a Sunday evening club performance would invalidate a policy of some eighty or ninety years standing.

The Lord Chamberlain was clearly outraged at this response. He instructed Johnston to inform the DPP that he felt that the play in question was quite unacceptable for public performance. On the one hand, he did not wish to create a disproportionately embarrassing situation, and of course the final decision would rest with the DPP; however, if the Royal Court performances created any significant public comment, he would feel obliged to reiterate his views on the 'desirability of proceedings, and if questioned as to his reaction would say that he had sent papers to the Director'.[143] He even went as far as to share his anger with the Queen. In a handwritten note to Johnston, dated 26 March 1968, Cobbold stated:

I mentioned last night to the Queen the present position about 'Early Morning'. Her Majesty agreed that this should be put firmly on the Attorney's [Attorney-General's] lap.

I also said I should be grateful if she would mention the Censorship bill to the Prime Minister . . . The Queen will do so.[144]

For an experienced head of the Royal Household, this was an astonishingly indiscreet note. It states categorically that the Queen had agreed to intervene directly with the Prime Minister over the Theatres Bill that was at that time in Committee stage in Parliament. It implies that the Queen shared the Lord Chamberlain's anger over the production of *Early Morning* and again categorically states that in her view the play should be a matter for the Attorney-General. The most likely interpretation of this statement is

---

[141] Ibid. Report of points made by Assistant Comptroller to the DPP at their meeting on 25 Mar. 1968.

[142] Ibid.

[143] Ibid. Report of points made by the Lord Chamberlain to the Assistant Comptroller on 25 Mar. 1968.

[144] Ibid. Note from Cobbold to Johnston, 26 Mar. 1968.

that, in the Queen's view, proceedings should be instituted by the DPP in the event of a club performance of *Early Morning*. This means that, according to the Lord Chamberlain, the Queen was prepared to speak to the Prime Minister, at one of her weekly meetings with him, on matters that were by this stage the affair of Parliament and of the Government's Law Officers.

There is of course no means of knowing whether the Queen actually did raise the issue of the 'Censorship bill' with Wilson at her weekly meeting: no formal record is published of these meetings between monarch and Prime Minister. And even if the Queen did indeed raise the matter with Wilson, she would have exercised no more than her constitutional right to 'be consulted, to encourage, and to warn'. However, Cobbold's indiscreet claim (provoked by fury at Bond's play) that the Queen was willing to express her views to the Prime Minister suggests a degree of excessive concern, bordering on panic, on the part of the Lord Chamberlain, and possibly the royal family, at the likely consequences of the Theatres Bill. One can only assume that the thought in their minds was this: if Bond could subject a historical queen to such withering scorn in his surreal farce, what might he not do to a reigning one? Cobbold's note also explains why Callaghan and Stonham were later instructed by the Prime Minister's Office to warn the Lord Chamberlain bluntly: if he spoke in the Lords debate against the Government's view of the Theatres Bill, it would be difficult to avoid giving the impression that he was expressing Her Majesty's point of view. Cobbold's subsequent insistence on speaking in the House of Lords against a bill supported at that juncture by the Government (having been firmly advised not to by the Minister of State) does serve to underline the degree of concern felt by the Palace at the prospect of a stage unfettered by censorship.

In the event, only one performance of *Early Morning* was given (prior to the passing of the Theatres Act) on 27 March 1968. Johnston reported to the Lord Chamberlain on 1 April that, for this one performance, a vice squad inspector joined the club without much difficulty; he was charged 7s. 6d. for membership and was able to buy two tickets at the same time: 'The police inspector told Nugent [DPP's office] he reckoned he was incorruptible, but after last night's performance was not sure.'[145] The Lord Chamberlain was informed on 4 April that the Attorney-General was now taking a more serious view of the matter, as it was possible for a police officer simultaneously to become a member and buy tickets. He was also informed that the police would interview the Royal Court authorities to warn them that the DPP was aware of and taking note of their intentions. Because of this pressure, the Royal Court

---

[145] Ibid. Report from Assistant Comptroller to Lord Chamberlain, 1 Apr. 1968.

cancelled the second performance of *Early Morning*, scheduled for 7 April, and instead presented a dress rehearsal to critics and selected guests, followed by a teach-in on stage censorship. Further pressure came from the Arts Council which decided to withhold its grant to the Royal Court during the build-up to the performance of *Early Morning*, partly because of the threat of legal proceedings.[146] Following the dress rehearsal and teach-in on 7 April, Esdaile (the theatre licensee) offered his resignation and demanded that of Gaskill as Artistic Director: Gaskill refused.[147]

The pressure exerted by the Lord Chamberlain was very effective in silencing the Royal Court for one last time, but it was a completely pyrrhic victory. A mere three months later the Theatres Act was on the statute book and the Royal Court was free to produce plays by Bond and other dramatists who for years had suffered the indignity of having their plays banned or cut to shreds by men whose social and political consciousness derived from an altogether different age. Gaskill took immediate advantage of this new freedom. In 1969, he presented at the Royal Court a full public production of *Early Morning* and productions of two other plays by Bond, which had previously suffered at the hands of the censor.

The abolition of censorship, as was made clear by Members of the Lords and Commons in their debates and by the report of the Joint Select Committee, was a political issue. Its abolition was a long-awaited conclusion to a battle fought on principle. Those opposed to the abolition of censorship were primarily concerned with protecting the reputation of the royal family and the political elite rather than with controlling obscenity and blasphemy. This point emerges with great clarity from the account given in this chapter. The Theatres Act of 1968 gave dramatists, for the first time since 1737, the same freedom of speech in the theatre as enjoyed by other writers and artists. The worries of the royal family, so far at least, have proved to be unfounded. No members of the royal family have been subjected on stage to the kind of offensive attacks that seem to have been feared in the mid-1960s by the Queen, her Lord Chamberlain, and her Prime Minister. The paparazzi and journalists of the popular press; television documentary makers; and, more recently, television scriptwriters have submitted the lives of members of the royal family to the most intrusive scrutiny. In marked contrast, since 1968, British dramatists have shown an almost total lack of interest in the royal family. While this may give rise to satisfaction in the Palace, it is at least arguable that a few offensive satirical attacks against royalty might in fact be preferable to such deafening indifference. Of course, things may change in future. But even if dramatists were to take

---

[146] See Hay and Roberts, *Bond*, 67.   [147] Ibid. 68.

a renewed interest in the lives of the royal family, they would still find themselves constrained by the law of libel and the general requirement not to use abusive and insulting words in such a way as deliberately to cause a breach of the peace. As Government ministers concluded in 1968, these constraints offer sufficient safeguards to all living persons, whatever their station in life.

8

The Aftermath: British Theatre following the Abolition of Statutory Censorship

LEGAL ACTION AFTER THE 1968 THEATRES ACT

Following the abolition of statutory theatre censorship in 1968, dramatists who had clashed repeatedly with the censor were now free to develop their ideas and ways of expressing them without having the irritation of knowing from the outset that they would face constant battles with the Lord Chamberlain over their choice of words, themes, and characters. Established writers such as Bond, John Arden, and Harold Pinter were able to explore in their work whatever aspects of human experience they chose and in whatever way. The quality and range of their mature work from the late 1960s would in itself provide more than ample justification for a stage freed from the muzzling constraints of censorship. In addition, a new generation of writers was soon to emerge, playwrights such as Howard Barker, Steven Berkoff, and, more recently, Mark Ravenhill and Sarah Kane, who have probed in their work complex patterns of experience with an imaginative and provocative use of words, deeds, themes, and characters. None of their plays would have been approved by the censor without significant cuts. Moreover, playwrights such as David Edgar, David Hare, Trevor Griffiths, and Howard Brenton have investigated in their work contemporary social and political issues with the kind of honesty that the censor would not have tolerated. Yet all of these playwrights, and many more, have helped to give British theatre of the late twentieth century a place of seminal importance in modern European culture. In short, it was as if the abolition of theatre censorship opened a floodgate of theatrical creativity.

A more trivial, but perhaps predictable consequence of the abolition of theatre censorship was the staging of numerous erotic revues in London's West End involving nudity and deliberately provocative sexuality. The first of these, *Oh! Calcutta!* (whose title was based on that of a painting by the French surrealist painter Clovis Trouille, in turn based on the pun 'O quel cul t'as'), was a celebration of slightly tacky eroticism compiled by Kenneth Tynan, with contributions from, amongst others, Jules Feiffer, Leonard Melfi, John Lennon, and even Samuel Beckett. From the mid-1950s, Tynan had established for himself a well-deserved reputation as one of London's most celebrated theatre critics. Since 1963 he had served as the flamboyant literary manager of the National Theatre, and had acquired something of the reputation of an *enfant terrible* in London's theatre world. *Oh! Calcutta!* was soon followed by a plethora of imitations: *Let my People come!*, *The Dirtiest Show in Town*, and Tynan's own follow-up show, *Carte Blanche*.[1]

Tynan had planned *Oh! Calcutta!* well before the abolition of stage censorship in Britain. In 1966 he had discussed with William Donaldson, producer of the Cambridge revue *Beyond the Fringe*, the notion of devising an entertaining *International Erotic Review*, with contributions from well-known writers, interspersed with dance and striptease numbers.[2] Any stage nudity that involved moving bodies would be immediately banned by the Lord Chamberlain. In view of this, and because of difficulties in finding a suitable cast and director in London, the decision was taken to open the revue in New York. Rehearsals began there late in 1968, but the revue did not finally open until June 1969. The New York critics hated it, but the audiences loved it. It ran until 1972 and then from 1976 for more than a decade. In 1970 *Oh! Calcutta!* opened in London in a revamped production directed by Clifford Williams at the Roundhouse, as no other venue would agree to stage the show. As Tynan's widow, Kathleen, wrote in her biography of her late husband:

The build-up to the London production was even louder and more hysterical than the one that preceded the New York opening. Would the revue be prosecuted by the Attorney-General under the provisions of the Theatres Act of 1968, as depraving and corrupting? Might Ken, as deviser, Michael White as producer, and Clifford Williams, as director, be arrested? John Mortimer was called in to give legal advice. He had no doubt that a production of *Oh! Calcutta!* would be at serious risk of prosecution, that the average jury might judge the repeated references to oral sex and sado-masochism to be depraving and corrupting; and that if a prosecution were to be launched, the chances of a conviction would be about fifty-fifty . . . During rehearsals the vice squad was despatched to keep an eye on proceedings. Elsewhere a battalion of Grundys went to work: Mary Whitehouse, and her Viewers' and Listeners' Association; a moral rearmer called the Dowager Lady Birdwood; and a Tory GLC [Greater London Council] Councillor called Frank Smith.[3]

The show opened on 27 July 1970 and was generally well received by the press. By the autumn it transferred to the Royalty Theatre in the West End

---

[1] Kathleen Tynan, *The Life of Kenneth Tynan* (London: Weidenfeld and Nicolson, 1987), 285.
[2] Ibid. 278.   [3] Ibid. 293.

and proved to be as popular in London as in New York. Attempts were made to bring a prosecution against the production, but four days after the opening, Sir Peter Rawlinson, the Attorney-General, decided on the evidence before him that there was 'no reasonable likelihood that a prosecution would be successful', and accordingly decided that no proceedings should be taken. Councillor Smith announced that the decision was 'a disaster for Britain', while the cast cracked a few bottles of champagne to celebrate.[4] The requirement in the 1968 Theatres Act that proceedings could only be brought, under the Act, with the agreement of the Attorney-General was intended to protect actors, directors, and writers from frivolous or vexatious prosecution. In this case, the provisions of the Theatres Act clearly achieved their intended purpose. Tynan had good cause to feel relief on this occasion, but he was, within two years, to lose another court case arising out of a completely different provision of the 1968 Theatres Act, namely Clause 4 concerned with libel. This was the unexpected outcome of his long and protracted battle to mount a production in London of *Soldiers* (1966) by the German playwright, Rolf Hochhuth.

Hochhuth's work had already been the subject of controversy in London when the Lord Chamberlain in 1963 had reluctantly agreed to give permission for a much cut version of his play *The Representative* to be performed by the Royal Shakespeare Company (RSC) at the Aldwych Theatre. This was a play that attacked the alleged failure of Pope Pius XII to speak out against the Nazi policy of mass extermination of the Jews, even when the SS began arresting Jews within sight of the Vatican in October 1943. Hochhuth's approach to his historical material involved attributing statements and dialogue to historical personages that they never uttered and confronting invented characters with historically real persons. Instead of making any sustained attempt to present a balanced view of the problems confronting Pius XII, the work presented an impassioned critique of the Pope's silence. The Lord Chamberlain insisted on significant cuts in the material before the play was presented by the RSC; he also insisted that a letter from Cardinal Giovanni Montini (subsequently appointed Pope Paul VI) should be added to the programme notes.[5]

Similar problems were caused to the Lord Chamberlain and his staff by *Soldiers*. In his initial report on the play, R. J. Hill commented to the Lord Chamberlain: 'I can see no future in the policy of giving official approval, if tacitly, to works of fiction, which since they impute words and actions to the living or recently dead, which they never uttered—must be untrue.'[6] This too

[4] Ibid.

[5] See BL, LCP Corr. 1963/3579 *The Representative*. Letter from Sir Eric Penn to O'Hara, 28 May 1963.

[6] BL, WB Corr. 1966/26 *Soldiers*. Report by R. J. Hill after reading the synopsis, 11 Jan. 1967.

was a play that offered a revisionist view of history, only this time the subject matter was concerned with English bombing raids on German cities. Always on the look-out for new material that would attract publicity and notoriety for the National Theatre, Tynan had requested a manuscript copy of *Soldiers* in the autumn of 1966. Churchill's state funeral had taken place in 1965, and here was a play that offered a completely different view of his role as a wartime leader allegedly driven to commit war crimes in his determination to defeat the Nazis. The play showed Churchill deliberately sanctioning the mass murder of civilians through the firestorm, terror bombing of Hamburg (Operation Gomorrah)[7] and possibly colluding in the death of a wartime ally, Poland's General Wladyslaw Sikorski.

Tynan managed to persuade the Artistic Director of the National, Sir Laurence Olivier, to support this choice of play for performance there, on the grounds that a subsidized theatre should present in its repertoire the kind of challenging material that would not normally be found in the repertoire of commercial theatres. He then embarked on a campaign of letter-writing to enlist further allies; to check whether the play was legally safe to perform; and to gain some impression of its historical accuracy. Arnold Goodman, Chairman of the Arts Council, thought the play was 'an eccentric choice for the National',[8] but did not wish to oppose any decision of the National Theatre Board to perform it. The lawyers of the National Theatre did not foresee any major problem with the play script, as Churchill was no longer alive. According to Tynan's widow, Sir Arthur Harris, Chief of Bomber Command, expressed the view that the play was a smear on 'Churchill, the War Cabinet *and* Bomber Command. He quizzed Hochhuth on his sources in a lengthy correspondence, and wondered whether he and Sir Laurence should not be told the nature of the playwright's private information.'[9] Hochhuth claimed to have been given information about the death of Sikorski by British secret service sources, which was deposited in a Swiss bank and could not be made public for fifty years. In view of the factual queries raised by Harris, Tynan persuaded Hochhuth to leave open the issue of how far Churchill was actively involved in Sikorski's death.[10]

Tynan knew from the outset that the main obstacle to any performance of *Soldiers* at the National would come from the Board. The Chairman of the Board was Lord Chandos, formerly Oliver Lyttelton, who (as Conservative MP for Aldershot) had served as President of the Board of Trade and Minister

[7] See 'Hamburg im Feuersturm, Teil 1, Operation Gomorrah', *Hamburger Abendblatt,* 19 July 2003. The casualty figures given in the article are: 34,000 people killed, 125,000 wounded and 900,000 made homeless.

[8] Tynan, *Kenneth Tynan,* 252.

[9] Ibid.   [10] Ibid.

of Production in Churchill's War Cabinet. Chandos had made it clear from the outset that he wanted the National to have nothing to do with the play.[11] In the end, his view prevailed. Despite the protracted attempts by Tynan and Olivier to support the case for a production of *Soldiers* at the National, a unanimous decision was taken by the Board on 24 April 1967 that 'the play was unsuitable for production at the National Theatre'.[12]

Tynan and Olivier subsequently announced that they intended to mount the play under the auspices of a company called St James's Players in the West End in the following January. Tynan duly submitted the text of *Soldiers* to the Lord Chamberlain on 29 July 1967 with a view to obtaining a licence to perform the play in the West End. The Reader, Heriot, wrote his report on 30 August. His main conclusion, though positive in tone, erected an insuperable obstacle for Tynan to negotiate: a licence for the play would only be given if permission was first obtained from the families of Churchill, Lord Cherwell, Viscount Alanbrooke, and Bishop George Bell.[13] In October, Tynan asked for an interview with the Lord Chamberlain to explore whether a club performance of the play might be tolerated. At this meeting, which took place on 24 October 1967, Cobbold refused to give any assurances about whether proceedings would be initiated if a club performance of *Soldiers* were to be mounted. At this point, Olivier had to pull out of the joint project because of ill health.

By the time of Tynan's abortive meeting with the Lord Chamberlain, the world première of *Soldiers* had already taken place in Berlin. Further productions followed in other European cities and in Toronto. The critical and audience response to these various productions was mixed.[14] Later that same year, after the abolition of stage censorship, Tynan was finally able to present *Soldiers* at the New Theatre in London on 12 December 1968. Despite bomb threats and hate mail sent to the theatre manager, the production was generally well received by audiences and critics. Then, without any prior warning, Edward Prchal, the Czech pilot of Sikorski's plane (who alone had survived the fatal plane crash off Gibraltar), issued a writ for libel against the theatre owner, the director of the production, and Tynan. Prchal had attended the opening night of *Soldiers* in Toronto, but had not expressed any view on the content of the play. His decision to issue a writ for libel under Clause 4 of the 1968 Theatres Act came as a bolt from the blue.

In view of the threat of legal action and faced with dwindling audiences, it was decided to take *Soldiers* off on 6 March 1969.[15] Four years later, in May

---

[11] Ibid.   [12] Ibid. 254.
[13] BL, WB Corr. 1966/26 *Soldiers*. Report by Heriot, 30 Aug. 1967.
[14] Tynan, *Kenneth Tynan*, 263.   [15] Ibid. 264.

1972, Tynan was found guilty of libel in the action brought by Prchal and had to pay £7,000 in damages and costs.[16] His ill-considered involvement in promoting a revisionist view of history had cost him dear. Not only did he lose the libel case, but he had destroyed any possibility of having a harmonious working relationship with the Board of the National Theatre and its chairman. In addition, after the *Soldiers* affair, Olivier increasingly distanced himself from Tynan. Ironically, a mere two months after losing the libel action, Tynan decided to quit his post at the National. After this successful libel action, no further productions of *Soldiers* took place in London until August 2004, when the tiny Finborough Theatre, a pub theatre in the Earls Court area of London, mounted a small-scale production of the play, which attracted generally favourable reviews. Hitherto, the threat of legal action associated with the play was evidently enough to deter any theatre manager from contemplating a production of the play.

The final attempt at legal action in the aftermath of the 1968 Theatres Act involved Mary Whitehouse and the National Theatre's 1980 production of Howard Brenton's *The Romans in Britain*. This was a powerful piece exploring how armies of occupation invariably treat people in the countries they invade as things or objects to be exploited and abused. The play makes a provocative parallel between the behaviour of the invading Roman armies in Celtic Britain in 54 BC and that of the British army in Northern Ireland at the time the play was written. Its sprawling structure moves the action in overlapping sequences from Roman to Saxon Britain and then to modern-day Northern Ireland. The real strength of the piece is to be found in its muscular, earthy dialogue and its ability to show, both visually and verbally, the matter-of-fact coarseness of invading armies of occupation.

In production, the scene that gave most offence occurs near the beginning of the play. Three Roman soldiers come across three naked Celtic men sunning themselves after a swim. The Romans kill two and attempt to bugger the third, a Celtic priest. The attempted anal rape is not altogether successful. As the third soldier claims to have lost his erection, he comments:

Arseful of piles. Like fucking a fistful of marbles. I mean, what do they do in this island, sit with their bums in puddles of mud all year long?[17]

Following the casual violence inflicted on Bosnian Muslims by their Serbian adversaries, and the sexual humiliation of Iraqi prisoners in Abu Ghraib by their American guards, it is perhaps easier for audiences today, than for audiences in the 1980s, to appreciate the sense of moral outrage that underpins

---

[16] Tynan, *Kenneth Tynan*, 315.
[17] Howard Brenton, *The Romans in Britain* (London: Eyre Methuen, 1980), 43.

Brenton's use of such disturbing visual and verbal imagery. At the time, there were many who simply took offence.

One of those was Horace Cutler, Conservative leader of the GLC who walked out in some anger from a preview of the production and threatened to suspend the grant made by the GLC to the National Theatre.[18] Another was Mary Whitehouse. She was a grammar school teacher, deeply imbued with the spirit of Moral Rearmament, who had dedicated her life from the age of 40 to liberating, as she saw it, the world of the broadcast and publishing media, as well as the theatre, from the burdens of blasphemy, smut, and sexual excess. Having founded the National Viewers and Listeners Association in 1963, she was tireless in her campaigns against Sir Hugh Greene, Chairman of the BBC from 1962, because of the material he sanctioned for broadcast. In 1976 she had also brought a successful private prosecution for blasphemous libel against the editor of *Gay News*, Denis Lemon, who was fined £3,500, and the publication itself £31,000, 'for publishing a poem in which Jesus on the Cross had masochistic, homoerotic feelings towards a Roman soldier'.[19] Given her zealous campaigning record, it was inevitable that *The Romans in Britain* would attract her attention.

Whitehouse never showed the slightest interest in the overall context in which a scene in a play took place: whether, according to Aristotle's definition, it was included 'to bring about a greater good, or to avert a greater evil'.[20] This meant that she ignored the contextual justification for the homosexual rape scene in Brenton's play, as a scene intended to produce a sense of revulsion at the behaviour of all invading armies. All that concerned her was that a 'dirty deed' was done in public. She therefore resolved to take legal action against the National Theatre production. In late October 1980, her legal team approached the Attorney-General, Sir Michael Havers, with the request that action be taken against the play under the 1968 Theatres Act.[21] On 27 November, the Attorney-General informed the barristers acting for Whitehouse that in his view there was no chance of a successful prosecution: he therefore declined to institute proceedings. On 17 December, Whitehouse and her legal advisers decided that, as no proceedings could be brought under the Theatres Act, the only avenue that could be pursued was a private prosecution under the

[18] Peter Hall, *Making an Exhibition of Myself* (London: Sinclair-Stevenson, 1993), 307.

[19] Denis Barker, 'Mary Whitehouse', *Guardian*, 24 Nov. 2001.

[20] Aristotle, *On the Art of Poetry* (London: Penguin Books, 1965), 71.

[21] Extracts from her autobiography, Mary Whitehouse, *A Most Dangerous Woman?* (Tring: Lion Publishing, 1982), are published on the website of MediaWatch-UK, the successor organization of the National Viewers and Listeners Association. This gives Whitehouse's diary entries for the autumn of 1980 on which the ensuing account is based: http://www.mediawatchuk.org/news%20and%20views/Romans%20in%20Britain.htm (accessed 28 Apr. 2006).

1956 Sexual Offences Act: this makes it an offence to procure by a male the commission of an act of gross indecency with another male in a public place. The Sexual Offences Act was designed to deal with men intent on masturbating or buggering others in public toilets. It was never intended that its provisions should apply to an artistic 'representation of an action'[22] in a public theatre. Much to his surprise and consternation, Michael Bogdanov, who had directed *The Romans in Britain* for the National Theatre, was served with a writ just before Christmas by Whitehouse's solicitors in which he was accused of procuring an act of gross indecency by staging the homosexual rape scene in the production. If found guilty, he faced a possible prison sentence of up to two years.

The committal hearing was held at Horseferry Road Magistrates Court on 29 June 1981. Bogdanov was represented by Lord (Jeremy) Hutchinson, with Geoffrey Robertson acting as his supporting defence counsel. Whitehouse was represented by John Smyth. Hutchinson argued persuasively that the Sexual Offences Act was never meant to cover the theatre, but Smyth made the point that there is no reference to this in the Theatres Act. The following day, the Stipendiary Magistrate delivered an almost apologetic verdict:

It appears illogical, but I must interpret the law as it stands and not as it might have been. I think it absurd that had Mr Bogdanov been a woman director he would have no case to answer, but as it stands that appears to be the law, and I must interpret it as it stands.[23]

Robertson now wrote to the Attorney-General and asked that he should issue a *nolle prosequi* in this case. This legal power (last used in a theatrical context by Queen Anne in the early 1700s to put an end to vexatious prosecutions brought against actors for uttering profane language in plays)[24] permits the Attorney-General 'to stop any prosecution if that is what he thinks the public interest requires'.[25] Robertson argued that this case represented a clear breach of Parliament's intentions in 1968 that proceedings against a play might only be taken with the express permission of the Attorney-General. Furthermore, Parliament had insisted that in the Theatres Act there should be a 'public good' defence available to playwrights and theatre practitioners. No such defence would be available in a case brought under the Sexual Offences Act. Havers declined to intervene, even though the prosecution brought against Bogdanov

---

[22] Aristotle, *Art of Poetry*, 38.
[23] Quoted from Geoffrey Robertson, *The Justice Game* (London: Vintage, 1999), 173.
[24] See Thomas, *Theatre in Europe*, 190.
[25] Robertson, *Justice Game*, 174.

was clearly intended to subvert the will of Parliament, as expressed in the Theatres Act.

The full trial at the Old Bailey opened almost a year later on 15 March 1982, some nine months after the final performance of *The Romans in Britain* had taken place. Because of Smyth's ill health, Ian Kennedy served as Whitehouse's barrister. On the second day of the trial, Kennedy called, as his main witness, Graham Ross-Cornes, who was Whitehouse's solicitor. At her request, he had attended a performance of *The Romans in Britain* (a play she had never seen), during which, in his view, he had seen an act of gross indecency:

He told of . . . witnessing an actor with his penis hand-held and erect, its tip protruding, advancing across the stage to place it on or against the naked buttocks of a trembling druid.[26]

Robertson persuaded Hutchinson to take the risk of asking where Ross-Cornes had sat in the theatre. His argument to his senior colleague was that the prosecution would have drawn attention to the fact if Ross-Cornes had been seated close to the stage. The gamble paid off. It emerged that Ross-Cornes had bought one of the cheapest back-row seats in the Olivier auditorium at the National, which is some ninety yards from the stage. Hutchinson mocked his parsimony and then asked him if he could be certain that he saw the tip of the actor's penis at a distance of ninety yards. When Ross-Cornes refused to budge from his assertion, Hutchinson proceeded to demonstrate how he may have been mistaken:

'What you saw, I suggest, was the tip of the actor's *thumb* . . .' (he slowly raised his right thumb, until it stood erect, protruding an inch from his fist) 'as he held his fist over his groin—like *this*.' Jeremy flung open his silk gown with his left hand while placing his right fist, thumb erect, over his own groin. It was a *coup de theatre* . . . The jurors stared transfixedly at the QC's simulated erection. The witness opened and closed his mouth. At last he rallied: 'I can't see clearly, Lord Hutchinson. Your gown is in the way.' Jeremy swivelled in his direction, holding the pose. The judge was speechless . . . Eventually, the crestfallen Mr Ross-Cornes had to admit that yes, he may have been mistaken. He could not rule out the possibility that it might indeed have been a thumb he had descried from the front row of the gods, and not the glans of the penis of Mr Peter Sproule.[27]

According to Robertson, this was the turning-point in the trial. But it was a curious one. The very next day, the Judge ruled that the Sexual Offences Act did apply to the theatre. Despite this favourable statement, Kennedy approached the defence barristers to inform them that he had decided to withdraw the case against Bogdanov. In her diary account, Mrs Whitehouse

[26] Ibid. 176.   [27] Ibid. 178.

made no mention of Hutchinson's cross-examination of Ross-Cornes; nor did she offer any explanation of Kennedy's decision, on his own initiative, to withdraw the action.[28] Writing in the *Guardian* on 28 October 2005, Mark Lawson offered the following explanation:

Kennedy told Whitehouse that he could no longer continue with the case. Bogdanov remembers standing in a corridor and hearing the prosecuting counsel, clearly on the phone to his employer. The wounded watchdog [Whitehouse], in a tetchy Newsnight interview afterwards, tried to insist that the organisation had withdrawn the threat to 'young Bogdanov', as she always called him, once their legal point was proved. But few believed her then or now: the buzz at the Bailey was that Kennedy had suffered a crisis of conscience.[29]

Kennedy, who is now a judge, has declined to comment on his reasons for withdrawing the action. However, the Judge who was trying the case at the time was greatly irritated at this decision. In his view, once a case had been presented by prosecuting counsel, it could only be withdrawn with the Judge's consent: Kennedy disagreed. The matter was finally resolved when Hutchinson and Robertson had a hastily arranged meeting with the Attorney-General. Rather than face an unseemly squabble between a Judge and senior QC over who had the power to withdraw a prosecution, Havers agreed to issue a *nolle prosequi*. Had he done so from the outset, a clear matter of principle would have been established: namely, that the Attorney-General would not permit the will of Parliament to be subverted in respect of the 1968 Theatres Act. This would effectively have closed all future loopholes for those interested, like Whitehouse, in bringing vexatious private prosecutions against plays and productions. The belated decision to issue a *nolle prosequi* removed the threat against Bogdanov, but the outcome left everyone dissatisfied.

Because of the unresolved action against Bogdanov, it took over twenty-five years before any theatre in Britain was prepared to mount a full professional production of *The Romans in Britain*. The first to do so was the Crucible Theatre in Sheffield, which presented a production of the play, directed by Sam West in February 2006. The theatre took legal advice first, but decided that there was now little threat of a prosecution. On the other hand, Bogdanov was concerned that the production would arouse new controversy:

[He] feared that there would be demonstrations again 'for all the wrong reasons'. The furore of 1980 is being replicated today by groups such as Christian fundamentalists opposing the regional tour of *Jerry Springer: The Opera* and Sikhs who forced the close of *Behzti* in Birmingham.[30]

---

[28] See: http://www.mediawatchuk.org/news%20and%20views/Romans%20in%20Britain.htm
[29] Mark Lawson, 'Passion Play', *Guardian*, 28 Oct. 2005.
[30] Louise Jury, ' "Romans in Britain" ready to revive old hatreds', *Independent*, 2 Feb. 2006.

In the event, the production passed off without any serious threat of legal or mob action. Again, however, the fact that a play was once associated with legal action was sufficient to deter, for decades, any theatre management from contemplating a production of the play.

THEATRE MANAGERS AND THEIR PERCEPTION OF CENSORSHIP ISSUES

The studious neglect of *Soldiers* and *The Romans in Britain* by British theatre managers since their first production raises the question of whether any form of covert censorship has replaced the statutory censorship formally exercised by the Lord Chamberlain. Isolated case histories do not provide a sound basis for drawing more general conclusions. The authors of the present volume therefore decided to use an empirical methodology based on questionnaire responses, supplemented by interviews or correspondence, to ascertain whether modern British theatre or company managers as a group have experienced any form of direct or indirect censorship since the Theatres Act of 1968.

In all 454 organizations were contacted in 2002–3: 43 community theatre groups; 161 theatre companies; 85 producing theatres; 55 London venues; 110 provincial venues. Each organization was asked the following questions, to which a yes or no response was required:

Has your theatre ever faced any **threat of prosecution** over the writing or producing of a play?

Has your theatre experienced any form of **direct censorship**?

> If yes, was this censorship exercised by: the Government; the Arts Council; the Regional Arts Board; the Local Authority; an individual taking legal action?

Has your theatre ever experienced any **indirect censorship**?

> If yes, was this through: sponsorship; advertisers; market pressure; a press campaign; advice from boards of governors?

A total of 184 replies were received, which marks a very high response rate to the questionnaire survey (40.5%) and therefore gives a statistically representative cross-section of views for that specific period (2002–3): 126 (or 68%) of the organizations contacted claimed that they had not been subject to any form of direct or indirect censorship; 58 (or 32%) of the organizations contacted claimed to have experienced some form of either direct or indirect censorship; 37.5% of community theatres appear to have experienced censorship activity of one kind or another; at the opposite end of the statistical spectrum, only

21% of provincial venues experienced any kind of overt or covert censorship activity.

The most important point to emerge from this survey is that the majority of theatre or company managers who replied (68%) claim not to have experienced any overt or covert form of theatre censorship. They have undertaken their task of pleasing different funding bodies (local authorities, Arts Council, and Regional Arts Boards), sponsors, audiences, playwrights, directors, designers, and actors without any sense of undue pressure coming from one group or another. They have faced the kinds of often conflicting demands that any theatre manager has to cope with in any modern European state: their lives involve a daily juggling act where the often contradictory needs of one group are counterbalanced by the vociferous claims of some other group. That is what it means to be a successful theatre manager.

A significant minority of theatre managers, however, did indicate in our survey that, in their view, they have been subject to undue pressure from one or more of the above groups of people. As always, the task is to determine where the perfectly normal interplay of market (and other) forces shades over into a more determined attempt by one group or another to exert an undue influence on the repertoire or the way the repertoire is presented.

7 respondents claimed to have experienced the threat of prosecution.

21 respondents claimed to have experienced some form of direct censorship:

in 3 cases there was direct Government intervention;

in 2 cases there was intervention by the Arts Council;

in 1 case there was intervention by a Regional Arts Board;

in 10 cases there was intervention by a local authority;

in 3 cases there was intervention by individuals or groups;

in 2 cases the source of intervention was unspecified.

37 respondents claimed to have experienced some form of indirect censorship:

in 6 cases, sponsors had applied pressure;

in 2 cases, advertisers had applied pressure;

in 11 cases, organizations had experienced market pressure;

in 1 case, a press campaign led to pressure;

in 13 cases, boards of governors had applied pressure;

in 4 cases, the source of pressure was unspecified.

In addition, in 5 cases, organizations admitted to having exercised self-censorship.

Where respondents agreed to be interviewed or contacted by e-mail, additional information was given to flesh out these bare statistics. In some cases, the theatre or company managers who were contacted agreed to have their comments attributed: in others, they asked to remain anonymous. Inevitably therefore, the background to the above statistical responses can only be illustrative. Generally, those productions that have caused most difficulties to theatre or company managers and that have provoked different forms of coercion or attempted coercion (from local authorities or individual councillors, receiving houses for touring groups, individuals, and diverse pressure groups) have tended to explore themes revolving around sex, violence, politics, or religion, sometimes intertwined. Where prosecutions have been threatened, they have involved libel or blasphemy.

THREATENED PROSECUTIONS

The touring group 7:84 became involved in a threatened libel action in 1972. They had just presented a production of the play *The Ballygombeen Bequest* by Margaretta D'Arcy and John Arden, to general critical acclaim, at the Edinburgh Festival. The production was then booked into the Bush Theatre in London, when it was cancelled a few days into the run. The play showed an Irish tenant being cheated by an absentee English landlord: 'Performances [in Edinburgh] would begin with the cast telling the audience that it was nothing to do with a Commander Burges in Sussex. "And then I'd give his telephone number," recalls [Gavin] Richards.'[31] Burges (now deceased) subsequently sued the playwrights for libel and in due course received an apology. In an interview given on 14 January 2003, Arden commented:

The Company (7:84) were warned by their lawyer that they could be included in the action if they didn't take the play off the stage. They did. We had to wait for five years before the case came to court. It was not only censoring the play but also our work in general because nobody wanted to commission work from us any more. We were regarded as unreliable and in trouble with the civil law.[32]

This reputation for unreliability was further compounded when D'Arcy was detained briefly under the Prevention of Terrorism Act in the late 1970s. D'Arcy's account of what happened is as follows:

In the late 70s I was travelling from Belfast to London. On the boat-train to Larne I was reading Fr. Raymond Murray's book about the Republican women prisoners

---

[31] Nicholas Wroe, 'Britain's Brecht', *Guardian*, 3 Jan. 2004.
[32] John Arden interviewed by Anne Etienne, 14 Jan. 2003.

in Armagh gaol. At Stranraer I was held and questioned under the Prevention of Terrorism Act. Among my documents was a letter from the Nottingham Theatre, saying they wanted to put on a play I had written with Arden, *The Non-Stop Connolly Show*. Although I was released without charge, the police informed the theatre of my arrest; as a result, the production was suddenly dropped.[33]

Arden described this as 'censorship by smear and insinuation'.[34]

Other examples of threatened prosecution because of libel were mentioned in the questionnaire returns and interviews but, as anonymity was requested, these cannot be discussed in detail. The issue of blasphemous libel did, however, attract a large amount of attention and publicity in 1998 in the town of Harlow in Essex. In February 1998, the Harlow Playhouse had booked the touring production of *The Complete Word of God (Abridged)* by the Reduced Shakespeare Company. This show had successfully toured to performance venues throughout the United Kingdom since 1995 and had met with considerable critical acclaim. In January 1998, Anthony Bennett, a solicitor from Harlow, took exception to the show on religious grounds and wrote to express his concern that the show was blasphemous to its producers, Mark Groucher and David Johnson, as well as to the Playhouse. The Company and the Playhouse replied that the play was not blasphemous and that it would be performed as planned unless payment of £200,000 was made to cover the costs incurred in cancelling the scheduled performances in Harlow and elsewhere. In a further letter, Bennett informed the Playhouse that he intended to bring a private prosecution for blasphemous libel against the Playhouse and the Company if the performances were not cancelled. As they were not cancelled, Bennett lodged a sworn affidavit with the Magistrates Court at Harlow to support a private prosecution against the Company and the Playhouse responsible for the production of *The Complete Word of God (Abridged)*. His affidavit listed thirty-three items where biblical figures were treated irreverently. The Company and the Playhouse refused to bow to the threat of prosecution, and none ensued. Bennett picketed the theatre and circulated 'Words of Warning' to the audience: all to no avail. However, his protests were echoed elsewhere in the country. In March 1998, the *Northern Echo* reported that church leaders in Darlington had 'branded a play "blasphemous" and called for its ban, three weeks before it was due to be performed in the town'. The report continued: 'The call came from the Reverend David Campbell, who saw an affidavit given to magistrates in Harlow, Essex, before a performance of *The Complete Word*

---

[33] E-mail from Margaretta D'Arcy to David Thomas, 12 Apr. 2007.
[34] Arden interview, 2003.

of God (Abridged) at Harlow Playhouse last month.'[35] Sporadic protests continued. In 2000–1, the production was booked into the Neptune Theatre, Liverpool. A few people stood outside the theatre on the opening night with banners 'asking the audience why they were going to see a show that was blasphemous'.[36]

GOVERNMENT INTERVENTION

Of the three cases of intervention by one of the Government's Law Officers, the Attorney-General, two can be outlined in further detail. In the first of these two instances, Max Stafford-Clark was rehearsing a production of G. F. Newman's play, *Operation Bad Apple*, for the Royal Court Theatre in 1982. The play dealt with the investigation of corruption in the Metropolitan Police by the Dorset Constabulary and suggested that corruption had reached the very highest echelons of the Metropolitan Police. The theatre received a letter from the Attorney-General saying that 'we might be in contempt of court as the case was still coming up and we might wish to reconsider'.[37] Despite this written warning, the company decided to go ahead with the production and was not in the event subject to any legal action.

In the second case, a production of *Maxwell: The Musical*, was brought to a halt by order of the Attorney-General in 1994 one week before the show was due to open at the Criterion Theatre in London. The play focused on the well-documented career of the press magnate and former Labour MP who had died in 1991. In an article in the *Sunday Times*, the barrister Sean Enright gave a highly critical account of the reasons for the Attorney-General's intervention, which was based on the claim that the musical might be prejudicial to a forthcoming trial. Enright argued that 'the idea of any potential juror seeing the musical and being gripped by prejudice is almost laughable'. The Attorney-General issued an injunction banning the planned production, which caused significant losses to the theatre and the actors involved. According to Enright, it also established 'a disquieting legal precedent'.[38]

[35] 'Outcry over play dubbed blasphemous', *Northern Echo*, 12 Mar. 1998.
[36] Sarah-Jane Leydon (Neptune Theatre, Liverpool) interviewed by Anne Etienne, 14 Jan. 2003.
[37] Max Stafford-Clark interviewed by David Thomas, 12 Jan. 2003. Stafford-Clark, former Artistic Director of the Royal Court Theatre, is now Director of Out of Joint Company.
[38] Sean Enright, 'Freedom of Speech—worth making a song and dance about', *Sunday Times*, 13 Feb. 1994.

INTERVENTION BY THE ARTS COUNCIL

Sir Peter Hall, in an interview given on 19 January 2003, explained how Arts Council officials advised him on the occasion of the production of *The Romans in Britain* that 'he should go easy if you want the grant for the National to go up. Be careful. It's quite right to do progressive plays, of course, but it's a question of how many.'[39] In his *Testimony* to the Camden Hall debate on *US*, the Vietnam War docudrama presented by the RSC in 1966, Hall expressed a trenchant critique of Arts Council policy:

The threat of grant standstill is a potent weapon and Whitehall knows it. Government now dominates the Arts Council. In the 1960s it was still a proudly independent body . . . In the Arts, governments have long realised that he who pays the piper can have a very big influence on the tune.[40]

This critical view of the Arts Council is one (as we shall see) that others in the theatre have shared. On the other hand, the Arts Council has had to cope with major structural changes over the past few decades, and frequent shifts in the level of government grant-in-aid for the Arts. This has made it difficult to sustain a consistent funding policy. In April 2002, the Arts Council of England and ten Regional Arts Boards merged to form a single organization, subsequently named Arts Council, England. The Chairman and the national Council are appointed by the Secretary of State for Culture, Media, and Sport,[41] which perhaps helps to explain why some theatre practitioners, rightly or wrongly, view Arts Council England as dominated by the government.

Perhaps inevitably, given the political nature of much of their work, community theatre groups have experienced more funding pressure than fixed venues. Some have ceased to exist altogether because their Arts Council funding has been completely axed. In many such cases, the decision to cut funding has been interpreted by the groups concerned as a political rather than an economic intervention. One respondent replied with the comment that the group for which he worked was stopped (through lack of funding) because it was politically effective. Precisely the same point was made in published format by 7:84 (England) when its Arts Council funding was terminated in

---

[39] Sir Peter Hall interviewed by Anne Etienne, 19 Jan. 2003.

[40] This debate held on 21 Jan. 2003 was organized to commemorate the 1966 production of *US*, directed by Peter Brook for the RSC. As Peter Hall was not able to attend, his views on the production and the theatre of the mid-1960s were read out by Michael Kustow.

[41] 'History of Arts Council, England', an information sheet prepared by the Arts Council, England, June 2004. See: http://www.artscouncil.org.uk/documents/information/HistoryACE_phpJGGeGy.doc

1984. In a programme note for their final touring production, *Six Men of Dorset*, the following claim was made:

> Why have they determined to cut 7:84 England? It's fairly obvious. Since 1971 we have been touring England and Wales, while our sister company has been touring Scotland, with first class theatre for working-class audiences. Our shows have been entertainments, but based on the lives, the struggles past and present of our audiences, and on the aspirations of those audiences for a better future. We look at our subjects, and the way we present them, and the way we work, from a socialist perspective—and we have refused censorship of any kind. We have become an integral part of the labour movement, bringing our shows to trades halls, clubs, village halls, all over the country, supporting working class struggles from the building unions' strike of '71 to the great miners' strike today. That is why we have been cut.[42]

During the Thatcher years, the withdrawal of Arts Council support for groups that were politically active was seen by such groups as a blunt but effective means of silencing unwanted opposition. This was never acknowledged by the Arts Council: quite the contrary. The Arts Council's 'Glory of the Garden' report of 1984 justified such cuts as the price to be paid for establishing regional centres of excellence. However, a link between government thinking and Arts Council policy was discerned by some. More recent initiatives by the Arts Council seem to suggest a continuing link between government (New Labour) thinking and Arts Council policy. The Arts Council's current priorities, as expressed in its policy document 'Ambitions for the Arts', resonate with Blairite concepts, such as cultural diversity, and the participation of ethnic minority groups in the Arts. But the policy of achieving cultural diversity is, in the Arts Council's view, not simply to be obtained through gentle persuasion: 'We also need to take positive action if we are to share our riches and achieve greater equality of opportunity.'[43] What this meant for London's theatres was a request from the London Arts Board in June 2001 to submit new cultural diversity plans in order to obtain Arts Council funding. London Arts even organized seminars to explain their aims. The consultation document issued to London's state-funded theatre companies by London Arts in 2001 stated:

> We wrote to you earlier this year explaining that we are seeking to establish how our support helps you to respond to London's cultural diversity. We would now like to sit down with you as an organisation that received fixed-term funding to discuss how you see your own work practice developing. Our objective is to work with you to

---

[42] Programme note for the touring production of *Six Men of Dorset*, which 7:84 toured 1–30 Sept. 1984.

[43] Arts Council Policy document, 'Ambitions for the Arts'. Quoted from 'Focus on cultural diversity: the arts in England, attendance, participation and attitudes', Research Report 34, Dec. 2003, Office of National Statistics.

provide guidance and advice where it will help and to find opportunities to show good practice. We will be looking for you to develop a plan to take this area of work forward, to review where you stand at the moment in relation to audiences, programming, staffing and governance. Then we will discuss and agree challenging and achievable targets that are appropriate for your organisation. These targets will form part of your future funding agreement with us.

A degree of potential coercion is clearly visible here and, on the evidence of the interviews conducted in 2003, it was equally clearly resented by some theatre managers. In this consultation document, it is suggested that Arts Council funding is in future to be linked to the way a theatre meets the cultural diversity targets imposed by the Arts Council. In effect, the performing arts are arguably to be used as a tool for social engineering.

Most of the criticisms of this policy, which were made in questionnaire returns or interviews, were given under conditions of strict anonymity. Theatre or company managers who feel threatened are understandably cautious about voicing any public criticism of their paymasters. However, even before he took over as Artistic Director of the National Theatre in April 2003, Nick Hytner was outspoken in his published critique of this latest Arts Council policy initiative:

We've been more comfortable with the kinder, gentler New Labour arts agenda, and we've learnt to speak the language of access, diversity and inclusion. We share aspirations with our political masters. We all of us want to play to as wide a public as we can find.

But there is a real danger in a relentless and exclusive focus on the nature of our audience. Performing artists, once under attack for apparently not paying their way, are now in the dock for attracting the wrong kind of people. And it doesn't matter whether what we do is any good or not. We have to call a halt to this. There's nothing inherently good about any particular audience. We mustn't judge the success of an artistic enterprise by its ability to pull an Officially Approved Crowd.[44]

Hytner here sums up a sense of resentment that is widely shared by his fellow theatre managers in London. None of them disagrees with the basic notion of widening access to culturally diverse audiences. What they reject is any suggestion, whether correct or incorrect, that their artistic policy should in effect be dictated to them.

LOCAL AUTHORITY AND POLICE INTERVENTION

Various examples of attempted or actual intervention by local authorities were given in the questionnaires, but most respondents requested anonymity.

---

[44] Nick Hytner, 'To hell with Targets', *Observer*, 12 Jan. 2003.

In some cases, plays on specific topics, such as freemasonry, gave offence to members of a local council and attempts were made to prevent the production; in other cases, controversial performers, such as Bernard Manning, were considered as too offensive to be allowed to perform in specific local authority theatres. Mention has already been made of the attempt by Cutler, leader of the GLC, to ban or curtail the production of *The Romans in Britain* by threatening to cut the GLC grant to the National. A similar threat was issued by Mike Garnett, a Conservative councillor in Harlow, when the Australian show, *The Puppetry of the Penis*, was booked for a run at the Harlow Playhouse in January 2003. In this show two actors 'manipulate (with charm and great aplomb) their genitalia into various shapes, objects and landmarks',[45] against a background of witty and entertaining dialogue. Garnett claimed that the show was 'sleazy and damaging to the theatre's reputation as a family venue',[46] and he asked the Playhouse management to cancel the show. Garnett informed the local press that 'he was prepared to propose a motion to Harlow Council to withhold the theatre's support grant [£750,000] if it continued to book adult shows'.[47] Fortunately for the Playhouse management, Garnett's stance was not shared by his fellow councillors who distanced themselves from any attempt to influence the theatre's artistic policy.

Other councils have not taken the same view. Vivyan Ellacott, Director of the Kenneth More Theatre in Ilford, reported that the Labour Group, forming the majority party of the London Borough of Redbridge Council, had complained in 2002 that the local theatre was not 'doing enough' for ethnic minorities. This was clearly part of the drive for cultural diversity in the Arts that, during Tony Blair's premiership, had already become a central plank of Arts Council policy:

In order to obtain the renewal of our annual Council grant (£74,000) the Labour Group required us to sign an undertaking agreeing to aim at staging shows that reflected the ethnic make-up of the Borough (i.e. 23% Muslim, 14% Afro-Caribbean etc). If we refused to sign this document they would withdraw the entire grant.[48]

The theatre refused to sign any such undertaking on the grounds that the council was attempting to engage in direct censorship. A debate in the local press followed, which became very heated as local elections were imminent. Ellacott explained what happened next:

The Conservatives rushed out a circular stating 'Vote Conservative and we promise never to censor the local theatre. Vote Conservative and we promise never to cut

---

[45] Advance publicity for the show published at: www.puppetryofthepenis.com/download/ukreturn.pdf. (accessed 28 Apr. 2006).

[46] 'Theatre defends "sleazy" show', *Citizen* (Harlow), 22 Jan. 2003.

[47] 'Sleaze Show must be stopped', *Herald* (Harlow), 23 Jan. 2003.

[48] E-mail from Vivyan Ellacott (Kenneth More Theatre, Ilford, Essex) to Anne Etienne, 19 Nov. 2002.

the grant of the theatre'. The Liberals denounced political correctness gone mad. At the last minute the Labour group offered a compromise: would we sign our intention 'in general terms' to support the Council in its multi-cultural efforts? Our Board of Governors refused to sign anything. In the May 6th election the London Borough of Redbridge was the only London borough to show a big swing to the Conservatives. The Conservatives won overall control. Problems over! However, an interesting warning to any local authority wishing to step into the minefield of 'censoring' the arts.[49]

In contrast to the various interventions by local authorities, which were mentioned, only one notification of intervention by the police was recorded. In 1990 a co-operative called Kickswift was touring a small-scale production of Steven Berkoff's *East*, a play depicting the anger, violence, and frustration of young people in London's East End. It was due to be performed in a pub theatre (The Hen and Chicken) in Bedminster, Bristol. Because the pub was rarely used for performances at the time, the company had to obtain an occasional licence from the local authority. At this point, the police intervened and asked for a copy of the script to be submitted to them. (As mentioned in the previous chapter, this right is given to the police in the 1968 Theatres Act if they have reason to believe that any performance may incite racial hatred, tend to deprave or corrupt, or lead to a breach of the peace.) It seems that the police were concerned at the violence depicted in the play and at its use of strong language. Although the reason for the police intervention was never made clear, the company suspected that the police may have been uneasy because the pub theatre was located close to Bristol City Football Club: in this case, the issue that might have troubled the police was a potential breach of the peace, arising out of performances of the play. Rehearsals were suspended for a week, while the company enlisted local journalists to mount a press campaign. After further negotiations between the police and the production manager, the company was eventually given permission to mount the production, which passed off without causing any breach of the peace.[50]

INDIRECT AND SELF-CENSORSHIP

The indirect censorship exercised by sponsors, advertisers, market pressure, or boards of governors is often difficult to quantify. One of those who responded, John Blackmore, Executive Director of the Octagon Theatre Bolton, felt that

---

[49] Ibid.
[50] Ashley Barnes interviewed by Anne Etienne, 14 Jan. 2003. Barnes, who directed the production for Kickswift, is now Artistic Director of Dead Earnest Theatre.

market pressure should not be described as censorship.[51] On the other hand, he went on to admit that the pressure to make the economics work does have a compromising effect on the programme: 'if you have a couple of winning shows, you can take more risks on the programme afterwards.'[52] The dilemmas posed by the economic pressures facing any theatre manager were particularly well summarized by Graham Whybrow, Literary Manager of the Royal Court Theatre:

A progressive theatre with artistic vision will try to pull towards art and pull the audience towards art, but within available financial resources. If the theatre tried to programme what the audience wants to see (based on what it wanted to see in the past), the theatre will be moving towards the audience and neglecting art.[53]

It was very clear from the responses received from managers of theatres in the provinces that the policy of many was indeed dictated by what their audiences wanted to see.

At its most sophisticated, the evaluation of what an audience would be prepared to watch is underpinned by an annual questionnaire survey and focus group meetings. This is the case at the Library Theatre in Manchester. As a result of this research, the theatre manager concluded, for instance, that there would not be a viable audience in the north-west for the controversial work of Sarah Kane. (Her play *Blasted*, for instance, is a disturbing account of murder, rape, and cannibalism in a Leeds hotel room following a bomb blast.) Her plays could only be shown in Manchester to a minority audience, and would therefore not be financially viable.[54] In other cases, managers rely on gut instinct in deciding what their audiences will accept by way of challenging new work. Even while doing so, some are aware that this involves a subtle form of self-censorship. Rob Swain, who was until mid-2003 Artistic Director of Harrogate Theatre, summed up this dilemma with great clarity:

As Artistic Director I obviously want to choose a range of plays that are going to entertain and stimulate our distinctive local audience and part of that judgement inevitably involves excluding a large range of produced and new plays from our repertoire. For example if Mark Ravenhill had sent me a first copy of *Shopping and F***ing* there is absolutely no way I would have been able to produce it on the main stage here because I know the reaction it would have got from this local audience, funders, potential sponsors, advertisers and my Board of Directors. Whilst nobody would put direct and obvious pressure on me to not produce certain plays, I know

---

[51] John Blackmore (Octagon Theatre Bolton) interviewed by Anne Etienne, 15 Jan. 2003.
[52] Ibid.
[53] Graham Whybrow (Royal Court Theatre) interviewed by Anne Etienne, 19 Jan. 2003.
[54] Christopher Honer (manager of the Library Theatre, Manchester) interviewed by Anne Etienne, 14 Jan. 2003.

the reaction that certain plays would receive from all the above bodies and interested groups, and therefore in the current economic and cultural climate of Harrogate there is a large degree of self-censorship on my part. Censorship is invisible and insidious and whilst the current funding and resources of theatres like this remains as it is, 'risks' which may break out of this self-imposed censorship will always be difficult to take.[55]

This thoughtful and mature response is typical of many other successful theatre managers who have to strike a pragmatic balance between what is desirable artistically and what is feasible economically. In the process, however, market forces are inevitably exercising what Swain sees as 'an invisible and insidious' form of censorship.

Dramatists have clearly suffered from this silent and invisible form of censorship. This is not only true of Kane and Ravenhill, but is perceived to be the case by other playwrights who were contacted. Berkoff, for instance, wrote on 31 December 2001:

While I have experienced little censorship from any authority or organisation, I have experienced total censorship from organisations in the performing arts. Known as a radical playwright and performer, I have established a large young and student following, both in Britain and other parts of the world. Given this fact, that I probably do have the largest young audience in Britain who religiously study my works, I nevertheless have faced a total blackout from all major subsidised theatres.

The National gave me space to do 2 shows 10 years ago which were immensely successful. We never heard back. This is a form of censorship—maybe of a different kind but no less pernicious and deliberate.[56]

A related but quite different sense of disenchantment was expressed to us in a letter written by Edward Bond on 14 December 2002:

You will know about my earlier relations with the theatre censor and the law courts. . . . The cultural censorship is more profound and far-reaching. English language theatre is dominated by Hollywood and Broadway. Plays are chosen for production if they are likely to be sources of a lot of money—on film, or TV or on American stages. This has engineered its own type of directing and acting. As the texts are anodyne—or emptily shocking—ways of disguising and invigorating them have to be invented . . .[57]

In view of his profound disenchantment with what he sees as the consumerist ethos that is shaping modern British theatre, Bond has chosen to work with French-speaking actors in Paris (and Belgium); there, in his view, the problem of language is not yet as corroding as it is in Britain.

---

[55] Letter from Rob Swain, Artistic Director, Harrogate Theatre, to Anne Etienne, 5 Dec. 2002.
[56] Letter from Steven Berkoff to Anne Etienne, 31 Dec. 2002.
[57] Letter from Edward Bond to Anne Etienne, 14 Dec. 2002.

Yet another form of disillusionment with English actors was expressed by Arnold Wesker, who claimed that he had experienced, not indirect, but direct censorship exercised by members of the RSC:

The one play that I believe was manifestly censored . . . is my play *The Journalists*. This play was contracted by the RSC, a date for rehearsal set, the characters cast from the RSC company. When the roles were offered to the actors they refused to perform the play. It is the first—and last—time this has ever happened . . . We will never really know why the actors refused to perform the play.[58]

Dramatists whose work is morally or socially challenging have inevitably suffered from the silent censorship exercised by theatre managers attempting to cater for the tastes of older, predominantly middle-class audiences. But as Berkoff, Bond, and Wesker assert, in their view dramatists can also be subjected to forms of direct and indirect censorship if their work is no longer seen to fit the cultural and aesthetic expectations and preconceptions of contemporary directors and actors.

Sometimes, the pressure to please an unadventurous audience has led to bruising encounters between touring companies and the managers of theatres receiving touring plays. When Volcano Theatre Company toured their production of *Macbeth—Director's Cut* in 1998–9, their interpretation of Lord and Lady Macbeth drew for its inspiration on the behaviour of the mass murderers Fred and Rosemary West. One provincial theatre manager was so irate at the production that he 'wrote to the Minister of Culture [Chris Smith] and asked to have our grant withdrawn and said we would never play in [his theatre] again'.[59] The company had experienced similar pressure when it toured an experimental piece in 1994–5 called *After the Orgy*, based on the work of Jean Baudrillard. One scene included a pornographic video recording that was shown on an eight-inch monitor at the very back of the stage: although the monitor was only just visible, the scene was considered unacceptable by a theatre manager in the Midlands and had to be cut for the performance at that theatre. To avoid any further difficulties with theatre managers, the company decided to replace the offending material with a video recording showing Benny Hill. Perhaps unsurprisingly, Volcano Theatre Company has never considered approaching sponsors, as they themselves consider that their work would be regarded as involving too much risk. On the other hand, the company is funded by the Arts Council and has never experienced any form of overt or covert pressure from that source.[60]

[58] Letter from Arnold Wesker to Anne Etienne, 17 Dec. 2002.
[59] Fern Smith (Volcano Theatre Company) interviewed by Anne Etienne, 14 Jan. 2003.
[60] Ibid.

Even self-censorship can come in many guises. Stafford-Clark found himself subject to severe political pressure from Jewish organizations when he began rehearsing Jim Allen's play *Perdition* for the Royal Court in 1987. The play purported to be a documentary piece showing how Zionists collaborated with the Nazis to fight for their own when Jews were evacuated from Budapest during the war. There was a furious response from Jewish organizations and immense pressure was applied to the theatre. Finally, Stafford-Clark decided to cancel the production at 48 hours notice. In his view, however, it was not simply a question of caving into political pressure. He had lost faith in the author who was prepared to include some facts that came to light but not others. Because of this, in Stafford-Clark's judgement, the play was based more on fiction than fact and could no longer be defended as a piece of documentary theatre.[61] His decision to cancel the production just before it was due to open brought a barrage of criticism from all those who wanted to see the controversial play (which was later presented at the Edinburgh Festival). In taking this action, Stafford-Clark declined to be swallowed up in a revisionist quagmire of the kind into which Tynan had earlier blundered over *Soldiers*. On the other hand, by cancelling the production at the very last moment, he laid himself open to the charge of bowing to political pressure. Ken Loach, the director of the Royal Court production, wrote in Allen's obituary in 1999: 'Previous attacks were as nothing compared to the Zionist fury unleashed when the play was being rehearsed. To Jim's disgust . . . the play was withdrawn.'[62]

PROTESTS, MOB VIOLENCE, AND DEATH THREATS

During the course of our survey, a number of respondents mentioned that they had been subject to pressure from individuals or small groups whose objections to a particular production were based on a fundamentalist religious faith. One of the more striking developments in the first decade of the new millennium has been the decision taken by religious pressure groups to expand their activities and to assemble instant mobs to protest or riot against specific plays and productions. The awesome power of the Internet and mobile phone messages have both been utilized to call together, not a few isolated protestors, but large street mobs. The scenes of mass protest aimed at specific plays and productions in Birmingham in 2004 and London

---

[61] Max Stafford-Clark interviewed by David Thomas, 12 Jan. 2003.
[62] James Burleigh, 'Dramas played out off-stage', *Daily Telegraph*, 21 Dec. 2004.

in 2005, and the death threats issued against writers or directors, are grimly reminiscent of similar scenes played out in Berlin and Leipzig during the 1920s and early 1930s.[63]

The first play to provoke mass protest, which developed into a violent riot, was Gurpreet Kaur Bhatti's black comedy *Behzti* (Dishonour) which had its première on 9 December 2004 at the studio of the Birmingham Repertory Theatre (the Rep). Written by a young Sikh woman, it addresses the issue of sexual abuse and hypocrisy in the Sikh community; in particular it shows the administrator of a Sikh Temple (Gurdwara) exploiting his position of authority to rape and control young men and women. A young woman Min is raped by the administrator Sandhu behind a screen while her mother is actually present in the Temple. Min is then beaten up by other women in the Temple who were themselves once Sandhu's victims. In her review of the production for the *Independent*, Helen Cross wrote:

It is offensive, and furious and bloodthirsty and angry in all the right places. Set mainly in the Gurdwara, the Sikh place of worship, this searing comedy features rape, abuse, murder, violence—while still managing to be hugely funny, touching and tremendously important . . . This play is much more mature and impressive than Kaur Bhatti's earlier *Behsharam* (Shameless). Braver, edgier and less frantically funny, this is particularly searing when pressing not only the bruise of religious hypocrisy but also the hidden wounds of female aggression, violence and despair. The actors rise effortlessly to the passion of the material . . . The best drama takes risks, kicks out and offends, and the best writers expose hypocrisy and pretence where they find it. Gripping and essential.[64]

Members of the Sikh community indicated even before the play opened its run that they were unhappy at the setting and some of the language used. Meetings were arranged between Sikh elders and the director and writer. Yasmin Wild, playing the role of Min, indicated that the cast were uneasy about the compromises that were made as a result: 'It may be a mistake to consult because it makes people think that they have a voice in the creative process.'[65] Some swear words and jokes were omitted, but the writer and director refused to yield to the demand that the setting of the play should be changed from a Sikh temple to a community centre. Initially, members of the Sikh community engaged in peaceful protests outside the theatre when the production opened. Then, according to a report in *The Times* on 22 December

---

[63] See Günther Rühle, *Theater für die Republik 1917–1933* (Frankfurt am Main: S. Fischer, 1967).

[64] Helen Cross, 'Gripping and essential: an offensive yet searing comedy', *Independent*, 21 Dec. 2004.

[65] Harriet Swain, 'Talks with Sikhs "backfired" on theatre', *Guardian*, 29 Dec. 2004.

2004, the demonstrations were hijacked by more extreme Sikh activists.[66] On Saturday, 18 December, protesters from the 400-strong crowd stormed into the theatre: windows were smashed, fire alarms set off, and back-stage equipment was damaged. Several police officers were hurt, three arrests were made, and over 800 people had to be evacuated from the main house at the Rep which was staging a Christmas show for a family audience. On Monday, 21 December, talks were held with the West Midlands Police and the Sikh community leaders. The police did not insist that the production should be halted but warned that the situation was likely to escalate. Stuart Rodgers, Executive Director of the Rep, decided after this meeting that he had no alternative but to cancel the production:

It is now clear that we cannot guarantee the safety of our audiences. Very reluctantly, therefore, we have decided to end the current run of the play purely on safety grounds. Sadly, community leaders have been unable to guarantee to us that there will be no repeat of the illegal and violent activities that we witnessed on Saturday. It remains a matter of great concern to us that illegal acts of violence can cause the cancellation of a lawful artistic work.[67]

The theatrical community in Birmingham rallied around in immediate support of the play and its author. The Birmingham Stage Company offered to mount a new production or a rehearsed reading of the play. However, as repeated death threats were made against the author who had to move into hiding, she asked that no further attempt should be made to produce her play or even organize a reading of it.[68]

Violence had clearly triumphed over the rule of law and the right of an audience to see a challenging play. However, a lot of public support was given to Bhatti by many fellow Asian writers and journalists. Typical of this was an editorial written by Sunny Hundal for *Asians in Media*:

The author doesn't want to talk about abuse or corruption in a community hall, she wants to talk about such issues in a Sikh Temple. This context is important and I'm not surprised she stuck by it. Are most Sikhs 'disgusted' by the play? Well not the ones I've talked to who have seen it. Yes it might be provocative but so what? So was the *Passion of Christ* but I didn't see Jews burning effigies of Mel Gibson and destroying cinemas.[69]

Equally staunch was the support of playwrights and directors across the racial spectrum. The *Independent*, on 21 December 2004, published a cross-section of views. The playwright Hanif Kureishi stated:

---

[66] 'Extremists hijacked play protest', *The Times*, 22 Dec. 2004.
[67] ' "Demeaning" play axed over safety fears', *Daily Telegraph*, 21 Dec. 2004.
[68] 'Threats to writer halt nationwide readings', *The Times*, 22 Dec. 2004.
[69] Sunny Hundal, 'The violent reaction to *Behtzi* is despicable and hypocritical', *Asians in Media*, 20 Dec. 2004: http://www.asiansinmedia.org/news/article.php/theatre/746 (accessed 21 Dec. 2004).

This is why we have art, so people are able to say things that are challenging and that some may not want to hear. The Sikh community requires liberalism as much, if not more, than anyone else. I think the Sikh community should be ashamed that it is destroying theatres. Destroying a theatre is like destroying a temple.[70]

Jatinder Verma, Artistic Director of Tara Arts, wrote: 'I am extremely disappointed, both for the writer and theatre—but also for the community. It is a sad day.'[71] Hytner, Director of the National Theatre, commented: 'It is desperately sad that we live now in a climate where the taking of offence is thought to be sufficient excuse for violence and intimidation.'[72]

Shortly after this outbreak of Sikh mob violence, a group of Christian activists showed that they too were capable of taking direct action. The spark that ignited their carefully choreographed protest was the planned broadcast of *Jerry Springer—the Opera*, a musical that had been running in London since 2003. It had opened at the National early in 2003 and then transferred, because of popular acclaim, to the Cambridge Theatre in the West End in October 2003. Throughout its long run in the London theatre,[73] the show attracted enthusiastic reviews, won numerous awards including the Best New Musical in the 2004 Olivier awards, and was not subject to any adverse attention from fundamentalist groups. All this changed when the BBC announced that it intended to broadcast the musical on 8 January 2005 on BBC2. Suddenly the BBC was deluged by protests.

The BBC received some 50,000 complaints by e-mail and by telephone over the Christmas and New Year period. Mark Thompson, Director-General of the BBC, commented in *The Times* on 8 March 2005 that 'many seemed to have come from a small number of sources'.[74] This electronic campaign was led by the website of an organization called Christian Voice. Prior to the screening of *Jerry Springer*, the Christian Voice website encouraged supporters to e-mail the BBC, and its Director-General, and to telephone the BBC and Ofcom (the independent regulator and competition authority for the UK communications industry).[75] In addition, it asked supporters to 'meet in front of your nearest BBC Venue Saturday evening for a peaceful prayer vigil'.[76] These 'vigils' took place on the night of the broadcast and in

---

[70] *Independent,* 21 Dec. 2004.   [71] Ibid.   [72] Ibid.
[73] When it finally closed at the Cambridge Theatre in 2005, the show had run for 609 performances.
[74] Mark Thompson, 'Why I stand by my decision to broadcast Jerry Springer—the Opera', *The Times,* 8 Mar. 2005.
[75] *'Jerry Springer—the Opera* on BBC2 Saturday 8 January 2005', http://www.christainvoice. org.uk/Springer1.html (accessed 11 Jan. 2005).
[76] 'Christian Voice—Prayer Vigils', Ibid.

London attracted over 150 vocal protestors. Subsequently, BBC executives involved with the production received anonymous telephone calls that were abusive and threatening, their names having been placed by Christian Voice on their website. (It should be noted, however, that Christian Voice had not encouraged any violence and had asked for a peaceful protest.)[77] The BBC employed a private security firm, Rubicon International, to protect these executives: the same firm protects BBC staff from threats of extremist attacks in Iraq.[78] Despite this pressure, the BBC refused to give in and the show was broadcast. Phone calls and e-mails received after the broadcast were evenly divided between those who supported the broadcast and those who were offended by it. Amongst leading journalists who commented on the hysteria, William Rees-Mogg was a lone voice in criticizing the BBC for its decision to broadcast the opera. For him, 'its callow sophistication is too repulsive'.[79] His view was countered by a robust and combative piece written by Libby Purves in which she praised the BBC for not giving into what she called 'fear and bigotry'.[80] On 7 March, in the Stationers' Livery Lecture, the Director-General of the BBC commented that 'the openness [of the BBC], along with the wider openness of our whole society, is under threat'. He went on to argue that 'the voices of those who would wish to limit [freedom of speech] seem to be getting more strident'.[81] This view was countered by a representative of Christian Voice who stated: 'This is not an issue of freedom of speech, but a case of broadcasting people not knowing the civilised limits and having to be told them.'[82]

Once the opera had been broadcast, attention shifted from the BBC to the provincial theatre tour of the opera. Letters of warning were sent by Christian Voice to venues that had expressed an interest in receiving the touring production. These stated amongst other things:

We are at this moment preparing charges of the criminal offence of blasphemy for service upon those responsible for broadcasting the show on BBC2, and those responsible for staging it at the Cambridge Theatre.

Should any regional theatre stage 'Jerry Springer the Opera' this autumn [2005], we shall be looking to prosecute them as well. We shall be especially keen to prosecute since the BBC broadcast, because anyone staging the show will now be doing so as a

---

[77] Adam Sherwin, 'Security guards step in after Springer opera death threats', *The Times*, 10 Jan. 2005.
[78] Christopher Morgan and Ben Dowell, 'TV chiefs given guards over Springer', ibid., 9 Jan. 2005.
[79] William Rees-Mogg, 'Wash your mouth out, Auntie', ibid., 10 Jan. 2005.
[80] Libby Purves, 'Bullies, bigots and the brave', ibid., 11 Jan. 2005.
[81] ' "Springer" row a threat to free speech—BBC chief', ibid., 8 Mar. 2005.
[82] Ibid.

deliberate act of provocation, knowing full well that the show is highly blasphemous and extremely offensive to Almighty God and to Christian believers.

In addition to that, many local theatres are supported by an organisation of friends or by public money, and the use of Council Tax-payers' money being used to subsidise an offensive, disgusting, blasphemous production will be hard for local Councillors to justify.[83]

In mid-March, *The Times* reported that many venues were intimidated by the threats of protest and prosecution.[84] But in the event, the tour got under way, the protests were sporadic, and, at the time of writing, no prosecution has been brought.

The Director-General of the BBC, as well as many reviewers and journalists, gave detailed accounts of *Jerry Springer—the Opera*, which carefully explained what they saw as its clearly focused, moral purpose. Ofcom was asked to judge whether the broadcast programme had infringed broadcasting standards: it ruled that the BBC was not in breach of infringing broadcasting standards by broadcasting the opera. In its adjudication, Ofcom gave a detailed summary of what it considered to be the real (as opposed to imagined) satirical intentions of the piece:

Ofcom appreciated that the representation of religious figures was offensive to some people. Their main concern arose from the depictions of figures at the heart of the complainants' religious beliefs. However, the show addressed moral issues in the context of a contemporary setting and contained a strong message. The show's effect was to satirise modern fame and the culture of celebrity. The images that caused the most offence were part of a 'dream' sequence serving as a metaphor for the fictional Jerry Springer and his chat show. In Ofcom's view, these were not meant to be faithful or accurate descriptions of religious figures, but a product of the lead character's imagination. Even as he lay dying, the fictional Jerry Springer still saw his life through the lens of his confessional show.[85]

None of these explanations satisfied Christian Voice and its sympathizers. In a subsequent initiative against the BBC, undertaken by another evangelical group, the Newcastle-based Christian Institute applied for a judicial review of the BBC's broadcast of the piece on the grounds that 'the programme breached the BBC's charter and broke the Human Rights Act by discriminating against Christians'.[86]

[83] http://www.christianvoice.org.uk/springer10.html (accessed 21 Apr. 2005).

[84] Jack Malvern and Dan Sabbagh, 'Christian voices silence Springer. A pressure group is forcing regional theatres to cancel *Jerry Springer—the Opera*', *The Times*, 16 Mar. 2005.

[85] *Jerry Springer: The Opera*, BBC2, 8 Jan. 2005, 22:00. Not in breach. Ofcom broadcast bulletin 34, 9 May 2005.

[86] 'Christian group takes BBC action', BBC News, 14 Mar. 2005: http://news.bbc.co.uk/1/hi/entertainment/tv_and_radio/4347845.stm. (accessed 21 Apr. 2005).

THE FUTURE: CENSORSHIP AND FREEDOM OF SPEECH

The Lord Chamberlain considered it his duty to censor plays that might give offence and disturb the peace. This produced two centuries of anodyne theatre. One of the roles of the theatre is to give offence, to provoke, and to push forward boundaries. As always, the question is: how far can one go? Jean Racine had to measure every word he wrote with infinite care, but he still offended powerful courtiers in the world of Louis XIV. Ibsen, when he wrote *Ghosts*, offended his contemporaries so profoundly that initially no one would read or produce his play. Ibsen commented in 1882: 'A writer must not leave his people so far behind that there is no longer any understanding between them and him. But *Ghosts* had to be written.' Threatened by activists of many different persuasions, should the theatre bow to pressure and remain silent? Should the theatre be willing to acknowledge the sensitivities of minorities living in Britain's modern multicultural society and exercise a degree of self-censorship? How freely can the theatre afford to speak out in future when addressing topics that might give offence to one or other cultural group?

So far individuals on the fringes of British Sikh or activist Christian groups have either used or threatened violence in an attempt to silence the work of a particular author. Hitherto there has been no pressure from Muslim activists because no playwright or theatre group in Britain has tested how far the Muslim community is prepared to go before violence erupts. If violence continues to break out as a result of the intervention of extremist pressure groups, it may only be a matter of time before Clause 6 of the 1968 Theatres Act is invoked and the theatre is once again subject to politically expedient censorship because its repertoire threatens a breach of the peace.

As the account given in this volume demonstrates, successive British governments since 1737 showed little enthusiasm for freedom of expression in the theatre. The likely future attitude of government on issues of freedom of speech is uncertain. The Blair Labour Government, for instance, in response to pressure from Muslim organizations, attempted unsuccessfully in 2006 to bring legislation on to the statute books that would have limited freedom of expression both in print and in performance on questions of religion. It is therefore by no means clear that future governments will see it as their primary duty to defend freedom of speech at all costs. The theatre will inevitably find itself at the heart of the struggle between those committed to freedom of artistic expression and those who, in pursuit of a doctrinaire vision of one kind or another, would seek to impose limits on what may be said on stage or anywhere else. The outcome of that struggle will determine whether the theatre in Britain remains free in future to explore serious cultural, social, religious, and political issues, or whether it will once again find itself muzzled or even silenced by government censorship or subject to new forms of cautious self-censorship.

Conclusion

The introduction of statutory theatre censorship in Britain in 1737 had a profound and constraining effect on the theatre until its abolition in 1968. In this volume, we have shown how and why in the late eighteenth century and throughout the nineteenth century there were no effective challenges to the statutory theatre censorship introduced by Walpole. During this lengthy period, playwrights and sympathetic Members of Parliament were primarily concerned with the monopoly over legitimate drama given to the two London patent theatres by the Licensing Act. Although this monopoly was successfully challenged in the provinces, it was not finally swept away in London until the 1843 Theatres Act; this Act, however, left in place the statutory censorship powers given to the Lord Chamberlain in the 1737 legislation. The three Parliamentary Select Committees on theatrical matters held during the course of the nineteenth century (1832, 1866, 1892) were all primarily concerned with the licensing of theatres and, later, music halls; in none of them was any significant attention given to the issue of theatre censorship.

It was not until a new generation of talented and vocal playwrights emerged at the turn of the century (led by Shaw and Granville Barker) that the system of statutory theatre censorship was seriously challenged. From the outset, government ministers and civil servants decided to respond to this challenge with a policy of deliberate inertia. We have shown in our account how they repeatedly acknowledged in private the absurdities of the theatre censorship system exercised by the Lord Chamberlain but then decided to 'let sleeping dogs lie'. As far as the Home Office was concerned, the system may have been absurd but it 'worked well in practice'. When challenged in Parliament, ministers were briefed by their civil servants to assert, quite incorrectly, that theatre censorship was exercised from within the Royal Prerogative and therefore was not a matter for the House of Commons. In reality theatre censorship was exercised under statute law and therefore could be challenged in the House of Commons. This calculated policy of obfuscation on the part of Home Office officials was pursued consistently during the early decades of the twentieth century. As a result, Parliament was repeatedly misled by ministers who were wrongly briefed and who were disinclined to pursue the matter further. Even when, in 1949, the Prime Minister, Attlee, sought clarification on the issue from the Lord Chancellor's department, the clear-cut and correct ruling given was never made public. It was not until the 1968 Theatres Act was passed that the issue was finally and effectively resolved.

Our account has also revealed further reasons why theatre censorship took so long to be abolished during the twentieth century. In the first place, the theatrical profession was hopelessly divided. Generally, commercial theatre managers welcomed censorship because, in their view, it provided them with a useful safeguard against vexatious prosecution. Playwrights and directors, on the other hand, were generally opposed to censorship because of the innumerable constraints it imposed on what might be written and how plays might be performed. Secondly, the attempts to abolish theatre censorship in 1909 and 1949 coincided with periods of such momentous political change that the issue of theatre censorship was pushed to the sidelines. Thirdly, we have documented the way two monarchs opposed the attempt to abolish theatre censorship in 1909 and 1966–8. In 1909 Edward VII, in clear breach of his constitutional role, adamantly refused to countenance the abolition of theatre censorship. This was a significant factor in the Asquith Government's decision to ignore the recommendations of the 1909 Joint Select Committee to replace, with a voluntary system, the theatre censorship provisions of the 1843 Theatres Act. In the period 1966–8, Elizabeth II, acting this time within the accepted constitutional framework of consultation between monarch and Prime Minister, applied pressure on Wilson in an ultimately failed attempt to retain protection for 'living persons' represented in stage plays. Although the precise nature of any exchanges between the Queen and Wilson on this topic has not been made public, the Lord Chamberlain claimed in 1966 that he had *'The Queen's authority to speak'* on the issue to civil servants, government ministers, and the House of Lords. His final intervention in the House of Lords in 1968 (for which he did not claim to have the Queen's authority to speak) involved a breach of normal constitutional propriety. By attempting to suggest an amendment on the issue of protection for living persons, he was in effect opposing a bill which, at that juncture (despite the earlier concerns of the Prime Minister expressed in Cabinet) had full government support. Although the Government made forceful attempts to dissuade him from speaking, in particular he was informed that his intervention might be misinterpreted as a plea from the Palace, Cobbold (with Wilson's last-minute permission) insisted on making his speech in the House of Lords, though to no avail.

Statutory theatre censorship in Britain was finally abolished with the passing of the 1968 Theatres Act. This resolved the previous, deliberately engineered confusion between the Royal Prerogative and statute law, and for the first time gave to playwrights in Britain the same freedom under the law as is enjoyed by other writers. We have shown that this reform was made possible by the simultaneous efforts of playwrights, directors, critics, and Members of both Houses of Parliament. The abolition of statutory theatre censorship coincided with other significant reforming measures (in respect of homosexuality, divorce, and abortion) that were passed by Parliament. All were first mooted, supported, or steered through Committee or Parliament by Jenkins, one of the great reforming Home Secretaries of modern times. Despite his modest assertion that he had been lucky enough to strike 'a liberal hour', it is at least arguable that, without his vigorous input, statutory theatre censorship would not have been abolished and that the policy of deliberate inertia, previously adopted by successive governments, would have prevailed.

Our investigation of attempts to bring prosecutions under the 1968 Theatres Act suggests that several vexatious prosecutions may have been prevented by the requirement that the permission of the Attorney-General should be obtained before any prosecution may be brought under the Act. However, the experience of Bogdanov, who was prosecuted under the Sexual Offences Act when he directed *The Romans in Britain* for the National Theatre in 1980, suggests that the wording of the 1968 Theatres Act needs to be modified (as in the draft bill of 1949) so that the permission of the Attorney-General is required before *any* criminal prosecution arising out of the performance of a play may be brought against any named manager, director, actor, or playwright.

The questionnaire survey of theatre and company managers in Britain permitted us to gauge the responses of this group at a particular point in time, namely 2002–3. The survey took place at a relatively stable moment in Britain's theatre history, which perhaps explains why the majority of managers who were contacted claimed to have no experience of direct or indirect censorship. The challenges to government policy which had been expressed by community theatre groups in the 1980s were a thing of the past, and it was not until December 2004 that specific productions were to be targeted by religious activists, some of whom were prepared to engage in violent protest and to issue threats against individual practitioners or playwrights. The survey conducted for this volume therefore may have elicited responses from theatre and company managers at a time when things were unusually and deceptively calm.

Following the riots and protests in Birmingham in 2004 and London in 2005, the theatre in Britain faces the possibility of a completely new kind of censorship. Using e-mail flaming, aggressive mass text messages, violent mob action, and threats of physical violence or death directed against individuals, extremist pressure groups of one kind or another may launch further attempts to coerce playwrights, directors, and actors into silence. The best defence against all such attempts is resolute government and police action against threatened or actual violence and unequivocal public support for freedom of speech. Neither can be taken for granted.

The European Convention on Human Rights supports freedom of expression, but within certain limits. Article 10, Section 1 states: 'Everyone has the right to freedom of expression, this right shall include freedom to hold opinions and to receive and impart information and ideas without interference by public authority and regardless of frontiers.' On the other hand, Article 10, Section 2 states: 'The exercise of these freedoms, since it carries with it duties and responsibilities, may be subject to such formalities, conditions, restrictions or penalties as are prescribed by law and are necessary in a democratic society . . . for the prevention of disorder or crime, for the protection of health or morals, for the protection of the reputation or rights of others . . . '[1] The theatre in modern Britain finds itself caught in the same tension that faced those who drafted these Articles in the European Convention on Human Rights. There is a fundamental human right to freedom of expression. But this right will inevitably be tempered by the rights of others. Many of these rights of others are spelled out in the 1968 Theatres Act. But today, in part because of the pressures of a multicultural society, which is itself the product of globalization, new demands for protection from insult and affront are being made.

Successive governments in Britain between 1737 and 1968 showed no interest at all in the issue of freedom of speech in the theatre: nor was there any widespread public interest in the issue until the 1960s. It is of course pleasing to see the theatre in Britain once again igniting passionate debate. However, there is an obvious unease in government circles at the 'clash of cultures' that is now a feature of modern British social life. In addition, some protestors, who feel that their 'rights' have been offended by playwrights or theatre practitioners, have begun to threaten or to use violence directed against individuals or artistic institutions. In view of this, it remains to be seen whether the theatre will be free to provoke passionate debate in future.

---

[1] *The European Convention on Human Rights and its Five Protocols,* 1950–66, Section I, Article 10: Sections 1 and 2, http://www.hri.org/docs/ECHR50.html.

Select Bibliography

Primary Source Material

The British Library

Additional Manuscripts

Add. 45290–45297	Correspondence and papers of William Archer
Add. 59895	Letters of H. H. Asquith
Add. 41206–41252	The Campbell-Bannerman Papers
Add. 59690–59703	The diaries of James Chuter Ede
Add. 56462 B	Gerald Gardiner Papers
Add. 45985–46118	The Viscount Gladstone Papers First Series
Add. 50508–50592	Shaw Papers: Series I
Add. 63409	Society of Authors Archive. Benn Levy 1932–57

The Lord Chamberlain's Correspondence Files 1900–68

LCP Corr.	Correspondence on plays which were given a licence.
LR Corr.	Correspondence on plays which were refused a licence.
WB Corr.	Correspondence on plays in the Waiting Box category.

The Royal Archives [formerly held at Windsor]

Box 251	1909 Censorship Committee.
Box C440	Theatres Act 1843 (1905–30).

Bodleian Library Department of Western Manuscripts

MSS	H. H. Asquith Papers (1–152).
MSS	Robert Harcourt Papers (648 and 681).
MSS	Gilbert Murray Papers (167).
MSS	Clement Attlee Papers (77–93 and 143).

Records of the House of Lords and House of Commons

Hansard (Lords and Commons)—transcripts of speeches and questions in Parliament from 1803.

Licensing Act 1737 (10 Geo. 2, c. 28).

Enabling Act 1788 (An Act to enable Justices of the Peace to license theatrical representations occasionally under the restrictions therein contained) (28 Geo. 3, c. 30).

Report from the Select Committee on Dramatic Literature, 2 Aug. 1832.

Theatres Act 1843 (Act for Regulating Theatres) (6 & 7 Vict., c. 68).

Report from the Select Committee on Theatrical Licenses and Regulations, 28 June 1866.

Report from the Select Committee on Theatres and Places of Entertainment, 2 June 1892.

Report of the Joint Select Committee on Stage Plays (Censorship), Nov. 1909.

Report of the Joint Select Committee on Censorship of the Theatre, 19 June 1967.
Theatres Act 1968 (c. 54).

House of Lords Library

SAM A/33; SAM A/155–57 Viscount Samuel Papers.

London Metropolitan Archives

A/PMC97	Annual Reports 1901–13. Public Morality Council (London)
A/PMC/98/1–33	Annual Reports 1931–63. Public Morality Council (London)
A/PMC/53	Miscellaneous letters, 1963–4
A/PMC/54	Miscellaneous letters, Committee on Stage Plays, Radio and Television (1965)
APMC/15	Meetings of Stage Plays Sub-Committee, 1957–65

The National Archives

CAB 128	Cabinet Minutes (CM and CC Series) 1945–75
CAB 129	Cabinet Memoranda (CP and C Series) 1945–75
CAB 134	Cabinet: Miscellaneous Committees: Minutes and Papers 1945–78
FCO 13/154	Foreign and Commonwealth Office: Proposed legislation on theatre censorship and possible implications on relations with foreign countries 1967
HO 45	Home Office Papers 1839–1979
HO 300	Home Office: Entertainments (ENT Symbol Series) Files 1951–81
LC 7	Lord Chamberlain's Department: Records of Licensing of Entertainments and Theatres 1660–1901.
LO 3	Law Officers' Department: Law Officers' Opinions 1889–1948
LCO 2	Lord Chancellor's Office and Lord Chancellor's Department: Registered Files 1850–1984
MEPO 2/11076	Metropolitan Police: Office of the Commissioner: Correspondence and Papers 1967–9. Theatres Act 1968: observation on the proposed bill to abolish censorship in theatres: amendment of Police General Orders and Instructions
PREM 13	Prime Minister's Office: Correspondence and Papers 1964–70

University of Sussex

Sx MS 37	Benn Levy Papers, University of Sussex Special Collections.

University of Warwick Modern Records Centre

MSS.154/8/100–105	Richard Crossman Papers, Diary Transcriptions
MSS.076	William Wilson Papers

William Wilson Private Archive

Parliamentary Papers, Theatre Censorship File.

Primary and Secondary Sources: Theatre and Censorship

Adams, J. Q. (ed.), *The Dramatic Records of Sir Henry Herbert* (New Haven: Yale University Press, 1917).

Aldgate, Anthony, *Censorship and the Permissive Society: British Cinema and Theatre, 1955–1965* (Oxford: Clarendon Press, 1995).

Bawcutt, N. W., *The Control and Censorship of Caroline Drama: The Records of Sir Henry Herbert, Master of the Revels, 1623–73* (Oxford: Clarendon Press, 1996).

Chambers, E. K., *The Elizabethan Stage*, 4 vols. (Oxford: Clarendon Press, 1923).

Cibber, Colley, *An Apology for the Life of Mr. Colley Cibber* (1740), ed. Robert Lowe, 2 vols. (London: John C. Nimmo, 1889).

Clare, Janet, *'Art made tongue-tied by authority': Elizabethan and Jacobean Dramatic Censorship* (Manchester: Manchester University Press, 1990).

Conolly, L. W., *The Censorship of English Drama, 1737–1824* (San Marino: Anderson, Ritchie & Simon, 1976).

Craig, Alec, *The Banned Books of England and other Countries* (London: Allen & Unwin, 1962).

De Jongh, Nicholas, *Not in front of the Audience: Homosexuality on Stage* (London: Routledge, 1992).

—— *Politics, Prudery and Perversions* (London: Methuen, 2000).

Dutton, R., *Mastering the Revels: The Regulation and Censorship of English Renaissance Drama* (London: Macmillan, 1991).

Etienne, Anne, *Les Coulisses du Lord Chamberlain: la Censure Théâtrale de 1900 à 1968* (unpublished Ph.D. dissertation, Université d'Orléans, 1999).

Findlater, Richard, *Banned* (London: MacGibbon & Kee, 1967).

Firth, Sir Charles Harding, and Rait, Robert S. (eds.), *Acts and Ordinances of the Interregnum, 1642–1660*, 3 vols. (London: HMSO, 1911).

Gaskill, William, *A Sense of Direction* (London: Faber, 1988).

Johnston, John, *The Lord Chamberlain's Blue Pencil* (London: Hodder & Stoughton, 1990).

Knowles, Dorothy, *The Censor, the Drama and the Film* (London: Allen & Unwin, 1934).

Liesenfeld, Vincent J., *The Licensing Act of 1737* (Madison: University of Wisconsin Press, 1984).

Marshall, Norman, *The Other Theatre* (London: John Lehmann, 1947).

Marwick, Arthur, *The Sixties: Cultural Revolution in Britain, France, Italy and the United States* (Oxford: Oxford University Press, 1998).

Nicholson, Steve, *The Censorship of British Drama, 1900–1968*, 3 vols. (Exeter: University of Exeter Press, 2003–8 [forthcoming]).

Nicholson, Watson, *The Struggle for a Free Stage in London* (London: Archibald Constable, 1906).

Owen, Susan J., *Restoration Theatre and Crisis* (Oxford: Clarendon Press, 1996).

Robertson, Geoffrey, *The Justice Game* (London: Vintage, 1999).

Ruffhead, Owen (ed.), *Statutes at Large*, 8 vols. (London: Henry Woodfall *et al.*, 1763).

Shellard, Dominic, Nicholson, Steve, and Handley, Miriam, *The Lord Chamberlain Regrets: British Stage Censorship and Readers' Reports from 1824 to 1968* (London: British Library Publishing, 2005).

Stephens, John Russell, *The Censorship of English Drama, 1824–1901* (Cambridge: Cambridge University Press, 1980).

Thomas, David (ed.), *Theatre in Europe: A Documentary History. Restoration and Georgian England 1660–1788* (Cambridge: Cambridge University Press, 1989).

Thomas, Donald, *A Long Time Burning. The History of Literary Censorship in England* (London: Routledge & Kegan Paul, 1969).

Tynan, Kathleen, *The Life of Kenneth Tynan* (London: Weidenfeld and Nicolson, 1987).

Wickham, Glynne, *Early English Stages 1300 to 1600*, 4 vols. (London: Routledge & Kegan Paul, 1959–2002).

Secondary Sources: The Political Background, 1737–1968

Bagehot, Walter, *The English Constitution*, 4th edn. (London: Kegan Paul & Trench, 1885).

Briggs, Asa, *The Age of Improvement, 1783–1867* (London: Longman, 2000).

Campbell, John, *Roy Jenkins: A Life* (London: Weidenfeld and Nicolson, 1983).

Cross, Colin, *The Liberals in Power, 1905–1914* (London: Barrie & Rockcliff, 1963).

Crossman, Richard, *The Diaries of a Cabinet Minister*, 3 vols. (London: Hamish Hamilton and Jonathan Cape, 1976).

De-la-Noy, Michael, *The King Who Never Was: The Story of Frederick, Prince of Wales* (London: Peter Owen, 1996).

Dickinson, H. T., *Walpole and the Whig Supremacy* (London: Hodder, 1973).

Foreman, Amanda, *Georgiana, Duchess of Devonshire* (London: HarperCollins, 1999).

Gash, Norman, *Sir Robert Peel: The Life of Sir Robert Peel after 1830* (London: Longman, 1972).

Grigg, John, *Lloyd George: The People's Champion, 1902–1911* (London: Harper-Collins, 1997).

Harris, Kenneth, *Attlee* (London: Weidenfeld and Nicolson, 1982).

Jefferys, Kevin, *Anthony Crosland* (London: Richard Cohen Books, 1999).

Jenkins, Roy, *Mr. Balfour's Poodle* (London: Collins, 1954).

—— *A Life at the Centre* (London: Macmillan, 1991).

Jones, Mervyn, *Michael Foot* (London: Victor Gollancz, 1994).

Lamb, Richard, *The Macmillan Years, 1957–1963: The Emerging Truth* (London: John Murray, 1995).

Langford, Paul, *The English Satirical Print, 1600–1832: Walpole and the Robinocracy* (Cambridge: Cambridge University Press, 1986).

Magnus, Philip, *King Edward the Seventh* (London: John Murray, 1964).

Marshall, Dorothy, *Eighteenth Century England* (London: Longman, 1962).

Morgan, Kenneth, *Labour in Power, 1945–1951* (Oxford: Oxford University Press, 1984).

Nicolson, Harold, *King George V: His Life and Reign* (London: Constable, 1953).

Pearce, Edward, *Lines of Most Resistance: The Lords, the Tories and Ireland, 1886–1914* (London: Little, Brown, 1999).

—— *Reform! The Fight for the 1832 Reform Act* (London: Jonathan Cape, 2003).

Pimlott, Ben, *Harold Wilson* (London: HarperCollins, 1992).

Plumb, J. H., *Sir Robert Walpole*, 2 vols. (London: Cresset Press, 1956 and 1960).

Thatcher, Margaret, *The Path to Power* (London: HarperCollins, 1995).

Williams, Basil, *The Whig Supremacy, 1714–1760* (Oxford: Clarendon Press, 1939).

Ziegler, Philip, *Wilson: The Authorised Life of Lord Wilson of Rievaulx* (London: Weidenfeld and Nicolson, 1993).

Index